WILD
guide

North East England

Hidden Places, Great Adventures
and the Good Life

Sarah Banks

T0287045

Sandham Bay p39

WILD
guide

Roseberry Topping p178

Contents

Regional
Overview

Ashgill Force p163

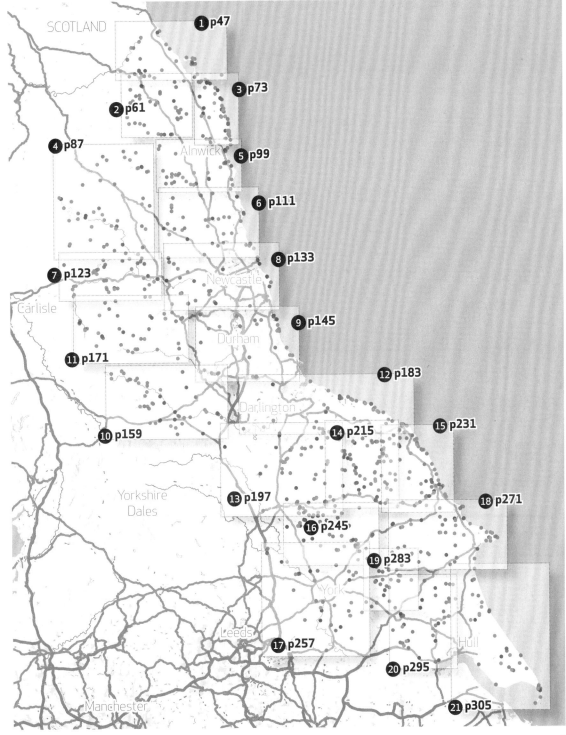

SCOTLAND

1 p47

2 p61

3 p73

4 p87

Alnwick

5 p99

6 p111

8 p133

7 p123

Newcastle

Carlisle

9 p145

Durham

11 p171

12 p183

Darlington

14 p215

15 p231

10 p159

Yorkshire Dales

13 p197

18 p271

16 p245

19 p283

York

Leeds

17 p257

Hull

20 p295

Manchester

21 p305

Harbottle Lake p77

Introduction

If you yearn for the wilderness, then the North East can offer you every kind of wild place you could possibly imagine. Whether it's soaring peaks and cliffs, dramatic valleys and magnificent waterfalls or tranquil rivers, lakes and beaches, it has everything covered. The beauty of this region is the astonishing variety of its landscape interwoven with a fascinating history, ranging from sacred Neolithic sites to post-industrial and wartime ruins. Moors, meadows and ancient forests are all laid out, ready for you to explore this wonderful and diverse landscape.

Wild frontiers to Yorkshire's 'Land's End'

This book takes in the former battlegrounds of the Scottish borders to the tip of Spurn Point, facing its own conflict with the sea, and stretches from the North Pennines and Hadrian's Wall across the North York Moors to the coastlines of Northumberland and Yorkshire. It is a celebration of the most beautiful, lesser-visited places, where you will find secret locations for wild swimming, walking and exploring, along with unique places to eat and stay.

The diverse topography of this area begins in Northumberland where the River Tweed marks much of the border with Scotland, reaching the sea at Berwick-upon-Tweed. Guarding the north-west boundary are the Cheviot Hills, formed 390 million years ago by intense volcanic activity and eroded into the smooth, round hills and valleys we see today.

The Northumberland coastline is a succession of sweeping sandy bays, undulating dunes, rocky promontories and remote islands. The Whin Sill, a layer of igneous dolerite, stretches from Berwick to Teesdale, and some of the region's most cherished landmarks are built upon its outcrops: Hadrian's Wall, the castles of Bamburgh, Lindisfarne and Dunstanburgh and the resistant lip over which the Tees dramatically plunges at High Force waterfall.

Sycamore Gap, Hadrian's Wall p120

One of the largest expanses of heather moorland in England covers the North York Moors, running from the steep slopes of the Cleveland Hills in the north-west to the towering cliffs of the Yorkshire coast. This is a Jurassic coastline, formed 150 to 200 million years ago, and like the Dorset Jurassic coast it is fertile ground for fossil hunters, with ammonites, belemnites, bivalves and dinosaur footprints regularly discovered. Inland, an outcrop of chalk was carved by fast-running streams 18,000 years ago to form the unique deep valleys of the Yorkshire Wolds. The plain of Holderness stretches to the boulder-clay cliffs of the coast, the fastest eroding coastline in Europe, and the precarious spit of land that is Spurn Point.

Standing stones to ironstone mines

For millennia, people have hunted, settled and farmed here, leaving behind mysterious, sacred and beautiful reminders of their presence that you can see and touch today.

Seek out the Neolithic Duddo Five Stones in Northumberland or the remarkable Rudston Monolith in East Yorkshire and ponder the significance of these sites for people 4,000 years ago. The Iron Age is marked by hill forts; Northumberland alone has 271 of these ancient monuments, which have remained relatively undisturbed since their last occupation 1,500 years ago, having escaped stone pilfering and ploughing.

The Romans built forts, camps and roads and left one of their most important legacies here: Hadrian's Wall, constructed in ad 122, guarded the northern frontier of the Roman Empire. The 7th century was the golden age of the Kingdom of Northumbria, which stretched from the Forth to below the Humber. Under powerful kings – Edwin, Oswald and Oswiu – Northumbria became one of northern Europe's leading cultural and Christian centres, producing scholars such as Bede, Cuthbert and Aidan – and the astonishing Lindisfarne Gospels. St Paul's Monastery in Jarrow, home of the Venerable Bede, partly survives as the chancel of St Paul's Church.

Northumbria, which fragmented into four areas under the Vikings, was under Danelaw when the Normans conquered in 1066, building castles at Norham, Pickering, Skipsea and Elsdon. Monasteries and priories grew up and flourished here from the 12th century, later destroyed by Henry VIII in the

11

Kirkham Priory p238

dissolution of the monasteries. Their glorious ruins survive at Rievaulx, Kirkham and Byland. The Middle Ages brought 500 years of wrangling between the English and the Scots. From the 14th to the late 17th century, fortified bastle houses, such as Black Middens in Tarset, Northumberland, were built to protect against the Border Reivers and are testimony to this terrifying time.

The Industrial Revolution of the 18th and 19th centuries had a huge impact on this region. Deposits of lead ore and other minerals generated a prolific lead mining industry in Weardale, while at Rosedale in the North York Moors mines sprang up around a massive iron ore industry, including a railway around the valley. This industrial exploitation has sculpted today's landscape, but wilderness has thankfully returned to these peaceful, rural dales; the ironstone railway is now a spectacular walking and cycling route, and the relics in the landscape are a chapter in the North East's rich history.

A Sense of the Wild

Picture yourself on a deserted beach in Northumberland, sand between your toes and the crash of the waves in your ears; or gazing at the dark skies over Dalby Forest with the Milky Way shining above you; or perhaps walking behind a waterfall before plunging into the pools below or sitting beneath a centuries-old oak in the tranquillity of an ancient woodland. These are all places where we regain our sense of awe, reconnect with nature and enjoy experiences that nourish our soul. They are all within these pages and are free for those who make the small effort to find them. Think of this book as a starting point; there are hundreds of spots to explore and no doubt you will discover secret places and enjoy thrilling adventures of your own.

In doing so, I wish you a wild and wonderful time!

Sarah

adventure@wildthingspublishing.com

Finding your way

Most places listed are on a public right of way, permissive path, open-access land or benefit from long-use rights. However some places, usually marked 🛈, may not have such clear rights. **You will need to make your own judgment about whether to proceed or seek permission from the landowner.**

An overview map and directions are provided, but the latitude, longitude for each location, provided in WGS84 decimal degrees, is the definitive reference and can be entered into any online map site, such as Google, Bing or Streetmap. The latter two provide Ordnance Survey mapping overlays, which show footpaths. OpenStreetMap increasingly shows paths, too. Print out the map before you go, or save a 'screen grab'. Map apps such as ViewRanger or Memory-Map are useful, and you can also enter the co-ordinates into your smartphone GPS or car sat nav (enable 'decimal degrees'). Postcodes are provided for convenience, but only provide a rough location. If you have paper maps, look up the equivalent National Grid reference in the conversion table at the back of the book. If a parking place is mentioned, always make your own judgment and be considerate. Where two places are named in the title, the focus of the text is always the first. Walk-in times given are one way only, allowing 15 mins per km, which is quite brisk. Abbreviations in the directions refer to left and right (L, R); north, east, south and west (N, E, S, W) and direction (dir). There are also: National Trust (NT), English Heritage (EH), Royal Society for the Protection of Birds (RSPB), National Nature Reserve (NNR) & Youth Hostel Association (YHA).

Wild & responsible

1. Fasten all gates and only climb them at the hinges.

2. Keep your dogs under close control, especially around livestock and in nature reserves.

3. Take your litter home, and gain good karma by collecting other people's.

4. If you wash in streams or rivers, use only biodegradable soap, or none at all.

5. Take special care on country roads and park considerately, to allow room for a tractor or truck.

6. Take map, compass, whistle and waterproof clothing when venturing into remote or high areas.

7. Always tell someone where you are going, and do not rely on your mobile phone.

Cornelian Bay p219

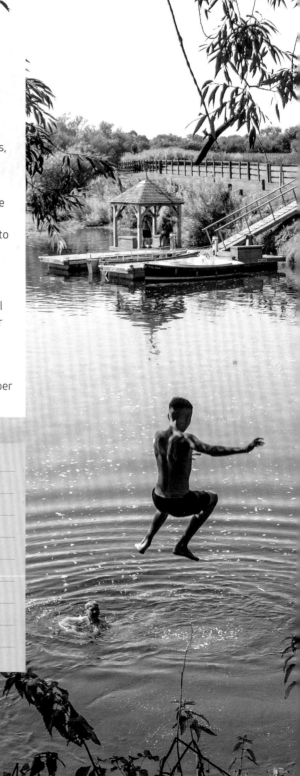

Best for
Wild swimming

Whether you're a seasoned wild swimmer who plunges into icy waters or someone who prefers the occasional dip to cool off on a hot day, there is a myriad of beautiful places to swim in the North East, including tranquil rivers, shimmering lakes and secret moorland tarns.

Bear in mind that just because a river or lake is on a footpath or open access land, this doesn't mean you have a legal right to swim there. Places marked with a 🏊 may be used by swimmers, but there may be no official right to swim, or rights may be discouraged. Always be discreet and choose a spot away from anglers. If asked to leave, do so politely.

The weather, heavy rainfall and localised pollution can all affect water quality and pose risks, so always make your own safety assessment. It is also important to consider biosecurity; the transition of invasive species from one body of water to another via our costumes can have devastating consequences. So, after each swim remember three simple steps: check, clean, dry.

Twizel Bridge, River Till p40

Irving Pool, River Coquet p77

Harbottle Lake p77

Lambley Viaduct, River South Tyne p115

Gainford, River Tees p149

Whorlton, River Tees p149

Swallowship Pool p116

St John's Chapel, River Wear p164

Meeting of the Waters, River Greta p149

Brian's Pond p187

Beningbrough, River Ouse p250

Be safe

1 Never swim alone, and keep a constant watch on weak swimmers.

2 Cold water can dramatically decrease swimming ability, create cold shock and cause drowning through panic. Know your limits, enter slowly and stay close to the shoreline.

3 Never jump into water unless you have thoroughly checked for depth and obstructions.

4 Avoid strong currents, such as those directly under large waterfalls or weirs, or those found in river rapids during floods: they can drag you under.

5 Always make sure you know how you will get out before you get in.

6 Wear footwear if you can.

7 Avoid direct contact with blue-green algae, and be wary of water quality in lowland areas during droughts and heavy rain. Cover cuts with plasters if worried, and if you develop flu-like symptoms tell your doctor you have been in a river.

Best for
Boats & floats

An expedition on a kayak, canoe or stand-up paddleboard (SUP) allows you to see the countryside from a different perspective. The North East's historic rivers, the Tyne, Tees, Wear, Derwent and Esk, all provide excellent starting points for an aquatic adventure, as do the tranquil canals of Pocklington, Driffield and Selby with their abundance of wildlife.

Kayaking and SUP, in particular, have seen a huge surge in popularity thanks to cheaper inflatable craft which are lighter and much easier to transport. This makes them perfect for weekend adventures and gentle paddling on sheltered waterways, but less suitable for rapids or places exposed to the elements. When planning a trip, always be mindful of the weather, wind strength and direction, flow, weirs and tidal rivers.

For some of the rivers mentioned in this book, and all of the canals, you will require a licence to paddle, which you can buy from British Canoeing, the Canal and River Trust or directly from some navigation authorities.

Ebchester Boathouse, River Derwent p127

Best for
Waterfalls & gorges

There is no doubt that a waterfall is a sensory feast, whether it is the awe we feel watching one in full spate; the walk through a picturesque valley to seek one out; hearing the clamorous flow of water before we see it; or the thrill of leaping off the ledges of a waterfall into a deep plunge pool below.

From the highest to the longest waterfalls in England, at High Force and Cauldron Snout, to pretty moorland cascades in picturesque fern-filled gorges, this region boasts some of the finest falls in the country. Many are found in the valleys of the North York Moors around Goathland and in the deep clefts of the Cheviot Hills, where moorland burns tumble through rocky ravines.

Before jumping into a pool below a waterfall, always check its depth and for any obstructions – even if you have taken the leap before – as water levels change throughout the seasons and can vary after heavy rainfall.

Slitt Wood Waterfalls p163

Be safe ⚠

1 Never jump into the centre of a waterfall, as the undercurrents can be very powerful there.

2 Never jump into pools that haven't been checked for depth.

3 Never descend something you can't climb back up. If in doubt, scramble up the gorge, not down.

4 Wear a wetsuit, to avoid hypothermia and protect from cuts. In narrow gorges wear a helmet, due to the danger of rock falls.

5 Beware of flash flooding after heavy rainfall upstream.

Best for
Secret beaches

Miles of pristine, dune-fringed beaches and secluded coves hug the Northumberland coastline yet many are deserted. Some of the hidden beaches require a longer walk-in, like those on Holy Island, which only adds to the pleasure in discovering them.

Yorkshire's sandy beaches are interspersed with charming fishing villages that cling to the rugged cliffs. Between these you will find coves, many only accessible by a steep clamber down or with the help of a rope, such as Port Mulgrave. On Durham's Heritage Coast the secluded cove of Hawthorn Hive is reached through an ancient wooded dene.

One of the most enjoyable ways of discovering these beaches is by walking the coastal paths. You will be rewarded with spectacular coastal scenery and the chance to spot seals, dolphins and porpoises; you can also scramble down to your own secret cove.

Check tide times before heading out as some beaches are best accessed, or are only accessible, during low tide. And remember – these beaches do not have lifeguards, so take care with rip currents and rocks.

Be safe

1 Never swim alone.

2 Be aware that rip currents can form when there is heavy swell or surf. These circulate water back out to the back of the breaking waves.

3 Rips often occur around the edge of coves or between surf breaks on longer beaches.

4 To escape a rip current swim perpendicular, in line with the shore.

5 Never jump or dive into water unless you have checked it for depth and obstructions. When looking down, water always appears deeper than it is.

6 Do not disturb seals or pups.

Best for
Sacred & ancient

In the North East you can genuinely travel through time. In the space of a day, you can touch a Bronze Age standing stone, climb an Iron Age hill fort and walk Hadrian's Wall, or rest by a medieval stone cross.

There has been a human presence in North East England for almost 10,000 years. One of the earliest, most important sites in Britain for evidence of Mesolithic people is Star Carr at the former site of a shallow post-glacial lake to the west of Scarborough.

Each generation has left its mark and the landscape here is littered with ancient crosses, stone circles, burial cairns, rock art and holy wells, which help create a picture of how our ancestors lived.

Many of these monuments are sited in glorious surroundings, often high on a hill with magnificent vistas, leading us to contemplate the significance of such places, such as the rock art at Lordenshaw, the standing stones of Simon Howe and the round barrow at the Seven Sisters on Copt Hill.

Lilla Cross p223

Best for
Easy Peaks & scrambles

When you find yourself in a beautiful landscape, there is an almost irresistible temptation to gain some higher ground to get a better view; that might be climbing a small hill or taking on a steeper, tougher ascent but once you are up there, the rewards are laid out before you.

The Cheviot understandably appeals to hill walkers who want to conquer Northumberland's highest summit. However, many other hills, such as the Iron Age hill forts of the Breamish Valley or Yeavering Bell, offer an easier, shorter climb for equal satisfaction along with spectacular views. The Cleveland Hills have several peaks to summit, and the walk-up Cringle Moor is a great adventure hike for children.

For the more adventurous, scrambling and bouldering adds an extra adrenalin-fuelled challenge, testing our strength, skill and judgment. Many of the bouldering sites here are suitable for a range of abilities, from beginners to the more experienced.

Corby's Crags rock shelter p94

Best for
Woods, meadows & wildlife

As storytellers know, there is an almost primeval attraction to losing yourself in a deep, dark wood. Being surrounded by trees with only birdsong as a soundtrack is at the heart of forest bathing, where we slow down and connect with nature.

Wondrous woodlands are found across the North East, from the botanical delight of the juniper forests in Upper Teesdale to Durham's ancient wooded coastal denes and the magnificent Kielder Forest, home to the largest population of red squirrels in the country.

Wandering through traditional hay meadows at Hannah's Meadow and Barrowburn feels like you're stepping back in time; almost half the UK's upland hay meadows are in the North Pennines, with fields brimming with characteristic northern species of wildflowers such as wood crane's-bill and melancholy thistle.

Along the coast thousands of seabirds – puffins, gannets and kittiwakes – flock to the chalk cliffs of Flamborough each year, and the Farne Islands harbour important breeding colonies of seabirds and grey seals. Dolphins and seals are frequently sighted along the entire coastline, and minke whales are commonly seen off the Yorkshire coast.

Barrowburn hay meadows p81

Best for
Ruins & follies

The ruins we see scattered across the landscape are chapters in a history book, each page a window on the past. From Roman ruins to crumbling castles, splendid monastic remains to resistant bastles, the North East is steeped in atmospheric sites.

As the northern outpost of the Roman Empire, this region abounds with remnants from this time. The hamlet of High Rochester nestles within the ruined ramparts of a Roman fort. These borderlands contain all manner of fortresses – from bastle houses built to defend against the Border Reivers to ruined castles that pepper the coastline from Dunstanburgh to Scarborough.

Religious ruins are found in abundance, ranging from tiny chapels and abandoned churches to glorious abbey ruins, many destroyed during Henry VIII's dissolution of the monasteries in the 16th century, such as Rievaulx Abbey in Yorkshire. Elaborate follies are visual reminders of an 18th-century fad for absurd decorative monuments.

Vestiges of mine workings and old machinery are dotted across Weardale and the North York Moors, and in the other-worldly terrain of Sunk Island, military ruins surface from a woodland grove.

Sheriff Hutton Castle p237

Best for
Slow food & drink

With its rich moorland, fertile pastures and extensive coastline, the North East has a bounty of farmers, fishermen and artisan food and drink producers, meaning you will feast on the best seasonal, local cuisine.

Part of discovering a new region is delving into its gastronomic scene, which gives us an insight into the area's cultural history. Virtually free of food miles, buying local supports the craft producers and farmers, as well as the eateries that are often important community hubs.

You can tuck into a seafood platter from a coastal beach shack, stock up for a picnic at a rural farm shop, sample honey at the farmers market, buy heritage-breed meat from the village butchers or pick your own strawberries at a family-run farm.

The North East is brimming with friendly village inns, cosy pubs and a growing number of microbreweries serving craft beers, ciders and gins. Some of these hostelries are also gastropubs where you can fine dine; others are unchanged from times gone by with cosy log fires, real ales and a good supply of northern warmth and humour.

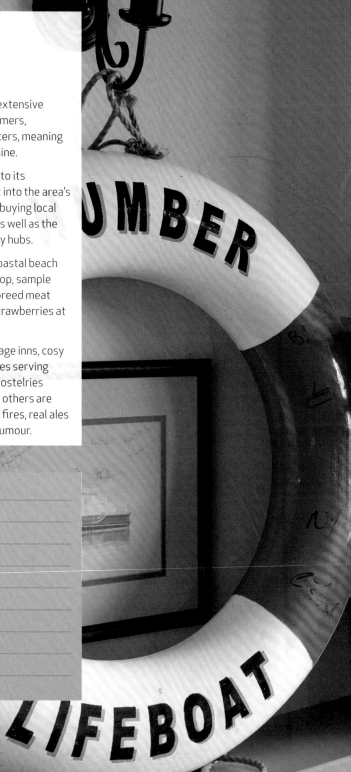

Crown & Anchor, Kilnsea p304

£9.50

Pork in Thatchers - Tender pieces of
pork in a rich cider gravy
served with choice of potatoes + veg £9.50

Best for
Wilder camping & rustic havens

An important part of planning a wild adventure is staying somewhere with the wilderness on your doorstep. With so many wonderfully run places to stay, the North East has something to suit all tastes and budgets.

You can rest your head in an enchanting hand-crafted chapel on wheels with a roll-top copper bath or pitch your tent at a coastal campsite and watch the sun setting over the bay.

There are some excellent hostels offering budget-friendly accommodation, and for those seeking a place to themselves, choose from a cosy old farmer's cottage, a log cabin in the dunes or a Land Rover Defender with a roof-top tent for your own memorable road trip.

What they all have in common are beautiful locations. Those in search of a truly wild experience might wild camp responsibly in the hills or dunes. However, this is not always legal or practical, so the next best thing is a back-to-basics wild-camping site or one of the remote bothies managed by the Mountain Bothies Association.

Wild camping

1 Camp above the highest fell wall, well away from towns and villages.

2 Leave no litter, remove other people's, and don't bury litter.

3 Do not light any fires, even if there's evidence that fires may have been lit by others.

4 Stay for only one night.

5 Keep groups very small – only one or two tents.

6 Camp as unobtrusively as possible, with inconspicuous tents that blend into the landscape.

7 Do not trespass and seek permission.

8 Perform toilet duties at least 30m (100ft) from water, and bury the results with a trowel. Take toilet paper and sanitary products home in a plastic nappy / dog poo bag.

NORTHERN BORDERS

Our perfect weekend

→ **Discover** the Neolithic singing stones of Duddo, crowning a hill with vistas towards Scotland

→ **Plunge** into the River Till beneath historic Twizel Bridge, crossed by armies en route to Flodden Field

→ **Climb** the spiral staircase at Norham Castle, a place that so inspired J. M. W. Turner, he painted it time after time

→ **Enjoy** a glass of fizz at the Old Dairy's rustic al fresco champagne bar, soaking up spectacular views of the Cheviot Hills

→ **Marvel** at the 19th-century murals adorning the walls of Lady Waterford Hall, painted by a woman ahead of her time

→ **Follow** in the footsteps of the pilgrims to Lindisfarne, then hop across rock pools to St Cuthbert's Island to watch the seals frolicking

→ **Wander** through the grass-fringed dunes at Ross Back Sands, a remote, wild beach with a castle at either end

→ **Dip** your toes in the River Tweed, then dare to make the short swim to Scotland

England's final frontier stretches along the Scottish border, from the rolling hills of the Cheviots in the west to the beautiful, dune-fringed beaches of the east coast. A region visitors often pass through to and from Scotland, this area is incredibly scenic, peppered with remote hamlets, winding rivers, ruined castles, sacred sites and its own tidal island – the cradle of early Christianity.

It's hard to believe a place so tranquil was once the scene of interminable border warfare, which from the 12th century saw the town of Berwick-upon-Tweed change hands between the English and the Scots 13 times, finally surrendering to the English in 1482.

The principal river here, the Tweed, forms a natural border between England and Scotland for its final 17 miles, entering England at Coldstream and flowing into the North Sea at Berwick. Famed as one of the world's finest salmon fishing rivers, it is also the starting point for many water-based activities, from wild swimming to paddleboarding and kayaking. The islet of Canny Island, upstream of Norham Bridge, provides a unique opportunity to swim the short distance from England to Scotland.

Not surprisingly, with such a turbulent history, castles still dominate the landscape. The sublime Norham Castle, perched high above the tumbling Tweed, was one of the most important fortresses in the region. Its pink-hued ruins were a major draw for J. M. W. Turner, who produced several haunting and atmospheric images of the castle.

Equally wistful are the ruins of Etal Castle in the charming estate village of Etal, built as a defence against the Scots and captured by James IV in 1513, days before the Battle of Flodden, where he became the last monarch in Great Britain to die in battle. The battlefield trail is one of the best in the country.

Sacred sites abound, including the 4,000-year-old Duddo Five Stones, a Neolithic circle of stones. They are also known as the 'singing stones', as when the wind blows, legend has it the unusual grooves in the rocks create a musical sound.

But, undoubtedly, the holy island of Lindisfarne is the region's most revered treasure as the bedrock of early Christianity. Unsurprisingly, this tidal island is hugely popular; however, a short walk from the main village leads to three unspoilt and deserted sandy beaches. For visitors seeking tranquillity, cross just before high tide, when the day-trippers are leaving – some shops and cafés may close, but the peace and solitude of this remarkable place will be all yours.

HIDDEN BEACHES

1 CHESWICK SANDS

A magnificent dune-backed sandy beach that stretches for miles with views towards Berwick to the north and a perfect vista of Holy Island to the south.

→ Heading N on A1, after Haggerston, take a R signposted for Cheswick and continue for about ½ mile. Take R after sharp bend then take next L. Continue through village and over railway bridge to parking area on L and beach.
2 mins, 55.7179, -1.9348 🏕🏖

2 COCKLAWBURN BEACH

Hidden down a winding lane, this beautiful sand and rock beach is backed by grassy dunes. Perfect for swimming and with some fascinating rock pools. Look out for seals and dolphins.

→ Heading N on the A1, take a R turn at roundabout onto A1167 then first R to Scremerston. After church take L turn, following road which swings sharply to the L then take first R. Continue across level crossing to end of road then R onto road leading to parking by beach.
2 mins, 55.7321, -1.9568 🏕🏖🏊

3 ROSS BACK SANDS

A spectacular, remote sandy beach and dunes, with Lindisfarne Castle at one end and Bamburgh at the other. Often deserted, this is a contender for Northumberland's most wild and beautiful beach.

→ Heading N on A1, turn R after Belford, signed 'Warren Mill'. Turn L at T-junction, signed 'Easington', then R, signed 'Ross', and park on verge before Ross Farm (NE70 7EN S/c cottages). Continue a mile on foot along lane and through dunes. Budle Bay sands and nature reserve are a mile to the S.
20 mins, 55.6351, -1.7734 🏕🏖

4 COVES HAVEN

Situated at the far north of Holy Island, this beautiful, remote sandy beach is backed by high dunes, with cliffs at the eastern end. On our visit we spotted deer scampering through the dunes. Rock pools at LT. Often overlooked by visitors.

→ Heading N on A1, turn R, signposted 'Holy Island', and continue 3 miles across tidal causeway to main car park before village. Turn L and L again out of parking, following unsigned lane to farm buildings then farm track N, keeping straight for 1 mile. At field end, head N onto dunes to Coves Haven.
30 mins, 55.6875, -1.7992 🏕🏖🏊🚻

5 SANDHAM BAY

To the east of Coves Haven is another of Holy Island's remote bays, hidden behind high dunes near Emmanuel Head. The lovely sandy beach is more likely to be visited by birdwatchers than sunbathers. The huge white pyramid is a navigation tower warning ships of hidden reefs off the coast.

→ As for Coves Haven, then at field end, head NE onto dunes towards pyramid.
30 mins, 55.6853, -1.7879 🏕🏖🏊🚻

6 THE LINKS BEACH

This is the most westerly of Holy Island's remote north-coast beaches. When the tide recedes, the sand stretches all the way to Goswick Sands on the mainland. The island-end of the beach feels less exposed, as it backs up against the dunes and cliffs of Snipe Point. Lots of LT rock pools here too.

→ Heading N on A1, turn R, signposted 'Holy Island', and continue for 1¾ miles and turn L up bumpy track to Snook car park (55.6843, -1.8349). Beach is just over the dunes.
2 mins, 55.6893, -1.8352 🏖🏊🚻

7 FISHERMAN'S HAVEN

Picturesque cove backed by rocks and low cliffs. Look out for seals, dolphins and

porpoises. Amazing views up and down the coast. Nice for an evening swim.

→ From Berwick, follow Castlegate (A1167) to roundabout and take R turn onto Northumberland Ave. Continue for ¾ mile to Green Havens car park and steps to beach (TD15 1NE).

5 mins, 55.7759, -1.9961

RIVERS & WATERFALLS

8 ETAL WEIR, RIVER TILL

Fun swim spot at the end of pretty Etal village. Some rapids to play in and deeper pools for swimming, with paddling by the small weir. Grassy bank and picnic tables.

→ Heading N on B6354 in Etal village, turn L and continue past castle on L to a small parking area by river.

2 mins, 55.6491, -2.1201

9 TWIZEL BRIDGE, RIVER TILL

In a picturesque gorge, beneath a lovely Tudor arch bridge, this section of the Till has some deep pools for swimming, paddleboarding or kayaking. There is a midway beach by the weir with shallower water.

→ Located just off the A698, midway between Cornhill-on-Tweed and Norham. Find parking

on L just after bridge at 55.6826, -2.1838. Follow footpath signed 'Twizel Castle' by parking area, then drop down to riverbank and follow path around. Deeper pool and paddleboarding launch near bridge. Continue to weir for beach and swim spot at 55.6836, -2.1866.

5 mins, 55.6837, -2.1867

10 FORD BRIDGE, RIVER TILL

An accessible deep pool with a rope swing on a meander of the river by the stone bridge, with shallow entry from a small beach. Also good for paddleboarding and kayaking. Near Ford Bridge Campsite.

→ Head W out of Ford, crossing B3654 and stone bridge to large parking area almost immediately on L behind trees.

2 mins, 55.6303, -2.0982

11 UNION CHAIN BRIDGE, RIVER TWEED

A wide, fast-flowing stretch of the River Tweed beneath the iconic Union Chain Bridge, with a small island from where you can swim or launch a paddleboard/kayak. Caution in high water.

→ Head NE out of Horncliffe, then take L turn to Union Chain Bridge. Parking possible for one car on verge on L, just past Chain Bridge

Honey Farm (TD15 2XT). Pass through gate before bridge, follow footpath to island on L.
5 mins, 55.7551, -2.1073 ⚓⚓

12 NORHAM, RIVER TWEED

A peaceful, calm and easily accessible section of the River Tweed. Upstream is Norham Bridge and Canny Island, where you can swim the short distance from England to Scotland. Scenic riverside walks with further picnic and paddling spots can be found along this lovely stretch.

➔ From Norham village centre, follow road N down to river for ¼ mile to parking area. Follow path L to beach and swim spot. Canny Island is ½ mile upstream at 55.7166, -2.1736.
1 min, 55.7222, -2.1647 ⚓⚓⚓⚓

13 HORNCLIFFE, RIVER TWEED

A hidden beach and pleasant spot for a picnic and paddle. Shallow entry to deeper water. Popular with salmon fishermen. You can follow the riverside path downstream all the way to the majestic Union Chain Bridge.

➔ In Horncliffe village, park in The Square (55.7416, -2.1146) and go down Tofts Lane to footpath on L and track down to river through gate.
10 mins, 55.7418, -2.1172 ⚓⚓⚓⚓

14 ROUTIN LYNN WATERFALL

On a path leading up to Goatscrag Hill, this pretty, secluded waterfall is situated in a hidden ravine, falling about 6m into a clear, brown pool of the Broomridgedean Burn.

➔ From Ford, follow the B6353 in the direction of Heatherslaw, then turn L at end of village towards Kimmerston. After 1½ miles, turn L at T-junction and continue for 1¾ miles to parking on R by roadside on no through road (55.6231, -2.0276). Follow footpath opposite (worn signpost for Routin Lynn Farm) for 100m, listening for rushing water to L. Follow path through woods down to falls.
10 mins, 55.6247, -2.0300 ⚓⚓

SACRED & ANCIENT

15 HOLY ISLAND

Cut off from the mainland twice a day, as the North Sea sweeps over its causeway, this tidal island is steeped in history. In ad 635, St Aidan arrived from Iona and founded his monastery here. The Christian message then flourished throughout the world, and the island has since remained a place of pilgrimage. You can walk the 3-mile Pilgrim's Way, marked out with poles along the sand – only to be attempted on a receding tide.

→ Holy Island is well signed from the A1 after Fenwick and is reached via a 3-mile causeway at LT. Most people cross as the tide is receding, spending LT on the island. Others prefer to remain on the island for HT, which is often quieter. Whether you choose to walk the Pilgrim's Way or drive, it is essential you consult the tide times and plan carefully before crossing. Park in Chare Ends car park (TD15 2SE).
5 mins, 55.6764, -1.8037

16 LINDISFARNE PRIORY
One of the most important centres of Christianity, established by St Aidan in ad 635, Lindisfarne Priory was also the home of the venerated St Cuthbert, who lived and died here. There is an EH entry fee, but you can wander around the outside of the ruins for free. The neighbouring parish church of St Mary the Virgin, the oldest building on Holy Island, has an interesting display about the Lindisfarne Gospels.

→ Lindisfarne is reached via a 3-mile causeway from the mainland, only accessible at LT, so check the crossing times carefully. From Chare Ends car park (TD15 2SE), follow signposts to the priory and church.
10 mins, 55.6680, -1.8009

17 DUDDO FIVE STONES
Situated on the crest of a hill, this striking Neolithic/Bronze Age circle of five standing stones has been weathered into strange shapes over its 4,000-year existence. There is a gap in the circle where a sixth stone once stood. There are glorious views of the Cheviots and towards the River Tweed and the Scottish Border.

→ 500m W of Duddo, you come to a small sign for Duddo Stone Circle on R. Park carefully on grass verge. Follow signposted permissive path N for ½ mile through two fields to circle.
20 mins, 55.6869, -2.1120

18 ST CUTHBERT'S ISLAND
This small island, which appears at LT just off Lindisfarne, is where St Cuthbert first tried to live as a hermit until he realised its proximity to Holy Island meant the monks could still holler across to him. He subsequently retreated to the more remote Farne Islands. Walk across at LT, take a pew on the rocks and watch as the resident seals put on a show for you.

→ From Lindisfarne, head past the priory and church to a footpath through a gate leading to the beach and the island.
5 mins, 55.6677, -1.8063

ROCK ART

19 ROUTIN LYNN ROCK ART

The largest carved outcrop of rock art in Northern England, this huge slab of pale grey stone is covered in decorative cup and ring marks. Although hidden in the trees, it is accessible, being by the roadside. Combine with visit to Routin Lynn Waterfall.

➜ As for Routin Lynn Waterfall but from parking, turn R and walk for a few metres to a clearing in the woods on L and path leading to the stone.

5 mins, 55.6247, -2.0276 ✝ 🍴

WILDLIFE WONDERS

20 FARNE ISLANDS NATURE RESERVE

Between 15 to 28 rocky islands scattered off the coast of Seahouses, depending on the level of the tide. From April to July this is one of the best seabird colonies in the UK, with more than 23 different species of birds, including 43,000 puffins who come to mate here each year. The islands are also home to colonies of Atlantic grey seals, with 2,000 pups born each year. On Inner Farne there is a chapel and Victorian lighthouse.

➜ Seahouses is the gateway to the Farne Islands, with boat trips from the harbour, including sunset visits, seal cruises and an Inner Farne landing trip.

5 mins, 55.6319, -1.6273 🚗

21 FORD MOSS

Explore the wild landscape of this former colliery set in a hollow at the top of the hill, with stunning views across the Till Valley and the Cheviots. Its most striking feature is the large brick chimney, part of a former coal mine. Circular route through wet and uneven terrain around the reserve. Look out for buzzards and kestrels.

➜ From Ford follow the B6353 for almost 1 mile then turn R along an unmarked road signed 'Ford Moss'. Limited parking on grass verge on L. Access to the reserve is through a 5-bar gate and track.

5 mins, 55.6308, -2.0559 🍴🐾🚶‍♂️🧭

LOST RUINS & CASTLES

22 LINDISFARNE CASTLE

This 16th-century fortress, which crowns a volcanic plug known as Beblowe Crag, was built from stone taken from the abandoned Lindisfarne Priory. Near the castle are some lime kilns, which are some of the largest

examples of their kind in the country. Make sure to visit the lovely walled garden designed by Gertrude Jekyll.

→ The castle is clearly visible and well signed from Lindisfarne village.
20 mins, 55.6690, -1.7847 ⬚⬚⬚⬚⬚⬚

23 NORHAM CASTLE

One of the finest border castles, set high on a grassy mound on the S side of the River Tweed. First built around 1121, it was one of the most important strongholds in this once turbulent region, besieged at least 13 times and most frequently attacked by the Scots. It finally fell to James IV's heavy cannon in 1513, shortly before his defeat at Flodden Field. Beautiful, majestic ruins to explore.

→ In Norham village, 6 miles SW of Berwick-upon-Tweed; located on minor road off B6470 (from A698). Car park (TD15 2JY).
2 mins, 55.7214, -2.1508 ⬚⬚⬚

24 TWIZEL CASTLE

Romantic ruins of a medieval castle standing above a bend of the River Till. Nice views towards Scotland. Afterwards head to the river for a swim.

→ There is a parking bay next to Twizel Bridge (55.6831, -2.1832). Follow fingerpost uphill

through the woods, which open out to a field where the castle is situated.
10 mins, 55.6840, -2.1879 ⬚⬚⬚

25 ETAL CASTLE

A ruined 14th-century castle built by Robert Manners as a defence against Scots raiders. It fell to James IV's army before his defeat at Flodden Field. Explore the picturesque village of Etal afterwards and enjoy a picnic by the riverside.

→ From Wooler, follow the A697 for 7½ miles, then take a R signed Ford and Etal onto the B6354 for ½ mile. Turn L, continuing on B6354 for 1½ miles through Heatherslaw to Etal village. Plenty of parking near entrance.
2 mins, 55.6474, -2.1199 ⬚⬚⬚

26 STEEL END FORT

Ruined tower and section of fort situated by the harbour, originally built to protect the island and Lindisfarne Castle from Dutch raids in the 1670s. As it was never rebuilt or redesigned, it is a rare example of late 17th-century defence structures.

→ Head towards the castle and as you approach the beach, turn R towards a promontory and the fort.
10 mins, 55.6681, -1.7957 ⬚⬚

26

HERITAGE SITES

27 FLODDEN BATTLEFIELD

A battlefield with more than just a memorial stone to mark the Battle of Flodden; here you can follow the battlefield trail on information boards at key spots to discover what happened on that fateful day in 1513, when James IV became the last British monarch to die in battle, changing the course of history forever.

→ Travelling N on the A697, at Crookham take the L turn to Branxton, passing through the village to Flodden Field battle site. Parking on L. Follow footpath sign to monument and battlefield trail.

5 mins, 55.6288, -2.1766 🚶

28 FORD AND ETAL ESTATES

One of Northumberland's best kept secrets, these two picture-postcard villages have a combination of heritage attractions, including ruined castles, white-washed cottages, cafés, pubs and the lovely River Till for a swim or riverside picnic. Make sure to visit the spectacular watercolour murals at Lady Waterford Hall in Ford.

→ From Wooler follow the A697 for 7½ miles, then turn R onto B6354, where Ford and Etal villages are well signed.

5 mins, 55.6312, -2.0877 🚶 🍴

COSY PUBS & MICROBREWERIES

29 THE BLACK BULL AT ETAL

Attractive village hostelry and the only thatched pub in Northumberland, managed by Cheviot Brewery, who brew their beer just up the road from here.

→ Etal, Cornhill-on-Tweed, TD12 4TL, 01890 820200

55.6480, -2.1175 🍴 🍺 🍷

30 THE BLUE BELL INN

Traditional coaching inn serving good pub grub. Decent selection of real ales from local breweries. Friendly, attentive staff.

→ Crookham, Cornhill-on-Tweed, TD12 4SH, 01890 820789

55.6373, -2.1436 🍴 🍺 🍷

31 THE CHEVIOT TAP

The onsite tap bar for the Cheviot Brewery, with a rotating range of food available on Friday nights. Plenty of outdoor seating. On chillier evenings, cosy up inside and toast S'mores over the open fire. Bell tents and

28

29

pods. Kids will love the curious and friendly alpacas. Gorgeous location.

→ Slainsfield, Cornhill-on-Tweed, TD12 4TP, 0191 389 7102

55.6478, -2.0823 🍴🛏️🅿️

SLOW FOOD

32 THE OLD DAIRY AT FORD

An old milking parlour with a rustic outdoor champagne bar, excellent coffee and occasional baked goods, which you can enjoy while soaking up glorious views of the Cheviots. There is also a barn packed with antiques and vintage curios to browse. A unique place.

→ Ford, Berwick-upon-Tweed, TD15 2PX, 01890 820325

55.6296, -2.0876 🍴🛏️🅿️📷

33 BOES AT HEATHERSLAW

Overlooking the River Till, this popular café in the old corn mill serves Tregothnan, a tea grown in England. Light lunches, tapas and sharing platters.

→ Heatherslaw Mill, Heatherslaw, Cornhill-on-Tweed TD12 4TJ, 01890 560267

55.6390, -2.1076 🍴🛏️🅿️

34 PILGRIMS COFFEE HOUSE

Independent ethical coffee house and roastery serving out of a repurposed shipping container on Lindisfarne. Nice outdoor seating area. Opening hours vary depending on tidal crossings.

→ Pilgrims Coffee House & Roastery, Marygate, The Holy Island of Lindisfarne, TD15 2SJ, 01289 389109

55.6713, -1.7999 🍴🛏️🅿️

35 THE LAVENDER TEAROOMS

Traditional tearoom with a pretty front garden and friendly staff serving local specialities. Don't leave without trying their singing hinnies, a type of sweet griddle cake. Also a village shop and post office.

→ Etal Village, Cornhill-on-Tweed, TD12 4TN, 01890 820761

55.6478, -2.1169 🍴

36 CORNHILL-ON-TWEED VILLAGE SHOP

A popular family-run village shop and so much more. As well as groceries, the shop offers home baking, including quiches and cakes, picnic lunches, soup, deli and filled rolls. Popular with the locals.

→ Main Street, Cornhill-on-Tweed, TD12 4UH, 01890 883313

55.6468, -2.2267 🍴🅿️

FISH & SEAFOOD

37 LINDISFARNE OYSTERS

On the site of oyster beds established by the 14th-century monks of Lindisfarne Priory, the family-run farm sells high-quality Pacific oysters grown on the seashore within the Lindisfarne NNR. Order online. Home delivery.

→ West House, Ross Farm, Belford, NE70 7EN, 01668 213870

55.6259, -1.7888 🍴

38 COULL'S FISH AND CHIPS

Tasty fish and chips served by a friendly team. Eat in or take away – a good spot to enjoy them is overlooking the bay at Greens Haven, with sweeping coastal views.

→ 11 Castlegate, Berwick-upon-Tweed, TD15 1JS, 01289 331480

55.7713, -2.0068 🍴

CAMP & SLEEP

39 THE BARN AT BEAL

Small, popular family-run campsite and the closest one to Holy Island at less than a mile to the causeway. There are 11 pitches and 16

hardstanding. Book in advance in high season. The barn has a restaurant, coffee shop, bar and breathtaking views from the terrace.

→ Beal Farm, Beal, Berwick-upon-Tweed, TD15 2PB, 01289 540044
55.6780, -1.8958 ▲

40 FORD BRIDGE CAMPSITE

Small, friendly campsite in the shadow of the Cheviots and with views of Ford Castle. Nearby is Ford Bridge, with a lovely swim spot. Dog-walking field.

→ Second Linthaugh Farmhouse, Cornhill-On-Tweed, TD12 4TQ, 07825 001425
55.6248, -2.1090 ▲

41 THE BLACK BULL INN

Village pub serving quality locally sourced food and a good selection of local ales. Also offers tastefully furnished accommodation named after local valleys, castles and rivers.

→ The Black Bull Inn, 2-4 Main Street, Lowick, TD15 2UA, 01289 388375
55.6491, -1.9828 ◁ 🍴 ♀ 🛏

42 THE COLLINGWOOD ARMS

Beautifully situated, laid-back, modern country house hotel with views over the River Tweed towards Scotland. A creative menu, with a focus on fish and game, served in the brasserie or restaurant. Antiques and roll-top baths in the rooms.

→ Main Street, Cornhill-On-Tweed, TD12 4UH, 01890 882424
55.6470, -2.2262 ◁ 🍴 ♀ 🛏

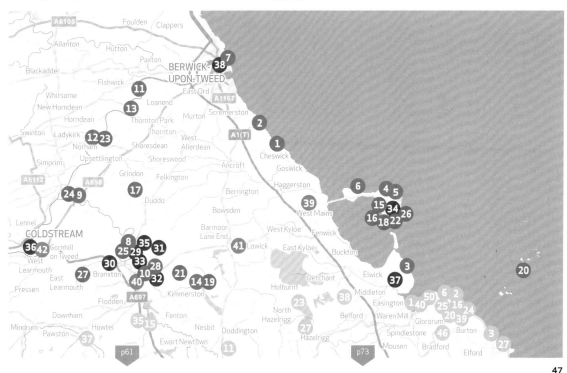

THE CHEVIOTS

Our perfect weekend

→ **Hike** through the College Valley on the slopes of the Cheviot to enjoy a refreshing dip in the Three Sisters Waterfall

→ **Delve** into the mysterious Cateran Hole, a smugglers' cave on a remote moor

→ **Scale** Yeavering Bell for splendid views of the Cheviots and Ad Gefrin, the summer palace of the kings of Northumbria

→ **Drop** into Doddington Dairy Milk Bar, which has been serving up ice creams since it was built by a farmer in the 1930s

→ **Climb** up to Ros Castle for spectacular views and spot the seven castles visible from its summit

→ **Visit** two legendary caves that take their name from St Cuthbert: a hillside hideaway with stunning views across the Milfield Plain and a huge sandstone shelter

→ **Pack** a picnic and explore the River Breamish. If you are feeling energetic, there are countless hill forts to conquer

→ **Leap** into the deep plunge pool beneath Linhope Spout, a dramatic 18m waterfall

A range of rolling hills, hidden valleys and waterfalls plunging into crystal-clear pools, far from the crowds, make the Cheviots the perfect destination for adventurers.

Straddling the English-Scottish border, these rugged upland peaks form a curvaceous backbone, with the broad-backed Cheviot at their heart, formed 390 million years ago when volcanic lava cooled to form its distinct shape.

As the highest mountain in Northumberland, the Cheviot is a magnet for walkers, but this area boasts many other thrilling summits, including the second highest peak, Hedgehope Hill, considered to have better views than its famous neighbour.

On the edge of the Cheviots, double-peaked Yeavering Bell and Humbleton Hill can be climbed in a couple of hours, in turn offering a sense of achievement and magnificent vistas.

Two of the Cheviot's most beautiful steep-sided valleys are the College and Harthope valleys, providing a springboard for exploration. Hiking through the College Valley offers sublime scenery with an exhilarating scramble at the craggy Hen Hole above the Three Sisters Waterfall.

The remote Harthope Valley has always attracted walkers, including 18th-century poet Sir Walter Scott and novelist Daniel Defoe. Scott described it as 'one of the wildest and most romantic' places.

Many of the region's spectacular falls await water lovers: magical Hethpool Linn, Harthope Linn with its natural water slide and Linhope Spout, plunging 18m into a legendary deep pool.

The picturesque river setting of the Breamish Valley is ideal for family picnics along the haugh land. An astonishing number of prehistoric hill forts were built here by ancient Britons 2,300 years ago; faint circles in the ground, the remains of timber roundhouses, can be seen in many, including at Brough Law.

To the east, Bewick is the gateway to further adventures: a scramble up Ros Castle for one of the best views in the North East; bouldering at Hepburn Crags and hunting for Berthele's Stone. Crawl through Cateran Hole, a smugglers' tunnel, and seek out caves where St Cuthbert once rested. Around this time, the 7th-century kings of Northumbria created a summer palace at Ad Gefrin, one of the 20th century's most remarkable archaeological discoveries.

You will spot red squirrels, peregrines and elusive feral goats grazing the slopes of the Cheviots, and the sighting of the remarkable Chillingham wild cattle, which live in ancient alder and oak forests, where they have roamed free of human interference for more than 1,000 years, is one you will never forget.

WATERFALLS

1 LINHOPE SPOUT, LINHOPE BURN

Spectacular chute of water into a deep plunge pool where daring souls can leap off various ledges into the clear, cool waters of the Linhope Burn. Situated in a pretty glade surrounded by the Cheviot Hills, this is the perfect spot for a picnic and a paddle in the shallows of the beck.

→ Travelling N on the A697 from Longframlington for 12½ miles, pass through Powburn then take L turn signposted 'Breamish Valley' and keep on through village, past pretty paddling and picnic spots, to end of public road. Continue 1½ miles on foot through hamlet and onto open moor. Signed to spout below on R.

45 mins, 55.4474, -2.0678 🚶🏕️⛺🏊⛴️🍴

2 HARTHOPE LINN, HARTHOPE BURN

Magical, hidden waterfall and plunge pool in a tiny, wooded gorge at the foot of the Cheviot and Hedgehope Hill. Further fun upstream above the falls, where a cataract has created a natural water slide.

→ Signed 'Harthope Valley' from the Anchor Inn in Wooler. Park at road end at Langleeford (55.4939, -2.0790) and walk 2 miles up Harthope Burn. Pass through gate on L to find falls.

60 mins, 55.4766, -2.1158 🚶🏕️⛺🏊⛴️🍴

3 HETHPOOL LINN, COLLEGE BURN

Screened by trees beside a footpath, a channel of deep pools has formed between the cleft of the rock walls of College Burn, leading from the waterfall. A magical place for a summer's evening dip.

→ Head N from Wooler on the A697 and after 2½ miles keep L onto the B6351. Continue for 4 miles through Kirknewton and take L for Hethpool. Continue past Hethpool House to car park on L. Walk back along road to gate on R and footpath signposted 'St Cuthbert's Way'. At second field cross stile on L, pass through field then a second field and cross footbridge to reach paths down to burn on R.

20 mins, 55.5500, -2.1569 🚶🏕️⛺🏊⛴️🍴

4 THE HEN HOLE AND THREE SISTERS WATERFALL

This dramatic gorge cuts an enormous slice out of the steep, west-facing slopes of the mighty Cheviot, creating a channel for the Three Sisters Waterfall, which pours into the Hen Hole. An outstanding location in the College Valley, it is arguably the most beautiful rift in Northumberland. End your journey here or scramble on for a finale at the summit of the county's highest hill (see The Cheviot entry).

→ Limited number of free parking passes issued each day for car park at Hethpool, obtained from College Valley website. From parking at Mounthooly Bunkhouse (NE71 6TU), follow footpath behind bunkhouse, passing woodland on R and continuing through valley before turning a corner to Hen Hole and waterfall. Alternatively, park at Hethpool and follow burn to Mounthooly as above (extra 5 miles).

60 mins, 55.4760, -2.1794 🚶🏕️⛺🏊⛴️🚵🏔️

RIVERS

5 BREAMISH VALLEY, RIVER BREAMISH

Several pretty paddling and picnic spots along the flat banks of the River Breamish, surrounded by high, rolling hills. Perfect day out for families with younger children.

→ Directions as for Linhope Spout from A697 to Ingram, then continue past Bulby's Wood car park on R and park up on the haugh land alongside the river.

1 min, 55.4436, -2.0069 🐟🚶🏕️

SPECTACULAR SCENERY

6 COLLEGE VALLEY

An incredibly beautiful valley on the northern edge of the Cheviot Hills, cut through by College Burn, with steep-sided crags, cascading waterfalls and spectacular scenery. A haven for wildlife – red squirrels, peregrines and slowworms thrive here – and home to feral goats, apparently released from Holy Island by Medieval monks. With no cars, it is a walkers' paradise with miles of paths, including the RAF 100 Crash Trail, exploring WW2 plane crash sites; tranquil valley floor walks; and challenging higher route trails, including to the Cheviot.

→ Head N from Wooler on the A697 and after 2½ miles turn L onto the B6351. Continue for 4 miles through Kirknewton and take L for Hethpool. Continue to free car park on L. Or obtain a limited vehicle pass from the College Valley website to park at Mounthooly Bunkhouse and continue on foot to trails.
60 mins, 55.5162, -2.1799 🅰🏕🌲🐾🚲🅿🔲

HILLTOPS & FORTS

7 THE CHEVIOT

Northumberland's highest mountain (815m), with views across to the Lake District on a clear day. Its broad hump back looms from near and far; you can see why the range of hills bears its name. The valleys and slopes on its approach are well worth exploring, and there is a sense of achievement on reaching its summit. But as it plateaus at the top, you can often get better views from neighbouring Hedgehope Hill. The weather can change fast so take both care and the proper equipment.

→ Park at Langleeford, as for Harthope Burn. The route then ascends along public footpaths with the burn on your L. Continue to Cairn Hill, passing the pretty waterfall of Harthope Linn on the way. At Cairn Hill pick up the Pennine Way to take you to the summit. Also possible to reach the summit via College Valley.
6–7 hrs, 55.4786, -2.1454 🔲🏔🅰🏕🐾🅿🚲

8 HEDGEHOPE HILL

The second highest hill (714m) in the Northumberland National Park is often overlooked in favour of its more famous neighbour. However, the views from the summit of Hedgehope Hill are considered better than the vista from the flat-topped Cheviot.

→ Directions as for Linhope Spout. Instead of dropping down to waterfall, continue along

track, taking a R before sheep pens to summit hill. OS map as well as appropriate clothing and footwear necessary.

2–3 hrs, 55.4719, -2.0903 🌊🏔🏕🅿🚌🐕♿

9 HUMBLETON HILL IRON AGE HILL FORT

Reach the summit of this hill (298m), retracing the site of a bloody, one-sided battle retold in Shakespeare's *Henry IV, Part 1*. The Battle of Homildon Hill (1402), which saw English forces, commanded by Harry Hotspur, battle Scottish forces on the hill's lower slopes, was deemed a triumph for the longbow. Follow the circuit around the hill, then climb to the hill fort and defence enclosures, dating back to the Iron Age, for fabulous views.

➜ Follow the A697 N from Wooler for just over 1 mile, then take a L for Humbleton to verge parking. There is an interpretation board just along the lane on R with directions to hill fort.

5 mins, 55.5483, -2.0538 🌊🚶🏕🅿🚲♿

10 YEAVERING BELL HILL FORT

This short, sharp scramble to Northumberland's largest Iron Age hill fort is well worth the effort for the stupendous views on the way up and from the 361m double-peaked summit. Good views of Ad

Gefrin, the 7th-century palace of King Edwin, which sits below it. Keep an eye out for the elusive feral goats.

➜ Head N from Wooler on the A697 for 2½ miles, then turn L onto the B6351 for 2 miles to parking on L by track. Follow track past cottages to gate and footpath sign to Yeavering Bell.

50 mins, 55.5573, -2.1156 🌊🚶🏕🅿🚲♿

11 DOD LAW AND ROCK ART

Climb to Dod Law, the highest point on Doddington Moor (187m), for magnificent views across the Cheviots and Milfield Plain. This archaeologically rich moor has Iron Age enclosures, Bronze Age burial cairns and a number of carved stones. There is a cup-and-ring-marked stone near the high point of the hill, and another lies in a gap among the ferns at the base of the hill at 55.5844, -1.9995.

➜ From Wooler follow the B6525 N for 2½ miles to Doddington. Park in village (55.5848, -2.0038) and head uphill past a cross on L. Opposite, find footpath onto moor. Head L round the gorse bushes to find rock art at 55.5844, -1.9995. For hill fort, follow footpath to 55.5785, -1.9938.

5 mins, 55.5789, -1.9945 🌊🚶🏕🅿🚲♿🛐

12 BREAMISH VALLEY HILL FORTS

An invigorating hill walk, with stunning views, visits five hill forts – or you could just visit one. Brough Law, an impressive Iron Age hill fort with a double ring of fallen defensive walls, is easily reached and makes a superb vantage point from where to admire the impressive terraces of neighbouring hills.

→ From the Breamish Valley car park at Bulby's Wood (NE66 4LT), W of Ingram, near Powburn off the A697. Cross road and follow signpost for Brough Law. There are waymarkers if you wish to continue to the other hill forts.

2 mins, 55.4412, -1.9892 🚶🧍🪧🚲📷♿️↩

13 ROS CASTLE

Being the highest of the Chillingham Hills (315m), this is one of the finest viewpoints in the area, boasting extensive views of seven castles on a clear day. A handy topograph has been built into the wall at the summit to help locate them, as well as a 3,000-year-old Iron Age hill fort. A short climb for a lot of gain.

→ Follow directions for Hepburn Woods but continue for almost ½ mile to lay-by parking on L at 55.5177, -1.8736. Follow footpath. Moderate climb; path uneven in places.

15 mins, 55.5216, -1.8729 🚶🧍🪧🚲📷♿️↩

SACRED & ANCIENT

14 AD GEFRIN ROYAL SUMMER PALACE

Once the summer palace of the kings of Northumbria and one of the most important sites in 7th-century Britain. King Æthelfrith, King Edwin and his queen consort, Æthelburga, and St Oswald all resided here. Some of the most momentous events in early northern English history took place here, including the first conversions to Christianity. Having existed under the radar until now, Ad Gefrin is in line for a multi-million-pound visitor centre, which aims to put it on a par with Sutton Hoo.

→ Head N from Wooler on the A697, and after 2½ miles turn L on to the B6351 for 2 miles. As the road turns to the R, there is a track to the left where you can park. Cross the road to find a path leading to Ad Gefrin site. Ad Gefrin sits beneath the shadow of Yeavering Bell, whose summit is probably the best place from which to view the site.

2 mins, 55.5680, -2.1172 ✝️

15 MAELMIN HENGE & TRAIL

Fascinating trail with faithful reconstructions of an Anglo-Saxon timber henge, cult centres, based on the nearby

4,000-year-old Milfield North Henge. There is also a Dark Age House based on three houses discovered at Woodbridge Quarry that date between ad 410 and 570. Excellent interpretation boards around the site. A must-vIsit for prehistory buffs.

→ Head N on the A697 from Wooler. The car park is on the R just before the village of Milfield. The trail starts behind the trees.
2 mins, 55.5963, -2.0977 🕇🚲

16 HETHPOOL STONE CIRCLE

This easily overlooked Late Neolithic double stone circle, situated on a gravel river terrace at the head of College Valley, is extremely rare in the north of England. A large circle of ruined stones remains, with isolated stones lying to the north and evidence of others beneath the ground. The site was likely ploughed during Medieval times, disturbing the circles.

→ Head N from Wooler on the A697, and after 2½ miles turn L onto the B6351. After 3½ miles turn L, signposted 'Hethpool'. Pass Hethpool House and cross cattle grid to car park on L. Circle is 250 yards along road to R.
2 mins, 55.5439, -2.1720 🕇🚲🚶

17 CHURCH OF ST GREGORY THE GREAT

Historic church housing an ancient stone relief of the adoration of the Magi, set in the wall north of the chancel arch. Social reformer Josephine Butler (1828–1906) is buried in the graveyard, and there is a mausoleum for the Davidson family. Davidson was chandler to Horatio Nelson, and his monument can be seen on the hill across the valley.

→ Head N from Wooler on the A697, and after 2½ miles turn L onto the B6351 for 3 miles to Kirknewton. Parking on L opposite church.
2 mins, 55.5659, -2.1388 🚲🕇

18 BLAWEARIE CAIRN

High up on Bewick Moor, this interesting Bronze Age cairn comprises large upright stones surrounding a ring of smaller stones containing cists, with a small cairn of stones in the centre. A spectacular location that feels remote but is easily reached. There is a hill fort and cup-and-ring-marked stones nearby (55.4880, -1.8779) and a ruined shepherd's hut set among crags for scrambling. The views from here are immense.

→ Travelling N on the A697, after Powburn and sawmill site, turn R onto B6346 for 2 miles,

then turn L towards Old Bewick. Parking on verge on R by farm/cottages. Follow footpath up through two gates and turn L, following track all the way to cairn on L.
30 mins, 55.4946, -1.8714 🏊🚶🏍🚲🚶

19 HOLY TRINITY CHAPEL, OLD BEWICK

A secluded 12th-century chapel hidden up a track in a hollow surrounded by woods next to a trickling stream. Inside, in the chancel, is an intriguing stone effigy of a 14th-century woman, which may have been the work of a school of sculptors from the Alnwick area.

→ Holy Trinity is at the end of a lane

immediately N of Old Bewick, between Eglingham and East Lilburn. Park along the verge.

2 mins, 55.4931, -1.8940 ✚

20 ST PETER'S CHURCH, CHILLINGHAM

A charming little country church housing an extraordinarily ornate 15th-century tomb of Sir Ralph Grey and his wife Elizabeth FitzHugh.

→ From Chillingham, pass the castle entrance on R then take next R to church at end.

1 min, 55.5273, -1.9033 ✚

HOLY WELLS & CAVES

21 KING'S CHAIR AND PIN WELL

A rather lovely walk through a magical glen among the hills behind Wooler leads to the Pin Well, where young ladies made a wish for their love on May Day. Look closely and you will see tiny crooked pin heads in the water. The rocky outcrop above is called the King's Chair, where a Scottish King is said to have observed a battle.

→ From Wooler follow the A697 S for ¾ mile towards Earle to lay-by parking on R at 55.5343, -2.0186. Then follow footpath past quarry, keeping left to follow a very narrow

path to the Pin Well, hidden away on L.
15 mins, 55.5374, -2.0224 🚶🏔️❓

22 CUDDY'S CAVE

An astonishing cave, also known as St Cuthbert's Cave, in a huge sandstone rock resembling an elephant's foot on a hillside where, according to local folklore, the devil hanged his granny.

→ Head S out of Doddington on the B6525 for 1 mile then turn L and continue to parking by gate on L, where you will see the cave on the hill. Head straight towards the cave and look for a small white pipe across the barbed-wire fence and paths up to it.
5 mins, 55.5731, -1.9949 🏰💚❓🖼️

23 ST CUTHBERT'S CAVE

Cave set within an overhanging sandstone outcrop where monks carrying St Cuthbert's body are said to have rested while fleeing Viking invaders in ad 875. Memorials to the Leather family, who once owned the cave, can be seen on the sandstone outcrops.

→ From Belford follow the B6349 W for 2¼ miles, then turn R for 2 miles. Turn R again for 1½ miles then R for ½ mile to NT car park.
20 mins, 55.6109, -1.9079 💚🚶⛱️

24 CATERAN HOLE

You could easily pass by this hidden cave on Bewick Moor without even noticing it is there. Once used by smugglers, the tunnel is around 35m in length, set in the gritstone of Cateran Hill. You can enter the cave via steps. Torch required.

→ Follow directions as for Hepburn Woods but continue for almost 2 miles to lay-by parking at 55.5153, -1.8426. Follow footpath across moor for ½ mile, then take L for 450m. Look carefully for a stone carved 'CH' and arrow L. Follow this path and keep looking out for hole on R.
25 mins, 55.5068, -1.8397 🔽🥾🏔️❓🖼️🧭♿

RUINS

25 HEPBURN BASTLE

A ruined 16th-century fortified tower house on the southern boundary of Chillingham Park. Great views across the Till Valley and Cheviots beyond. Afterwards, head into Hepburn Woods to seek out Berthele's Stone (see entry).

→ Travelling N from Eglingham on the B6346 continue for 5 miles, passing Old Bewick, then after 2 miles take R turn to parking in Hepburn Woods car park

(NE66 4EG) on R. Walk back down road
to bastle through gate on R.
5 mins, 55.5169, -1.8898 🚗

BOULDERING

26 HANGMAN'S ROCK

A large precariously balanced sandstone
rock situated on top of the hill overlooking
Old Bewick on Bewick moor. At the top of the
hill are a Celtic Iron Age hill fort and some
cup and ring markings.

→ As for Blawearie Cairn but go through
second gate and after a couple of hundred
metres cross the fence on the right by a stile
and head diagonally up the hill towards the
pine trees and the rock beyond.

20 mins, 55.4896, -1.8897 🚶🧗🔌❓🚗

27 BACK BOWDEN DOORS

Part of the same rocky outcrop as
neighbouring Bowden Doors, this Fell
Sandstone crag is situated in a sheltered
position with glorious views to the west. It
offers plenty of routes across all grades.
The superb open crag of Bowden Doors is a
little further south and more technical, with
steep climbs popular with outdoor groups.

→ From Belford head W on the B6349 Wooler
Road and continue for 3 miles. Turn R at
Hazelrigg sign and follow this for ¾ mile to
brow of the hill and parking by a steel gate
on R (55.5934, -1.9047). Pass through gate
onto open access land to reach crag. For Back
Bowden Doors, return to B6349 and turn R to
parking at 55.5830, -1.8518 on L and crag on
R. Raven's Crag is just below.

5 mins, 55.5937, -1.8998 🚶🔌🚗

28 BERTHELE'S STONE

A humungous stone, the size of a small
barn, that has detached from the crags
above. It is very well hidden but worth
the hunt when you find it on a wooded
slope in a clearing of trees, surrounded
by ferns, mosses and lichen. The stone is
apparently named after a forestry worker.
Further bouldering opportunities at
Hepburn Crags.

→ Travelling N from Eglingham on the B6346
continue for 5 miles, passing Old Bewick, then
after 2 miles turn R to parking in Hepburn
Woods car park (NE66 4EG) on R. Follow
footpath through woods, taking fork on L
to a path on L (55.5110, -1.8839) straight
up into woods until you reach a series of
disappointing boulders. Turn R and you will see
Berthele's Stone.

20 mins, 55.5109, -1.8818 🏔🔌🗿🚗

30

WILDLIFE WONDERS

29 CHILLINGHAM WILD CATTLE

One of the world's last remaining herds of wild cattle, rarer than the most endangered tiger, whose gene pool is so isolated that every animal is a genetic clone. Held up as sacred beasts, the cattle were sacrificed to the gods by pre-Christian pagans. They are potentially dangerous and can only be visited with a warden.

→ Wild Cattle Pavilion, Chillingham Castle, Chillingham, Alnwick, NE66 5NP, 01668 215250

2 mins, 55.5286, -1.9023

30 BRANTON LAKES NATURE RESERVE

Peaceful, hidden nature reserve in a former sand and gravel quarry with two large lakes and grazed grassland, providing diverse habitats for birds, wildlife and plants, including adders, great white egrets, kingfishers and brown hares. Footpaths and bird hides. Bring binoculars.

→ Travelling N on A697, ½ mile after Powburn take L towards Branton. After ¾ mile there is a metal gate on R and parking.

2 mins, 55.4421, -1.9256

LOCAL FOOD

31 INGRAM CAFÉ

Café in the heart of the Breamish Valley with outdoor seating area, serving up cakes, soup, scones and bacon butties. Bike park available. Open 10am – 4pm daily. Gifts and local products for sale.

→ Wardens Lodge 68, Alnwick, NE66 4LT, 01665 578100

55.4408, -1.9702

32 DODDINGTON DAIRY MILK BAR

You will easily spot this popular ice-cream parlour by the large cow standing outside. Built by a local dairy farmer in the 1930s, the updated milk bar offers a wide selection of award-winning ice creams and shakes from Doddington Dairy. Light lunches, cakes and teas also available.

→ 11 South Road, Wooler, NE71 6QE, 01668 282357

55.5444, -2.0092

33 THE BOSK

Coffee house, wine bar and B&B in a nice village setting. Menu specials on certain nights as well as regular dishes. Modern, airy interior and outdoor terrace.

31

32

Dogs welcome outside.

→ 5 The Old Barn, Branton, Alnwick, NE66 4LW
55.4413, -1.9321 🍴🏠

34 CHATTON VILLAGE STORE

Family-run village shop stocking local Northumbrian produce, including seasonal veg, takeaway food and drink and delicious tray bakes.

→ Chatton, Alnwick, NE66 5PU, 01668 215375
55.5492, -1.9128 🍴

COSY PUBS

35 RED LION INN

An 18th-century inn once frequented by sheep drovers from the north and now a friendly local pub serving good food and ales. B&B.

→ Main Road, Milfield, Wooler, NE71 6JD, 01668 216224
55.5986, -2.1044 🍴🏠

36 THE PERCY ARMS

Village pub serving homemade dishes with an emphasis on fresh, locally sourced seasonal ingredients. Lovely patio with cabins for al fresco dining. Rooms.

→ Main Road, Chatton, NE66 5PS, 01668 215244
55.5489, -1.9133 🍴🏠

COTTAGES & B&BS

37 THE BOTHY AT REEDSFORD

Pretty whitewashed Northumbrian cottage situated in a sheltered, sunny spot in the remote and scenic Bowmont Valley. Spectacular sunsets. Games room and rustic dining barn and a stream down the lane with a rope swing.

→ Crabtree & Crabtree Cottages
55.5862, -2.1708 🏠

38 THE BOATHOUSE AND FOLLY

Breathtakingly beautiful open-plan boathouse with floor-to-ceiling windows and a veranda overhanging the lake. A stunning location and perfect for a special occasion.

→ Middleton Hall, Belford, NE70 7LF, 01668 219677
55.6143, -1.8519 🏠

39 CHILLINGHAM MANOR B&B

Beautiful Grade II listed manor house offering comfortable and stylish rooms and Mhairi's full Northumbrian breakfasts, including bespoke Manor Bangers.

→ Chillingham, NE66 5NP, 01668 215614
55.5279, -1.9042 🍴🏠

BUNKBARNS & HOSTELS

40 WOOLER HOSTEL & SHEPHERD'S HUTS

Friendly hostel and a good base for exploring the Cheviots and Scottish Borders. Traditionally hand-crafted

Northumbrian shepherd's huts (sleep 2–3) which replicate those used by shepherds on the Cheviot Hills. Dogs allowed in the huts.

→ 30 Cheviot Street, Wooler, NE71 6LW, 01668 281365
55.5436, -2.0151

41 MOUNTHOOLY BUNKHOUSE

Beautifully situated bunkhouse at the head of the College Valley, sitting below the Cheviot. Sleeps 24 in versatile accommodation, including a family annexe. Can be booked as a whole. On both the Pennine Way and St Cuthbert's Way.

→ Mt Hooley, College Valley, Wooler, NE71 6TU, 01668 216358
55.4968, -2.1894

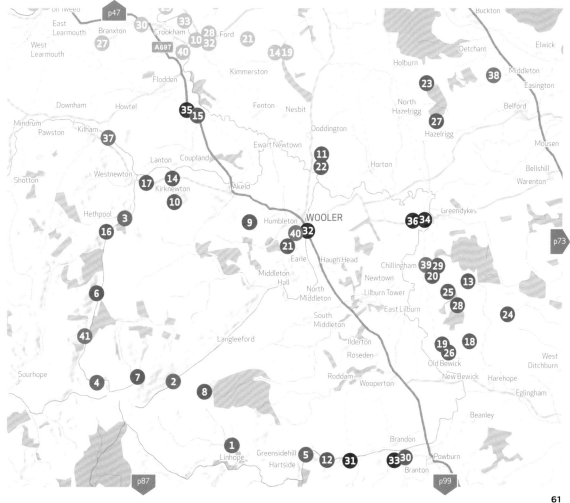

ALNWICK & EMBLETON BAY

Our perfect weekend

→ **Wait** for the tide to recede at Harkess Rocks near Bamburgh Lighthouse and bathe in one of the large rock pools that are revealed

→ **Swim** through natural caves, arches and pools at Rumbling Kern and leap into the surf

→ **Pitch** your tent at Budle Bay Campsite for spectacular sunset views over the sands

→ **Spot** the praying monks in the grounds of Hulne Priory, then picnic beside the River Aln below

→ **Visit** the cross, marking the spot where King Malcolm III of Scotland was slain in the 1093 Battle of Alnwick

→ **Call** in at L Robson & Sons Fisheries in Craster to collect oak-smoked kippers for breakfast

→ **Sample** a beer from the microbrewery at the Ship Inn at Low Newton and sit outside and watch the waves crash on the beach

→ **Delight** in the kaleidoscope of tulips planted in Howick Hall's Botticelli Meadows, then follow a magical woodland trail to a hidden cove

Pristine golden sands guarded by mighty fortresses, secluded bays and traditional fishing villages – not to mention superb seafood – word is spreading that Northumberland has a coastline to rival the best in Britain.

You could be forgiven for thinking this means the beaches are thronged with people. While Bamburgh, with its imposing 11th-century castle and endless silver sands, attracts a fair number of visitors, there are plenty of quiet beaches to find peace and solitude, even at the height of summer.

Bamburgh itself has a cluster of curiously named bathing pools, revealed at low tide. Choose your favourite: Cat Pool or The Gun, Aa'd Lads or Aa'd Lasses Pool. Ours is the Egg Pool: an oval pool refreshed at high tide by the deep, sapphire-blue waters of the North Sea.

The glorious 62-mile Northumberland Coastal Path offers some of the best shoreside walking in the country, taking in several secluded beaches in this area.

From the only west-facing harbour on the east coast, Beadnell's long, sheltered bay stretches south to jumbled rocks at Snook Point, an unspoiled section of beach. The adventurous may wish to try shore diving around the reefs of Beadnell Point to view the rusting wreck of the MV Yewglen.

The pint-sized village of Low Newton, and its cream-washed Victorian cottages built for local fishermen, huddles around a large grass square with an 18th-century pub tucked in the corner, overlooking the sea. There are few greater pleasures than sitting on the green here, tucking into a crab sandwich, with a glass of craft ale.

Dramatic Rumbling Kern, a small beach in a rocky cove with incredible geological features in the sandstone rocks, is a thrilling coasteering location.

For food lovers there is an abundance of flavoursome local fare to tempt the palate, from rustic seafood shacks to sea-view pubs and the world-famous Craster oak-smoked kippers.

For history buffs the ornamental grave of sea rescue heroine Grace Darling lies in the graveyard of St Aidan's Church, also worth visiting to see the 1,400-year-old Bamburgh Bones in its atmospheric crypt.

A few miles inland lies the historic market town of Alnwick with its majestic castle and award-winning gardens. Enjoy peaceful riverside walks through Hulne Park to the delightful ruins of a Carmelite priory, then browse the shelves of world-famous Barter Books, which has armchairs for relaxing and reading, open fires and an excellent café.

BEAUTIFUL BEACHES

1 BUDLE BAY

Glorious bay of LT sand flats, quickly covered by an incoming tide. Part of the Lindisfarne NNR and a haven for waders and wintering wildfowl. There are some industrial remains to explore, including an old jetty. Spectacular sunset beach. Take extreme care with mud flats and do not cross the mouth of the bay.

→ Best reached from parking along The Wynding (NE69 7DD) in Bamburgh and following the coastal path N for a spectacularly scenic walk.
30 mins, 55.6104, -1.7663

2 BAMBURGH CASTLE SANDS

Sensational beach with the magnificent Bamburgh Castle towering above the dunes. Walk down The Wynding for superb views back across the beach and castle. Good for surfing.

→ Signed Bamburgh from A1 near Belford. Turn L for parking down The Wynding, dir Golf Course (NE69 7DD). After houses on R (300m) find two car parks for beach.
5 mins, 55.6130, -1.7130

3 ST AIDAN'S DUNES, SEAHOUSES

Beautiful, long, dune-fringed sandy beach with Bamburgh Castle as a backdrop.

→ Head N out of Seahouses on the B1340 dir Bamburgh. After a mile park on R opp turn-off for Shoreston.
2 mins, 55.5893, -1.6674

4 BEADNELL BAY

Gorgeous horseshoe-shaped bay with pristine sands backed by grassy dunes and the only west-facing harbour on the east coast. Miles of dune-fringed beach and shallow waters, perfect for swimming and paddle sports.

→ For quieter south end of beach, approach from High Newton, parking in Newton Steads car park (NE66 3DF). For north end, follow B1340 N for 3 miles to Beadnell village.
2 mins, 55.5326, -1.6286

5 EMBLETON BAY

One of Northumberland's most spectacular beaches, this wide sandy bay with clear waters stretches beneath the dramatic ruins of Dunstanburgh Castle.

→ In Embleton take the B1399 S and turn L on to W.T. Stead Rd then immediately R onto Sunny Brae and keep L. Take L at end of road, which then turns sharply to the R. Take next L turn towards the golf course and parking at Dunstan Steads. Walk through dunes to the beach.
5 mins, 55.4972, -1.6102

HIDDEN BEACHES

6 THE EGG POOL, HARKESS ROCK POOLS

One of several LT rock pools for plunging near Stag Rock Lighthouse, each with their own name (check out the information board). The large oval Egg Pool warms up quickly on a sunny day.

→ From Bamburgh continue along The Wynding for ½ mile to parking (55.6158, -1.7243). Find pools below cottages, past lighthouse and 200m beyond.
5 mins, 55.6171, -1.7259

7 FOOTBALL HOLE BEACH

Small but beautiful bay of pale sand surrounded by dunes. Look out for seals and occasional dolphins.

→ The beach is most easily accessed by walking N from Low Newton (approx. 10 mins). No direct road access means it is relatively quiet.
10 mins, 55.5232, -1.6198

8 NEWTON HAVEN BEACH

Large, sandy and rocky beach in a fabulous location near the wonderful Ship Inn.

→ From High Newton, follow signs to Low Newton and parking after ½ mile in Low Newton car park on R.

5 mins, 55.5127, -1.6172 ⛵🚽

9 CRASTER PLUNGE POOL

Two large, deep plunge pools within rocks opening out to the sea, en route from Craster to Dunstanburgh Castle. The first one you reach is possibly the best one.

→ From Craster head N in the direction of Dunstanburgh Castle to pools on R.

5 mins, 55.4772, -1.5928 🌊🏊▽🍴🚽

10 RUMBLING KERN

Hidden sandy cove and thrilling coasteering spot with leaps and jumps from a series of vertical sandstone walls, as well as stacks and caves to swim through. Fascinating geological features.

→ From the Alnwick bypass (A1) take the B1340 turn-off at Denwick and follow signs to Longhoughton. At Longhoughton follow the B1339 N and after 1 mile turn R towards Howick to parking at Sea Houses Farm, where the road turns sharp L along the coast. Follow farm track just N of the farm to the cove.

5 mins, 55.4492, -1.5873 🌊🍴🏊▽🍴🚽

11 HOWICK HAVEN

Sandy cove just S of Rumbling Kern with LT rock pools and ledges.

→ Reached by following coastal path S of Rumbling Kern. Parking at same car park.

10 mins, 55.4458, -1.5882 🌊🏕🏊🚽

12 HOWICK HALL BEACH

Secluded cove at the end of the Howick Burn. Footbridge across burn. Mostly rocky beach with some LT sand.

→ Reached via the Long Walk (1½ miles/15 mins) from Howick Hall Gardens (fee) or by following coastal path S from Rumbling Kern (use same car park). Howick Hall has one of the best coastal gardens in the UK, including an arboretum with 11,000 trees grown from seeds collected in the wild since the 1980s.

15 mins, 55.4403, -1.5932 🌊🏕🏊🚽

13 SUGAR SANDS

Sheltered and secluded sandy beach, one of several pretty coves along this stretch of the coast.

→ As for Howdiemont Sands, then follow coastal path N for 600m. Alternatively, access via coastal path S of Howick.
5 mins, 55.4372, -1.5899 🖼️ⓘ

14 HOWDIEMONT SANDS
Lovely secluded sandy beach with dunes accessed at the end of a farm track.

→ From Longhoughton, turn R opp church and continue for ½ mile to Low Stead Farm. Continue through farm to car park; honesty box for parking. If closed there is a small parking area in front of gate. Alternatively, park at Boulmer beach car park and walk N on coastal path.
2 mins, 55.4341, -1.5862 🖼️⛺⛺ⓘ

RIVERS

15 RIVER ALN, HULNE PARK
Just upstream of Monk's Bridge in Hulne Park. Beautiful beach with paddling and deep enough for a longer swim. Perfect picnic spot. Ruins and follies to explore in the park.

→ In Alnwick, park in Ratten Row at entrance to Hulne Park (55.4167, -1.7166). Follow Red route, passing Duchess Bridge. Just after Monk's Bridge, find beach a few yards upstream. (Park opens 11am – 7pm in summer. Closes 5pm winter).
40 mins, 55.4255, -1.7235 🚶‍♂️🌲🐟🚶ⓘ

CASTLES & RUINS

16 BAMBURGH CASTLE

Perched above an outcrop of the Great Whin Sill, this superbly situated 11th-century coastal fortress has panoramic views of Holy Island, the Farne Islands and Bamburgh village. Once the capital of the 7th-century kings of Northumbria, the castle site has been occupied since at least the last Iron Age.

→ Travelling N on the A1, turn off at Adderstone services and follow the B1341. Bamburgh is about 5 miles. Alternatively, take the more leisurely B1340 coastal road.

5 mins, 55.6089, -1.7099 🅿🅿🅿

17 DUNSTANBURGH CASTLE

Standing on a remote headland these iconic 14th-century ruins, with their impressive gatehouse and twin-towered keep, are reached by a beautiful walk along rugged coast.

→ From Craster, the 1½-mile walk to the castle is well signposted.

30 mins, 55.4893, -1.5950 🔽🚶🏠🏛🏺🔲

18 HULNE PRIORY

Situated in Hulne Park, Alnwick Castle's former hunting ground, these stunning 13th-century fortified ruins are possibly the first Carmelite priory in Britain. Look out for the eerie statues of praying monks. A picturesque hillside setting, and the riverside below is great for picnics.

→ In Alnwick, find parking in Ratten Row at entrance to Hulne Park. Follow red route to ruins. Return on same route or complete circular walk.

50 mins. 55.4351, -1.7429 🏺🌳🚶🏛✝

19 ST LEONARD'S HOSPITAL CHAPEL

Lying in ruins near Alnwick Castle, this rare example of a medieval hospital was founded around the 12th century by Eustace de Vescy for the poor, elderly and sick and was annexed to Alnwick Abbey in 1376. Also visit nearby Malcolm Cross.

→ From Alnwick, leave town across the Lion Bridge, with castle on R, and continue to lay-by on R at 55.4254, -1.7016. Walk back along road to ruins across road.

2 mins. 55.4229, -1.7044 🅿🔲

FOLLIES & MEMORIALS

20 GRACE DARLING'S GRAVE

The Gothic-style memorial to sea rescue heroine Grace Darling is found in the graveyard of St Aidan's Church. The

lighthouse keeper's daughter became a national heroine after rowing to rescue survivors from a shipwreck. The church's crypt houses the Bamburgh Bones: the remains of 110 Anglo-Saxons unearthed in the dunes near Bamburgh Castle and laid to rest here. The rows of ossuary boxes containing human bones are an extraordinary sight.

→ St Aidan's Church is in the centre of Bamburgh. Park in Glebe Field car park (NE69 7AE, seasonal) or the Links Road car park opp castle.

5 mins, 55.6079, -1.7179 ✝

21 MALCOLM III CROSS

This stone cross marks where Malcolm III, King of Scotland, was slain in the Battle of Alnwick in 1093, one of two battles fought near the town. Malcolm and his son were killed by an army of knights led by Robert de Mowbray, Earl of Northumbria, and their bodies interred at Tynemouth Priory.

→ From Alnwick, leave town across the Lion Bridge, with the castle on the R, and continue to lay-by on R at 55.4254, -1.7016. Walk towards roundabout and find gate to cross on R.

2 mins, 55.4263, -1.7006 🅿🖼

WILDLIFE & DARK SKIES

22 EMBLETON QUARRY NATURE RESERVE

A community-owned nature reserve with various interesting habitats, including rare Whin grassland on the Whinstone ridges of the old quarry. Designated dark-sky site with pristine skies, as good as those found in parts of Kielder.

→ In Embleton, travelling N on the main street (B1339), turn R into Quaker's Row to find gate into reserve (NE66 3XS).

1 min, 55.4983, -1.6362

LOCAL SEAFOOD

23 BAIT AT BEADNELL

Take-away food shack in a converted shipping container serving up freshly caught lobster and paella, which you can tuck into on the beach. Open 9am – 4pm. Occasional one-meal suppers. Booking advised.

→ Beach Car Park, Beadnell, Chathill, NE67 5EE 55.5519, -1.6287 🍴

24 CREEL AND REEL SEAFOOD TRAILER

Tuck into seared scallops with garlic butter and toast or monkfish and chorizo skewers from this funky seafood trailer that pitches up in a car park beneath Bamburgh Castle.

→ Links Road, Bamburgh, NE69 7AX,
07595 981399
55.6041, -1.6975 🍴

25 THE POTTED LOBSTER

Fish restaurant with a relaxed vibe
overlooking Bamburgh Castle. Superb
menu of fresh, locally sourced seafood,
featuring smoked haddock chowder, crab and
Lindisfarne oysters – not to mention their
delectable potted lobster. Booking advised.
→ The Potted Lobster, 3 Lucker Rd,
Bamburgh, NE69 7BS, 01668 214088
55.6064, -1.7171 🍴

26 L ROBSON & SONS FISHERIES

Fourth-generation business that has been
producing world-famous oak-smoked kippers
and salmon for more than a hundred years.
→ 9 Haven Hill, Craster, Alnwick, NE66 3TR,
01665 576223
55.4722, -1.5929 🍴

COSY PUBS

27 THE OLDE SHIP INN, SEAHOUSES

Almost every inch of this seaside pub is
decked out in nautical nick-nacks, with a
floor made from ship's decking and cosy
wood-panelled snugs resembling cabins.
Real ales and pub grub on offer. Beer
garden with harbour views.
→ Main Street, Seahouses, NE68 7RD,
01665 720200
55.5822, -1.6523 🍴

28 THE JOLLY FISHERMAN INN

Tuck into a steaming bowl of moules-frites
or opt for the Jolly Fishboard at this historic
pub which people flock to for its excellent
seafood menu. Stunning sea views from the
terrace at the back.
→ Haven Hill, Craster, Alnwick, NE66 3TR,
01665 576461
55.4723, -1.5924 🍴

29 THE JOINERS ARMS

Rustic-chic gastro pub serving locally
sourced food with a contemporary twist.
Five boutique-style rooms with gilded
armchairs and enormous baths. The perfect
place for a romantic weekend away.
→ Newton-by-the-Sea, Alnwick, NE66 3EA,
01665 576 239
55.5196, -1.6297 🍴

30 THE SHIP INN, LOW NEWTON
Deservedly popular pub in the corner of a square just a pebble's throw from the gorgeous beach at Low Newton. Fish caught by local fishermen, lobster from Newton Bay, free-range meat, good coffee and live music. Microbrewery producing 20 different beers.
➜ Low Newton-by-the-Sea, Alnwick, NE66 3EL, 01665 576262
55.5140, -1.6200

31 FISHING BOAT INN
Gorgeous modern pub serving real ales and excellent fish and seafood dishes. Terrace with beautiful views of the bay. Stylish accommodation, including the rustic Cabin's Cove with full-width windows to the sunrise.
➜ 14-15 Boulmer Village, Boulmer, Alnwick, 01665 577750
55.4213, -1.5807

32 THE PACK HORSE INN, ELLINGHAM
Traditional village pub with cosy bar, log fire and low-slung beams, serving decent pub grub and local ales. Beer garden. B&B.
➜ Ellingham, Chathill, NE67 5HA, 01665 589292
55.5254, -1.7353

CAFÉS & RESTAURANTS

33 CARNABY'S CAFÉ, CHATHILL
Light and airy industrial-chic café situated just off the A1. Flavoursome, seasonal menu, including an amazing selection of salads and frittatas. Serves pizzas from the truck in the evenings. Kids' play area. Dogs welcome outside.
➜ Brownieside, Chathill, NE67 5HW, 01665 579061
55.5076, -1.7399

34 SALT WATER CAFÉ, BEADNELL
Start the day with a proper Northumbrian breakfast or opt for pancakes at this popular village café in the heart of Beadnell. Across the road, and part of the same team, is the Craster Arms with a pleasant beer garden and B&B.
➜ The Wynding, Beadnell, Chathill, NE67 5AS, 01665 720333
55.5566, -1.6377

35 BEADNELL TOWERS
Homely boutique hotel serving pub classics in the seaside village of Beadnell. You can also pop in for a drink after a bracing walk on the beach. Individual rooms to suit all needs; families, dog-friendly, accessible.

➜ The Wynding, Chathill, NE67 5AY, 01665 721211
55.5561, -1.6376

36 EARL GREY TEA HOUSE, HOWICK HALL
Sip from a cup of Earl Grey tea in the place where it was created. The blend was invented at Howick Hall by the 2nd Earl Grey, British prime minister from 1830 to 1834, using Bergamot to offset the taste of lime in the water from the hall's well.
➜ Howick, Hall, Alnwick, NE66 3LB, 01665 572232
55.4507, -1.6097

37 TREEHOUSE RESTAURANT, ALNWICK
A magical restaurant in the treetops, with twinkling lights and a roaring fire. This is one of the largest treehouses in the world.
➜ The Alnwick Garden, Denwick Lane, Alnwick, NE66 1YU, 01665 660320
55.4142, -1.6978

38 THE SCHOOL HOUSE COUNTRY KITCHEN
Licensed country kitchen in a converted school offering up a fresh, seasonal menu, including tasty brunches, afternoon tea, pizza and sandwiches. They run the Apple Inn across the road, which has rooms.

45

→ The School House, Belford, Lucker,
NE70 7JL, 01668 219114
55.5626, -1.7592 🍴

39 R CARTER & SON BUTCHERS
Dubbed 'carnivore heaven', this award-winning butcher, baker and sausage-roll maker has been in business since 1887. High-quality meat, homemade pies and its own cured bacon.
→ 3 Front St, Bamburgh, NE69 7BW,
01668 214344
55.6067, -1.7166 🍴

CAMP & GLAMP

40 BUDLE BAY FARM CAMPSITE
No-frills campsite with stupendous sunset views over Budle Bay. No toilets or showers. £15, pay on arrival.
→ B1342, Bamburgh, NE69 7AL, 07707 299430
55.6091, -1.7569 ⛺

41 DOXFORD FARM CAMPING
Small, quiet campsite with level pitches on a working farm with miles of woodland and lakeside walks. Also bell tents and luxury glamping pods.
→ Doxford Farm, Chathill, NE67 5DY,
01665 579456
55.4943, -1.7056 ⛺

47

42 COAST AND CASTLES CAMPING
Family-friendly campsite and glamp site with grass camper-van pitches near the beach at Boulmer. Basic facilities, pop-up bar and communal seating area. Campfires and BBQs encouraged!
→ Boulmer Road, Longhoughton, Alnwick,
NE66 3NU
55.4260, -1.6069 ⛺

43 OLD RECTORY, HOWICK
Glamping bell tent with a wood-burning stove in the grounds of a Georgian rectory that has great access to a hidden beach at Howick Haven.
→ Old Rectory, Craster, Alnwick, NE66 3LE,
01665 577590
55.4521, -1.5957 🏕

44 NORTHUMBERLAND FARM
Wake up early enough to help the farmer on his morning rounds, checking the animals at this family farm, part of the Featherdown Farm collection. Canvas hideaway with en suite. Honesty shop stocked with local goodies, from home-reared lamb to local oysters.

48

→ Featherdown.co.uk
55.5708, -1.6686 🏖

45 TREES AT TUGHALL
Minimalist-style cabin for two with a huge picture window near the beautiful sands of Beadnell Bay. There's no Wi-Fi to distract you, so it is the ideal place for a digital detox.
→ Trees at, Tughall, Chathill, NE67 5EN, 07593 437255
55.5410, -1.6724 🏖

46 BAMBURGH UNDER CANVAS
Five Lotus Belle tents with proper beds and bedding, a wood-burning stove and views of the Cheviot Hills. No kids. Pets allowed.
→ Glororum, Bamburgh, NE69 7AW, 07791 963926
55.5917, -1.7286 🏖

47 MIDDLEMOOR FARM HOLIDAYS
Quirky hideaway in a glamping narrowboat called Moonraker, safely docked on dry land. There's a cabin bed and the option of an al fresco shower. Miss Ellie sleeps 6 or opt for one of the showman's wagons. Fire pits and countryside views.
→ Middlemoor Farm, North Charlton, Alnwick, NE67 5HP, 07976 900668
55.4997, -1.7501 🏖

RUSTIC HAVENS

48 THE BATHING HOUSE
Surely one of the most romantic settings possible. This iconic, Grade II listed cottage perches on the cliff edge above a beautiful sandy cove, with panoramic views out to sea from every window.
→ The Bathing House, Howick, Craster, NE66 3LB, 01697 746777
55.4508, -1.5879 🏖

49 LOOKOUT COTTAGE
Hunker down in this snug cottage, once a lookout used to combat smuggling on the coastline. Features from its past are still in place, including the original bunkers where the coastguards once slept. Perfectly positioned above Embleton Bay.
→ Low Newton-by-the-Sea, Alnwick, NE66 3EQ, National Trust
55.5171, -1.6207 🏖

50 GREY HERON LODGE
Nestled in the dunes of beautiful Budle Bay Sands, this log cabin, with its own sandy beach, is the perfect beach bolthole for 6.

→ Stablewood Cottages, Lucker Steadings, Lucker Road, Lucker, NE70 7JQ, 01668 219607
55.6137, -1.7481 🏖

51 CALDER COTTAGE
Cosy cottage for two with fresh, contemporary interiors, log burner and gorgeous sea views of Embleton Sands.
→ Calder Cottage, Embleton. Crabtree & Crabtree holiday cottages
55.4963, -1.6321 🏖

KIELDER TO COQUETDALE

Our perfect weekend

→ **Scramble** up to the mythical Drake Stone, Northumberland's biggest boulder, to discover a magical hidden lake

→ **Follow** in the footsteps of the Victorians through an ancient, wooded valley to reach a spectacular waterfall

→ **Head** off the beaten track for an exhilarating ride along Kielder Forest Drive and admire the views from Blakehope Nick

→ **Imagine** being a soldier marching around Chew Camp, the highest Roman site in England

→ **Hunt** out the bastle houses, the fortified farmhouses that hint at the region's turbulent past

→ **Wander** through flower-rich ancient hay meadows, then take a dip in the cool, clear waters of the River Coquet

→ **Immerse** yourself in the sound and patterns of the lake in Kielder's mesmerising Wave Chamber

→ **Spend** the night in the remote Green Bothy, then explore England's largest area of rare blanket bog

→ **Gaze** up at pristine, twinkling skies from Stonehaugh's Star Dome Pavilion

Remote Cheviot moorland, rough fells, deep forests and peaceful river valleys, the contrast with the sandy beaches and castles of Northumberland's east coast could not be greater.

With 27 miles of scenic shoreline, Kielder Water, surrounded by England's largest forest, dominates this untamed western corner. Europe's largest man-made reservoir is the base for many water adventures, including sailing, paddleboarding and canoeing, with most of the amenities along the south shore where the bulk of visitors congregate.

But take yourself off to the tranquil north shore and it is a different story. As red squirrels parkour between the branches of the soaring Sitka spruce and ospreys hunt over the water, the landscape takes on the character of a Highland forest. Pine-fringed trails lead to the Belling Peninsula with its peaceful shoreline picnic spots overlooking the glistening water.

Not to be missed is the epic road trip along Kielder Forest Drive, a journey to be savoured, taking you through the far reaches of this infinite upland forest with panoramic views.

Tranquillity prevails, but it wasn't always this way. If Britain ever had a wild west, it must surely have been here. With 500 years of cross-border warfare and clashes between rival kinship groups, this was once a very dangerous place to live. The Border Reivers (from which the word 'bereaved' originated) raided farmsteads, stealing livestock. Black Middens Bastle is the start of the fascinating Tarset Bastle Trail.

The Otterburn Ranges are the second-largest live-firing range in the UK, but also an unspoiled expanse of countryside to explore, covering one-fifth of the national park. Quite fitting that the Roman camps of Brigantium and Chew Green are sited nearby. Beyond are the upper reaches of the Coquet Valley. The River Coquet starts as a trickle in the Cheviot Hills and flows through a remote valley with several idyllic swim spots. For a moorland swim, plunge into Harbottle Lake after a hike to the Drake Stone.

Some of the most precious habitats in England, and even Europe, thrive here: upland hay meadows, unique peat bogs and ancient woodland. On a warm summer's day, the vibrant slopes of Barrowburn Hay Meadows are a delight to wander through, as are Butterburn Flow's rare peat bogs in the Kielder Mires.

This is one of the best places in Northumberland's International Dark Sky Park to stargaze. On a clear evening, you can look up at millions of stars, the Milky Way and the Andromeda Galaxy, 2.5 million light years away, all visible with the naked eye.

WATERFALLS

1 HINDHOPE LINN WATERFALL

Spectacular waterfall with a refreshing plunge pool in an enchanting dell of old Scot's Pine and larch, reminders of the ancient forests here.

→ Park at Blakehopeburnhaugh car park at the N end of Kielder Forest Drive, off the A68. Pass through gate over River Rede onto gravel track and after a few yards take R turn onto woodland path.

20 mins, 55.2936, -2.3489 🪧🏕️⛰️🚶

2 HARESHAW LINN WATERFALL

Cross six charming bridges through ancient woodland to a spectacular 9m waterfall. There are several smaller falls on the way up; the second one in a secluded setting has a delicious plunge pool (55.1574, -2.2514). This beautiful, wooded valley was a favourite with the Victorians, who came here for recitals and performances.

→ Bellingham is 17 miles N of Hexham on the B6320. Take the Otterburn/Redesmouth road from the main street and turn L immediately after crossing stream to car park (NE48 2BZ or 55.1453, -2.2520). Well-signposted circular walk of 3 miles.

60 mins, 55.1627, -2.2499 🪧⛲⛰️🚶

RIVERS & LAKES

3 IRVING POOL, RIVER COQUET

Idyllic swim spot surrounded by open meadows and moorland. Plunge pool, some rapids and a small waterfall.

→ Follow the River Coquet from Rothbury and B6341 to Alwinton. Cross River Coquet at Linbriggs farm and continue ¾ mile to park by river.

2 mins, 55.3593, -2.1748 🐾⛲⛰️⛲

4 BUCKHAM'S BRIDGE, RIVER COQUET

Remote valley where the Buckham's Walls Burn joins the River Coquet and once the haunt of whisky smugglers. Nice spot for paddling and picnics.

→ Follow directions for Shillmoor Irving Pool and continue for 1½ miles to bridge.

1 min, 55.3681, -2.2064 ⛰️🐾⛲🐾📷

5 HOLYSTONE, RIVER COQUET

Delightful meadow-side riverbank next to footbridge with some shade from trees. Paddling and deeper pools for swimming.

→ Head S out of Harbottle, then just before Sharperton (before the river bridge) turn R and continue for just under ½ mile to parking on L and footpath across field to bridge and riverbank.

2 mins, 55.3222, -2.0687 🐾⛲🐾

6 HARBOTTLE LAKE

Secluded moorland tarn just over the brow from the mythical Drake Stone, perfect for a wild swim after a hike up the Harbottle Hills. Shallow entry at NE corner.

→ As for Drake Stone, then descend hills to lake.

5 mins, 55.3323, -2.1316 ⛰️⛲🔽🐾✴️

7 SWEETHOPE LOUGHS

Freshwater lake with shallow bay. Organised open-water swimming as well as paddleboarding and kayaking. A lovely sand lake if you want a wild swim, with lifeguard support.

→ Travelling N on the A696 from Kirkwhelpington, after 1 mile turn L at crossroads. Continue for 3 miles, keeping L at fork to sign for Sweethope Loughs on L. For outdoor swimming, contact H2oTrails, Northumberland 07737 300470, h2otrails@outlook.com

2 mins, 55.1361, -2.0860 🐾

8 BELLING PENINSULA, KIELDER

Stroll along the pine-fringed north shore of Kielder Water to the secluded, wooded peninsula at Belling Crag, a 15m-high sandstone wall of an old quarry, now partly submerged by the reservoir along with The Belling, a farm that now lies beneath the lake. Experience the sounds and sight of the water in the Wave Chamber art installation.

→ Park at Kielder's Hawkhope car park and follow the Lakeside Way for ¾ mile, then turn L onto narrow path of the peninsula.

30 mins, 55.1876, -2.4798 🏊🚶🏕

9 PATTERSON'S PAUSE, KIELDER

Secluded valley with a unique curved suspension bridge over the Lewisburn inlet leading to a stone table top and chairs, perfect for a picnic, with lovely views back across the water. Look out for herons down by the shore and buzzards overhead.

→ Park at Matthew's Linn car park (55.2053, -2.5576) and follow footpath beneath the C200 bridge towards the inlet. Cross suspension bridge and head uphill to Patterson's Pause on R.

20 mins, 55.2050, -2.5641 🚶🏊🏕🐕

10 THE GOATSTONES

On a quiet moorland knoll at the S end of Ravensheugh Crags, and with commanding views all around, this quartet is a rare example of a four-poster stone circle. One of the stones is decorated with cup and ring marks, with 13 markings on the flat surface of the stone. A lovely, peaceful site.

→ Follow the B6320 S from Wark for 2½ miles to R turn onto Ward Lane. Continue for 3 miles to lay-by parking opposite Manor House. Follow track up towards Ravensheugh Crags, and stones are just above track on L after crags.

5 mins, 55.0666, -2.2685 ⛰🐕🚶

11 CHEW GREEN

The highest Roman site in England at 442m, this large marching camp near the Scottish border is in one of the most remote corners of the country. Excavations in the 1930s uncovered six components to the site, all built at different times, possibly starting in ad 79. Just the earthworks remain, best seen by climbing up the road past the car park. You can follow in the footsteps of Roman soldiers

by walking a stretch of Dere Street, the old Roman road it sits upon.

→ Follow the River Coquet from Rothbury and B6341 to Alwinton. Cross River Coquet at Linbriggs farm and continue for 10 miles to a parking area on the L just before the road swings to the L and climbs steeply. Follow footpath to site or climb up road for views across.

5 mins, 55.3706, -2.3337 ⛺♿📷🏕🚶🧍

12 BREMENIUM ROMAN FORT

For two centuries this was the Roman Empire's northernmost fort. Built in the late first century ad, north of Hadrian's Wall, it provided warning of attacks from the north and guarded Dere Street Roman Road. It was destroyed in the mid-fourth century ad, and over subsequent centuries, the small hamlet of High Rochester has grown up within the fort's walls, including two bastle houses.

→ The fort is 8½ miles N of Risingham on the A68 and a short distance from the village of Rochester. Park at Camien Café, the last café in England (Rochester, Newcastle upon Tyne, NE19 1RH) and follow the footpath behind the café. There is a permissive path around the defensive circuit of the fort where parts of the standing Roman walling are visible on the S, W

and N sides, and gateways still exist on the N and W sides.

10 mins, 55.2820, -2.2649 📷♿🧍

13 THE DRAKE STONE

Known for its healing powers, this mythical 9m sandstone boulder, originally known as the Dragon Stone, and reputedly used in druidic rituals, teeters on the top of the Harbottle Hills. A beautiful walk up with spectacular views towards the Cheviot range and a magical moorland tarn to bathe in on the other side.

→ As for Harbottle Castle, but from the parking cross road and head R to footpath sign on L after a few yards. Cross field to gate and follow forest perimeter N through another gate and onto narrow track up to the Drake Stone. Adhere to signs re MOD activity here.

30 mins, 55.3338, -2.1267 🚶⛺📷📷

HOLY WELLS

14 LADY'S WELL

Enveloped by a grove of trees, this bewitching glassy pool with its Victorian stone cross is reputedly where the Anglo-Saxon St Ninian preached to and baptised Christian converts. The Roman monk St

Paulinus is also believed to have baptised 3,000 Northumbrians at this spot, which abuts the old Roman road, during Easter week in ad 627. The ancient spring is so pure it provides water for the village. An atmospheric and tranquil place.

→ Head W from Rothbury on the B6341 for 4 miles, then turn R onto Greenside Bank. Continue for 3 miles, crossing bridge over river and taking next L to Holystone village and parking. Footpath to the well is signed. Go through a gate and along a field boundary to trees.

5 mins, 55.3204, -2.0762 ♿🐕♀

15 ST CUTHBERT'S WELL

When St Cuthbert came to Bellingham, he blessed a natural spring (Cuddy's Well), which appears to have remarkable healing properties. The well has never dried up and its water is used for baptisms in St Cuthbert's Church. Afterwards, follow the riverside path upstream to the Jubilee Park picnic area by the bridge.

→ From Bellingham village follow the footpath sign to the river. The well is at the bottom of some steps below the church.

5 mins, 55.1427, -2.2561 ✝🐕

LOST RUINS

16 BLACK MIDDENS BASTLE HOUSE

Built between the 16th and 17th centuries to protect against border raids, this thick-walled bastle house lies in an isolated spot on the N side of the Tarset Valley. An exterior staircase leads to the first-floor living quarters. Follow the Tarset Bastle Trail (information board on site) to see more of the valley's fortified farmhouses, then call in at the charming Holly Bush Inn in Greenhaugh.

→ From Greenhaugh, pass pub on L, then take R at brown signpost. Well signposted from here for 3¼ miles.

2 mins, 55.2037, -2.3580 ⛰🚶📷

17 RUINED LOW ROSES BOWER

A remote, abandoned farmstead on the edge of Wark Forest with a curious outside toilet, the Long Drop Netty, perched on a gorge above the Warks Burn. The drop is reputed to be the longest of its kind in England. After exploring the ruins, wander down to the tumbling burn and a small plunge pool, Black Pool. The Star Dome Pavilion in the forestry village of Stonehaugh offers superb views of pristine starry skies.

21

→ From Wark head W in the dir of Stonehaugh for ½ mile to where road swings to L. Keep L and continue for 3½ miles past farm at Hetherington. Continue, then turn L at forest entrance to parking by footpath at Roses Bower Farm on L. Follow footpath through one field then into meadow and ruins ahead. Continue along footpath to burn.
5 mins, 55.0863, -2.3117 🏔🏕🎣👤

18 HARBOTTLE CASTLE
Built under Henry II as a defence against the Scots, this ruined medieval castle overlooks the River Coquet. It was also the home of Henry VIII's sister, Margaret Tudor, widow of James IV of Scotland, allowing her to remain close enough to continue to influence Scottish politics. Substantial earthworks survive as well as portions of the shell keep and inner bailey curtain wall. Splendid valley views.
→ From Rothbury follow the B6341 for 4 miles, then turn R onto Greenside Bank for 4½ miles to car park at end of village on R. Follow footpath through field to castle.
5 mins, 55.3372, -2.1082 📷🧭

19 SWINBURNE TITHE BARN
One of the prettiest barns you will come across, this charming building was used to collect tithes from farmers in the Middle Ages to bolster the local church. Gorgeous situation and views.
→ Heading N on the A68, take L turn for Great Swinburne and follow road to church and parking area. Walk past church and you will see the barn ahead of you through gate.
5 mins, 55.0763, -2.1046 🏔📷

DARK SKIES

20 STAR DOME PAVILION
Built in 1957 to house forestry workers, this forestry village is known for its dark, starry skies. Set in a wildflower meadow, the Star Dome, with its planted green roof, is a purpose-built stargazing site. The small observatory here also runs events.
→ From Wark head W in the dir of Stonehaugh for ½ mile to where road swings to L. Keep L and continue for 3½ miles past farm at Hetherington. Continue, then turn L at forest entrance and continue to Stonehaugh village and pavilion.
2 mins, 55.0793, -2.3300 🌟🔭

FORESTS & MEADOWS

21 BARROWBURN HAY MEADOWS
Stroll through stunning ancient upland hay meadows, a blaze of colour in June and July,

19

20

enjoying wide vistas and the song flight of skylarks. The two fields behind the farm are an SSSI, with more than 60 species of plants. The upper reaches of the River Coquet may beckon for a quick dip. An absolute delight.

→ Follow the River Coquet from Rothbury and the B6341 to Alwinton. Cross River Coquet at Linbriggs farm and continue for 6 miles to parking at Wedder Leap car park on L. Best meadows are behind the farmhouse.
10 mins, 55.3867, -2.2125 🚶🏕️🐾🐕

22 KIELDER FOREST DRIVE

A thrilling 12-mile road trip and one of the best ways to experience England's largest forest, taking in the breathtaking scenery of this isolated upland landscape. One of the highest and most remote roads in the country, it feels a million miles from anywhere (see Blakehope Nick entry).

→ From Kielder village, follow signs for Kielder Castle. Pass the castle on R and car park on L to get onto the 12-mile Forest Drive. Toll £3 at machine. Road is surfaced but becomes an unsealed gravel forest track. A 4x4 isn't essential, but you do need to drive with care as there are loose stones, the weather can be changeable and there is no mobile signal.
5 mins, 55.2344, -2.5790 🅿️🔽🔲📷

23 BUTTERBURN FLOW, KIELDER MIRES

The largest of the ancient Border Mires that drape over the landscape like a wet blanket, the desolate moorland of Butterburn Flow is a truly memorable place, with only the occasional otherworldly cries of curlew to break the silence. In summer the tiny white heads of cloudberry dance above hummocks of sphagnum moss. No paths and wet terrain. The River Irthing passes through here, perfect for a refreshing swim.

→ Continue a mile W of Gilsland, over bridge and uphill past Gilsland Spa. Continue for another 1½ miles and take 'no through road' R turn over cattle grid. Continue for 7 miles along track to bridge over River Irthing.
2 mins, 55.0827, -2.5323 🅿️🔲🏕️🐾🐕❄️

HILLTOPS & BOULDERING

24 OUTER GOLDEN POT, OTTERBURN RANGES

Some of the national park's most beautiful scenery lies within the Otterburn Ranges, partly crossed by public roads and, when the flags aren't flying, you can also travel on military roads. This (the old Roman road of Dere Street) is one of the best viewpoints from which to admire the ranges; you can observe

the training targets which sit alongside the mounds of three Bronze Age cairns.

→ Follow the River Coquet from Rothbury and the B6341 to Alwinton. Cross River Coquet at Linbriggs farm and continue for 8 miles to parking on R by a Falklands War memorial.
2 mins, 55.3594, -2.3111 🚶🏔️⛺🚗🍴

25 MOTE HILLS, ELSDON

Situated on a spur above Elsdon Burn, Mote Hills is one of the best examples in England of an early 12th-century Norman motte and bailey castle. The huge earthwork was built during the reign of William the Conqueror to guard the wild frontier but abandoned in 1157 by Henry II in favour of a sturdier stone-built castle at Harbottle. Excellent local pub, café and church where St Cuthbert's coffin rested. Leave on the Morpeth road (B6342) to appreciate the scale of the structure.

→ From Rothbury follow the B6341 for 11½ miles to Elsdon and parking. Follow road past village hall to earthworks.
5 mins, 55.2354, -2.0997 🔄🏔️📷

26 BLAKEHOPE NICK

The highest point on the Kielder Forest Drive at 457m is marked by The Nick, an intriguing viewing shelter whose design frames

segments of the surrounding landscape and the endless skies above. Stop and take in the wildness of this remote upland terrain, enjoying panoramic views towards Kielder.

→ From Kielder village, follow signs for Kielder Castle. Pass the castle on R and car park on L to get onto the 12-mile Forest Drive. Toll £3 at machine. Road is surfaced but becomes a gravel forest track. The Nick is roughly halfway along on L.
2 mins, 55.2793, -2.4535 🏔️📷

27 WINTER'S GIBBET

A lone gallows stands on the highest point of an old drovers' road on Benshaw Moor, reminding visitors of a grisly murder. William Winter was hanged here and left until his clothes rotted off. Stunning views across Benshaw Moor, an area of wild open access heathland, peatland and blanket bog, currently undergoing rewilding.

→ Head E out of Otterburn on A696, then take the B6341 road for 3 miles. The Gibbet is on the R. Park in lay-by opposite.
5 mins, 55.2112, -2.0611 🏔️

28 GREAT WANNEY CRAG

An impressive sandstone crag situated in an isolated yet commanding position above

moorland and forest. Walk through beautiful peatland surrounded by the bobbing white heads of cotton grass in spring and summer. A good mix of routes across all grades with some easier bouldering on the ground.

→ Travelling N on the A696 from Kirkwhelpington take a L after ¾ mile signposted 'Sweethope Loughs'. Continue for 3½ miles, keeping L and passing entrance of Sweethope Loughs to parking on R at Fourlaws Forestry Commission lay-by (55.1404, -2.0908). Follow footpath up to crags.
20 mins, 55.1451, -2.1072 🚶🔽🏔️⛺

CAFÉS

29 SIMONBURN TEAROOM

Charming tearoom with a beautiful garden in a gorgeous village. Great for walkers and cyclists. Also does B&B. Dry storage for cyclists.

→ 1 The Mains, Simonburn, NE48 3AW, 01434 681321. Open spring until clocks go back in autumn.

55.0575, -2.2032

30 FOUNTAIN COTTAGE AND B&B

Friendly café and a good place to refuel after a walk to the beautiful Hareshaw Linn waterfall. All day breakfasts, sandwiches and light bites. Secure storage for bikes.

→ Fountain Cottage, Bellingham, NE48 2DE, 01434 239224

55.1451, -2.2537

COSY PUBS

31 THE STAR INN, HARBOTTLE

Stylish, relaxed and popular pub serving meals, including pizzas, to eat in or take away from the Italian kitchen in its courtyard. The setting and pub are lovely but the food really sets it apart. Also the village shop and tourist information point.

→ Harbottle, Morpeth, NE65 7DG, 01669 650221

55.3362, -2.1054

32 BLACKCOCK INN

Friendly, family-run 16th-century coaching inn in the small village of Falstone, which sits below the dam of Kielder reservoir on a loop of the River North Tyne. Pleasant riverside walks and an interesting churchyard next door.

→ Falstone, Hexham, NE48 1AA, 01434 240200

55.1804, -2.4352

33 ANGLER'S ARMS

Friendly and unpretentious with decent pub grub. Located at the end or the start of the Kielder Forest Drive and handy if you are staying at the campsite. Vegan and Vegetarian options. Outside seating.

→ Kielder, Hexham, NE48 1ER, 01434 250230

55.2338, -2.5818

34 BATTLESTEADS HOTEL & RESTAURANT

It is not surprising that this village pub and hotel is Northumberland's greenest. Sustainability is at the core of their business, with a carbon-neutral heating and water system, organic toiletries and locally sourced food.

→ Wark on Tyne, Hexham, NE48 3LS, 01434 230209

55.0859, -2.2206

35 THE PHEASANT INN

Expect flavoursome, home-cooked food and a good range of beers at this friendly family-run

country inn, which has beams, open fires and portraits of the locals on exposed stone walls. Picnic benches by the brook for summer days.

→ Shilling Pot, Stannersburn, Hexham, NE48 1DD, 01434 240382
55.1729, -2.4374

36 BARRASFORD ARMS

Kick back in the cosy bar of this award-winning 19th-century inn, which offers an excellent menu, using locally sourced seasonal produce, and a good selection of beers from nearby microbreweries. Beer garden with views across the North Tyne Valley. Country pub accommodation.

→ Barrasford, Hexham, NE48 4AA, 01434 681237
55.0544, -2.1318.

CAMP & GLAMP

37 RAVENSCLEUGH CAMPSITE, B&B & WILD SWIMMING

Rustic campsite with a beautiful wild swimming pond on a family farm, with pitches in the orchard, valley or on the hill – camping as it used to be. Views across the Rede Valley. Shared access to the family's bathroom and shower. Very friendly hosts. Also B&B. Non-campers can swim for a small fee.

→ Ravenscleugh, Elsdon, NE19 1BW, 01830 520896
55.2162, -2.1069

38 KIELDER CAMPSITE

One of the most remote campsites in England, hidden away in the depths of Kielder Forest with no mobile signal and limited Wi-Fi. Pristine skies for stargazing. Tents have their own camping field.

→ Kielder, Hexham, NE48 1EJ, 01434 239257
55.2372, -2.5910

39 BELLINGHAM CAMPSITE

Larger eco-friendly campsite with level pitches and good facilities, including a shop selling local produce. Kids' play area and games room. Wool-insulated glamping pods also available. Excellent walks nearby and access to pleasant stretch of river from Bellingham.

→ Bellingham, Hexham, NE48 2JY, 01434 220175
55.1375, -2.2595

40 ELF KIRK VIEWPOINT CAMPING

Overnight camping for camper vans at various locations in Kielder Forest, including Elf Kirk Viewpoint with beautiful views over Whickhope Inlet and the dam; Hawkhope car park; Tower Knowe and at the back of the Angler's Arms in Kielder village. £10 per night. Pay at Kielder Castle car park and Tower Knowe or at Angler's Arms. Sorry no tents.

→ Kielder Castle, Kielder, NE48 1ER
55.1686, -2.4813

41 SYCAMORE COTTAGE & GLAMPING PODS

Spacious glamping pods on a traditional hill farm where you can gaze up at star-filled skies from your bed or take in magnificent views over Hadrian's Wall from the canopy-covered terrace. Black Hut has a striking, double-ended, outdoor roll-top bath.

→ 1 Front Street, Barrasford, Hexham, NE48 4AA, 07793 868277
55.0547, -2.1322

42 WILD NORTHUMBRIAN

Gorgeous off-grid, rustic-chic dwellings in a serene setting abundant with wildlife.

Choose from a yurt in the trees, an antique shepherd's hut or a magical hand-crafted cabin. Outdoor kitchens, Hikki Scandinavian wood-fired outdoor baths, compost loos and a pretty stream with a rope swing.

→ Thorneyburn Old Rectory, Tarset, NE48 1NA, 01669 650166
55.1829, -2.3381 🏕

43 HESLEYSIDE HUTS

Fairy-tale glamping in a hand-crafted chapel on wheels. Copper bath and a sumptuous bed in the eaves, tucked away on the 4,000-acre Hesleyside Estate, home of the Border Reiver Charlton family for 750 years. Two delightful cabins, three charming shepherd's huts and ancient woodland trails to explore. Marshmallows to toast under starry skies.

→ Hesleyside Huts, Estate Office, Hexham, NE48 2LA, 01434 220068
55.1464, -2.2848 🏕

BOTHIES & BUNKHOUSES

44 SPITHOPE BOTHY

Small bothy, with a wood burning stove, on an old drovers' route across the border. Bring fuel to replenish wood store.

→ 2 miles N of Byrness on A68. NE19 1TR. Check for latest updates at Mountain Bothies Association.
55.3443, -2.3668 🏕

45 ROUGHSIDE BOTHY

In a stunning location on a rustic former farm. Open fire and compost loo. Popular with walkers.

→ No vehicles allowed in forest. Park in gateway on N side of road at Bower before the bridge over the burn. Check for latest updates at Mountain Bothies Association.
55.1433, -2.4006 🏕

46 GREEN BOTHY

Remote bothy in Wark Forest with three separate rooms sleeping 6 plus. Head NW to find Kielder Mires, England's largest area of blanket bog and its most tranquil place. Wood burning stove. Open fire.

→ No vehicles in forest. Park along roadside in Stonehaugh at 55.0796, -2.3255. Check for latest updates at Mountain Bothies Association.
55.1011, -2.4089 🏕

47 WAINHOPE BOTHY

Cosy former working farm, with original features, hidden in the remote forests of Kielder. Closed April to September so as not to disturb the breeding ospreys.

→ Located 2½ miles E of Kielder on NE side of water. Hawkhope car park (NE48 1BH) or Kielder Castle. Check for latest updates at Mountain Bothies Association.
55.2256, -2.5189 🏕

48 FLITTINGFORD BOTHY

An old shepherd's hut by a drovers' road adopted by the Mountain Bothies Association. Located near Kielder Water, it has room for 4. Open fire. Take water.

→ Check for latest updates at Mountain Bothies Association.
55.1914, -2.3889 🏕

49 TARSET TOR BUNKHOUSE & BOTHIES

Glamping site in a super location on the edge of Kielder Forest in a Dark Sky Reserve. Timber eco buildings, including a stylish bunkhouse sleeping 16–20 and four bothies sleeping up to 8. Small number of camper-van and camping pitches.

→ Greystones, Lanehead, Tarset, Hexham, NE48 1NT, 01434 240980
55.1654, -2.3271 🏕

RUSTIC HAVENS

50 SKY DEN TREE HOUSE, CALVERT KIELDER

Stunning architecture-designed treehouse, sleeping 4, in the heart of Kielder Forest with a spectacular opening roof to reveal the UK's darkest skies. Amazing wildlife experience. Spot red squirrels and osprey. Excellent accessibility for all accommodation.

→ Kielder Forest Park, Calvert Trust Kielder, NE48 1BS, Canopy and Stars.
55.1634, -2.5326 🏕

51 THE BOTHY, CHURNSIKE LODGE

Former gamekeeper's lodge in the grounds of a Victorian hunting lodge on the edge of Wark Forest and one of the most remote locations in the whole of England for those in search of peace and solitude.

→ Churnsike Lodge, Brampton, CA8 7BB, Airbnb
55.0874, -2.5278 🏕

52 TUTOR'S LODGE

Sensational off-grid bolthole up a 3-mile track in the wild, rugged hills of the Upper Coquet Valley. The cottage with its striking modern extension is one of several holiday homes on the eco-conscious 36-acre Kidlandlee Estate.

→ Kidlandlee, Harbottle, Morpeth, NE64 7DA, 01669 650472
55.3824, -2.1409 🏕

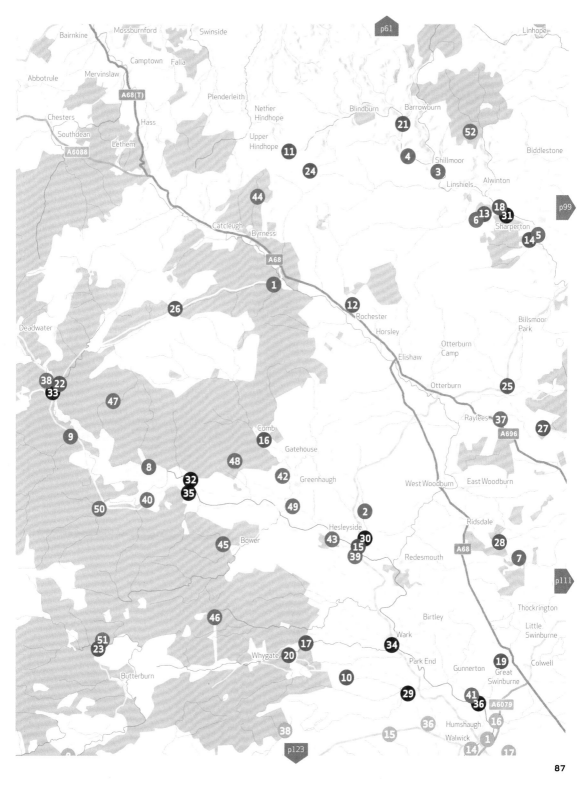

ROTHBURY & SIMONSIDE

Our perfect weekend

→ **Scale** the three peaks of the Simonside Hills for a fabulous view across to the Cheviots

→ **Row** across the River Coquet to visit a Medieval hermitage carved out of the rock

→ **Climb** up to Corby's Crag, an ancient rock shelter, and look down on the view that inspired a poster for the *Lord of the Rings* film

→ **Walk** through the dunes at Alnmouth to find a deserted, ruined chapel, then tuck into freshly caught lobster at the Fish Shack in Amble

→ **Ponder** the mysteries of the prehistoric cup and ring marks at the Lordenshaw hill fort

→ **Scale** the slopes of an Iron Age hill fort in magical Thrunton Woods to find McCartney's cave chiselled into the rock face

→ **Spot** the sun on the summer solstice through the mysterious hole in Thompson's Rock

→ **Camp** for the night in the rugged, undulating dunes of Druridge Bay, a glorious and remote sweep of pristine white sands

The Northumbrian market town of Rothbury, huddled in the shadow of the distinctive Simonside Hills and surrounded by beautiful scenery, makes an excellent base for exploring the heart of Northumberland and the magnificent sandy beaches of this coastline. It is little wonder that the Victorian inventor and industrialist Lord Armstrong chose to build his remarkable home and gardens here at Cragside.

With an easily recognisable craggy profile, the Simonside Hills provide a dramatic backdrop to the central reaches of the Coquet Valley. The hills' spiritual significance to the Bronze Age people, 5,000 years ago, is apparent in the prolific number of burial cairns and rock carvings adorning the slopes and summits.

These wild and rugged hills are steeped in legend and folklore, where duergars – dangerous dwarves – lurk in the shadows, appearing at night to prey on lost travellers. In reality, the creatures to look out for include adders, red grouse, wild goats – and red squirrels in the forests below.

A ramble to the summit at Simonside, along the easy-to-follow ridge line, makes for an adventurous hike with scrambles, wonderfully contorted rocky outcrops and stupendous 360-degree views of the Cheviot Hills and coastline from the top.

On the eastern slopes of the hills is the curious Thompson's Rock, a mystical holed stone orientated so that when the sun sets during the midsummer solstice, a burst of sunlight creates a spectacular diffraction of its rays.

Below the Iron Age hill fort at Lordenshaw is one of the largest clusters of cup and ring marks in the country, with 100 carved marks, from simple cups to more elaborate ringed cups and grooves, dating back to the early or late Neolithic period.

The primary river, the Coquet, winds its way through the Coquet Valley to the gentler plains of the valley floor at Rothbury, where there are plenty of places to swim. By following many of the riverside paths, you will soon stumble upon a secluded spot to take a dip.

To the east, Northumberland's glorious sandy beaches sweep south: dune-fringed Alnmouth with a tiny chapel hidden in the dunes; the long stretch of sand at Warkworth with views across to Coquet Island, where puffins come to breed in summer; and wild and windswept Druridge Bay, in whose rolling dunes you could quietly lay your head for the night, drifting off to the sound of tumbling waves and waking as the sun rises over the sea.

BEAUTIFUL BEACHES

1 ALNMOUTH BAY

Wide sandy beach with dunes split into three beaches. It is possible to cross the estuary by kayak or boat to the opposite 'island' to visit the ruins of St Waleric chapel (see entry) and wild beach to S. Beware of strong currents.

→ In Alnmouth, access from parking in Riverside Road and through dunes to beach.
5 mins, 55.3855, -1.6105

2 DRURIDGE BAY

A sweeping expanse of pristine white sands backed by dunes make up this remote beach and nature reserve. Beautiful bay. The dunes provide some shelter but it can be windy here, which means you may almost have the place to yourself.

→ 3 miles S of Amble (A1068), pass turn-off for Druridge Bay Country Park (NE61 5BX, see Ladyburn Lake entry) and continue ¾ mile for next L (unsigned, opp Red Row turn-off). Park at far end of lane. Path leads to middle of Druridge Bay (500m) with a low dune hill to the R.
5 mins, 55.2760, -1.5717

3 WARKWORTH BEACH

Beautiful stretch of pale golden sands backed by dunes, with views across to Coquet Island.

→ From A1068 N of Amble (NE65 0XB) head through Warkworth and take R along narrow lane on N side of bridge to car park at end, ½ mile. Walk through dunes to beach.
5 mins, 55.3516, -1.5945

4 SEATON POINT

Quiet beach near Boulmer, popular with local swimmers and good for a HT swim. Call in at the gorgeous Fishing Boat Inn afterwards.

→ From Boulmer follow coast road S for 1 mile. As road veers to R, take L turn onto a track to park. Beach is just at the end.
2 mins, 55.4060, -1.5805

RIVERS & LAKES

5 WARKWORTH HERMITAGE, RIVER COQUET

Row or swim across the pretty River Coquet to the fascinating Medieval hermitage carved out of the rock face, once a private chapel. Look out for the unusual multi-trunk yew.

→ From behind Warkworth Castle follow the path upstream along the river for 300m to where the little ferry boat usually waits to cross. Beaches upstream.
10 mins, 55.3462, -1.6206

6 THRUM ROCKS, RIVER COQUET

Gorge with plunge pools and flat rocks, popular with local kids.

→ 1 mile E of Rothbury on riverside path. Or parking at 55.3088, -1.8904 and trodden path to riverbank. No entry from mill.
2 mins, 55.3084, -1.8930

7 ROTHBURY STEPPING STONES, RIVER COQUET

Stepping stones across the river with deeper pool to the right for an upstream swim. Good spot for families with children.

→ In Rothbury, head towards Cragside on the B6344. Turn R opp almshouses for parking and river. Follow footpath downstream for further river access points. Note it is only possible to swim/scramble to Thrum Rocks, as private signs and barbed-wired fence by mill.
1 min, 55.3098, -1.9061

8 BEGGARS RIGG, RIVER COQUET

A shingle beach on a meander of the River Coquet as it cuts across a meadow in the

shadow of the Simonside Hills. Good for picnics and paddling, with occasional pools for swimming.

→ Parking at Beggars Rigg car park. Follow river path L for 500m to a kissing gate on L and then follow path into field to river beaches.

10 mins, 55.3042, -1.9296

9 PAUPERHAUGH BRIDGE, RIVER COQUET

A peaceful stretch of the River Coquet beneath the attractive stone five-arch Pauperhaugh bridge. Nice spot for a picnic and paddle.

→ From Rothbury, follow B6344 for 3 miles to Pauperhaugh and parking in pull-in over bridge.

2 mins, 55.2887, -1.8435

10 LESBURY WEIR, RIVER ALN

A pretty weir pool near Alnmouth, sheltered by trees.

→ Just N of Alnmouth roundabout (A1068) at Hipsburn find footpath/gate on L, 100m before new river bridge at Lesbury. Roadside parking in either Hipsburn or Lesbury.

10 mins, 55.3966, -1.6371

11 LADYBURN LAKE, DRURIDGE BAY

A freshwater lake with a nice jetty, surrounded by woods and meadow. Organised water sports available here. There are stepping stones halfway around the lake which kids love hopping across. Picnic tables. Open daylight hours.

→ From Amble follow the A1068 S for 2¾ miles, then take L turn signed 'Druridge Bay Country Park'. Parking is first L up the rise, in the water sports car park. One-hour free parking at machine.

1 min, 55.2938, -1.5780

LOST RUINS & CASTLES

12 EDLINGHAM CASTLE

Situated on the riverside, the captivating ruins of this 14th-century castle have an astonishing leaning tower. Also worth a visit is the neighbouring 12th-century St John the Baptist church with its small window slits in the tower, possibly used by archers. Perfect for a summer picnic and a game of hide and seek.

→ Follow the B6341 S from Alnwick for 6 miles, then R turn for Edlingham village and parking by church.

2 mins, 55.3768, -1.8184

12

13

14

13 RUINED MORTUARY CHAPEL, ALNMOUTH

Nestled in the lee of the sand dunes, where herons and oystercatchers circle above the mud flats, this ruined chapel is a beautiful place to visit at the end of the day when the sandstone is illuminated by the setting sun. The chapel dates back to the 19th century and was built on the site of the ancient parish church of St Waleric's, destroyed in a flood in 1806. Although just a few yards from Alnmouth beach, its relative inaccessibility makes for a peaceful visit.

→ Only accessible from beach on kayak or paddleboard. Otherwise, from Alnmouth follow the B1338 to roundabout, then turn L onto the A1068 for 1 mile to parking on L (55.3760, -1.6219). Cross road to footpath to Buston Links and chapel.
15 mins, 55.3839, -1.6135 ✝🖼🛈🚶

14 LOW CHIBBURN PRECEPTORY

Just behind the Druridge Pools lie the ruins of a Medieval Hospitaller preceptory. It had several uses, ranging from a hospital to a dowager house, before it was destroyed by French invaders in 1691.

→ Park on the verge along the Druridge Pools beach road at 55.2630, -1.5687. Follow the path, marked by a fingerpost, inland through trees and two fields to see the preceptory ahead of you.
20 mins, 55.2623, -1.5832 🛈🚶

15 WARKWORTH CASTLE

Sitting above a loop of the River Coquet, this mighty Northumberland fortress was inhabited by the influential Percy family between the 14th and 17th centuries. Worth the EH entry fee. Afterwards, you can admire its majestic setting by following the riverside walk to the hermitage (see entry).

→ Signposted in Warkworth, 7½ miles S of Alnwick on A1068. Car park at NE65 0UJ.
5 mins, 55.3453, -1.6117 🚻🔣🍴

HILLTOPS

16 SIMONSIDE, SIMONSIDE HILLS

This justifiably popular summit has magnificent panoramic views of the Cheviots and the Northumberland coastline. The spiritual importance of these wild, windswept hills to Bronze Age people is evident by the number of burial cairns on the slopes and crags. After reaching the 430m hilltop, continue along the ridge to explore the contorted peak of Old Stell Crag, which stands on an ancient stone barrow,

15

16

then head onto Dove Crag (fun bouldering). However, beware the Simonside Duergars, malevolent dwarves of folklore who reside in the rugged hills and lure unwitting travellers to their doom. Bivvy in Croppy's Hole to the NE of Selby's Cove.

→ Park at the Simonside Forestry Commission car park (NE65 7NW). Follow track through woodland to clearing before Simonside, then continue up steep stepped ascent to summit. Head along ridge to further crags.
45 mins, 55.2823, -1.9640 🅥🛈⛰🖼

ROCKS & CAVES

17 CORBY'S CRAGS ROCK SHELTER

Enjoy superb sunsets over the Cheviot Hills from this large, natural sandstone shelter where prehistoric activity has been discovered, including Mesolithic flints and an Early Bronze Age cremation in a pottery vessel. By day, skylarks hover, willow warblers dart and the views are impressive enough to have inspired a poster for *The Hobbit* film, which features the evocative ruins of Edlingham Castle and the viaduct as the backdrop.

→ On the B6341 heading towards Alnwick, just past L turn for Edlingham village, park at

the viewing lay-by on L at 55.3837, -1.8013. Walk a few metres uphill to access track on R ascending hill. Cross small burn, and shelter is in crags to R.
10 mins, 55.3810, -1.8015 ♿🛈🖼🚶

18 GIMMERKNOWE

At the W end of the escarpment overlooking Rothbury, this south-facing cluster of boulders and small buttresses is great for early evening scrambles and bouldering as the sun is setting. To the immediate S lie extensive earthworks from Old Rothbury hill fort. Combine with further bouldering at Ship Crag to NE.

→ From Rothbury follow high street W then take R turn before church uphill on Gravelly Bank. Turn sharp R onto Hillside E to street parking. Follow Pennystane Lane, then turn R opp walled garden onto track for 500m to crags on R.
30 mins, 55.3129, -1.9275 ♿🛈🖼🚶

19 MCCARTNEY'S CAVE

Hidden in an enchanted forest landscape, this tiny cave has a Gothic entrance carved part way up a large sandstone rock on the side of Callaly Crag. It is said to have been hewn by a monk named McCartney, from nearby Callaly,

as a quiet retreat for his studies. Watch out for mischievous hobgoblins who dwell here and play tricks on passers-by.

→ From Whittingham follow Callaly Road for 1½ miles to parking by woods on L at 55.3845, -1.9091. Take a map. Follow worn path into woodland circling Castle Hill Fort. Lots of fallen trees. Path climbs towards Callaly Crag and cave is on R. Continue to Callaly Crag for views and bouldering.
30 mins, 55.3783, -1.9056 🚶🅿️⛰️🅥

20 THOMPSON'S ROCK

This huge stone at the base of The Beacon on the Simonside Hills has a mysterious 3-inch diameter hole that is said to directly align with the midsummer sunset. At the winter solstice the sun's light reaches four-fifths along the hole in the rock in the other direction.

→ Park in Lordenshaw car park (NE65 7NW) and follow the path up towards The Beacon. As the path levels out, bear R on the grass path towards a scattering of rocks. Thompson's Rock is the largest square boulder.
5 mins, 55.2824, -1.9291 ⛰️🚶📷

21 LORDENSHAW ROCK ART

Contemplating these great slabs of rock peppered with patterns carved thousands of years ago, you get a sense of our connection with the past. Occupying a spectacular setting overlooking the Cheviots, this is possibly the largest concentration of rock art in the UK, with 100 carved cup-and-ring-marked rocks dating back to the early or late Neolithic period. Motifs vary from simple cups to more complex ringed cups, grooves and longer channels. Main Rock is at 55.2832 -1.9190, Horseshoe Rock is at 55.2871 -1.9212 and Channel Rock is at 55.2885 -1.9120. Also earthworks of an Iron Age hill fort.

→ Located about 2½ miles S of Rothbury. Park in Lordenshaw car park (NE65 7NW) and follow the grass track N. Signpost and QR code with rock info.
2 mins, 55.2874, -1.9152 📷⛰️🚶

INDUSTRIAL HERITAGE

22 GREAT TOSSON LIME KILNS

This is the best-preserved lime kiln in the Northumberland National Park. There were once 400 of these kilns spewing smoke across the valley. This one is unusual as it was designed by the architect George Reavell of Alnwick in 1888 for Lord Armstrong of Cragside. Beautiful views of the Cheviot Hills.

→ From Rothbury head S on the B6342, then R onto Whitton Bank Rd for ½ mile. Then take R onto Carterside Rd for 1½ miles. At road end turn L to parking and kiln after ½ mile on R.
1 min, 55.3030, -1.9585

23 CRAGSIDE

A well-known NT site but worthy of a mention. Cragside has a vast, wild feel to it, with rocky outcrops, towering trees and demanding trails. Its pinetum, planted around 140 years ago to recreate a North American landscape, includes Douglas fir, Caucasian fir, noble fir and western hemlock, and is home to five of the top ten champion trees, the tallest of their kind in the country.
→ Rothbury, Morpeth, NE65 7PX, 01669 620333
5 mins, 55.3137, -1.8855

LOCAL FOOD

24 SCOTT'S OF ALNMOUTH

Award-winning, well-stocked deli with a focus on homemade goodies and hot drinks to takeaway to the beach. Excellent coffee, cakes, cheeses, charcuterie and smoked fish. Friendly staff.

→ 15–16 Northumberland Street, Alnmouth, NE66 2RS, 07590 564963
55.3877, -1.6124

25 BERTRAM'S

Cosy licensed café with a pretty courtyard serving delicious, home-cooked food. Run by a mother-and-daughter team and the perfect place to refuel after a day at the beach. Open 7 days a week, 9am – 7pm. Also does B&B.
→ 19 Bridge Street, Warkworth, NE65 0XB, 01665 798070
55.3484, -1.6115

26 THE RUNNING FOX BAKERY

Wonderful artisan bakery with four coffee shops throughout Northumberland. The original bakery opened here in 2011, followed by Longframlington, Shilbottle and Longhoughton. Their foxy picnics, which come in various sizes, are perfect to pick up and take to the beach.
→ 2–4 Riverside, Felton, Morpeth, NE65 9EA, 01665 660721
55.2967, -1.7105

27 FISH SHACK, AMBLE

Rustic harbourside café, built from an old boat, serving excellent seafood, including Amble lobster, Seahouses kipper and traditional fish and chips. Dine in one of the cute beach huts or grab a table overlooking the busy harbour.
→ 29 Harbour Road, Amble, Morpeth, NE65 0AP, 01665 661301
55.3368, -1.5769

COSY PUBS & RESTAURANTS

28 NORTHUMBERLAND ARMS

Award-winning gastro pub with a large outdoor area to enjoy a drink or dine al fresco with views over the River Coquet. Pub classics and traditional puddings.
→ The Peth, West Thirston, Felton, Morpeth, NE65 9EE, 01670 787370
55.2957, -1.7103

29 ANGLERS ARMS, WELDON BRIDGE

Traditional 18th-century Northumbrian coaching inn situated on the banks of the River Coquet and once popular with travellers from Scotland. Serves real ales and excellent food. Nice covered beer garden to the side.
→ Weldon Bridge, Longframlington, Morpeth, NE65 8AX, 01665 570655
55.2810, -1.7852

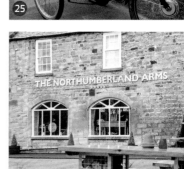

30 THE RED LION INN, ALNMOUTH

Popular post-beach pub with a pizza oven and beer garden and a viewing platform overlooking the Alnmouth estuary. Good food and local beers. Cosy bar and rooms.

➜ 22 Northumberland Street, Alnmouth, Alnwick, NE66 2RJ, 01665 830584
55.3883, -1.6128

31 THE WHITTLING HOUSE

Laid-back country restaurant with characterful interiors and 10 beautifully furnished rooms, including a bed for your pup. Alternatively, pop in for a drink or leisurely lunch after a stroll along Alnmouth beach.

➜ 24–25 Northumberland St, Alnmouth, Alnwick, NE66 2RA, 01665 463001
55.3885, -1.6129

CAMP & GLAMP

32 ALNHAM FARM

Semi-wild camping in a wildflower meadow with spacious pitches and basic facilities, including running water and portaloos. You will need a torch as there is no electricity, which means the skies are so dark you may spot the Milky Way twinkling above.

➜ Westgate House, Alnwick, NE66 4TJ, 01669 630210
55.3935, -2.0054

33 WALKMILL CAMPSITE

Posh wild-camping site in a great location, nestled in a meander of the River Coquet among woodland and wildflowers. Basic facilities, plenty of space. A 30-minute walk to the beach.

➜ Walkmill Nr, Guyzance, Warkworth, NE65 9AJ, 01665 710155
55.3333, -1.6417

34 THE CHRISTMAS FARM

Small organic family farm with a wild-camping site. Compost toilet, standpipe with fresh water and campfire for toasting marshmallows. Glorious views and a beautiful situation. April to September.

➜ The Christmas Farm, Longframlington, Morpeth, NE65 8DA, 01665 570113
55.3160, -1.7973

35 HUTS IN THE HILLS

Marvel at pristine night skies from the star-gazing roof of this gorgeous shepherd's hut at the foot of the Cheviot Hills. Five huts of

various sizes, each crafted with reclaimed oak and insulated with sheep's wool, with antique outdoor baths overlooking spectacular scenery. Hampers available.

→ Prendwick Farm, Alnwick, NE66 4UZ, 01669 630273
55.4042, -1.9983

36 SHORESIDE CAMPING HUTS

Camp above a wild, sandy beach in these stylish off-grid camping huts with amazing sea views. The huts can only be reached by foot along St Oswald's Way coastal path.

→ Alnmouth, Alnwick, NE66 3BE, 01665 830554
55.3955, -1.5983

37 WOODLAND CHASE GLAMPING

Sleep beneath a woodland canopy in a palatial treehouse or laze with a book on the shaded veranda of the Saddler's and Crofter's Cabins. In keeping with the natural surroundings, the buildings have all been created using materials from the family farm. Sorry, no kids.

→ Woodland Chase, Felton, Morpeth, NE65 9NT, 07931 334275
55.3159, -1.7162

38 THE BADGER & THE BEAR OUTDOOR ADVENTURE CAMPSITE

A wild-camp experience in A-frame shelters with the chance to learn some survival skills. Great for an outdoor family adventure, even for those who are seasoned campers.

→ Thistleyhaugh Farm, Longhorsley, Morpeth, NE65 8RG, 077033 335132
55.2772, -1.7997

RUSTIC HAVENS

39 LEMMINGTON LODGE

Contemporary cedar-clad lodge tucked away in a semi-woodland setting, with sliding doors onto a terrace with spectacular views across the Vale of Whittingham to the Cheviot Hills. The ideal getaway for a family holiday.

→ Lemmington Cottages, Lemmington Estate, Alnwick, NE66 2BD, 07887 630340
55.3932, -1.8418

40 WESTFIELD HOUSE FARM

Sleep beneath magical night skies in these Farrow-and-Ball-painted shepherd's huts with wood-fired hot tubs. Situated in a hay meadow overlooking beautiful countryside, each of the four huts has a campfire with a

tripod grill for al fresco meals. All mod cons but no Wi-Fi. Also B&B.

→ Westfield House Farm, Rothbury, NE65 7LB, 01669 640089
55.3237, -1.9803

41 CRAGEND GRANGE

Rare-breed working farm with B&B (including floor mattresses in double room for children) and a self-catering renovated worker's cottage on the edge of Cragside with lovely views. Free-range hens, British rare-breed cattle, goats and sheep.

→ Cragend Farm, Rothbury, Morpeth, NE65 7XN, 01669 621533
55.3018, -1.8641

42 BRINKBURN MILL

Hidden away at the bottom of a peaceful, wooded valley is this characterful former mill. Now owned by the Landmark Trust, this cosy bolthole for 4 is next door to the 12th-century priory.

→ Longframlington, Morpeth, NE65 8AR, Landmark Trust
55.2786, -1.8169

MORPETH & WANSBECK

Our perfect weekend

→ **Explore** the delightful Hartburn Grotto, created as a changing room for 18th-century bathers, and follow the passageway leading to the burn

→ **Clamber** over the spectacular rocky outcrop of Shaftoe Crags and seek out the Jubilee Stone

→ **Enjoy** a drink at the historic King's Arms overlooking the picturesque harbour at Seaton Sluice

→ **Climb** the stone staircase at Rothley Castle, a ruined Gothic folly in a magnificent setting on a craggy, heather-clad hill

→ **Tuck** into tea and fruit scones at Kirkharle Courtyard, the birthplace of Capability Brown

→ **Hop** across the stepping stones at the River Wansbeck in Bothal and look out for native, white-clawed crayfish beneath the water

→ **Play** a game of French cricket on the low-tide sands at Cambois Beach, which runs from Blyth Harbour to the Wansbeck Estuary

→ **Admire** the romantic ruins of Mitford Castle, then enjoy a paddle and picnic down by the river

The River Wansbeck starts its course as an inland rivulet of water, rising on the rugged moors above Sweethope Loughs, known locally as The Wanneys, weaving its way through a gentle, pastoral landscape and pouring into a wide estuary south of Newbiggin-by-the-Sea.

As we leave behind the 'Wilds of Wannie', the name Tynesiders gave the land where Border Reivers ran amok on the upper reaches of the Wansbeck, the scenery changes. Here you will find undulating meadows, broad-leaved trees, ponds and large country house estates, including Wallington and Belsay. You could be forgiven for thinking you had stepped into one of Gainsborough's 18th-century paintings of a sedate English countryside. Not surprising, maybe, as Capability Brown was born at Kirkharle in 1715, a village which honours him with a courtyard of artisan shops and a café.

Cycle along quiet country lanes or stroll along riverside paths in this pleasant corner of Northumberland, stopping off at charming cafés: a pot of tea and a slab of cake at Capheaton Village Tearoom or the cheese-lover's afternoon tea at the Cheese Loft Café in Blagdon.

But this is just part of the story; there are also plenty of wild adventures to be had. The magnificent gritstone outcrop at Shaftoe Crags provides the ideal setting for a day's adventuring. The fascinating geology, rich in ferns, includes rock shelters and Iron Age burial mounds. The same outcrop of coarse-grained pebbly sandstone also appears in the ruined hilltop Gothic folly at Rothley.

The River Wansbeck offers some idyllic stretches for secret swims, particularly in Lady Chapel Woods at Bothal. Its tributary, the Hart Burn, is the location for the fairy-tale Hartburn Grotto, an astonishing two-room shelter carved out of a natural cave. For paddleboarders or those seeking a longer swim, the Riverside Park at Wansbeck has easy access to the water. The man-made lagoon at Bolam has a jetty for launching canoes, with secluded picnic spots and a wild-camping site opposite.

While the beaches on this stretch of coastline are lesser known, there are gems to discover. The historic harbour at Seaton Sluice, with its ingenious sluice gates, has a beautiful sandy beach for swimming and paddleboarding. Cambois Sands, once blighted by the ugly backdrop of Blyth power station, has an immense sweep of beach at low tide, with footpaths along the dunes. Newbiggin-by-the-Sea, recognised by the quirky 'Couple' statue out at sea, boasts stunning sunrises and sunsets. An abundance of marine life graces the bay: dolphins and seals – and if you're lucky, porpoises and whales.

RIVERS & LAKES

1 LADY CHAPEL WOODS, BOTHAL, RIVER WANSBECK

This delightful woodland trail runs past the site of a ruined chapel to a dappled secret swim spot at a bend in the river with deep pools, little rapids and stone ledges. There are a couple of picnic benches in a clearing of the trees nearby. Look out en route for the Jubilee Well, dated 1887, and a curious, much-weathered coat of arms carved into the quarried rock face.

→ From Morpeth follow the A192 then the A196 towards Bothal. After 3½ miles cross river bridge, then take immediate L to car park (55.1698, -1.6232). Follow footpath through woods, passing little coat of arms, the well on the R and picnic benches on the L, then follow path down to beach at river bend. Other swim spots en route, including a deep pool at 55.1671, -1.6554.

25 mins, 55.1661, -1.6566 🏊🅿🏕🚶

2 BOTHAL CASTLE STEPPING STONES, RIVER WANSBECK

Stepping stones across the river in a pretty 19th-century estate village with honey-coloured houses, a castle and medieval church. A small suspension bridge, no longer in use, was built so the vicar could cross the river. Shallow paddling with deeper pool beyond the stones.

→ From Morpeth follow the A197 for 3½ miles to Bothal village. Parking near church or on the roadside near houses. From church look for a fingerpost pointing towards the river and follow path.

5 mins, 55.1718, -1.6238 🏊🚶

3 PLESSEY WOODS, RIVER BLYTH

Follow enchanted woodland paths down to the river for paddling and swim spots at the wooden jetty or head to a small beach at the bottom of the steep steps to the river (55.1115, -1.6289), where there is a deep pool. Take care as the riverbed has sharp rocks. Café at the visitor centre.

→ From the junction of the A1 and A19 at Seaton Burn, head N on the A1068 for 4½ miles. Country park is signed on L. Walk past visitor centre, through woods and head L to follow route down to riverside.

20 mins, 55.1178, -1.6281 🏊🅿

4 HUMFORD MILL, RIVER BLYTH

Stepping stones over the river leading onto a lovely riverside walk through Humford Woods. Shallow paddling here with deeper pools upstream by the weir.

→ From Bedlington follow the A193 from roundabout towards Blyth, turning R then R again, following track to parking at Humford Mill car park (NE22 5RT).

2 mins, 55.1194, -1.5809 🏊🚶🚶

5 MITFORD CASTLE, RIVER WANSBECK

Deep section of river, with a small beach downstream of the stone bridge, as it loops away from the pretty ruins of 11th-century Mitford Castle. The castle, which sits on a hillock above, became the HQ of notorious kidnapper Sir Gilbert Middleton in the 14th century and was used to hold prisoners.

→ From Morpeth follow the B6343 for 2 miles through Mitford, then take a L turn to cross bridge to parking on L. Follow footpath down from bridge on R. Best view of Mitford Castle is from gate opp church. Keep-out signs.

2 mins, 55.1633, -1.7342 🏊🅿📷

6 WANSBECK RIVERSIDE PARK, RIVER WANSBECK

A calm, smooth stretch of the River Wansbeck good for swimming, paddleboarding or kayaking, both up and downstream, with plenty of parking right next to the river.

→ Head E of Morpeth on the A197 for 5 miles, then turn R on to Sheepwash Road (A1068) and L on to Wellhead Dean Road, keeping L for parking at Riverside Park.
1 min, 55.1711, -1.5945

7 FONTBURN RESERVOIR

Small peaceful reservoir, with areas of wetland and scrub, located at the end of a track. Home to red squirrel, badgers and roe deer and with the Simonside Hills as a backdrop. There are woodland walks and beaches around the southern shore – perfect for picnics.

→ From Scot's Gap head N on the B6342 for 5 miles, then turn L along a track to parking at southern shore car park (L at end). Camper vans £10 overnight, payable at visitor centre.
2 mins, 55.2355, -1.9241

8 BOLAM LAKE

An abundance of wildlife can be found at this small lake, including red squirrels, roe deer and a bevy of mute swans. You can launch a canoe here for a small fee, payable at the visitor centre. There is a semi-wild campsite at the friendly Bolam Lake Camping Paddock opposite the country park.

→ Head N from Belsay towards Bolam for about 2 miles to signs for Bolam Country Park. Follow road to L for parking.
2 mins, 55.1315, -1.8718

BEAUTIFUL BEACHES

9 CAMBOIS BEACH

A long sweep of sandy beach, backed by rocks and dunes, sandwiched between the River Wansbeck estuary to the N and Blyth Harbour to the S.

→ From Blyth follow the A193 then the A189 to Brock Lane. Take exit towards Cambois/ Sleekburn/industrial zone. Continue for 2 miles to small car park and beach.
1 min, 55.1578, -1.5268

10 SEATON SLUICE HARBOUR

Situated at the mouth of the Seaton Burn, this small pretty harbour once exported coal, bottles and salt. In the mid-17th century Sir Ralph Delaval (of Seaton Delaval Hall) constructed sluice gates which trapped sea water at high tide and released it at low tide, preventing the harbour from silting up. A century later a cut was made through the headland to form a new harbour entrance, with gates at either end creating a basin

unaffected by the tide. It is backed by a beautiful sandy beach that stretches N for 2 miles to Blyth.

→ Off Links Road/Beresford Road (both A193) in Seaton Sluice village centre. Parking nearby and nice pub overlooking the harbour.
2 mins, 55.0837, -1.4744

RUINS, FOLLIES & CAVES

11 HARTBURN GROTTO

Built out of a cave as a two-room shelter with a fireplace and dressing room, this utterly captivating grotto was created in the 18th century so ladies could discreetly change before using the passage linking the grotto to the river to bathe in the Hart Burn. A delightful place next to the burn where you can take a dip.

→ From Hartburn, park in honesty box car park (55.1687, -1.8614), then turn L and walk for 5 mins along road to footpath sign on R into woods. Follow track which bears L and after another 5 mins the grotto is on the L. You can return same way or walk through the beautiful woods to loop back onto road.
10 mins, 55.1720, -1.8659

12 ST HELEN'S CHURCH, LONGHORSLEY

Empty shell of a Norman church off the beaten track on the banks of Paxtondean Burn. Volunteers are planting up wildflower areas, including inside the church. A peaceful place to wander around.

→ From Longhorsley continue for ½ mile S and look out for L turn. No parking here but continue through gate to parking by church.
2 mins, 55.2431, -1.7588

13 WALLINGTON HALL

NT country house surrounded by a landscape of lawns, lakes and woodland, including a delightful secret garden hidden in the woods. The lawns are carpeted with crocuses in spring. Riverside walks and cycle trails.

→ Heading N on the A696 from Belsay, continue for 4½ miles, then take R turn signposted 'Deanham'. Continue for 1 mile to R turn onto B6342, and car park for Wallington is on the L.
5 mins, 55.1522, -1.9563

14 ROTHLEY CASTLE

Sitting on a small hill among some impressive crags, the ruins of this 18th-century Gothic folly have glorious views across beautiful countryside. Built for the

Wallington Hall Estate, the central tower has two storeys, and you can climb the stone staircase to the second floor where the views get even better. Plenty of crags here for bouldering. A magnificent setting.

→ From Scot's Gap head N on the B6342 for just over 2 miles to verge parking at Rothley crossroads. Walk S along the B6342 to gate just after crags on L and follow footpath beside a stone wall on R. Near end of wall, veer L up to hilltop, where ruins will come into view.

30 mins, 55.1929, -1.9329 🏞🖼🧗🏕🚶🏔

15 SHAFTOE CRAGS

This superlative Tolkienesque landscape, with its jumble of boulders, terrific crags and rock shelters spread across a mile of moorland, has sweeping views of the Simonside Hills and the coast. Salter's Nick, a gap in the sandstone, was once used by smugglers for taking salt into Scotland and bringing whisky into England. Also seek out Queen Victoria's Jubilee Stone.

→ Travelling NW on the A696 from Bolam Lake, after ¾ mile turn L at a crossroads along a track for Shaftoe Crags. Continue to parking by a wall after first cattle grid. Walk up hill to crags.

15 mins, 55.1349, -1.9166 🏞🚶🏔🚗🏔

16 CODGER FORT

Sitting on top of a rocky crag, this striking 18th-century folly is a prominent feature for drivers on the B6342. Built by Sir Walter Blackett as part of the Wallington Estate, it continues to inspire debate as to whether it is a folly or was intended to defend the land and route through England during the 1745 Jacobite rebellion. Beautiful situation. Private land so roadside view only.

→ From Scot's Gap continue N for just over 2 miles to lay-by parking at Rothley crossroads on R at 55.2010, -1.9320. From the lay-by walk to the crossroads, turn R for a few yards to see fort on R from roadside. Fast road.

5 mins, 55.2051, -1.9316 🖼❓

17 ST ANDREW'S CHURCH, BOLAM

Beautiful Saxon church hidden down a track. It escaped destruction in a WW2 air raid when a bomb dropped on it failed to explode. The German pilot returned 60 years later to apologise for the attack. The tower dates from the late Saxon period, and a repaired leaded window is a testament to the bomb attack.

→ From Belsay, head N towards Bolam Lake for 2½ miles, then just past lake take a R turn

20

and continue for ½ mile to L along track to church and parking.
2 mins, 55.1376, -1.8565 🏰🏕️

18 STARLIGHT CASTLE

Reputedly the result of a bet to build a castle overnight, Starlight Castle was constructed by Sir Francis Delaval of the Seaton Delaval Estate in the mid-18th century. Standing high on Holywell Dene, this mini fortress would have had great views across the harbour in its day. Only a small section of wall survives.

➔ From Seaton Sluice Harbour, follow the A193 towards Hartley. Just after school on R, turn R to parking behind school. Find footpath down to river then take L to footbridge just past big pipe. Double back on opposite bank. Just before bench on L find steep path up to ruins.
10 mins, 55.0779, -1.4780 🏰🚶

19 CHURCH OF OUR LADY IN SEATON VALLEY

Tiny Norman church that was a private family chapel of the Delaval family for more than 700 years. Look out for the striking stone effigies of Sir Hugh Delaval and an unidentified lady.

➔ In Seaton Delaval, follow the A190 (The Avenue) towards Seaton Sluice. Just before

Seaton Delaval Hall, there is a slight bend to the L and parking space on R and gate to church.
2 mins, 55.0811, -1.4974 🏰

ART & CULTURE

20 NORTHUMBERLANDIA

An intriguing human landform sculpture, the Lady of the North is a reclining woman made from 1½ million tonnes of rock, clay and soil, reaching 30m high and ¼ mile long. You can follow footpaths around, up and over the mounds, and from the top you can see into the Shotton Surface Mine.

➔ Travelling S on the A1, take the exit towards Blagdon/Dinnington/Ponteland/Shotton. Turn L into Blagdon Lane (signposted Northumberlandia). After ¾ mile turn L into Northumberlandia.
2 mins, 55.0887, -1.6298 🥕🏕️⛰️

21 THE COUPLE STATUE, NEWBIGGIN

Two very realistic 5m-high bronze figures standing on a large platform, keeping watch over the sea. The artwork by sculptor Sean Henry divides opinion. You can decide for yourself.

➔ There is a large, free car park beside the Newbiggin Maritime Centre. The sculpture is

18

19

best viewed from further along the promenade (Promenade, Newbiggin-by-the-Sea, NE64 6DA). 5 mins, 55.1816, -1.5088

LOCAL FOOD

22 DRIFT CAFÉ

Friendly beach café near Cresswell Pond and a great place to refuel after a walk on the beach. Serves light lunches, soups, home-baked cakes, pizzas and fish and chips. Garden. Second-hand books and artwork for sale.

➔ Cresswell, NE61 5LA, 01670 861599
55.2373, -1.5463

23 CAPHEATON VILLAGE TEAROOM

Slabs of lemon drizzle and wedges of Victoria sponge are served at this eye-catching-green tin-hut village hall. Also soup and sandwiches. Very popular with passing cyclists. Open Sat and Sun, 10am – 3pm.

➔ Capheaton and District Institute, Silver Hill, Capheaton, NE19 2AA
55.1179, -1.9468

24 KIRKHARLE COFFEE HOUSE

Set within an 18th-century courtyard of artisan businesses and the birthplace of

landscape artist Capability Brown, this popular café serves teas, cakes and light lunches. Afterwards take a stroll around the Serpentine Lake.

➔ Courtyard, Kirkharle, NE19 2PE, 01830 540362
55.1367, -1.9803

25 BLACKSMITH'S COFFEE SHOP

Charming café in a converted blacksmith's serving delicious home-made food, including sandwiches, light lunches and salads, as well as a moreish selection of traybakes and cakes.

➔ Belsay Village, NE20 0DU, 01661 881024
55.1016, -1.8414

26 SEAGLASS EATERY

Seafront café serving Pilgrims Coffee and stotties with a delicious range of fillings, including Craster kipper fillet. Occasional bistro evenings. Double room available. Drying room for wetsuits and canoe/paddleboard storage.

➔ Promenade, Newbiggin-by-the-Sea, NE64 6DA, 07917 743777
55.1853, -1.5092

27 CASTAWAYS TEASHOP

Lovely café with sea view terrace serving locally sourced ingredients. Good pit stop if you are cycling the Coast and Castles Cycle Route. Open 7 days, 9am – 4pm.

➔ 32 Collywell Bay Road, Seaton Sluice, Whitley Bay, NE26 4QZ
55.0827, -1.4714

28 THE CHEESE LOFT CAFÉ

A cheese-lovers dream! An artisan cheese farm run by the Northumberland Cheese Company, with a lovely café upstairs in the rafters. The cheeses are made from cow's, sheep's and goat's milk, with varieties such as Kielder, Cheviot and Hadrian's to sample.

➔ The Cheese Farm, Green Lane, Blagdon, NE13 6BZ, 01670 789798
55.0872, -1.6956

29 THE CHEESE SHOP, MORPETH

You will find more than 160 different cheeses, including local, national and European specialities, at this one-stop cheese store, one of the largest cheese retailers in the North East.

➔ 6 Oldgate, NE61 1LX, 01670 459579
55.1676, -1.6914

30 THE BLAGDON FARM SHOP

Large farm shop on the Blagdon Estate with a bakehouse selling homemade ready meals. Also a high-quality butchery and deli with an excellent cheese counter.

→ 16–18 Milkhope Centre, Berwick Hill Road, Blagdon, NE13 6DA, 01670 789924

55.0793, -1.6622 🍴

FRIENDLY PUBS

31 THE BLACKBIRD, PONTELAND

Characterful village pub, once a 14th-century castle, standing on a historic site where a peace treaty was signed between Henry III and Alexander of Scotland. It still retains some original features, including a Tudor fireplace. The menu is rustic: country pub classics with a modern twist.

→ Blackbird Inn, North Road, Ponteland, NE20 9UH, 01661 822684

55.0512, -1.7426 🍴 🛏

32 THE KING'S ARMS

Popular historic pub serving quality food and good selection of beers. In summer take a seat on the front patio overlooking beautiful Seaton Sluice Harbour. When it is a little chillier, enjoy a beer next to the log fire inside.

→ The Harbour, Seaton Sluice, NE26 4RD, 0191 237 0275

55.0843, -1.4718 🍴

CAMP, GLAMP & SLEEP

33 TRANWELL FARM CAMPSITE

Small off-grid campsite with 12 pitches mown into the long grass. Stargazer bell tent in its own setting and shepherd's hut with solar panel. A short walk from the pub. Green Camping Club site. April to October.

→ Gubeon Wood, Tranwell Farm, Morpeth, NE61 6BH, 07947 598832

55.1425, -1.7215 ⛺

34 ABBEYFIELD GLAMPING

Sink into the feather bedding on the double bed above the cab of this gorgeously quirky restored Bedford TK horsebox, which sits in a pretty meadow by ancient woodland. Lovely decked terrace to the side with a fire pit to snuggle around. Ideal for couples or small families.

→ Abbeyfield Stables, Mitford, Morpeth, NE61 2YU, 07403 318392

55.1649, -1.7121 🏕

35 LOTTIE'S CABIN, HILLSIDE HUTS

Inspired by lodges in the Canadian Rocky Mountains, this gorgeous two-storey luxury cabin is set within a natural woodland overlooking a wildflower meadow with breathtaking views of the coast. There are three other huts and cabins to choose from.

→ Hillside, Earsdon Hill Farm, Morpeth, NE61 3ES, 07767 668400

55.24931, -1.68976 🏕

36 ROTHLEY LAKEHOUSE

Large, spacious lake-front house with magnificent views, perfect for a family gathering. The house was a former shooting lodge, and the lake was inspired by Capability Brown, who was born near here. Sleeps 16.

→ Longwitton, NE61 4JY. National Trust Cottages.
55.2120, -1.9318

37 CAPHEATON SCHOOL HOUSE

Old black and white photographs on the walls recall the school days of this cosy cottage, which has lovely lake views and is part of the Capheaton Estate. A cosy wood burner, squashy sofas and throws make for a comfortable stay.

→ Capheaton Hall, Capheaton, NE19 2AB,
0191 375 8152
55.11787, -1.94574

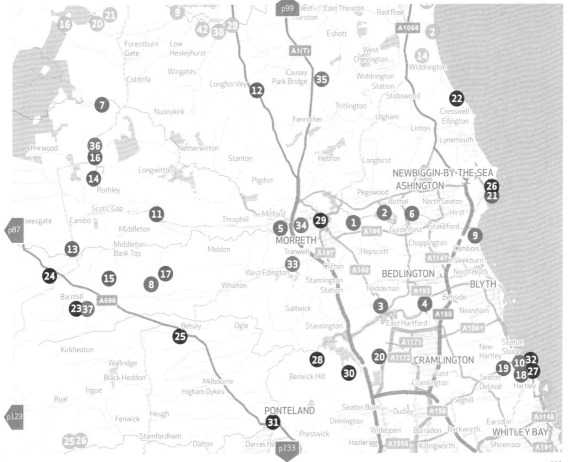

HADRIAN'S WALL

Our perfect weekend

→ **March** from Steel Rigg to Housesteads along Hadrian's Wall, the northernmost frontier of the Roman Empire

→ **Descend** to the Devil's Water to bathe in the secluded Swallowship Pool

→ **Visit** the 1,000-year-old yew tree in St Cuthbert's churchyard

→ **Gaze** up at star-studded skies above Cawfield Quarry in the lee of the Great Whin Sill, then hunker down with a drink at the Milecastle Inn

→ **Swim** beneath the arches of the monumental Lambley Viaduct, once used for transporting coal and lead from the surrounding mines

→ **Stay** at the 18th-century Causeway House on the old Roman road, the only house in Northumberland still thatched in heather

→ **Hike** through ancient woodland to the ruins of a Medieval peel tower at Staward Gorge

→ **Paddleboard** on the River North Tyne at Chollerford, then explore the ruins of Chesters Bridge Abutment, keeping an eye out for kingfishers

In an outstanding feat of Roman engineering, Hadrian's Wall dips and dives across the Northumberland countryside like a rollercoaster, piggybacking on the Great Whin Sill. So resistant to erosion is this hard black dolerite that wherever it reaches the surface, it forms a remarkable landscape feature, a geological peculiarity that makes the wall so striking.

Emperor Hadrian built the wall in ad 122 to form a barrier marking the north-west corner of the Roman Empire. Scattered along the wall's route are temples, forts, turrets and milecastles. With so much to see, it can be daunting to know where to begin.

One of the best sections lies between Steel Rigg and Housesteads, passing through the evocative Sycamore Gap. Walltown Crags is a spectacularly well-preserved stretch with stupendous views, and Cawfield Quarry is a mesmerising place to spend an evening, with millions of stars twinkling in the night sky above a shimmering lake.

The wall is just one part of this World Heritage Site. Often overlooked are the lovely Brocolitia Temple of Mithras and the impressive riverside ruins of Chesters Bridge Abutment, which lie on the opposite bank to the baths of Chesters Roman Fort. Recycled stone from the wall can be seen at tiny St Giles Church in Chollerton, where a Roman altar has been flipped over and used as a font. Ruined Thirlwall Castle benefited from pillaged stones, which were used to build it in the 12th century.

This area is well set up for visitors. The AD122 Hadrian's Wall Country Bus shuttles between Hexham and Haltwhistle, stopping at the main sites, enabling you to choose how much of the wall you wish to walk before catching the bus back to your starting point. The state-of-the-art YHA The Sill is an excellent base for exploring the area, with plenty of good campsites and pubs to suit all tastes too.

Just as dramatic are the wall's loughs, wild upland waters formed by glaciers in the last ice age. The smallest of these is Crag Lough, its shoreline bordering a wooded glade along the wall's route and an alluring diversion for a secluded swim.

Plenty more water adventures can be enjoyed in the rivers North Tyne and South Tyne at Chollerford and Featherstone. Set up camp for the day at one of the sheltered beaches along the River Allen in dramatic Staward Gorge and explore the ancient woods and splash in the river. Nearer Hexham, the captivating Swallowship Pool on the Devil's Water is a bewitching place, with reflections of the gorge's sandstone walls rippling across its tranquil waters.

RIVERS & WATERFALLS

1 CHOLLERFORD, RIVER NORTH TYNE

Deep section of the Tyne upstream of Chollerford bridge and weir, with several entry points along the riverside path. Calm, smooth stretch for swimming and paddleboarding. Also jetty at George Hotel in Chollerford.

→ Chollerford is 3 miles N of Hexham. Parking at Chesters Roman Fort (closes 5.30pm). Walk along road to roundabout, cross bridge and follow riverside path upstream.

20 mins, 55.0310, -2.1184

2 LAMBLEY VIADUCT, RIVER SOUTH TYNE

Follow a pretty woodland path along the South Tyne Trail to a pebble beach with swim pools beneath the imposing Lambley Viaduct, which crosses the River South Tyne here in a series of elegant stone arches. The 260m-long structure once carried trains from Alston to Haltwhistle, transporting coal and lead from the surrounding mines.

→ Follow the A689 N to Lambley. After Lambley village take R turn and follow road for 1¼ miles to Lambley Viaduct South Tyne Trail car park on L at 54.9298, -2.5015. Follow way-marked trail, then cross viaduct, then footpath to R to footbridge to pebble beach on other side.

20 mins, 54.9191, -2.5085

3 FEATHERSTONE CASTLE, RIVER SOUTH TYNE

A superb, accessible swimming spot near Featherstone Castle with a suntrap of a sandy beach on hot days. Deeper water in the middle of the river but plenty of shallows for paddling and flat rocks on the opposite bank for jumping. Beautiful situation. River can be flashy here.

→ On the A69 heading towards Carlisle, 1 mile beyond the Haltwhistle turn-off, turn L on to Bellister Bank and continue for 1 mile, then take a slight R turn and continue for a further mile, passing Haltwhistle Campsite, to parking on R before footbridge over river. Follow footpath on L of riverbank to beaches.

5 mins, 54.9415, -2.5141

4 FEATHERSTONE BRIDGE, RIVER SOUTH TYNE

Swim spot beneath the stone arch bridge with beach and deep pools. Easy access and huge slabs of rock to sunbathe on. Be mindful as the river can reach high levels here.

→ On the A69 heading towards Carlisle, 1 mile beyond the Haltwhistle turn-off, turn L on to Bellister Bank and continue for 1 mile, then take a slight R turn and continue for ½ mile, passing Haltwhistle Campsite, to lay-by parking before stone bridge and access to river.

1 min, 54.9506, -2.5078

5 TYNE GREEN, RIVER TYNE

Good access to the River Tyne for a swim or paddleboard/kayak launch from steps and jetty by the 18th-century bridge surrounded by beautiful parkland and mature trees.

→ From Hexham follow Haugh Lane straight across roundabout onto the A6079, then turn L onto Tyne Green Road and signs to country park (NE46 3HR) and parking.

2 mins, 54.9779, -2.1004

6 PLANKEY MILL, RIVER ALLEN

Beautiful wooded riverside walks with access to beaches through the trees. Also check out beach, rocky slabs and pretty pools further downstream at 54.9449, -2.3152. Wild camping available at Plankey Mill farm. Just turn up and pay.

→ 3 miles SW of Haydon bridge on the A686. After Langley, take R turn, signed 'Plankey Mill/Lough Green', then continue for 1 mile to L turn for Plankey Mill. Continue, then descend the hill to parking at the riverside campsite.

Best pools are a ¾-mile walk downstream. Upstream to NT Allen Banks, mainly paddling.

15 mins, 54.9468, -2.3170 🚶🏊🧍🏕️⛰️

7 SWALLOWSHIP POOL, DEVIL'S WATER

Deep, clear pool on the evocatively named Devil's Water beneath the sandstone walls of a gorge that creates a beautiful reflection in its calm waters. Beach and paddling. Reached via a lovely woodland walk, this is a delightful location.

→ Lay-by parking by Kingswood Education and Outdoor Centre (NE46 1TP), N of Linnels Bridge on the B6306. Take footpath into woods. Continue past Duke's House to fork in path near ruins of Five Gates House. Turn R along path through Scots Pines. Turn R when path ends and follow path above Devil's Water to steep, uneven path to burn and pool.

30 mins, 54.9555, -2.0672 🏊🏕️🧍🚶☕⛰️

8 CRAMMEL LINN, RIVER IRTHING

Spectacular 7.5m waterfall with pool on wild moor strewn with derelict military tanks, as adjacent to military training area. Check red flags. Popular spot on a hot day.

→ Head 1 mile W of Gilsland, over bridge and uphill past Gilsland Spa. Continue for another

1½ miles and take 'no through road' R turn over cattle grid. Find parking by signed footpath on R after 1 mile, on far edge of forest.

10 mins, 55.0202, -2.5637 🚂🏕️🏊🚶

LAKES & LOUGHS

9 CAWFIELD QUARRY LAKE, HADRIAN'S WALL

Picturesque reservoir in a former quarry at the base of one of the most scenic stretches of Hadrian's Wall as it clings to the sheer crags of the Whin Sill. A Dark Skies Discovery site. A peaceful place to watch the sun go down and the stars come out. 'No swimming' signs.

→ Cawfield is clearly signposted from the Military Road. Park in Cawfield's car park by the lake.

1 min, 54.9930, -2.4499 🧍🏕️📷

10 CRAG LOUGH

The most magical of the four lakes along the wall, Crag Lough sits directly below the sheer Whin Sill crags. Beautiful situation. It is a natural eutrophic lake, so be mindful of blue-green algae.

→ As for Sycamore Gap but continue along path to woodland on L. Just before gate a small path leads down to shore. Alternatively,

pass through gate to open meadow
and shoreline.

20 mins, 55.0061, -2.3656 🏊⛰🏕🚶

11 BROOMLEE LOUGH

Large lake surrounded by open moorland
near Housesteads Roman Fort/Hadrian's
Wall. Marshy, shallow shore in places but
deeper in SE corner beneath Dove Crag. NT
specifies no swimming here as SSSI.

→ Housesteads Fort is well signposted along
the B6318 Military Road. Follow path up past
fort to Hadrian's Wall path heading E. Continue
½ mile to Milecastle 36 and beat a path over
open-access land for 300m.

25 mins, 55.0215, -2.3234 ⛰🏕❓

SACRED & ANCIENT

12 STEEL RIGG TO HOUSESTEADS, HADRIAN'S WALL

With immense views, a magical lake and
a famous tree, this section of Hadrian's
Wall is almost unrivalled in its dramatic
features and magnificent vistas towards
Housesteads Fort. As you walk the wall,
you are literally following in the footsteps
of the Roman soldiers who manned this
outpost of the empire.

→ Steel Rigg is well signed from the B6318.
From the car park (NE47 7AN), follow the
Hadrian's Wall footpath to Housesteads for
3½ miles. Then return by the excellent AD122
Hadrian's Wall Country Bus, which stops at all
the main sites.

2 hrs, 55.0134, -2.3304 🚶🏕🚲📷

13 WALLTOWN CRAGGS, HADRIAN'S WALL

Walk this stunning and spectacularly
preserved section of the wall, as it snakes
and twists along the dramatic crags of the
Whin Sill, to be rewarded with stupendous
360-degree views. One of the best places in
the country for stargazing.

→ Follow the track marked 'lightweight
vehicles only' to parking spot at 54.9894,
-2.5085 and footpath sign for Hadrian's Wall
path. Head for dramatic Whin Sill crags and
climb to turret at top for great views back.

2 mins, 54.9911, -2.5092 🐕🚲📷🚶🧗

14 CHESTERS BRIDGE ABUTMENT

Impressive remains of the Roman bridge that
carried Hadrian's Wall across the River North
Tyne. The bridge was built in two phases,
between ad 122 and ad 192, and is now on dry
land, as the River Tyne has shifted some 20m
since its construction. This tranquil riverside

117

location, with its herons and kingfishers, is less frequented than Chesters Fort on the opposite bank, whose Roman baths you can see from here.

→ Park at Chesters Fort car park (fee if not EH member), then walk along the B6318 to roundabout and cross bridge to gate on R to riverside walk to bridge ruins.

20 mins, 55.0252, -2.1358 🚶 ⛺ ⛓ 🚆

15 BROCOLITIA, TEMPLE OF MITHRAS

A lesser-known site along Hadrian's Wall, these fascinating remains of a Roman temple just below Carrawburgh Fort, or Brocolitia, are dedicated to Mithras, a sun god worshipped by soldiers. The cult of Mithras, who according to legend entered a cave and killed a sacred bull, placed great emphasis on honour and military prowess, and Temples of Mithras were fairly common in civilian settlements near Roman forts. The temple was built around ad 200 but destroyed 150 years later and although several existed along Hadrian's Wall, this is the only one that can be seen today.

→ 3¾ miles W of Chollerford on the B6318. Car park NE46 4DB (fee).

10 mins, 55.0338, -2.2225 ✝ ⛓ ⛺ ⛺

16 ST GILES CHURCH, CHOLLERTON

A 13th-century church housing Roman monolithic columns from Coriosopitum (Corbridge Roman site) and an upturned Roman altar, now used as a font, which sits just inside the doorway.

→ The church is to the W of the village of Chollerton, just off the A6079. Limited parking at front of church. Path leads to church.

2 mins, 55.0417, -2.1095 ✝

17 BRADY'S CRAG

Small sandstone outcrop with a freestanding boulder and a series of small walls to the E, where there is a little cave shelter. A beautiful situation, hidden away behind an ancient church that stands on the site of a historic 7th-century battle. Views across to the silhouette of Hadrian's Wall. Ideal for family bouldering on a summer's evening.

→ Approximately 600m N of the B6138 Military Road, 1½ miles SE of Chollerford. Park at St Oswald's Chapel lay-by on L (55.0190, -2.0999). Follow footpath around the R-hand side of church. Pass through gate and continue downhill to R towards a red-brick structure. Head for stile over fence and follow track to L past the gorse to crag on R.

10 mins, 55.0234, -2.0959 🌊 🪨 🧗

18

RUINS

18 THIRLWALL CASTLE

Perched above the Tipalt Burn in a landscape once riven by border feuds, this 12th-century castle was rebuilt by John Thirlwall around 1330, from stone pillaged from Hadrian's Wall, to withstand Scottish raids. Today its thick bastle walls have been colonised by plants, and raucous jackdaws wheel above and roost in the stone crevices.

→ From Gilsland travel E on the B6318 for 1½ miles to Thirlwall View car park, off the B6318, after Longbyre at 54.9862, -2.5360. Follow footpath over railway line to castle.
10 mins, 54.9888, -2.5338 🌫️🚶🛈

19 STAWARD PEEL

Ruins of a Medieval peel tower, gatehouse and ditches situated on a highly defensible oval promontory overlooking the River Allen as it cuts through Staward Gorge. The tower was first built from timber then demolished and rebuilt in stone using recycled Roman masonry. Only three of the substantial thick stone sides are preserved, but the views over the gorge are worth the climb. There is a lovely pool, easily reached, in the river below to cool off after the hike up.

→ Follow directions for Plankey Mill then take the footpath signposted 'Staward Peel (1 mile)' through the woodland. Narrow, uneven paths, eroded in places. When you come to the clearing of the gorge, take the steep path on the L to reach the peel tower (brown route).
45 mins, 54.9413, -2.3146 🌫️🚶🛈

ANCIENT TREES & WOODLAND

20 LETAH WOOD

Ancient woodland and the last wild daffodil wood in Northumberland. Visit in early spring for daffodils, followed by carpets of wild garlic. A lovely place for families with small children, who will enjoy playing in the Letah Burn and scampering along the trails.

→ From Juniper head E through village and continue for 1½ miles, then take L onto Hill Rd to find small parking area on L in front gate at entrance to the woodland.
2 mins, 54.9411, -2.0949 🛈🚶🌿

20

21 ANCIENT YEW, ST CUTHBERT'S CHURCH

Three noble yews stand in St Cuthbert's churchyard; the largest behind the church is almost 1,000 years old, predating the church, with its enormous girth held together by thick iron straps. The pair of yews in front

21

of the church may be 500 years old. The 15th-century church is the only perpendicular-style church in Northumberland, with parts dating back to the 12th century. The remains of a 7th-century Saxon cross, with Roman altar stones at its base, also stands in the churchyard, suggesting the site has a longer sacred history. Picturesque hamlet and walks.

→ From Bardon Mill, take the A69 E for ½ mile to signpost for Beltingham on R. Follow road then take R again for Beltingham. Parking in front of church.

1 min, 54.9699, -2.3302 🅿 ✝

22 SYCAMORE GAP

It takes something special to upstage a World Heritage Site but one tree in Northumberland just about manages to do it. The most photographed tree in the country stands in a dramatic dip in the wall, a channel chipped away by meltwater flowing beneath ice sheets that once covered the area. To see it for real is quite an experience, all the more captivating as you stumble upon it side on, without immediately recognising it as THE tree.

→ From Steel Rigg car park, continue E along the wall for 1 mile.

45 mins, 55.0034, -2.3738 📷 🔲

23 ALLEN BANKS AND STAWARD GORGE

The largest area of ancient and semi-natural woodland in Northumberland, with a deep gorge carved out by the River Allen, this 100-hectare NT-managed site is made for adventures. There are numerous marked trails of varying terrain to follow and idyllic riverside picnic spots.

→ Located 5 ½ miles E of Haltwhistle, 3 miles W of Haydon Bridge, ½ mile S of A69. Pay and display at Allen Banks.

1 min, 54.9704, -2.3170 🅿 🚶 ⛴ 🏔 ⛰

INDUSTRIAL HERITAGE

24 STUBLICK CHIMNEY

Looming over the landscape, this 30m-high stack was originally the vent at the end of a long flue that billowed out lead fumes from Langley lead smelting mill a mile away. The mill closed in 1887 but reservoirs, flues and watercourses, as well as this chimney, are reminders of the industries that once characterised this area.

→ Travelling E from the crossroads at Langley on the B6305, you will see the chimney on the R after ¾ mile. Park in lay-by on L and cross road to reach chimney.

3 mins, 54.9443, -2.2507 🏞 📷

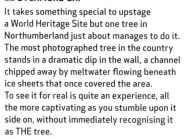

25 DUKESFIELD ARCHES

Two graceful Gothic arches hidden in woodland in the valley of the Devil's Water are all that remain of the once-important Dukesfield Smelt Mill, the largest in the country for a century from the 1670s. Afterwards, head back to the bridge for a paddle in the burn.

→ From Hexham take Causey Hill Road to Juniper (5 miles). Continue through village, crossing bridge over Devil's Water. At junction turn L then just after bridge find parking on R by gate at entrance to woods (54.9172, -2.0903). Follow track to arches on L.
5 mins, 54.9164, -2.0930

CAFÉS & PUBS

26 THE GARDEN STATION, LANGLEY

A restored Victorian railway carriage hidden in a tranquil woodland garden with an occasional tearoom serving delicious food on vintage china. Gardens open every day, all year round. Café is open weekends. Best to check ahead.

→ Langley-on-Tyne, Hexham, NE47 5LA, 01434 684391
54.9456, -2.2692

27 THE TWICE BREWED INN

Popular country inn and B&B situated just below Hadrian's Wall. On-site brewery with own ales. Dark skies location with observatory. Good option when Kielder is busy. Parking for camper vans overnight with permit from reception.

→ Bardon Mill, NE47 7AN, 01434 344534
54.9958, -2.3910

28 MILECASTLE INN

Traditional friendly pub serving excellent home-cooked food and ales. Pull up at one of the tables at the front for amazing sunset views over Hadrian's Wall. Two s/c cottages.

→ Military Road, Haltwhistle, NE49 9NN, 01434 321372. Ring ahead if walking from a campsite in case of early closure. No dogs inside.
54.9879, -2.4456

29 CORBRIDGE VICAR'S PELE TOWER

Quirky micro gin bar in a 14th-century defensive pele tower in the grounds of St Andrew's Church and once used as a vicarage. Good selection of real ale, beer and wine.

→ Market Pl, Corbridge, NE45 5AW, 07565 801463
54.9742, -2.0193

30 THE RAT INN, ANICK

Idyllic village-green setting and spectacular views across the surrounding countryside. The menu at this old drover's inn, now a gastropub, features local produce, some grown in the pub's grounds, including rhubarb for a chutney that is served with local pork and black pudding terrine.

→ Anick, Hexham, NE46 4LN, 01434 602814
54.9842, -2.0743 🅿️ 🍴

31 THE ANGEL OF CORBRIDGE

Possibly the oldest inn in Northumberland, dating back to 1569, this is a popular village pub and hotel with a fish and chip shop, Angelfish, at the rear. Corbridge has riverside walks and independent shops, including a wonderful homeware store, RE, in Bishop's Yard.

→ Main St, Corbridge, NE45 5LA,
01434 632119
54.9737, -2.0175 🅿️ 🍴 🚩

CAMPSITES & HOSTELS

32 HADRIAN'S WALL CAMPSITE

Scenic campsite right next to Hadrian's Wall with stunning sunrise and sunset views. Grass and hard-standing pitches and good facilities. Small hut for backpackers to prepare food and eat in inclement weather. Also a bunk room with two rooms sleeping 4 and 6 people. Bell tents and shepherd's huts.

→ Tilery, Melkridge, Haltwhistle, NE49 9PG,
01434 320495
54.9855, -2.4226 🔺

33 HALTWHISTLE CAMPING & CARAVANNING

Small, secluded riverside campsite in a clearing of the NT-managed Bellister Wood. A peaceful location and haven for wildlife, with access to river and superb walking country. Good facilities.

→ Burnfoot Park Village, Haltwhistle,
NE49 0JP, 01434 320106
54.9520, -2.4948 🔺

34 WINSHIELDS CAMPSITE

Traditional campsite situated at the foot of Hadrian's Wall and the Pennine Way. Walkers and cyclists £10 pn. Walk in and off. Lovely bunk barn, sleeping 5 in one room, with lounge, table and chairs. Perfect for walking the wall. Not suitable for large tents.

→ Twice Brewed, Military Road, Bardon Mill,
Hexham, NE47 7AN, 07968 102780
54.9947, -2.4007 🔺

35 RYE HILL FARM

One of the most secluded campsites in Northumberland, this small site has flat pitches sheltered by mature beech trees on one side and open vistas on the other. Kids will love meeting the ponies, sheep and hens, as well as cooking up a feast in the mud pie kitchen. Games barn with table tennis and pool table.

→ Rye Hill Farm, Slaley nr Hexham, NE47 0AH,
01434 673259
54.9159, -2.0637 🔺

36 GREENCARTS CAMPSITE

Beautifully situated campsite on a working farm with a dorm-style camping barn, sleeping 11, and bunk house with 2 rooms. Grass and hard-standing pitches. Log baskets available for camping fires. Open April to October.

→ Greencarts Farm, Humshaugh, NE46 4BW,
01434 681320
55.0400, -2.1819 🚩

37 YHA THE SILL

State-of-the-art youth hostel built of stone, glass and wood to blend in with the surrounding landscape. Next door to The Sill and the popular Twice Brewed pub. Excellent base for exploring the wall without a car as it is one of the stops on the excellent AD122 bus route.

→ Military Road, Once Brewed, Bardon Mill,
Hexham, NE47 7AN, 0345 260 2702
54.9960, -2.3889 🚩

38 HAUGHTONGREEN BOTHY

Stone sanctuary in Wark Forest S of Kielder forest, near Hadrian's Wall and Green Lough Nature Reserve.

→ Just N of Hadrian's Wall and Greenlee Lough. No vehicles in forest. Overnight pay and display at Cawfield Quarry (54.9929, -2.4502), NE49 9PJ. Check for latest updates at Mountain Bothies Association.
55.0357, -2.3336 🚩

GLAMPING

39 LANGLEY DAM GLAMPING

Six unique 'Langley Longboat' cabins situated beside Langley Dam reservoir with superb views across the water and moors beyond. Own private patio with fire pit and rustic seating. Within walking distance of beautiful Allen Banks and Staward Gorge for swimming in the river. A short drive from Hadrian's Wall. Breakfast packs and children's playground.

→ Langley Dam, Langley, Hexham, NE47 5LD, 07711 288350
54.9418, -2.2692

40 PEAT GATE SHEPHERD'S HUT

Charming handmade shepherd's hut tucked away in a wildflower meadow by a babbling brook, with superb views across the valley. Generous welcome pack, thanks to the very friendly owners who live across the way.

→ Peat Gate Shepherd's Hut, High Burnfoot, Haltwhistle, NE49 0JJ, Sykes Cottages
54.9234, -2.5045

RUSTIC HAVENS & B&B

41 CAUSEWAY HOUSE

Charming 18th-century farmhouse and the only house in Northumberland still thatched in heather. Situated on the Stanegate, the old Roman road, near Vindolanda Fort, it is ideally placed for exploring Hadrian's Wall. Landmark Trust property.

→ Henshaw, Hexham, NE47 7HD, Landmark Trust
54.9910, -2.3721

42 THE WAITING ROOM, STAWARD STATION

Cute holiday cabin renovated from the 19th-century Staward station ticket office on the disused railway line between Haydon Bridge and Allendale. Garden and fire pit. Beautiful location. You can look out over Staward Gorge from the top of the bridge at the end of the platform.

→ Staward Station, Langley-on-Tyne, Hexham, NE47 5NR, 07410 627497
54.9317, -2.3025

43 LAVERICK COTTAGE, HEXHAM

Perched on the hillside with sweeping countryside views and a short distance from Hadrian's Wall, this old farm worker's cottage has been stylishly furnished.

→ Stay on the Hill, Fourstones, Hexham, NE47 5DX, 07939 121785
55.0068, -2.1689

44 PEEL COTTAGE

Tiny, single-storey NT cottage, with stunning views, sitting in the shadow of Hadrian's Wall. Sleeps 2.

→ Once Brewed, Hexham, NE47 7AW, National Trust Cottages
55.0008, -2.3879

45 SPRINGWELL COTTAGE

Former 18th-century farm worker's cottage in the lee of Hadrian's Wall. Sleeps 6 so ideal for families exploring the wall. NT.

→ Twice Brewed, Bardon Mill, Hexham, NE47 7AW, National Trust Cottages
54.9975, -2.3882

46 DILSTON MILL B&B

The owners here embraced the 'slow' movement long before it became popular, providing a peaceful stay in a self-service B&B in a converted historic watermill on the banks of the Devil's Water. There is also a cute studio for two and gardens beyond a bend in the river.

→ Dilston Mill, Corbridge, NE45 5QZ, 01434 633493
54.9654, -2.0401

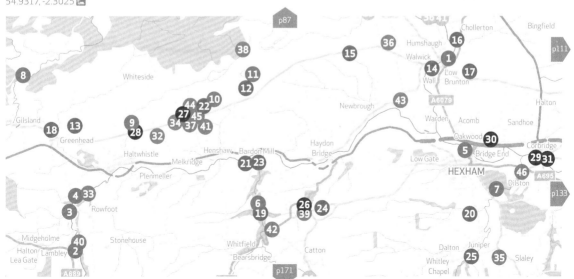

TYNE & WEAR

Our perfect weekend

→ **Follow** the Derwent Valley walk to the Nine Arches Viaduct, a masterpiece of Victorian railway engineering

→ **Enjoy** chargrilled lobster at Riley's Fish Shack overlooking King Edward's Bay

→ **Bathe** in the natural tidal pool at Cullercoats Bay, used by local swimmers in the 19th century

→ **Hop** across rock pools to St Mary's Island and climb the 137 steps of the lighthouse for magnificent views along the coast

→ **Climb** up to the Penshaw Monument, a replica of a Greek temple, for far-reaching views towards Durham Cathedral and the North Pennines

→ **Stroll** through the ancient woodland of Whittle Dene and pick out your favourite fairy-tale cabin

→ **Explore** the ruins of St Paul's Monastery, home of the Venerable Bede, the father of English history

→ **Bring** your binoculars to Marsden Rock, one of the best places for birdwatching in England

Tyne and Wear is a place that exists in people's minds and memories but, in fact, it disappeared as an official region in 1986 after multiple reshuffles of north-east county boundaries. The cities of Newcastle, Gateshead and Sunderland were the industrial and spiritual heart of this area, and evidence of the part they played in its history is everywhere around.

It would be easy to look at a map and see only the cities, but great efforts have been made to preserve the wild and unspoilt areas, as well as the rich industrial heritage here. The Derwent Valley walk is a perfect example; its railway once carried half a million passengers a year as well as coal and steel to feed the region's industry. Now it is a wild, green spine running the length of the Derwent Valley, where reintroduced red kites wheel above the forests surrounding the Nine Arches Viaduct below. A short climb through the woods leads to the wistful ruins of Old Hollinside Manor.

Causey Arch, the oldest surviving single-span railway bridge in the world, crosses a scenic gorge in an ancient woodland recolonised by nature since the railway closed. An early morning visit is rewarded with an uplifting chorus of birdsong.

Ancient woodland covers just one per cent of the total land area in Northumberland. Enchanting Whittle Dean in Ovingham is a rare fragment of these woods, so precious that the local community has formed a group to look after what remains.

For those interested in spiritual history, this area holds a special place as the home of the Venerable Bede, the monk who first recorded the history of the English people. The 7th-century St Paul's Monastery in Jarrow was his home, and with its superb library it became the cradle of European art and culture.

The area's magnificent coastline combines miles of sandy beaches and rugged cliffs. The dramatic limestone stack of Marsden Rock, surrounded by cliffs and caves, is a mecca for birdwatchers, holding the largest seabird colony in the North East, including thousands of pairs of nesting kittiwakes, fulmars and cormorants.

The Marsden Grotto pub is a unique bar built into the caves. Further north is Whitley Bay with its own part-time island. Cullercoats, once an artists' colony, has sea cliffs for coasteering and a tidal pool for bathing. For seafood, Riley's Fish Shack in Tynemouth is one of the best beach cafés in the country, with deckchairs to relax in as you sample a delicious platter of the latest catch. Walkers will enjoy home-baked quiche at Dulcissima in pretty Matfen.

HIDDEN BEACHES

1 TABLE ROCKS TIDAL POOL, CULLERCOATS

A natural tidal pool near Cullercoats beach, expanded for swimmers in the 19th century with steps cut into the rocks. The Whitley and Monkseaton Bathing Club, formed in 1910, made good use of the pool and also had changing facilities. Cullercoats is a great spot for some thrilling coasteering, with lots of overhangs, cracks and cliffs.

→ In Cullercoats find street parking off Windsor Crescent. The pool is at the bottom of a slipway reached from the pavement.
5 mins, 55.0405, -1.4314

2 WHITBURN BEACH

Secluded sand and shingle beach with some rock pools, often overlooked in favour of the busier beaches nearby. Look out for Finn's Labyrinth, a circular maze of medieval design, created by Sean Hesa in memory of his dog.

→ Park at Souter Lower car park and follow coastal path S for about 550m and path to beach.
10 mins, 54.9594, -1.3559

3 MARSDEN BAY

A beautiful bay with dramatic cliffs, sea stacks, caves and Marsden Rock, and home to one of England's most important seabird colonies with thousands of fulmars, kittiwakes, cormorants and gulls. Above the bay is The Leas, a long stretch of grassy land for kite-flying, walks and cycling.

→ From the A1(M) take the A194 then the A1300 to South Shields. At the coast turn R onto the A183 coast road and park in the first car park on L.
5 mins, 54.9785, -1.3783

4 ST MARY'S ISLAND, WHITLEY BAY

A miniature, part-time island reached via a short causeway between tides. The surrounding nature reserve has rock pools, clifftop grassland, a beach and wetland habitats. The lighthouse, completed in 1898 on a hazardous coastline for ships, was in operation until 1984. Climb the 137 steps to the top of the lighthouse for spectacular views of the coast.

→ From Whitley Bay, head N on the A193 for 1½ miles, then turn R into The Links. Follow for ½ mile to parking.
1 min, 55.0691, -1.4526

RIVERS & LAKES

5 WHITTLE DENE RESERVOIR

As well as being an osprey-breeding site, this group of small lakes near Hadrian's Wall attracts a variety of birdlife. There are paths around the lakes with access to the waterside. Bird hides and picnic area.

→ Travelling W along the B6318 Military Road from Heddon-on-the-Wall, cross bridge over reservoir, then turn L at crossroads to lay-by parking on L. Walk back to crossroads to access reserve and hides, taking care as busy road.
5 mins, 55.0067, -1.9000

6 EBCHESTER BOATHOUSE, RIVER DERWENT

The boathouse stands next to a weir which forms a large, wide, calm pool on the River Derwent, giving easy access to the water for kayaks, paddleboards and swimmers.

→ Driving W through Ebchester on the A694, turn R on to the B6309, Chare Bank, and the boathouse is on the L at the bottom of the hill. Limited parking on a lay-by by the boathouse.
2 mins, 54.8932, -1.8438

7 ST PAUL'S MONASTERY

Home of the Venerable Bede, the monastery at Jarrow was one of Europe's most influential centres of learning and culture in the 7th century. The ruins are of the medieval monastery but part of the Anglo-Saxon monastery survives as the chancel of St Paul's Church. The dedication stone of St Paul's Church, set above the chancel arch as you enter the west door, gives the date of ad 687, making it the oldest such stone in the country.

➜ From the Jarrow Interchange, follow the A185 E towards the docks, then take first L, following signs for Bede's World, then R turn to parking by St Paul's church at Church Bank, NE32 3DY.

1 min, 54.9804, -1.4722 ✝ 🐾

8 ST EBBA'S CHURCH

St Ebba's was founded in the 12th century, and the graveyard has remnants of the ramparts of a Roman fort that once stood on this high terrace above the Derwent. The graves include that of Joseph Oley, 'the last of the swordmakers of Shotley Bridge'.

➜ The church entrance is on Shaw Lane, off the A694, Vindomora Rd, through Ebchester. There is street parking directly in front of the church.

1 min, 54.8937, -1.8399 ✝

9 MATFEN STANDING STONE

Created using a single piece of stone, this roadside Bronze Age standing stone is 2m high and 1m wide at the top, with deep grooves caused by water erosion on all sides. If you look closely, you will see cup marks near the base.

➜ Stone is found just under 1 mile S of Matfen, next to Standing Stone Farm. Parking on verge/lay-by.

1 min, 55.0285, -1.9494 🐾

10 PENSHAW MONUMENT

Visible from miles around, this much-loved local landmark is a 21m replica of the Temple of Hephaestus in Athens. It was erected between 1844 and 1845 to commemorate John Lambton, 1st Earl of Durham and Governor General of British North America. An image of the monument even appears on the badge of Sunderland Football Club. Great views of the surrounding landscape.

→ Located on the A183, 1 mile from the A19. Limited parking at the bottom of Penshaw Hill or nearby at Herrington Country Park.
5 mins, 54.8830, -1.4808

ANCIENT WOODLAND

11 WHITTLE DENE ANCIENT WOODLAND

A delightful, rare fragment of ancient woodland cared for by the local community. A wander through the magical glade of Whittle Dene is an absolute joy, with its beautiful trees, pretty stream and relics from a watermill that hint at its industrial past. At the southern end some rustic cabins are hidden among the trees.

→ Follow the A695 W to Ovingham from the Prudhoe direction. Take R at roundabout, crossing Ovingham Bridge to parking in the village. Find footpath behind the church into woods. Whittle Dene lies beyond the initial woodland.
15 mins, 54.9780, -1.8871

RUINS & INDUSTRIAL HERITAGE

12 OLD HOLLINSIDE MANOR

Occupying a commanding position above the country park, this 13th-century manor house was known locally as the Giant's Castle, owing to the stature of the members of the family who lived there.

→ Directions as for Nine Arches Viaduct. The footpath to the manor is a short way to the E of the viaduct.
15 mins, 54.9342, -1.7100

13 DERWENTCOTE STEEL FURNACE

Built around 1730, this is the earliest and most intact steel-making furnace in Britain. It was powered by water from the Derwent and made iron and steel for local industry. Afterwards, visit the ruined 18th-century workers' cottages behind the forge down by the river.

→ From Rowlands Gill follow the A694 for 3 miles to signposted parking on L. Cross road and follow Forge Ln for few yards to furnace.
5 mins, 54.9031, -1.7980

14 CAUSEY ARCH

Built in 1726, Causey Arch is the oldest surviving single-span railway bridge in the world. Measuring 32m long and 24m high, it crosses a picturesque ravine in ancient woodland. Paddling in the burn. Bouldering opportunity at Causey Quarry. Cute café by the car park.

Today's Catch

OD, HAKE, Herring
TUNA, Swordfish
moked Haddock, Lemon
sole
Salmon, TigerPrawns
urbot, Brill
Samphire, Haddock

18

→ Causey Arch Car Park, Marley Hill, NE16
5EJ. Walk through woodland and follow path,
crossing footbridges, to arch.
10 mins, 54.8973, -1.6878

15 NINE ARCHES VIADUCT
The 150m viaduct was built in 1867 because
the Earl of Strathmore refused to allow the
railway to pass through his nearby Gibside
estate. It now carries cyclists and walkers
through the country park. Footpaths take you
down from the viaduct onto riverside meadows
below for a better view of the arches.
→ There are car parks at the Land of Oak and
Iron Heritage Centre and Thornley Woodlands
Centre on the A694 between Winlaton Mill
and Rowlands Gill. From either of these you
can access the Derwent Walk, which runs
through the centre of the park and leads to
the viaduct.
30 mins, 54.9335, -1.7197

LOCAL FOOD

16 RILEY'S FISH SHACK
Pull up a deckchair at this acclaimed seafood
bar and grill operating out of two converted
shipping containers on beautiful King
Edward's Bay. The food is amazing; tuck into

delicious, chargrilled monkfish, mackerel
and lobster and savour the experience at
one of the best seafood restaurants in the
North East.
→ King Edward's Bay, Tynemouth, NE30 4BY,
0191 257 1371
55.0187, -1.4204

17 THE VIEW
Modern glass-fronted beach café with
stunning views across Cullercoats Bay.
Terrace with canopies and heaters and heated
beach huts. Breakfast, lunch and snacks. 9am
– 6pm Mon – Fri, 9am – 5pm weekends.
→ Longsands Beach, Grand Parade,
Tynemouth, NE30 4JA, 0191 253 5459
55.0304, -1.4304

18 LATIMER'S SEAFOOD HATCH
Start the day with a kipper in a bun at this
friendly food hatch serving up local, fresh fish.
Sit at tables overlooking the sea where, if you
are lucky, you may spot dolphins or porpoises.
Seafood picnic boxes to take to the beach and
a well-stocked seafood and deli counter.
→ Shell Hill, Bents Road, Whitburn, SR6 7NT,
0191 529 2200
54.9447, -1.3648

19 THE CAFÉ AT BRADLEY GARDENS
Set in an original 19th-century glasshouse in
the grounds of a secret garden, this lovely café
serves up lunches, soup and homemade cakes.
Suntrap terrace and a cosy log burner for
cooler days. Open 9am – 4.30pm Tues – Sun.
→ Sled Lane, Wylam, NE41 8JH, 01661 852176
54.9660, -1.8044

20 MARSDEN GROTTO PUB
This gastro beach bar, Europe's only cave
pub, has been partly dug into the cliff
face and fronted with a more conventional
building that opens onto the beach with
spectacular views.
→ Coast Road, South Shields, NE34 7BS,
0191 455 6060
54.9770, -1.3776

21 BLACK HORSE, BEAMISH
Popular 17th-century country pub perched
high on a hill overlooking the Beamish Valley,
serving good pub classics using locally
sourced ingredients. Rooms and beautifully
situated Huckleberry Cottage. A short walk
away from the Beamish Museum.
→ Red Row, Beamish, DH9 0RW, 01207 232569
54.8927, -1.6792

22 THE FEATHERS INN

Award-winning friendly country pub with oodles of character and charm.

→ Hedley on the Hill, Stocksfield, NE43 7SW, 01661 843607
54.9272, -1.8780 🍴

23 CHARLOTTE'S BUTCHERY

Bijou butcher's selling high-quality meat, with a girl butcher and friendly team at the helm. Charlotte is one of only a handful of female butchers in the country.

→ 15 Ashburton Road, Gosforth, NE3 4XN, 0191 285 1988
55.0027, -1.6348 🍴

24 BROCKSBUSHES FARM SHOP

Large family-owned farm shop selling a good range of local produce, fruit and vegetables, and prepared meals. Seasonal PYO soft fruits. Tearoom and kids' holiday events.

→ Corbridge, NE43 7UB, 01434 633100
54.9688, -1.9656 🍴

25 DULCISSIMA COFFEE HOUSE AND DELI

Relax with a coffee and cake on the café's garden terrace overlooking the beautiful estate village with its large green babbling stream and pretty stone bridges. Great pit stop for walkers and cyclists pedalling the quiet country lanes.

→ Matfen, NE20 0RL, 01661 886202
55.0408, -1.9542 🍴

26 THE BLACK BULL, MATFEN

Traditional, friendly country pub overlooking the pretty green of one of the most delightful villages in Northumberland.

→ Rose Cottage, Matfen, NE20 0RP, 01661 855395
55.0414, -1.9532 🍴

CAMP, GLAMP & SLEEP

27 PITCH ON THE WALL CAMPSITE

Unfussy, old-style campsite with basic amenities: portaloos and running water. Plenty of space in between pitches and it's in a really great location for walking and exploring Hadrian's Wall.

→ Heddon-on-the-Wall, NE15 0JB, 07733 114364
54.9956, -1.8419 ▲

28 BROCKWELL WOOD CAMPING

Back-to-basics wilderness campsite in 26 acres of Brockwell Wood, although only 7 miles from Newcastle. Map provided to help you pitch your tent. Forage for wood and have fun making your own campfire. You can buy meat at the farm to cook for your supper.

→ Blaydon Burn House, Burn Road, Blaydon-on-Tyne, NE21 6JR, 0191 414 2025
54.9534, -1.7477 ▲ 🔥

29 VALLEY VIEW CAMPING

Hilltop campsite with glorious sunset views overlooking the Tyne Valley.

Spacious, flat pitches with tons of space for kids to play and kites for them to borrow. Portaloo but no on-site shower facilities. The excellent Feathers Inn is a short distance away.

→ East Farm, Hedley on the Hill, Stocksfield, NE43 7SW, 07760 350508
54.9262, -1.8824 ▲

30 WILD CAMPING NORTHUMBERLAND

Unfussy, almost-wild camping site with superb sunset views over the Tyne Valley. Spacious pitches. Portaloo but no showers. Friendly hosts. Good pubs nearby.

→ Hedley West Riding, Hedley on the Hill, NE43 7SL, 07890 220643
54.9260, -1.8850 ▲

31 HIGH HOUSE BARN

High-end glamping on an 80-hectare farm and microbrewery in fully furnished bell tents. On-site restaurant serving up full English breakfasts, Sunday lunch and tea and cake. See how their beers are made on a tour of the brewery, with a tasting session at the end.

→ Matfen, NE20 0RG, 01661 725234
55.0227, -1.9218 🏕

32 DEFENDER CAMPING

Fully kitted-out Land Rover Defender with rooftop tent accommodation, enabling you to explore the rolling countryside and the stunning Northumberland coastline.

Operated by Northumberland 250, the folk behind a fantastic driving adventure route. Collect from various locations.

→ Northumberlanddefenders.com
54.9685, -1.6171 🏕

33 THE BANQUETING HOUSE

Become a lord or lady for the weekend with a stay in this extraordinary 18th-century Gothic folly, which looks down onto an octagonal pool and has splendid views to the Derwent Valley, on the edge of the Gibside Estate.

→ Burnopfield, NE16 6AA, 01628 825925, Landmark Trust
54.9220, -1.7182 🏕

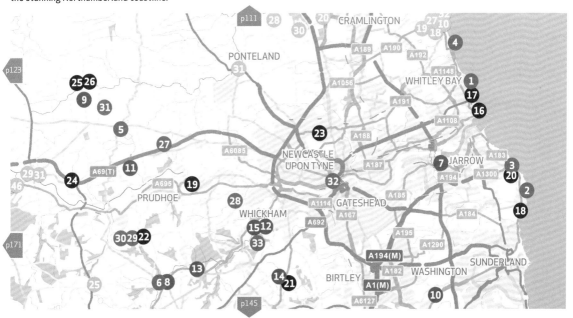

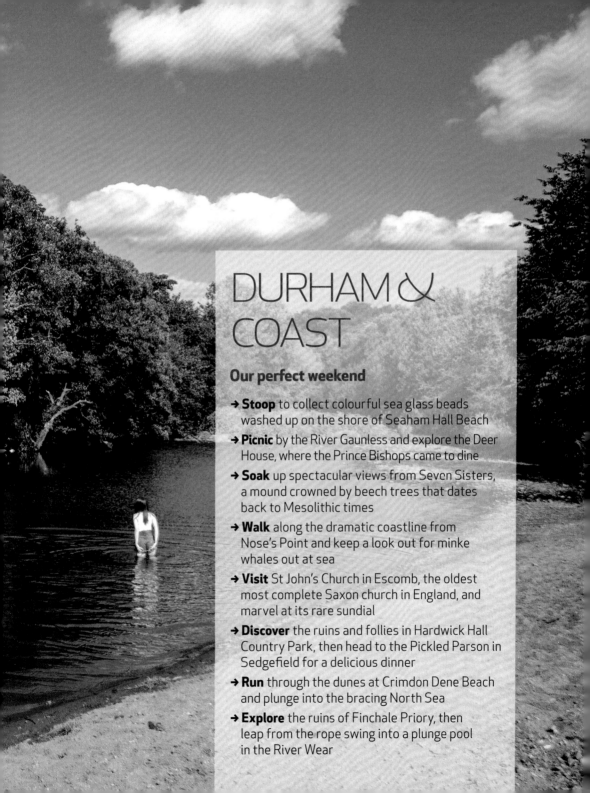

DURHAM & COAST

Our perfect weekend

→ **Stoop** to collect colourful sea glass beads washed up on the shore of Seaham Hall Beach

→ **Picnic** by the River Gaunless and explore the Deer House, where the Prince Bishops came to dine

→ **Soak** up spectacular views from Seven Sisters, a mound crowned by beech trees that dates back to Mesolithic times

→ **Walk** along the dramatic coastline from Nose's Point and keep a look out for minke whales out at sea

→ **Visit** St John's Church in Escomb, the oldest most complete Saxon church in England, and marvel at its rare sundial

→ **Discover** the ruins and follies in Hardwick Hall Country Park, then head to the Pickled Parson in Sedgefield for a delicious dinner

→ **Run** through the dunes at Crimdon Dene Beach and plunge into the bracing North Sea

→ **Explore** the ruins of Finchale Priory, then leap from the rope swing into a plunge pool in the River Wear

Stretching south along the coast, the sandy bays of Northumberland and Sunderland surrender to the wild and rugged Durham Heritage Coast, abundant in caves, stacks, denes and dramatic Magnesium Limestone cliffs clothed in rare wildflowers.

Rock rose, bee orchids, bloody cranesbill and grass of Parnassus thrive in these remarkable coastal meadows, only found in a few other places in England and nowhere by the sea. They support a wide range of insects, including, glow-worms, the Durham argus butterfly, extinct further north, and the rare Cistus Forester moth.

For all its unspoilt beauty, this area is far less visited than it deserves to be. In part, the legacy of coal mining is to blame. Colliery waste was routinely dumped into the sea, turning the sand and water black, dubbing these shores the 'black beaches'.

Following a multi-million-pound regeneration programme to remove tons of colliery waste, the coastline has thankfully recovered. The sea is blue again and beaches like Crimdon Dene boast a sandy shoreline popular with families. The little sandy beach in Seaham Harbour has been popular with wild swimmers for almost 150 years, since the local swimming club was founded.

Evidence of the past remains. The burnt-orange boulders strewn across the cinder-hued sand at Blackhall Sands, which featured in the 1971 cult movie *Get Carter*, resemble a Martian landscape. From dramatic Nose's Point, stroll along Blast Beach to stumble across fossils, pottery and the occasional deep-red pools of iron-rich water.

Cutting into these cliffs is Britain's largest and best-preserved gorge woodland at Castle Eden Dene, created by glacial meltwater eroding channels in the limestone escarpment. Hawthorn Dene, with its ancient oak and ash woodland, leads to a lovely, secluded beach beneath a brick railway viaduct.

With Durham Cathedral being the final resting place of St Cuthbert, this region is spiritually significant. Its importance was later symbolised when William the Conqueror granted the Bishops of Durham the title Prince Bishop, giving them almost regal powers in return for keeping the unruly north under control. One of their best-preserved residences, Auckland Castle, is surrounded by parkland, with the striking Deer House perched above the River Gaunless, a tributary of the River Wear and a delightful spot for a riverside picnic.

The lower reaches of the Wear meander through Durham's towns and villages, with many stretches ideal for wild swimming: the beaches near Finchale Priory ruins, Bishop Auckland and Witton-le-Wear. The wide, smooth stretch at Lumley Bridge in Chester-le-Street is ideal for a leisurely paddleboarding adventure.

HIDDEN BEACHES

1 SEAHAM SLOPE BEACH
Small sheltered sandy beach in Seaham Harbour with a picturesque black and white lighthouse at the end of the pier. People have been swimming here for almost 150 years, since the Seaham Harbour Swimming Club was founded in 1880. Flamingo Café nearby.

→ From Seaham follow the B1287 onto North Road/Terrace, then at roundabout take 1st exit, following road down to harbour and car park (SR7 7EE). Stairs to beach. Gated access is controlled as part of harbour, so check ahead because if the sea is rough the gates will be shut.

2 mins, 54.8389, -1.3257

2 SEAHAM HALL BEACH
One of the best places in Europe for sea-glass hunters as it was home to the UK's largest bottle works, the Londonderry Bottleworks, in the 19th century, which dumped heaps of glass into the North Sea to be tumbled and shaped by the waves over the years. Spot people doing the 'sea glass stoop' to collect these colourful gems.

→ Follow signs from Seaham town to Seaham Hall Beach car park at SR7 7AF, then take steps to the beach. Also North Beach Coffee Bar here.

5 mins, 54.8511, -1.3417

3 BLACKHALL ROCKS BEACH
The burnt-orange boulders strewn across the cinder-hued sand here resemble an alien landscape. The sulphurous smell comes from the sand, eroded from pyrite layers which break down to form yellow crusts of iron sulphate on exposure to air and water. Sea caves and amazing beach art by local artists. The Magnesium Limestone cliffs encourage rare flowers in spring and summer, including butterwort and grass of Parnassus.

→ Travelling S, turn L off the A1086 under a railway bridge to Blackhall Rocks Beach car park. Follow coastal path to steps down to the beach.

10 mins, 54.7469, -1.2717

4 BLAST BEACH
From dramatic Nose's Point, Blast Beach stretches out beneath cliffs cloaked with spectacular wildflowers. Walk to the large magnesium sea stack at its southern end and you will stumble across fossils, pottery, a WW2 pillbox and occasional deep-red pools of iron-rich water, reminders of its industrial past.

→ From Seaham follow the A182 S, signed for Nose's Point on L. Plenty of free parking at SR7 7PS. Steep path to beach.

2 mins, 54.8203, -1.3221

5 HAWTHORN HIVE
A remote sand and shingle bay at the end of a steep-sided coastal dene reached via paths through ancient woodland and hay meadows. Care with kids as beach shelves quickly.

→ Head S from Seaham on the B1432 and turn L signed 'Hawthorn'. Continue to road end and parking by bungalow (54.8066, -1.3418). Go through metal gate signed 'Hawthorn Dene', following track above dene. At end of track turn R through meadows then L, crossing railway track to steps down to beach.

30 mins, 54.8073, -1.3145

6 SHIPPERSEA BAY
Backed by steep cliffs, this beautiful, secluded cove is reached via a precarious dirt path known as the Goat Track.

→ Best reached from Hawthorn Hive beach. Continue S along coastal path. You will come to metal railings with Shippersea Bay below. Access is down a very steep and often slippery path. Ravine at S end is less steep.

5 mins, 54.8004, -1.3123

7 CRIMDON DENE BEACH

Miles of sandy beach backed by dunes and home to one of the most successful breeding colonies of Little Tern in the UK. Super eco café, Dunes, at N end. Quieter towards S end.

→ Head SE on the A1086 Coast Road from Crimdon to L turn signposted 'Crimdon Dene'. Continue to furthest car park at TS27 4DW.
2 mins, 54.7212, -1.2383 🏄

RIVERS & LAKES

8 ESCOMB LAKE

A secluded and sheltered lake, perfect for a summer picnic and swim. The best entry point is in the NE corner. The River Wear, also good for a swim, is right behind the lake. Escomb church is the most complete Saxon church in England (see listing).

→ Park in Escomb village by church and follow footpath between houses at back to lake shore.
5 mins, 54.6689, -1.7106 🏊🎪

9 LYONS LAKE, HETTON COUNTRY PARK

Nice lake for a paddle and picnic, situated in Hetton Lyons Country Park. You will need insurance to launch your own paddleboard/kayak or swim here. On-site café.

→ From Durham follow the A690 E for 4½ miles and turn R onto Robin Lane in West Rainton, signposted 'Hetton-le-Hole'. Continue for 3½ miles to parking off Down's Pit Lane, Hetton-le-Hole, DH5 9AR.
5 mins, 54.8244, -1.4413 🏊🎪🎪

10 ESCOMB VILLAGE, RIVER WEAR

This swim spot with a beach on the River Wear is an alternative to the lake at Escomb.

→ Park in Escomb village by church. Follow Dunelm Chare and footpath behind church to river.
5 mins, 54.6665, -1.7021 🏊🎪

11 COCKEN WOOD, RIVER WEAR

Hidden away in Cocken Wood on the opposite bank to Finchale Priory, this secluded swim spot on a meander of the Wear has deep pools, a rope swing and beach and the evocative ruins as a backdrop. Less well known than the opposite bank.

→ From Great Lumley, head S on Cocken Lane for 1¼ miles, then turn L onto Cocken Road and parking on R at Cocken Road car park (lay-by) at 54.8196, -1.5388. Follow path or steps down to beach area. Can be reached from priory side via footbridge, but site closes at 5pm.
10 mins, 54.8178, -1.5383 🏊🎪🎪🏄🎪🎪

12 FINCHALE PRIORY, RIVER WEAR

Beside the picturesque ruins of Finchale Priory, this meander of the River Wear is perfect for paddling and picnics. You can also cross the footbridge for beaches on the opposite bank (see Cocken Wood entry).

→ From High Carr Rd in Durham, at roundabout take 3rd exit on to Finchale Rd. Continue onto Old Pit Ln, then at roundabout take 2nd exit to stay on Old Pit Ln. At next roundabout take 3rd exit onto Finchale Rd/Ave, then L turn at prison. Road swings to R. Continue to parking at bottom of hill by priory (priory site closes at 5pm).

5 mins, 54.8187, -1.5403 🚻

13 LUMLEY BRIDGE, RIVER WEAR

A pleasant stretch of the river to paddleboard, easily accessed by a wide set of steps and jetty used by the rowing club at the Riverside Sports Complex by Lumley Bridge.

→ From Chester-le-Street follow the B6313 to Park Road N/A167, then turn L at roundabout onto Ropery Lane and Riverside car park.

2 mins, 54.8514, -1.5601 🏊

14 BISHOP AUCKLAND, RIVER WEAR

Popular with families and teenagers, this lovely stretch of the Wear has several beaches and is deep enough for a decent swim. Easy parking at the rugby club. Never feels overcrowded as there is plenty of room for everyone.

→ From Bishop Auckland, head NW on the A689. At roundabout take first exit onto High Bondgate, then continue on to Newton Cap Bank. Turn L onto Bridge Road and parking at rugby club.

5 mins, 54.6647, -1.6906 🏊🚻🥾

15 WITTON-LE-WEAR, RIVER WEAR

A pleasant stretch of the Wear with a beach area, paddling and a pool deep enough to swim in for up to 70m.

→ From Witton-le-Wear follow road, Clemmy Bank, S to Witton Bridge. Park on L just before bridge and follow riverside path downstream to swim spot.

5 mins, 54.6717, -1.7722 🏊🚻ℹ️

RUINS & FOLLIES

16 FINCHALE PRIORY

The ruins of a beautifully situated riverside priory founded on the site of the hermitage of St Godric, a retired sailor. It later became a holiday retreat for the monks from Durham Cathedral. Lots to explore plus lovely

riverside walks and swimming, best from the opposite bank (see entry).

→ From High Carr Rd in Durham, at roundabout take 3rd exit onto Finchale Rd. Continue onto Old Pit Ln, then at roundabout take 2nd exit to stay on Old Pit Ln. At next roundabout take 3rd exit on to Finchale Rd/ Ave, then L turn at prison. Road swings to R. Continue to parking at bottom of hill by priory. Open 10am – 5pm Apr to Oct, 10am – 4pm Oct to Mar. Car park gates are locked half an hour before closing.

2 mins, 54.8182, -1.5403 🚗🚶

17 DEER HOUSE, AUCKLAND CASTLE

Built in 1760 in the deer park of Auckland Castle, the centuries-old home of the Bishops of Durham, this ostentatious Gothic-revival eye-catcher cost £379 to build, a hefty sum at the time. As well as providing shelter and food for the deer, it had a first-floor dining room where guests of the bishops could enjoy the view of the castle and the countryside. This idyllic parkland is well worth exploring, with its medieval fishponds and paths, an ice house, a stone pyramid and a stunning bridge over the River Gaunless, which has some lovely pools for a dip.

→ In Bishop Auckland, park in main car park and head back towards park gates, following footpath past old castle, then turn L at end towards Deer House.

20 mins, 54.6687, -1.6666 🚗🏕🏊🚶

18 BEAUREPAIRE PRIORY

Beaurepaire means 'beautiful retreat', and this 13th-century manor house priory hosted three King Edwards in its time, as well as providing a haven for monks. It is an easily accessible ruin that you can explore and scramble over. The name has been corrupted to 'Bearpark' locally.

→ From Bearpark take Colliery Road right to end. Turn R and R again then L onto a track past woodland. Follow this for 1 mile to small bridge over river and parking in lay-by. Pass through gate on R up hill and ruins are ahead.

5 mins, 54.7891, -1.6236 🚗🏕🔭

19 COXHOE HALL

Once one of the county's finest houses and the birthplace of the poet and feminist Elizabeth Barrett Browning in 1806. After the industrial revolution blighted the landscape, the house was abandoned, becoming a POW camp. It was finally demolished in 1956. Little remains apart

20

from gateposts, a drive and a section of wall. A peaceful location with nice views.

→ From Durham follow the A177, then take the A688 at the Bowburn Interchange. At the roundabout, take the 2nd exit onto the B6291 to Coxhoe. At fork in road park by house on R, just before ruined gate posts. Follow road ahead then take R onto bridleway through woods, turning L at clearing.

15 mins, 54.7170, -1.4880 ▨▢

SACRED & ANCIENT

20 SEVEN SISTERS

Dating back to the Mesolithic period, this impressive mound crowned by beech trees sits atop Copt Hill. It was first excavated in the 19th century, but it was a second dig that revealed the burial mound to be 7,000 years old. Only five of the seven trees remain. Benches and fantastic views.

→ From Houghton-le-Spring follow the B1260 in the direction of Seaham. Entrance to the mound is on R opp the Copt Hill pub. Parking is tricky and access is required by gate to mound so best to park in Houghton-le-Spring and walk. Alternatively, have a pint in the pub and take a stroll up afterwards.

20 mins, 54.8366, -1.4514 ▢▨▨▨

21 ST MARY THE VIRGIN CHURCH

Standing high on the clifftop and overlooking the coast, this Anglo-Saxon church, dating back to the 7th century, is one of the 20 oldest surviving churches in the country. Worth a visit if you are in the area. Open 1 Jun to 8 Sep, Wed and Sat, 2pm – 4pm.

→ Park at Seaham Hall Beach car park, then cross road to follow footpath to Seaham Hall and church beyond.

10 mins, 54.8476, -1.3437 ✝▢

22 ST JOHN'S CHURCH, ESCOMB

The oldest, most complete Saxon church in England with the earliest surviving example of a sundial in its original setting. Built around ad 675, possibly using stone from Binchester Roman Fort, the church is a perfect example of Saxon architecture. It sits in a sub-circular churchyard, suggesting this may be an even older pre-Christian sacred site. The interior is a must-visit for its wealth of Saxon artefacts and interesting display boards. A footpath behind the church leads to the lovely Escomb lake.

→ From West Auckland follow the A68 N for 1½ miles, then turn R onto Greenfields Road for 1½ miles, then L onto Wigdan Walls Road

21

22

to Escomb. Parking is by church. The key hangs outside No 28 Saxon Green, behind the church.
1 min, 54.6660, -1.7080 ✝

WOODLAND & WILDLIFE

23 HARDWICK HALL COUNTRY PARK

A beautiful 18th-century country park with several ornamental features, including temples, grottoes, follies and lakes. To the NW of the park the lovely Gothic ruins of Bono Retiro and Bottle Pond are a haven for wildlife, including herons, damselflies and dragonflies. Hardwick Park has more than 10 species of these tiny winged creatures, which have been around since the time of the dinosaurs.

→ From Sedgefield follow the A177 for 1 mile. Park is signposted. Open dawn until dusk.
5 mins, 54.6544, -1.4681 🐾🏕🍴🅿

24 CASTLE EDEN DENE

Britain's best-preserved gorge woodland on Magnesium Limestone, this is a truly magical place steeped in myths and folklore. It is a survivor of the wildwood that once covered much of the country, having evaded clearance for agriculture due to its almost vertical, wooded valley sides. Oak, beech and ash, as well as ancient yew trees, here since at least Saxon times, grow alongside lush vegetation, including ferns, mosses and liverworts. Miles of footpaths lead you through the dramatic ravine past the Devil's Lapstone, Kissing Frog Stones and Gunner's Pool Bridge.

→ Heading S on the A19, after the Peterlee roundabout, take L turn after Old Shotton onto Passfield Way, then continue on Durham Way to Stanhope Chase and parking at SR8 1NJ.
2 mins, 54.7474, -1.3371 🐾🏕🅿🍴

25 HEDLEYHOPE FELL NATURE RESERVE

This is the Durham Wildlife Trust's largest reserve; the heathland stretches along the side of a valley, offering superb views. The heather, bilberry and cotton grass are home to 20 butterfly species, as well as lizards, slowworms, lapwing, skylark and curlew.

→ The reserve is located just E of Tow Law. It has 3 car parks: one at either end and the main car park next to the B6031 Tow Law to Cornsay Colliery road.
1 min, 54.7673, -1.7692 🏕📷🥾🚶🚶

25

26 MALTON RECLAIMED COLLIERY SITE

It is hard to believe that this site was once a colliery, now that its restoration has made it a home to wildlife. Oak woodland, hedgerows ponds and meadows are home to great crested newts, dragonflies and a host of other flora and fauna.

→ The reserve is 750m E of Lanchester, just off the A691. Park at the Malton picnic area, walk S over the bridge and past Officials Terrace – a reminder of its colliery past. Turn immediately L and walk down the track a short way to the reserve.

10 mins, 54.8122, -1.7236 🎋🦌🡒

27 LOW BARNS NATURE RESERVE

Former farmland and pits and now a delightful nature reserve abutting the River Wear. It is one of the best reserves in the region for wildlife thanks to its wide range of habitat comprising lakes and streams, reed beds, wet pasture and mixed woodland, including an extensive area of Alder. The circular walk passes several excellent bird hides. Coffee shop and small visitor centre on site. Closes at 4pm.

→ From the A68 follow the brown signs through Witton-le-Wear, turning R at the Victoria pub. Cross over the level crossing and

the reserve is ½ mile along the road on the R at DL14 0AG.

2 mins, 54.6780, -1.7518 🧍🦌🎋🍺

INDUSTRIAL HERITAGE

28 STONY HEAP FAN HOUSE

This huge piece of brutalist industrial architecture was once a ventilation fan housing for the now defunct Stony Heap Colliery. Almost hidden in undergrowth and liberally graffitied, it is a reminder of the scale of industry that once existed here.

→ On the A692 from Consett, take the fourth turning on the roundabout E of Leadgate onto Brooms Lane. Follow the road downhill to a crossroads. Turn L and the fan structure is on R next to two large fenced-off settling pools. Parking available next to the fan.

1 min, 54.8580, -1.7722 🏚

FRIENDLY PUBS

29 DUN COW INN

If it is good enough for the President of the US, this pub is definitely worth a visit. Prime Minister Tony Blair took George W Bush for a pint here when he was visiting the UK.

27

28

Traditional with lots of rooms for eating and drinking. Nice menu and good selection of draught ales on offer.

→ 43 Front St, Sedgefield, TS21 3AT, 01740 620894
54.6536, -1.4467 🍴

30 THE PICKLED PARSON

Modern British pub with a menu focused on produce from local artisan suppliers and farmers. The elegant and tastefully decorated building overlooks the green, and village church. Stylish rooms.

→ 1 The Square, Sedgefield, TS21 2AB, 01740 213131
54.6532, -1.4503 🍴🛏

CAFÉS

31 THE LOOKOUT

Contemporary light and airy café in Seaham Harbour Marina with a glass-roofed terrace overlooking the sea. Barista coffee, scones, cakes and panini. Fabulous sea views.

→ The Waterside, Seaham Harbour Marina, SR7 7EE, 0191 581 4087
54.8384, -1.3265 🍴

32 FLAMINGO BAR & CAFÉ

Quirky health-food café bar, with a sea view terrace, offering up tasty, nutritious dishes, lattes and smoothies. Dog friendly – inside and outside; they even have their own menu!

→ Unit 3 The Castleside, Seaham Harbour Marina, SR7 7EE, 07399 067840
54.8386, -1.3283 🍴

33 NORTH BEACH COFFEE BAR

Clifftop café bar above Seaham Hall Beach with an extensive breakfast menu, including full English and toast and oats, as well as sandwiches and cakes.

→ Seaham Hall Car Park, North Rd, Seaham, SR7 7AG, 0191 513 0484
54.8498, -1.3448 🍴

34 FIFTEAS VINTAGE TEAROOM

Atmospheric family-run 1950s-inspired tearoom serving up light lunches, delicious cakes, scones and afternoon teas on vintage china. Outside seating. Dog-friendly seating area.

→ 9 Market Pl, Bishop Auckland, DL14 7NJ, 01388 304886
54.6654, -1.6724 🍴

35 NUMBER FOUR

You are guaranteed a warm welcome at this traditional tearoom on elegant Sedgefield's high street. Varied menu, including lunches, an amazing array of cakes and pastries and baked goods. Very popular place for afternoon teas.

→ 4 High St, Sedgefield, TS21 2AU, 01740 623344
54.6536, -1.4508 🍴

CAMP & GLAMP

36 THE BARN AT EASINGTON

Small campsite on the edge of Hawthorn Dene. Grass pitches with no electric hook-up. BBQs and campfires encouraged. Fire pits available. Pretty walk through the dene to hidden Hawthorn Hive beach.

→ Thorpe Lea East, Easington Colliery, Peterlee, SR8 3UT, 07851 934678
54.8019, -1.3250. ⛺⚡

37 SHARPLEY CAMPING

Family-friendly campsite, perfect for exploring the Durham Dales and heritage coast. You can even spot the sea from various points on the site. Reasonably priced, well-spaced pitches. Plenty of space for kids to play. Four pods with wood-fired hot tubs and bell tents. Campfires allowed.

→ Salters Ln, Seaham, SR7 0NN, 07789 487698
54.8371, -1.4161 ⛺⚡

38 CRIMDON HOUSE FARM CAMPING

Tiny campsite on a busy working farm. Incredible sea views and path leading down to long sandy beach. Friendly, laid-back owners. No electric hook-up.

→ Coast Road, Hartlepool, TS27 3AA, 07974 610139

54.7217, -1.2525 △

39 WEST HALL GLAMPING

Wake up to the sound of birdsong in a luxury glamping lodge with all mod cons, including hot tubs, fire pit and patio, tucked away next to woodland by a trickling stream. Beautiful views and surrounding countryside.

→ Norburn Ln, Witton Gilbert, Burnhope, DH7 6TS, 07879 101497

54.8172, -1.6585 ⌂

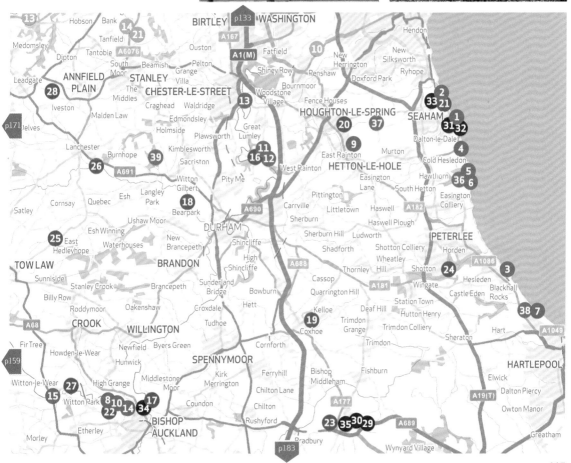

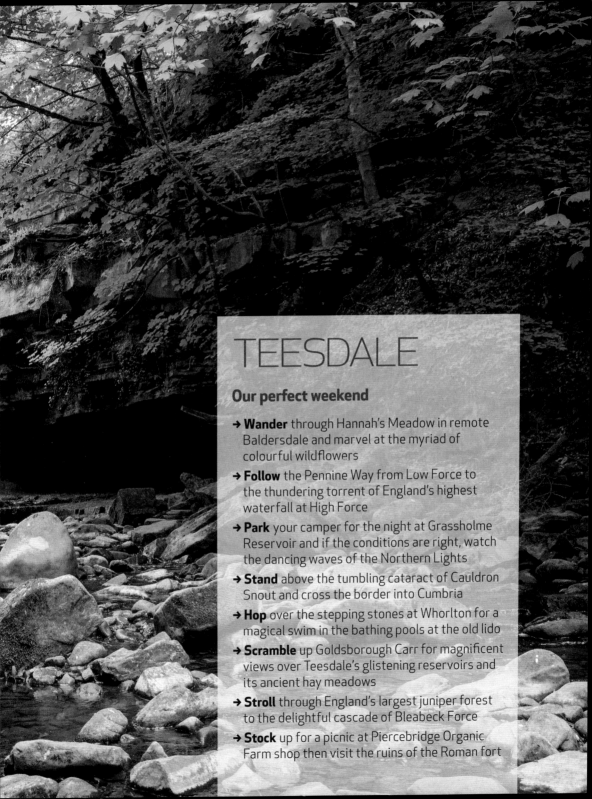

TEESDALE

Our perfect weekend

→ **Wander** through Hannah's Meadow in remote Baldersdale and marvel at the myriad of colourful wildflowers

→ **Follow** the Pennine Way from Low Force to the thundering torrent of England's highest waterfall at High Force

→ **Park** your camper for the night at Grassholme Reservoir and if the conditions are right, watch the dancing waves of the Northern Lights

→ **Stand** above the tumbling cataract of Cauldron Snout and cross the border into Cumbria

→ **Hop** over the stepping stones at Whorlton for a magical swim in the bathing pools at the old lido

→ **Scramble** up Goldsborough Carr for magnificent views over Teesdale's glistening reservoirs and its ancient hay meadows

→ **Stroll** through England's largest juniper forest to the delightful cascade of Bleabeck Force

→ **Stock** up for a picnic at Piercebridge Organic Farm shop then visit the ruins of the Roman fort

Often referred to as 'England's last wilderness', Teesdale is the north's hidden gem. For those already enraptured by its charms, this utterly beautiful area has it all: wild moorland, tumbling rivers, spectacular waterfalls, ancient hay meadows, fascinating geology and picturesque towns and villages.

It has fewer visitors than the Yorkshire Dales, yet its wildflower meadows are just as glorious, bursting into life in early summer, carpeting the landscape with a tapestry of colour. Lying in the North Pennines AONB, Teesdale is home to 40 per cent of the UK's last remaining upland hay meadows.

Strolling beside dry-stone walls along country lanes in midsummer, verges spilling over with bristly purple heads of melancholy thistle, delicate yellow buttercups and wood cranesbill, is an unforgettable pleasure, as is the sight of the wonderful Hannah's Meadow in Baldersdale.

Teesdale splits into Upper Teesdale, upstream of Middleton-in-Teesdale, and Lower Teesdale, towards Barnard Castle. East of this handsome market town are some of the loveliest stretches of the River Tees: beneath the ruins of Egglestone Abbey and along the Teesdale Way towards the Meeting of the Waters, a beauty spot painted by J. M. W. Turner. Further downstream is elegant Gainford, with one of the best pools on the Tees for a wild swim.

From Middleton-in-Teesdale, a succession of charming villages, including well-heeled Romaldkirk with its award-winning pub, and Cotherstone, famous for its cheese, give way to a wilder landscape punctuated with the distinctive white farmhouses of the Raby Estate.

A special feature is the rocky outcrop of Whin Sill, providing the drama for some of the area's most recognised landmarks. Teesdale does waterfalls in superlatives, with the highest falls in England at High Force and the longest at the equally impressive Cauldron Snout.

England's largest juniper forest is a botanist's dream. One of the first trees to colonise Britain after the last ice age, juniper thrives here; its arching braided branches, gin-scented foliage and purple berries line the rugged paths towards High Force. In the Moor House – Upper Teesdale NNR, a white crystalline marble in the rocks, Sugar Limestone, supports rare arctic-alpine plants, including the bright-blue spring gentian.

The shimmering blue oases are Teesdale's reservoirs, built to provide water for the thirsty cities of Teesside and popular with anglers and abundant in wildlife. Miles of paths edge the rocky shorelines, with plenty of secluded spots for picnics. Here you can also enjoy pristine night skies and some of the best views of meteor showers in the country.

WILD SWIMMING

1 GAINFORD, RIVER TEES

Idyllic spot on a bend in the River Tees with a wide pebble beach in one of England's prettiest villages. Paddling and deep pools for swimming. Afterwards, stop by the ancient churchyard of St Mary's then head to the Cross Keys for a gourmet pizza and a game of dominoes. Stan Laurel, of Laurel and Hardy fame, went to school here.

➜ Head W from High Coniscliffe on the A67 for 3½ miles. At Gainford, turn L onto High Green then continue to village green for parking near St Mary's church (54.5461, -1.7382). Follow riverside footpath through woodland behind church for 400m to beach.
10 mins, 54.5427, -1.7428 🏊🚶🅿🚻

2 GAINFORD SPA, RIVER TEES

A favoured swim spot with locals on the wooded banks of the River Tees, best suited to experienced swimmers as the entry is steep. The mineral spring flows from an artesian well and was discovered during an attempt to drill for coal in the 19th century, which instead uncovered the pungent sulphurous waters. Taking the waters was all the rage and the site gained popularity with the hope that Gainford would become a spa resort, but this never happened. The current well is a 2002 replica of the original 19th-century well.

➜ From Gainford head W along the A67 to lay-by parking after ½ mile. Follow the path down to the river to reach the spa.
2 mins, 54.5499, -1.7495 🏊

3 HIGH CONISCLIFFE, RIVER TEES

A pleasant stretch of the Tees between High Coniscliffe and Merrybent, with deep pools, shallow rapids and a large pebble and sand beach. Further beaches downstream.

➜ From Merrybent, head NW on the A67 for 1¼ miles in direction of Barnard Castle. At High Coniscliffe, pass St Edwin's Church on L and take R to street parking in West Close, Ulnaby Lane (54.5339, -1.6551), just before school. Cross road and follow footpath to L of turreted wall to riverside path. Avoid fishermen by continuing downstream. Follow grass path to beach. Continue downstream for other spots at 54.5243, -1.6512 and 54.5260, -1.6373.
10 mins, 54.5246, -1.6535 🏊

4 WHORLTON, RIVER TEES

Beautiful stretch of the Tees that was a public lido. Cascades tumble over stone slabs into various deeper swimming pools. There are several access points, depending on your aptitude, with a shallow entry point at 54.5257, -1.8316.

➜ Whorlton is 4 miles E of Barnard Castle. Park in Whorlton village and follow footpath in front of church over the wall and through graveyard. Follow steps on L down to river, then cross stepping stones to riverside path.
5 mins, 54.5266, -1.8349 🏊🅿🚻

5 EGGLESTONE ABBEY BRIDGE, RIVER TEES

Beneath the high arch of Egglestone Abbey Bridge the River Tees cuts through, forming a deep gorge with rocks and pools ideal for swimming. Daring young locals climb the rocks to plunge into the river beneath.

➜ Approx 1½ miles E of Barnard Castle. Take Newgate out of Barnard Castle, then turn R onto the road signposted for the A66. Follow this over Egglestone Abbey Bridge and turn R at the lights, where there is a lay-by on the R. Return to the bridge to find the Teesdale Way on the E side of the bridge. Descend to the bridge and pools.
5 mins, 54.5296, -1.8993 🏊🔽🚻

6 THE MEETING OF THE WATERS

The tumble of huge rocks where the River Greta and River Tees meet makes for a dramatic scene that inspired artist

J. M. W. Turner. It also forms deep pools, perfect for a cooling swim.

→ Approx 3 miles E of Barnard Castle. Take Newgate out of Barnard Castle, then turn R onto the road signposted for the A66. Follow this over Egglestone Abbey Bridge, turning L. Follow road to parking at various lay-bys at Manyfold Beck (W of Rokeby Hall). Follow Teesdale Way footpath, which skirts a field next to the river, through woods to Mortham Lane and the pools.

15 mins, 54.5251, -1.8707

WATERFALLS & CAVES

7 CAULDRON SNOUT WATERFALL

A tumbling succession of spectacular cataracts stretching more than 180m gives Cauldron Snout the title of the longest waterfall in England. The falls are just as impressive, if not more so, than its neighbour, High Force, just a few miles further S and, because of its remote location, you're likely to be the only one here.

→ From Middleton-in-Teesdale head N to Langdon Beck on the B6277. Turn L onto a small road (signposted 'Cow Green Reservoir') and continue for approx 2 miles to car park. The waterfall is almost 2 miles downstream of the reservoir, along a signed footpath. To approach the falls head on, find the Pennine Way, opposite Langdon Beck YHA, for a beautiful walk along the river (3 miles).

35 mins, 54.6528, -2.2891

8 HIGH FORCE WATERFALL, RIVER TEES

Chances are you will hear High Force before you see it. England's biggest waterfall drops a spectacular 21m over a shelf of ancient Whin Sill rock, a layer of dolerite formed from molten rock nearly 300 million years ago, into a swirling plunge pool below. Take time to marvel at the power of the thundering sheet of white water crashing onto the rocks below.

→ Such is the popularity of High Force that it has now garnered an entrance fee. However, to avoid the traditional tourist trail, park as for Low Force and walk 1½ miles upstream to a viewing platform. You can also stand, with care, above the falls to witness this force of nature from a different perspective.

35 mins, 54.6506, -2.1862

9 LOW FORCE, RIVER TEES

Lesser-known sister of thundering High Force, about 1½ miles downstream. There's

a deep, calm pool on a side channel by a wooded island accessible across dry rocks (54.6495, -2.1654) and a long gorge beneath the Wynch Bridge.

➜ Located 4 miles NW of Middleton-in-Teesdale on the B6277 (15 miles SE of Alston). Park at lay-by by junction, 200m after Bowlees Visitor Centre sign. Follow path down to bridge and falls (300m). Good basic riverside camping 1½ miles downstream on opp bank at Low Way Farm, Holwick (DL12 0NJ, 01833 640506).

5 mins, 54.6464, -2.1505 🏊🚻🚶

10 BLEABECK FORCE

A delightful, secluded waterfall a short stroll N of the more well-trodden path to High Force. This tributary of the Tees cascades over the waterfall before descending to meet its more famous counterparts. Admire the open views towards Cronkley Fell to the W.

➜ As for High Force above. Continue W along Pennine Way for 700m to falls, opposite quarry.

20 mins, 54.6463, -2.1960 🏊🍴🚶⛺

11 SUMMERHILL FORCE AND GIBSON'S CAVE

Several pretty woodland plunge pools with paddling, leading to a waterfall and large cave overhang with plunge pool. Easy access for paddling/swim halfway between the falls and the cave at 54.6525, -2.1439. The cave is named after William Gibson, a lovable 16th-century rogue who hid here while on the run.

➜ From Bowlees Visitor Centre car park (DL12 0XF), keep R to follow riverside path upstream to Summerhill Force then beyond for cave.

5–10 mins, 54.6528, -2.1414 🍴🏊🐕🚻

12 MILL FORCE

A bend in the River Greta, close to the town of Bowes, forms a wide pool and waterfall, perfect for swimming.

➜ From Bowes take the road S to Gilmonby. At the bridge over the river there is a small lay-by on R before bridge, where you will also find the footpath to the falls.

5 mins, 54.5145, -2.0134 🏊🚻🍴⛺🚶🚻

13 HUGGILL FORCE

A moorland stream which suddenly drops 7m, creating a dramatic waterfall in a gorge. Easily accessible and possible to walk up the gorge to the foot of the falls. Most impressive after rain.

➜ From Bowes, take the road S towards Gilmonby, then cross over the River Greta. At the junction take R turn signposted 'Sleightholme' to the road onto the moor to Huggill Sike. After just over a mile, park on verge of the field before Huggill Sike by the signpost for a bridleway. Then walk diagonally W over a small hill to Huggill Sike and the waterfall. To access falls, follow hill down and walk up the gorge.

5 mins, 54.5073, -2.0373 🏊🍴⛺🚻

14 HUDESHOPE BECK RIVER POOL

At a bridge over Hudeshope Beck a low waterfall forms a wide pool, creating a lovely, shaded swim spot in a river gorge.

➜ From the B6277 through Middleton-in-Teesdale, turn R on to Town Head to King's Walk on the L. Walk or drive ⅓ mile to a lay-by on L and the bridge above the pool.

2 mins, 54.6294, -2.0836 🏊⛺🍴🚻

15 HUDESHOPE BECK WATERFALL

Hudeshope Beck cuts a deep gorge, forming a pool and scouring caves into its banks. The pool makes a great swim spot and those daring enough might jump from the waterfall with care. Perfect secluded picnic spot with a bit of adventure.

➜ From the B6277 through Middleton-in-Teesdale, turn R on to Town Head to King's Walk on the L. Parking after ⅓ mile in lay-by

on L. Follow King's Walk to a section of steel barriers on the L to find the waterfall. Scramble down from either side of the bank and walk up gorge to pool.

15 mins, 54.6387, -2.0822 🚶🏊🚐🚶🏕🏞

16 GOD'S BRIDGE RIVER CAVE

A natural rock formation forming a bridge carrying the Pennine Way over the River Greta. The pools beneath the bridge are ideal for a refreshing dip, which you can share with the swallows that dart underneath it to collect mud for their nests. If water levels are high enough, you can swim through the tunnel it forms. A short distance away is a well-preserved lime kiln.

→ Travelling W from Bowes on the A66, after around 2 miles stop in the lay-by just to the E of the Pennine Way (54.5112, -2.0678). Walk down the path to join the Pennine Way, then around God's River Cottage and the bridge is in front of you. See if you can spot the family of weasels that live in the dry-stone wall next to the cottage. If coming from the E, a well-signposted underpass takes the Pennine Way under the A66.

10 mins, 54.5086, -2.0678 🏊🏞🚻

SCENIC RESERVOIRS

17 COW GREEN RESERVOIR

Located in a remote moorland setting equidistant between Cumbria and Co Durham, this vast two-mile-long reservoir occupies the site of a former natural lake. Its high altitude means conditions are too extreme for many waders and wildfowl, as it regularly freezes in winter. A traffic-free road runs alongside the gravel shoreline to the dam wall at the E end, where the water rushes over a long stairway to form Cauldron Snout (see entry).

→ From Middleton-in-Teesdale head up the dale to Langdon Beck on the B6277. Turn L onto a small road, signposted 'Cow Green Reservoir', and continue for approx 2 miles to parking and footpath around reservoir.

40 mins, 54.6680, -2.2907 🚶🚴🏞🚻

18 HURY RESERVOIR

Beautifully situated reservoir in the Baldersdale valley with the River Balder running through. There is a small picnic area by the dam wall and a gravel shoreline. Walk around the reservoir to find plenty more hidden picnic spots.

→ From Barnard Castle follow the B6277 to Cotherstone for 4½ miles, then take L turn

after village, signposted for the reservoirs, for 2 miles. Continue along Briscoe Lane to fork in road. Take L for N shore picnic spot. Parking on L after dam wall.

1 min, 54.5726, -2.0548 ▓▓▓

19 BALDERHEAD RESERVOIR

One of several reservoirs in Upper Teesdale that have been designated Dark Sky Discovery Sites, thanks to low light pollution and wide-reaching views. During a night visit you may see up to 2,000 stars twinkling above – and in the right conditions, the Milky Way and the Northern Lights. Camper vans can park up for the night here (and at nearby Selset Reservoir) for a fee.

→ Located approx 11 miles W of Barnard Castle. From Barnard Castle follow the B6277 to Romaldkirk, then follow the Balderhead road via Hunderthwaite. The reservoir is signposted at the entrance to the car park, approx 4½ miles along this road. No facilities. Water and toilet at Grassholme Reservoir. Overnight parking £10 payable online or at Grassholme Reservoir. Limited mobile coverage.

1 min, 54.5623, -2.1262 ▓▓▓

20 BLACKTON RESERVOIR

The middle reservoir in a chain of reservoirs on the River Balder. Beautiful scenery and walks from here; join the Pennine Way and walk to Hannah's Meadow (see entry), which is stunning in late spring and early summer. There is a nature reserve at the W end of the water, and from the dam wall you can see the dramatic movement of water from the overflow tunnel.

→ As for Hury Reservoir but take L turn at fork and continue to signs to Blackton Reservoir. A loose gravel road with potholes leads to parking at dam wall.

1 min, 54.5625, -2.0821 ▓▓▓▓

21 GRASSHOLME RESERVOIR

At this pretty, rural reservoir surrounded by stunning scenery you might spot ospreys hunting over the water. Teesdale Sailing and Watersports Club offers organised water sports here, including sailing, windsurfing and paddleboarding. Lovely circular walk. Small shop.

→ Take the B6277 from Barnard Castle towards Mickleton. Turn off at the W end of village, signed Grassholme Reservoir. Continue for 1 mile to car park (DL12 0PW) on R.

1 min, 54.5968, -2.0974 ▓▓▓▓▓

ANCIENT WOODS & MEADOWS

22 JUNIPER WOODS

Juniper trees date back 10,000 years and were one of the first tree species to colonise Britain after the last ice age. The juniper forest here in Upper Teesdale is the largest in England. Juniper is dioecious, which means it is either male or female, unlike most tree species. Sadly, several trees are suffering from *Phytophthora austrocedri*, a soil-borne pathogen that kills native juniper trees, noticeable in the bronze-coloured discolouration you will see.

→ Located 4 miles NW of Middleton-in-Teesdale on the B6277 (15 miles SE of Alston). Park at telephone box/lay-by, by junction, 200m after sign for Bowless Visitor Centre. Follow path down to Low Force then follow Pennine Way for 1½ miles towards High Force to reach juniper wood.

30 mins, 54.6498, -2.1815 ▓▓▓▓▓

23 HANNAH'S MEADOW

This remote location was once the home of recluse and unlikely TV celebrity Hannah Hauxwell, who lived for decades at Low Birk Hatt Farm, farming alone and using only traditional methods. In June and early

July these glorious species-rich upland hay meadows are a riot of colour with ragged robin, wood crane's-bill, yellow-rattle, adders-tongue fern and globeflower, plus rare species such as frog orchid and moonwort.

→ From Barnard Castle follow the B6277 to Romaldkirk, then follow the Balderhead road via Hunderthwaite. Roadside parking (54.5661, -2.1044) at the entrance to the reserve, 250m E of entrance to Balderhead reservoir. Follow the Pennine Way footpath S to meadows.

5 mins, 54.5629, -2.1014 🌼🔲🔺🏕🚶

24 THE TATTY FIELD, BALDERSDALE HAY MEADOWS

Stroll alongside old-fashioned flower-rich meadows in Baldersdale and marvel at the sheer diversity of plant life that flourishes here. The Tatty Field is a particularly striking example of these upland hay meadows. In any one upland hay meadow there can be more than 30 different plant species, and up to 100 in any one field. Nearby Hury Reservoir is a popular site for overwintering birds, such as the mallard, tufted duck and goosander. The meadows are cut in mid-July.

→ From Middleton-in-Teesdale follow the B6277 for 5½ miles. Before the village of

Cotherstone, take a sharp R and continue for 2 miles. At Briscoe Farm take L then first R uphill to dead end at Fiddler House for parking (54.5656, -2.0464). Walk back down hill to Briscoe Farm and take L along Briscoe Lane for meadows. Tatty Field is at 54.5704, -2.0502.

20 mins, 54.5704, -2.0502 🌼🏕🚶🔺

25 HAMSTERLEY FOREST

As the largest forest in Co Durham with miles of walking, cycling and horse-riding trails through deciduous and coniferous woodland, Hamsterley is a popular place. However, it is vast enough for you to be able to escape the well-trodden path. Explore the tranquillity of Low Redford Meadows, an SSSI with more than 100 species of plants and birdlife, including woodpeckers, pied flycatchers and nightjars, or enjoy a stroll through oak woodland alongside Bedburn Beck, particularly beautiful in autumn.

→ From Wolsingham follow road towards Hamsterley. Continue on minor road (Shull Bank) for 3½ miles then turn R just before Bedburn into Redford Lane. Take first L to parking at Low Redford.

5 mins, 54.6724, -1.8774 🚶🔲🏕♿

LOST RUINS & CASTLES

26 EGGLESTONE ABBEY

Charming ruins of a small monastery of Premonstratensian White Canons situated in a secluded part of the valley above the River Tees. Much of the 13th-century church remains as well as some living quarters. The monks extracted stone from the quarry below, which was then transported along the river to Barnard Castle and Durham, where it was chiselled into monuments, tombs and religious decorations. Swim spot below (see entry).

→ From Barnard Castle bridge, turn L onto The Sills then L onto Abbey Lane for 1 mile. The abbey is on the R. Alternatively, from Barnard Castle follow the riverside public footpath sign for the Teesdale Way to Abbey Bridge. Secluded swim spot beneath the ruins.

40 mins, 54.5309, -1.9041 ✝🔲🏕

27 BOWES CASTLE

The imposing ruins of Henry II's 12th-century keep stand on the site of a Roman fort, guarding the approach to the strategic Stainmore Pass over the North Pennines. Thanks to some Medieval recycling, the Normans were able to reuse the stone and

28

29

30

earthworks dug by the Romans. However, the English defeat at Bannockburn in 1314 meant the castle was in ruins by 1325. Only the keep remains, but it's a peaceful spot off the Pennine Way near scenic riverside walks.

→ From Barnard Castle bridge turn R on to The Sills/A67. Then L onto the Bowes Road (A67) for 3¾ miles. Then turn L at A66 junction. At the roundabout take the 3rd exit onto The Street. Castle on L with parking in village.

5 mins, 54.5168, -2.0135 🚗🎡

28 RABY CASTLE AND DEER PARK

Built in the 14th century by the powerful Neville family and home to Cecily Neville, mother of two kings of England, Raby Castle is one of the most impressive intact castles in the north of England. It was a parliamentary stronghold during the English Civil War. Beautiful deer park and walks. The kids will love the Plotters' Forest, a playground in the forest.

→ From the S, leave the A1(M) at Junction 58 and travel towards West Auckland, turning L onto the A688 towards Barnard Castle – Raby Castle is on the R-hand side.

5 mins, 54.5907, -1.8023 🏰💷🍽️

SACRED & ANCIENT

29 ST MARY'S OLD CHURCH, BRIGNALL

A small fragment of a 13th-century church with a walled graveyard which was once drawn by J. M. W. Turner. Romantic setting by the River Greta. Downstream is a gorge and pool.

→ From Brignall follow footpath adjacent to new church, which runs through field behind and over stream. After 500m take R path as you near river. Turn L for river gorge, with some pools after 200m. Continue further for the thundering Hell Cauldron rapids.

10 mins, 54.5052, -1.8822 ✝️🎡

30 PIERCEBRIDGE ROMAN FORT

Partially excavated remains of a 4½-hectare Roman fort dating back to around ad 270, possibly built on the site of an earlier military stronghold. It was located beside the major Roman road of Dere Street, linking York to Hadrian's Wall at Corbridge. Excavations have revealed a bathhouse in the SE corner and soldiers' barracks. Interesting site to explore in a pretty village that has an excellent pub, organic farm shop and riverside meanders along the Teesdale Way.

→ Travelling E on the A67 from Gainford, turn R on to the B6275, signposted 'Piercebridge'.

31

Turn R at the Fox Hole pub. Roadside parking by village green (54.5358, -1.6771). The fort lies in a field behind the row of houses just past the church, accessed via a driveway and gate to field.

5 mins, 54.5360, -1.6759 🚲🎡

31 PIERCEBRIDGE ROMAN BRIDGE

Very few Roman bridging sites have visible remains today, but these at Piercebridge are of a large bridge over the River Tees that once carried Dere Street, the main Roman road north from York. The Tees has shifted northwards since the bridge

was built, leaving the remains scattered several metres south of the current river. The bridge dates back to ad 150, earlier than the neighbouring fort (see entry), and the surviving remains suggest the original structure would have been about 123m long. Venture to the far end of the site to get a feel for the construction of the bridge and imagine its strength in its heyday.

→ Follow directions as for Roman fort but continue across bridge. Car parking on L next to the George Hotel (DL2 3SW). Follow riverside footpath at end of car park to a gate leading to the bridge.

10 mins, 54.5346, -1.6700

32 STANWICK CAMP

An excavated section of the ramparts of the huge first-century Iron Age trading and command post of the Brigantes, the most important tribe in pre-Roman northern Britain. There is more than four miles of ditches and ramparts enclosed in an area of 310 hectares. Nearby is the 13th-century Church of St John, which also sits within the earthworks of the camp and houses a Saxon cross shaft.

→ From Eppleby head S past primary school on R. After ½ mile turn L to T-junction then take L. After a few metres find parking on verge on R and small tatty board for camp on L. Go through hedge and follow wooden steps up to the camp and earthworks. For a longer walk, continue to end of earthworks, then turn R along road to church, then take footpath to the L of church back to the camp.

2 mins, 54.5064, -1.7249

33 BARNINGHAM MOOR ROCK ART

Several large rocks, some upright and others in the ground, carved with elaborate and highly decorative cup and ring marks near Wash Beck.

→ From Barningham head W to a mile beyond DL11 7DY (Haythwaite). Follow the track L for 600m up past the lake and along Wash Beck to Osmarill Gill. The best stone is situated 200m to the L.

15 mins, 54.4707, -1.9095

BOULDERING

34 GOLDSBOROUGH CARR

Isolated set of moorland gritstone buttresses with plenty of climbs and scrambling. Superb setting with spectacular views over Hury and Baldersdale Reservoirs and the colourful patchwork of hay

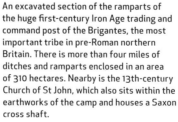

meadows of Upper Teesdale.

→ From Barnard Castle follow the B6277 to Cotherstone for 4½ miles, then take L turn after village towards reservoirs for 2 miles. Continue along Briscoe Lane, keeping L with Hury Reservoir on R. Keep L, with Goldsborough Carr visible on L. Park on grass verge and follow footpath to crag.

5 mins, 54.5552, -2.0734 🌄🧗‍♂️🐾

LOCAL FOOD

35 CROSS LANES ORGANIC FARM SHOP

The living-meadow roof of this family-run farm shop, with its grazing sheep, has become something of a local landmark as you power along the A66. Stock up on gourmet delights or enjoy a meal in the award-winning organic restaurant.

→ Cross Lanes, Barnard Castle, DL12 9RT, 01833 630619

54.5190, -1.9237 🍴

36 MAINSGILL FARM SHOP

One of the largest farm shops in the north, just off the A66, with a two-storey food hall. Butchery with meat sourced from the farm, including grass-fed beef aged for 28 days and artisan produce. Also home to a number

of exotic animals, including llamas, camels and ostriches.

→ East Layton, Richmond, DL11 7PN, 01325 718860

54.4723, -1.7626 🍴

37 BARNARD CASTLE FARMERS MARKET

Barney's Market is one of the north-east's most popular farmers markets offering a good range of regional artisan food as well as organic meat, cheeses, game and jams. First Sat of the month, Apr to Dec, on The Cobbles.

→ Barnard Castle Farmers Market, Horsemarket, Barnard Castle, DL12 8LY

54.5429, -1.9234 🍴

38 PIERCEBRIDGE ORGANIC FARM SHOP AND CAFÉ

A 121-hectare organic farm with an amazing multi-award-winning farm shop. On-site butchers selling homemade burgers, sausages, home-cured bacon and ham, as well as classic cuts of meat from its own cattle, pigs and lambs and vegetables from local farms. Wed to Fri 10am – 3pm, Sat 9am – 1pm.

→ The Green, Piercebridge, DL2 3SE, 01325 374251

54.5365, -1.6780 🍴

39 TEESDALE CHEESEMAKERS

A turophile's dream! The cheese-centric Café Cheesedale, run by husband-and-wife team Allison and Jonathan, serves up all things cheesy. There are also two cosy, off-grid shepherd's huts with B&B and almost a hectare of woodland and stream to explore.

→ Pond Farm, 11 Copley Lane, Butterknowle, DL13 5LW, 07887 676397

54.62218, -1.85613 🍴🛏️

FRIENDLY PUBS

40 THE ANCIENT UNICORN

Traditional coaching inn that has been the resting place for travellers across the Pennines for 400 years. Low-beamed bar with cosy log fire. Home-cooked food.

→ The St, Bowes, Barnard Castle, DL12 9HL, 01833 628576

54.5171, -2.0093 🍴🛏️

41 FOX AND HOUNDS, COTHERSTONE

Welcoming 18th-century country pub, overlooking the green in pretty Cotherstone, serving good traditional food and real ales. Cosy log fire or outside seating, and quoits on the terrace in summer.

→ Cotherstone, Barnard Castle, DL12 9PF,
01833 650241
54.5733, -1.9851 🍴

42 THE FOX HOLE

Located in a historic village, this friendly
roadside pub offers a local, organic,
free-range and artisan seasonal menu.
Contemporary open-plan decor; choose from
wellie bar or dining room and wood burners.
Terrace garden.

→ Piercebridge, Darlington, DL2 3SJ,
01325 374286
54.5381, -1.6766 🍴

43 ROSE AND CROWN

Family-run, creeper-clad 18th-century
coaching inn in a picturesque honey-stoned
Teesdale village. Popular with foodies,
thanks to its locally sourced modern British
menu, which includes Teesdale lamb, sharing
platters with local cheeses and scrummy
puddings. Traditional bar with flagged floors
and low beams. Dog hall of fame. Electric car
charging point.

→ Romaldkirk, Barnard Castle, DL12 9EB,
01833 650213
54.5939, -2.0097 🍴📷

CAMP, GLAMP & SLEEP

44 HIGH SIDE FARM

Campsite in miniature with only four tent
pitches and caravan/campervan pitches
on a dinky site. Also one glamping pod

situated away from the campsite. Glorious
views across Teesdale and Lunedale. Sorry,
adults only.

→ Highside Farm, Bowbank, Middleton-in-
Teesdale, DL12 0NT, 01833 640135
54.6083, -2.0851 📷

45 HILL TOP HUTS

A dozen simply furnished, insulated
glamping pods located on a field behind the
Moorcock Inn. Pick up locally reared meat
from the on-site shop to cook over the BBQ.
Panoramic views of the surrounding fells and
super walks from the door.

→ Hill Top, Eggleston, Barnard Castle, DL12
0AU, 07969 639852
54.6158, -2.0070 📷

46 SCARGILL CASTLE

The perfect romantic getaway created from
the ruins of a 16th-century castle. A stone
spiral staircase leads to the living area with
its polished oak floors. Snuggle in front of
the wood burner set within a Tudor fireplace
or lounge on the bateau lit and take in the
stupendous views across Teesdale.

→ c/o Marian Cottage, Lartington, Barnard
Castle, DL12 9BP, 01833 650573
54.4918, -1.9189 📷

47 THE COACH HOUSE AT SCARGILL LODGE

Converted former coach house (for couples)
whose traditional stone exterior belies the
light, bright and airy decor inside. Pergola-
covered courtyard with seating and BBQ.

Fabulous walks from the door. The Bothy
next door sleeps 4.

→ Scargill, Barnard Castle, DL12 9SY,
01748 850333
54.4976, -1.9478 📷

BUNKBARNS & HOSTELS

48 LANGDON BECK HOTEL

Located in a spectacular part of Upper
Teesdale overlooking the fells, this remote
country inn has two cosy bars and a lounge.
Rooms. Popular with cyclists and walkers on
the Pennine and Teesdale Ways.

→ Forest-in-Teesdale, DL12 0XP,
01833 622267
54.6760, -2.2293 📷

49 LOW WAY FARM, HOLWICK

Family-run working farm with a camping barn
comprising two separate barns either side
of the River Tees and near the Pennine Way.
Also two cottages. Sunday lunch available in
the Farmhouse Kitchen. Book ahead.

→ Holwick, Middleton-in-Teesdale, DL12 0NJ,
01833 640506
54.6377, -2.1332 📷

50 LANGDON BECK YHA

Small rural hostel with superb views across
the fells. Dorm and private rooms. Friendly,
helpful manager.

→ Forest-in-Teesdale, Barnard Castle, DL12
0XN, 03453 719027
54.6692, -2.2183 📷

43

48

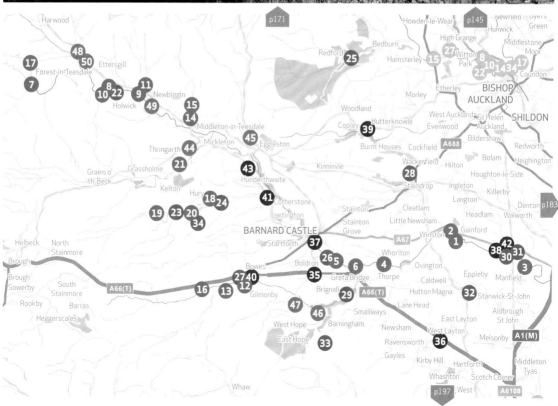

ALLENDALE & WEARDALE

Our perfect weekend

→ **Clamber** behind the spectacular Ashgill Force, then dip in the pools below

→ **Explore** the ruins of Nenthead Mines and see if you can spot rare minerals in the shallow beck

→ **Stroll** beside the waterfalls of Middlehope Burn in Slitt Wood to reach a secret tunnel to swim through

→ **Wander** through the ancient woodland of Baal Hill Wood to find the 400-year-old Bishop Oak

→ **Drive** from St John's Chapel to Langdon Beck for breathtaking moorland views along England's highest road pass

→ **Follow** Isaac's Tea Trail, an old merchant's route, to visit the delightful ruins of Rowantree Bastle

→ **Discover** the fascinating geology of the area, which gave rise to its mining past, at West Rigg Opencut where the Slitt Vein of quartz and fluorite is exposed

→ **Pack** a picnic to enjoy by the River Wear at St John's Chapel, then cool off in a beautiful natural bathing pool

This is a land of high road passes, wide valleys and rugged scenery. It is an exhilarating landscape whose geology gave rise to a huge lead mining industry, and although relics of this fervent industrial activity have profoundly shaped the land, wilderness has also reclaimed it.

This remote region, part of the North Pennines AONB, is famous for its deposits of lead ore and other minerals that formed around 290 million years ago. These valuable deposits were the foundation of the area's economy for many centuries.

As well as lead mining, which peaked in the 18th and 19th centuries, other commercially mined minerals included sphalerite (zinc ore), iron ores, fluorite and barium. Mining had a dramatic effect on the topography, leaving a legacy of settlements, spoil heaps, shafts and chimneys.

The compelling, sparse beauty here inspired the poet W. H. Auden, who was drawn to Rookhope, calling it 'the most wonderfully desolate of all the dales'. The ruins of Rookhope Arch hint at its industrial past.

There are many such relics to discover in this landscape: mine entrances, watercourses and ruined buildings are strewn across the valley at Nenthead, the highest village in England. It was the first purpose-built industrial village in the country, created by the Quaker-run London Lead Company in 1704. Now the Nenthead Mines Conservation Society provides underground trips to Carrs Mine.

The geology is laid bare at the disused ironstone quarry at West Rigg Opencut where the Slitt Vein, mainly quartz and some fluorite, is exposed at the surface, forming a protruding rib of rock along the centre that you can scramble over.

Swimming adventures abound with moorland tarns and abandoned quarries offering up secret swim locations. The River Wear flows through Ireshopeburn, St John's Chapel and Stanhope. Here the waters tumble over sandstone slabs into large bathing pools, creating idyllic swim spots.

Derwent Reservoir is a mecca for water sports, and the beautiful woodland gorges of the Derwent Valley contain some of the finest ancient sessile oak woodlands in the North East. The varied habitat is teeming with wildlife, including red squirrels, buzzards, kingfishers and roe deer.

Tremendous opportunities for walking, cycling, swimming, sailing and even skiing abound – the North Pennines are one of the snowiest parts of the UK – and there are ski resorts at Weardale, Allenheads and Yad Moss. Excellent budget-friendly hostels and traditional pubs contribute to the unpretentious authenticity of this entire area. This and the friendly welcome you receive make it ideal for those seeking the genuine wild experience.

WATERFALLS

1 ASHGILL FORCE

Spectacular 16m curtain waterfall that you can walk behind, by way of a rocky shelf, when not in flood. Off the beaten track in a beautiful deep gorge with pools for paddling and dipping in. Many smaller waterfalls further downstream with deeper pools. A haven for dragonflies.

→ Park in Garrigill (lay-by parking S of village at 54.7649, -2.3955). After a few hundred metres, follow footpath sign on L, then cross Windshaw Bridge to South Tyne Trail. Follow river upstream for 1 mile, passing small waterfalls and plunge pools.

35 mins, 54.7588, -2.3762 🏊🏼⛺🔆👤⛺🏕

2 SEVEN SISTERS WATERFALL

Pretty waterfall with seven falls upstream of the River Nent in Alston, with lots of rocks to hop over and pools to paddle in on the riverside walk to the bridge and falls.

→ From the market cross in Alston pass L of the Turk's Head to The Butts, then continue on to Gossipgate to follow the riverside footpath to the falls.

20 mins, 54.8152, -2.4298 🏊🏼⛺👤☂🏕

3 WHARNLEY BURN WATERFALL

This pretty hidden waterfall in a tranquil wooded ravine is reached by a short walk along the River Wear to its tributary, the Wharnley Burn.

→ Heading N from Castleside on the A68, take R turn at Allensford Park to car park. Cross road to footpath to L of bridge. Follow path upstream to waterfall.

5 mins, 54.8446, -1.8849 🏊🏼⛺👤🔆🏕

4 SLITT WOOD WATERFALLS

A picturesque trail through ash and wych elm woodland beside a series of waterfalls and pools. The step-like rocks are due to repeated layers of limestone, sandstone and shale wearing away at different rates. At the end of the trail are the remains of Slitt and Middlehope Mines, with pools and a tunnel you can swim through.

→ Travelling W along the A689 in Westgate (Front Street) look out for lay-by on R to park. Walk W along Front St, turning R just before the Primitive Methodist Chapel (one of the best preserved of its kind in the north). Follow footpath, keeping R at the houses with the burn on the R. Cross footbridge, pass High Mill and go through a kissing gate into the woods, following burn on L. A lovely 3-mile circular

walk leads to the old ironstone quarry at West Rigg Opencut (see entry).

5 mins, 54.7470, -2.1475 🏊🏼⛺🔆👤⛺🔆🏕

RIVERS & LAKES

5 KIRKHAUGH, RIVER SOUTH TYNE

Peaceful swim spot by new footbridge over the River South Tyne. Mostly paddling with some deeper pools and large pebble beach. Near Kirkhaugh station on Alston narrow-gauge railway. Perfect for picnics.

→ From Alston follow the A689 N for 2 miles towards Slaggyford. After Nook Farm Shop, find lay-by parking on L at 54.8352, -2.4752. Cross road to follow Pennine Way towards Dyke House, then continue over railway bridge at Kirkhaugh station. Cross field to footbridge over river.

20 mins, 54.8407, -2.4721 ☂⛺🔆👤🏕

6 STANHOPE OLD BRIDGE, RIVER WEAR

Deep pools with slabs and ledges beneath an attractive old stone bridge. Stepping stones further downstream towards village.

→ From Stanhope head W on the A689, then take L on to the B6278 to parking in lay-by on L just before bridge. Cross bridge to river

access on opp bank. Stepping stones at 54.7473, -2.0156.

2 mins, 54.7466, -2.0244

7 IRESHOPEBURN, RIVER WEAR

Just downstream of the old stone bridge is a hidden beach with shallows for paddling and deeper pools. Further downstream is a wide pool, popular with local swimmers.

→ Head W out of Ireshopeburn on the A689. Pass the Weardale Museum on the R, then take R over Coronation Bridge to a small parking space on R. Only space for one car so consider parking in the village and walking here. Find the slit in the stone wall of the bridge and follow the Weardale Way downstream to beach.

5 mins, 54.7420, -2.1936

8 ST JOHN'S CHAPEL, RIVER WEAR

Gorgeous natural swimming pool with falls just off the Weardale Way. Grassy bank for picnics and a wide beach.

→ Park in St John's Chapel (on the A689). Then walk to river and follow the Weardale Way riverside path downstream for ½ mile to pool.

15 mins, 54.7374, -2.1665

9 ALLENSFORD PARK, RIVER DERWENT

A very accessible shaded stretch of the Wear with deep pools for swimming, beaches and paddling for younger children. Café at campsite in park.

→ Heading N from Castleside on the A68, take R at Allensford Park to car park and river.

2 mins, 54.8476, -1.8765

10 TUNSTALL RESERVOIR

Flanked by ancient Backstone Bank Wood, this picturesque lake is part of the medieval estate of the Bishops of Durham. Picnic benches, large beach area and woodland walks. Beautiful place to visit early morning or evening.

→ Travelling W along Front Street in Wolsingham, take the R turn signed Tunstall Reservoir onto Leazes Lane for 2¾ miles, passing dam wall and continuing to car park on R.

1 min, 54.7656, -1.9000

11 DERWENT RESERVOIR

The second largest reservoir in the North East set in a stunning landscape with trails around its shoreline. Organised water activities available through the Derwent Sailing Club, including sailing,

paddleboarding, kayaking, windsurfing and open-water swimming sessions.

→ Well signed from the A68. Parking at the Derwent Reservoir visitor centre or Millshield picnic area (fee), or continue through Edmundbyers to Pow Hill Country Park, DH8 9NU, with free parking, café and trails.
3 mins, 54.8611, -1.9820 🏊🚶🚻

12 WESTGATE TARN

A pretty meadow-side tarn with spectacular sunset views across the valley. A remote, peaceful place.

→ Travelling E on the A689, turn L, signposted 'Side Head', after bridge at Daddry Shield. Continue for ¾ mile then make sharp R to Side Head and verge parking at road end (54.7462, -2.1539). Then follow footpath beyond for remote circular tarn hidden behind embankment (54.7479, -2.1504).
5 mins, 54.7480, -2.1507 🚻🏔🏊

13 COWSHILL TARN

A beautiful moorland tarn in a scenic location with splendid views. On access land but fenced. Please use your judgement or ask permission.

→ Follow the A689 to Cowshill and parking in village. Follow road uphill, then take bridleway on R after pub through field. Look for footpath sign onto access land, and tarn is ahead of you.
10 mins, 54.7620, -2.2324 ❓🏊🏔

14 THORNGREEN LIME KILNS

Some of the best-preserved lime kilns in the region, built into the hillside above Middlehope Burn and worked until the 20th century. They were once connected via a tramway to Thorn Green Quarry. An ingenious conservation method using mesh socks has helped repair cracks in the kilns caused by the cycle of heating and cooling.

→ From Allenheads head NE on the B6295 for 1 mile, then turn sharp L and after 300m turn R to see the kilns. Small parking bay above the kilns.
2 mins, 54.8142, -2.2420 🏛

15 ALLENDALE CHIMNEYS

Standing tall on Dryburn Moor, these two prominent chimneys were once part of the Allen Smelt Mill Flue System. The flue tunnel here, one of the best preserved in England, has collapsed in places revealing arched interiors where lead and silver

condensed to then be scraped off and removed. This wild, peaty moorland is criss-crossed by several ancient packhorse routes and has sweeping views of the dales below.

→ Leave Allendale Town on the B6295, then turn L after bridge and continue for ½ mile to junction and L turn for 2 miles to parking in lay-by (54.8714, -2.3018). Go through gate and follow footpath towards the chimneys and past the flue.

25 mins, 54.8777, -2.3014 ▲🚶📷🚻

16 ROOKHOPE ARCH
All that remains of Rookhope Smelt Mill is this ruined arch whose elegance belies its original function as a two-mile horizontal chimney that carried poisonous gases high onto the moor. Poet W. H. Auden had a lifelong love for this remote area, once the centre of the lead mining industry in the North Pennines.

→ From the B6295 in Allenheads, take the first right, signposted 'Rookhope', and continue for 5 miles to car park on L and arch on R. Combine with Groverake Mine (see entry).

1 min, 54.7815, -2.1188 📷

17 SHILDON ENGINE HOUSE
A 19th-century engine house and a reminder of a thriving lead mining community in an area rich in deposits of lead ore, or Galena. It was built in 1805 to house a Cornish pumping engine which prevented the lead mines below from flooding. Following its decommission, it was converted into apartments for mining families, then abandoned a century ago.

→ Blanchland is well-signed from main roads. Park in main village car park (honesty box), then turn L and follow the road uphill. The engine house is on the l

15 mins, 54.8543, -2.0647 📷

18 NENTHEAD MINES
Remote valley strewn with remains from the lead and zinc mining industries, including mine entrances, watercourses, abandoned buildings and the former smelting yard. Volunteers from the Nenthead Mines Conservation Society run regular open days, with underground tours of Carrs Mine and Brewery Shaft for a donation. Small museum displaying fascinating mineral collection.

→ From Nenthead (The Hive) head S to car parking on L and footpath to entrance to area of mines.

5 mins, 54.7843, -2.3370 📷🚶♿🚻🅿

19 GROVERAKE MINE
Nestled in a shallow Weardale valley, the Groverake Mine is an amazing sight when you come across it on the remote road between Allenheads and Rookhope. It was the last large-scale mine in Co Durham and has the only surviving headgear. Wandering around the site gives a vivid impression of the industrial past of these now-deserted rural hills.

→ From Allenheads, head E in the direction of Rookhope. After 2½ miles, lay-by parking is on L next to gate to mine.

2 mins, 54.7920, -2.1639 📷🅿

20 WEST RIGG OPENCUT
At this former ironstone quarry the Slitt Vein, quartz and a little fluorite, is exposed at the surface, forming a protrusion of rock along the middle. Look out for the narrow slits in its centre, where earlier miners attempted to work lead ore, predating the iron ore workings. Wander around the site or follow the footpath north, returning via the pretty waterfalls of Slitt Wood (see entry).

→ Travelling W along the A689 at Westgate (Front Street) take the R turn after the Hare and Hounds pub onto Scutterhill Bank for about ½ mile, then take L at the crossroads for a further

½ mile to parking and opencut mine on R and L.
1 min, 54.7475, -2.1399

21 ALLEN SMELT MILL

Remains of a smelt mill that was once the centre of the lead mining industry in the Allen Valley from the 17th to 19th century. The original flue tunnels and bunkers remain. The site is part of a restoration programme and access is by appointment only, but you get an excellent view from the gate. Nice café, Coffee and Kuriosities, and pretty riverside walks.

➔ Follow the B6295 N out of Allendale Town for 1 mile to the Allen Mill complex on R, just before bridge over river. Alternatively, follow the riverside walk from the town centre.
1 min, 54.9035, -2.2639

22 SIKEHEAD CHIMNEY

This monumental 15m-high chimney looms on the horizon of moorland south of Blanchland. A remnant of the Jeffrey Smelt Mill, it lies at the end of a flue running from the mill to the chimney. Bridleways and footpaths cross this remote area, and it would be easy to spend several hours exploring this graveyard of a once-booming industry.

➔ From Blanchland follow the sign for

Baybridge (½ mile). Cross bridge and follow signs for Stanhope for about 2 miles. Once on the moors, the first footpath running along the disused flue is on the R. There is a bridleway further along. The chimney is next to Sikehead Dams.
25 mins, 54.8127, -2.0713

RUINS & FOLLIES

23 WELL HOUSE BASTLE

The remains of this 17th-century bastle house date back to the days of the Border Reivers, when rival clans living in the 'debatable land' between England and Scotland raided farm steadings. You can see the original entrance and remains of the fireplace and chimney breast of the first-floor living quarters. Interesting display about the Border Reivers in the barn extension. Tie in with Epiacum Roman Fort.

➔ As for Epiacum Roman Fort but at signpost at top of hill, follow footpath L to bastle house.
5 mins, 54.8304, -2.4750

24 ROWANTREE STOB BASTLE

This enchanting ruin is hidden on the slope of a hill behind a line of ash trees. Despite its name, it is not located in a defensive

position and its walls are thin compared with traditional bastle houses. Despite its crumbling walls, and it being gently subsumed by wildlife and vegetation, its classic stone doorway, cut into a semi-circular arch, is remarkably intact. A delightful setting by Knockshield Burn. Perfect spot for a picnic.

➔ Follow the B6295 S from Allenheads for 5 miles to Sinderhope. At crossroads turn L and after ½ mile park on L by stone building with red shutters. Find sign for Isaac's Tea Trail on L and follow markers to bastle.
20 mins, 54.8555, -2.2516

25 ST ANDREW'S CHURCH AND HOPPER MAUSOLEUM

An abandoned church and striking mausoleum on Greymare Hill with spectacular views at each turn. The elaborate Baroque-style mausoleum, which dominates the church, was erected in 1752 by Humphrey Hopper of Black Hedley for his wife, Jane. Inside the church are details of the last marriage and baptisms to take place here in the 1950s.

→ Travelling N on the A68 from Allensford, pass Manor House Inn on L, then continue for 2 miles to R turn at crossroads at Kiln Pit Hill. Park in lay-by on R (54.8921, -1.9352). Walk up road to footpath on R to church.
10 mins, 54.8921, -1.9352 ✝🖼

SACRED & ANCIENT

26 EPIACUM ROMAN FORT

The unusual diamond-shaped layout and well-preserved ramparts of Epiacum Roman Fort, the highest stone-built fort in England, make it unique among forts in the Roman Empire. It was built around ad 120, at the same time as Hadrian's Wall, to control the surrounding lead and silver mines. Looking across the impressive defence ditches with spectacular views of the valley, one ponders what it would have been like to be stationed here. Uncommercial site where kids collect a sword, shield and trail from the 'Centurion's Hut' to travel back 1,000 years as a soldier in the Second Nervian Cohort.

→ From Alston follow the A689 for 2½ miles. Parking on L at Nook Farm Shop and Café.
5 mins, 54.8322, -2.4763 🖼🚴🔭

27 CHURCH OF THE HOLY PARACLETE, KIRKHAUGH

This small church with its unusual needle spire is the only church in the country with this dedication. An ancient stone cross, dating back to the 11th century, stands in the graveyard to the front of the church door. Cut from a single sandstone block, its survival is possibly due to its previous use as a gatepost, evident in the scars of holes on its side.

→ From Alston follow the A686 N. After ½ mile bear L (at Gate House) and continue for 2 miles to parking on verge by entrance to church.
1 min, 54.8386, -2.4695 ✝🚴

28 CHURCH OF ST JOHN THE EVANGELIST

The highest parish church in England, surrounded by a beautiful, wild churchyard. It was built in 1845 by the London Lead Mining Company to serve the mining

community of Nenthead. Look out for the ancient refectory table, used as an altar, and a medieval communion rail. While here don't miss the amazing miniature village in the neighbouring garden, which includes a castle, a mill and Big Ben, created by a former coal miner to raise money for charity.

→ From the Hive Café in the village centre, walk up the hill and follow Hillersdon Terrace to the church on R. Miniature village is a few metres beyond church gate on L.
10 mins, 54.7906, -2.3434 🐾

ANCIENT WOODLAND

29 THE BISHOP OAK, BAAL HILL WOOD
Owned by the Prince Bishops of Durham in the 14th century, this rare relic of ancient woodland has a majestic oak that is at least 400 years old, making it a sapling under James I. Originally an oak and birch woodland, there are also exotic species, including giant redwoods and monkey puzzle trees. Bluebells in springtime and rich in birdlife – willow warblers, redstarts and buzzards.

→ From Wolsingham head N on the B6296 for ¾ mile, then take L (No Through Road) to parking on verge at 54.7425, -1.8801. Walk on road to Baal Hill Farm, then follow hedge

L round farmhouse to gate with sign for woodland. Continue along path to find oak in clearing on L.
30 mins, 54.7488, -1.8956 🚻🚶

30 DERWENT GORGE AND MUGGLESWICK WOODS
A stroll through this dramatic gorge takes you through one of the finest ancient oak woodlands in the North East. Towering sessile oaks (with stalkless acorns) rise up from the steep slopes of the ravine, where you may spot buzzards and red kites gliding above the tree canopy. At the valley bottom there is a footbridge over the river which you can scramble down to.

→ From the A68 travelling N at Allensford Bank, take L, signed 'Wallish Walls', to parking on verge after ¾ mile, before Crooked Oak Farm. Follow footpath through oak woodland of the gorge to footbridge over river.
10 mins, 54.8370, -1.9136 🚻🚶🛇🚌📷

CAFÉS & LOCAL FOOD

31 THE HIVE AT NENTHEAD
Decorous former Wesleyan chapel, once the centre of the mining community, and

now a thriving village café and arts centre. Magnificent period features, including the old organ. Lunches, delicious cakes and scones using locally sourced ingredients.
→ The Hive, Nenthead, CA9 3PF, 01434 408040
54.7880, -2.3418 🍴

32 THE HEMMEL CAFÉ
Small, friendly café and craft shop in a converted milking barn with a lovely outside space and play area for kids. Tasty homemade food, including Sunday lunches (only in winter).
→ Heritage Centre, Allenheads, Hexham NE47 9HJ, 01434 685568
54.8022, -2.2200 🍴

33 THE NOOK FARM SHOP AND CAFÉ
Friendly roadside farm shop and café selling farm-reared beef and lamb, cheese, vegetables and homemade frozen meals. Below Epiacum Roman Fort (see entry). Overnight parking for camper vans.
→ Epiacum Roman Fort, Kirkhaugh, Alston, CA9 3BG, 07415 029398
54.8336, -2.4720 🍴

34 ALSTON WHOLEFOODS

This treasured ethical grocers and deli is a workers' co-operative that has been supplying an enormous range of local, regional, fair-trade and organic food for almost 25 years, including more than 40 different cheeses from its moreish cheese counter.

→ Market Place, Alston, CA9 3QN, 01434 381588
54.8122, -2.4389 🏠🍴

COSY PUBS

35 LORD CREWE ARMS

Enjoy a glass of Lord Crewe Brew in the atmospheric crypt bar, a medieval vaulted chamber beneath a beautiful country hotel in the honey-stone village of Blanchland. Dating back to 1165, this was once the guesthouse of Blanchland Abbey. Top-class seasonal food and accommodation.

→ The Square, Blanchland, Consett, DH8 9SP, 01434 677100
54.8482, -2.0545 🏠🛏🍴

36 ALLENHEADS INN

An 18th-century village inn and former home of the Beaumont family, one of the biggest mine owners in the North Pennines. Decked out with knick-knacks from a bygone age, the café is popular with cyclists on the C2C cycle route. Lock-up for bikes.

→ Allenheads, Nr Hexham, NE47 9HJ, 01434 685200
54.8027, -2.2200 🏠🛏🍴

37 DERWENT ARMS, EDMUNDBYERS

Traditional pub serving classic Northumbrian cuisine and local ales in a pretty village setting with breathtaking scenery on the doorstep, including nearby Derwent Water. Roaring fires and a nice beer garden at the front.

→ Edmundbyers, Consett, DH8 9NL, 01207 255545
54.8454, -1.9754 🍴🛏

38 THE CUMBERLAND INN

Good pub grub, local ales and cider are served at this friendly CAMRA award-winning pub. Great atmosphere, friendly staff, varied menu and reasonable prices. Great views from the large bay window.

→ Alston, CA9 3HX, 01434 381875
54.8118, -2.4417 🍴🛏

39 ALSTON HOUSE

Stylish hotel, pub, restaurant and café that welcomes walkers, cyclists, dogs and muddy

boots. Seasonal menu using local food producers. Bask in the beer garden on sunny days and cosy up by the roaring log fire in winter.

→ Townfoot, Alston, CA9 3RN, 01434 382200
54.8115, -2.4414 🍴🏠🛏

CAMPSITES & HOSTELS

40 HAGGS BANK CAMPSITE

Snooze in your hammock tent strung between the trees in the woodland patch or pitch your tent in the terraced wildflower meadow with breathtaking views across the valley. There is also a bunkhouse, ideal for large groups.

→ Nentsberry, Alston, CA9 3LH, 01434 382486
54.7997, -2.3649 ⛺

41 BOLBEC MANOR CAMPSITE

Friendly, well-maintained campsite with superb views over Muggleswick Moor and Derwent Water. BBQs and campfires allowed. Manor House Inn and small shop next door. Some traffic noise from A68.

→ Carterway Heads, Shotley Bridge, Consett, DH8 9LX, 07512 247102
54.8653, -1.9357 ⛺🔥

42 CARRS FARM

Wind- and solar-powered bunkhouse in a 17th-century converted barn with eco wood-burning stove and rain butt for harvesting water. Fully equipped kitchen. Accommodates 21 people. Three rooms. Spectacular views across Weardale.

→ Wolsingham, DL13 3BQ, 07592 744649
54.7156, -1.9037 🛏

43 BARRINGTON BUNKHOUSE

Bunkhouse sleeping 12 in the heart of the Weardale countryside. There are also a couple of tent pitches. Self-service continental breakfast. Right next to the pub. No mobile reception.

→ Barrington Cottage, Rookhope, DL13 2BG, 01388 517656
54.7804, -2.0975 🛏

44 HIGH KEENLEY FELL B&B

A working farm in beautiful surroundings with reasonably priced accommodation in a converted barn around a courtyard. Local produce and delicious cooked breakfasts.

→ High Keenley Fell Farm, Allendale, Hexham, NE47 9NU, 01434 618344
54.8974, -2.3254 🛏

45 ALSTON YOUTH HOSTEL
You are guaranteed a warm welcome from hosts Linda and Neil at this independent hostel tucked away in a tranquil woodland setting on the edge of Alston. Drying room, cycle store, good showers. Family and private rooms. Look out for red squirrels from the breakfast room window.

→ The Firs, Alston, CA9 3RW, 01434 381509
54.8092, -2.4419

46 NINEBANKS YOUTH HOSTEL
Family-run hostel and chalet in a beautiful location near Hadrian's Wall. Book a room, a wing, the chalet or the entire hostel. Self-catering or meal packs and catered options. Gather round the fire pit in the evenings to watch the sun set over the surrounding hills.

→ Hexham, NE47 8DQ, 01434 345288
54.8567, -2.3573

47 YHA EDMUNDBYERS
Independent village hostel in a former 17th-century inn with wooden beams and cosy rooms. Well placed for exploring Weardale. Private and shared rooms. BAA is the hostel's cosy in-house pub, situated next door. Campsite for tents only in the walled garden with great views.

→ Low House, Edmundbyers, Consett, DH8 9NL, 0345 260 3101
54.8453, -1.9737

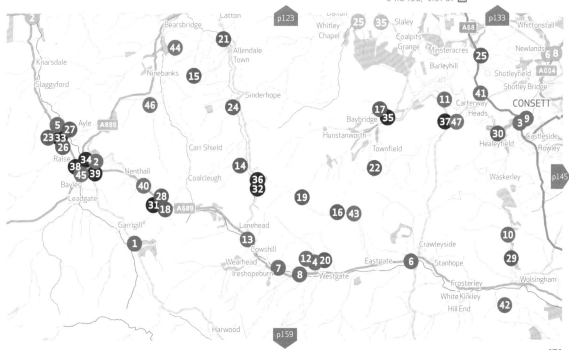

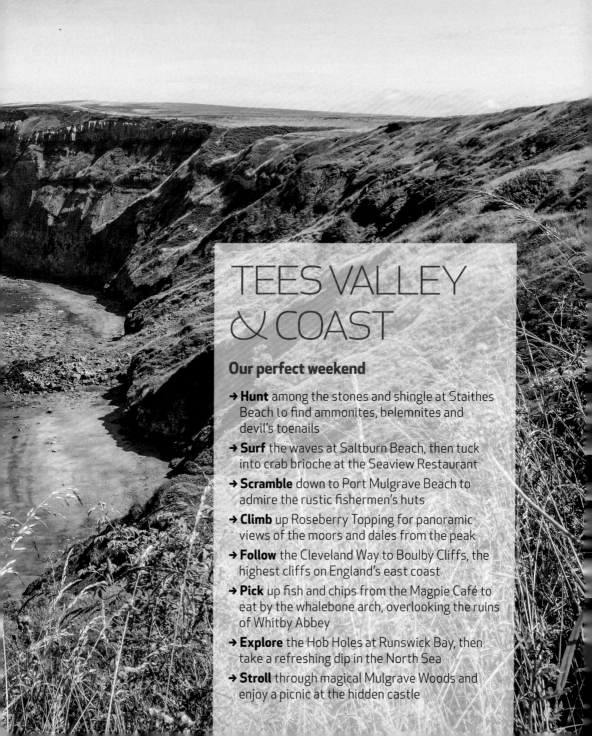

TEES VALLEY & COAST

Our perfect weekend

→ **Hunt** among the stones and shingle at Staithes Beach to find ammonites, belemnites and devil's toenails

→ **Surf** the waves at Saltburn Beach, then tuck into crab brioche at the Seaview Restaurant

→ **Scramble** down to Port Mulgrave Beach to admire the rustic fishermen's huts

→ **Climb** up Roseberry Topping for panoramic views of the moors and dales from the peak

→ **Follow** the Cleveland Way to Boulby Cliffs, the highest cliffs on England's east coast

→ **Pick** up fish and chips from the Magpie Café to eat by the whalebone arch, overlooking the ruins of Whitby Abbey

→ **Explore** the Hob Holes at Runswick Bay, then take a refreshing dip in the North Sea

→ **Stroll** through magical Mulgrave Woods and enjoy a picnic at the hidden castle

Sea life is a defining feature of this area, so it is no surprise to discover that Captain Cook's birthplace is here with a monument to his memory. Here the River Tees meets the sea, and the coastline offers picturesque fishing villages, towering coastal cliffs, romantic ruins, wooded valleys, hidden beaches and superb bays for surfing and swimming.

Tees Bay is an extraordinary industrial landscape centred around North and South Gare, built to offer vessels safe harbour following a great storm in 1861. The southern promontory at South Gare is a curiously compelling rewilded landscape, with its iconic green fisherman's huts nestled in the dunes and brightly coloured boats bobbing in Paddy's Hole. Here grey seals and harbour seals gather, and terns, guillemots and gulls wheel above.

To the south is Saltburn, with its eye-catching pier and the oldest working water-balanced incline tramway in Britain. Once famed for smuggling and fishing, it subsequently became a popular Victorian seaside resort, while today it has a more bohemian feel. Its incredible golden sands are a magnet for surfers, drawn by the clearly defined waves and constant stream of rip-able surf, with several surf schools for those starting out. Also worth exploring are Saltburn's three beautiful, ancient valleys: narrow, steep-sided wooded denes formed by melting glaciers at the end of the last ice age.

Between Saltburn and Whitby are some of the most exhilarating coastal vistas, including secret coves and hidden beaches: Cattersty Sands, Hummersea, Port Mulgrave, Kettleness and Saltwick Bay. Evidence of traditional industries that once thrived here is all around – fishing, ironstone and alum mining – remnants of which can be seen below Boulby Cliffs, the tallest cliffs on the east coast of England. In the 18th century the rugged recesses of this coastline provided shelter for smugglers, one of the less salubrious industries.

It is also called the Dinosaur Coast due to the large number and quality of the dinosaur footprints and fossils discovered here, dating back to the Jurassic Period, 150 to 200 million years ago. Staithes, Runswick Bay and Saltwick Bay are excellent places for fossil hunting, with ammonites, belemnites, devil's toenails (gryphaea) and tiny star-shaped crinoids frequently found.

The coastal scenery of this whole area is truly spectacular, with soaring cliffs clothed in wildflowers and an abundance of marine wildlife: common seals and grey seals, bottlenose dolphins and porpoises, while Minke, pilot and fin whales can be spotted from boat trips.

RIVERS

1 YARM, RIVER TEES

A tranquil stretch of river accessed via a small wooden platform, just behind the Blue Bell pub. A long swim or paddle upstream under the historic 14th-century bridge takes you out of town to picturesque countryside.

→ From Yarm head towards Egglescliffe, crossing the historic bridge. Parking can be tricky so turn L on Aislaby Road to park on verge by school playing fields (54.5125, -1.3624) and walk back along the Teesdale Way, which comes out opp pub. Take footpath at side of pub onto riverside path to jetty.

10 mins, 54.5117, -1.3540

2 NEWSHAM HALL, RIVER TEES

A secluded meander of the River Tees as it winds through lovely open countryside, with an entry point from the grass bank.

→ Take the Aislaby road from Egglescliffe (S of Stockton-on-Tees) and bear L (straight on) for Newsham Hall. Continue to parking bay on L after 1 mile. Follow Teesdale Way sign diagonally across field to river.

5 mins, 54.4909, -1.4102

3 PRESTON PARK, RIVER TEES

Very accessible swim spot from the floating pontoon in Preston Park, with the possibility of an upstream swim to Yarm bridge.

→ Situated 2½ miles N of Yarm on the A135. Well signed. Free parking at Butterfly World, TS18 3RH. Head towards play area and river to find pontoon.

5 mins, 54.5355, -1.3375

4 SCALING DAM RESERVOIR

Surrounded by wild heather moorland, this large freshwater lake offers organised stand-up paddleboarding, kayaking and open-water swimming sessions.

→ Located between Guisborough and Whitby, directly off the A171, TS13 4TR

3 mins, 54.5035, -0.8561

5 NORTH EAST WAKE PARK

Organised open-water swimming from May to Oct (£5). Rules to follow and pre-booking essential. You can also launch your own stand-up paddleboard or kayak.

→ Bishopton lake, Stockton-on-Tees, TS21 1EY, 07492 693 602. Swimmers use main car park. For stand-up paddleboard and kayak launch use the Lakeside car park.

3 mins, 54.5779, -1.4360

HIDDEN BEACHES

6 SOUTH GARE

Created in the 19th century, this man-made spit of land juts into the North Sea to protect ships entering the Tees estuary. The reclaimed land and breakwater are now a haven for birdlife as well as harbour seals and grey seals. Nestled in the dunes are around a hundred photogenic green fishermen's huts. Across Coatham Sands to the south are the prominent cliffs of Hunt Cliff and Hummersea, while across the estuary is the futuristic landscape of North Gare, the inspiration for Ridley Scott's *Bladerunner*. It is a fascinating place where nature is slowly claiming back the land.

→ From Redcar follow the A1042 for 1½ miles, then continue onto South Gare Road for 2 miles, passing private road sign (everyone does), almost as far as the lighthouse. Ample parking at Paddy's Hole.

2 mins, 54.6358, -1.1369

7 MARSKE-BY-THE-SEA

Sandy beach with calm waters for swimming. Easy parking overlooking the sands. The Headland Espresso coffee van is often parked up here.

→ From Marske-by-the-Sea, follow coast road along seafront to second car park (Headland car park, TS10 3RF) on R.
1 min, 54.6051, -1.0351 🏊🚲

8 SALTWICK BAY

Small, sandy cove. In summer watch the sun rise and set here in a day. At LT wander on the scars, frequented by wading birds, crabs and tiny sea creatures. Good fossil hunting and look out for jet too, much favoured by Victorian funeral goers and revived by goths. Shipwreck of trawler, *Admiral Von Tromp*, is snared by rocks around Black Nab to the south.

→ From Whitby follow Abbey Lane into Hawkser Lane. At signs for holiday park turn L. Drive down lane until you reach wooden barriers. Park and walk down steep path to beach.
10 mins, 54.4847, -0.5873 🏕🚻📷⦿🐚

9 STAITHES

This tiny beach next to the harbour is great for fossil hunting. Be careful of rockfall from cliffs at the south end of the beach. Call in at The Cod and Lobster pub afterwards.

→ From Whitby follow the A174 N for 10 miles, then turn R onto Staithes Lane and car park on R. Walk down hill to old village and harbour/beach.
15 mins, 54.5586, -0.7891 📷

10 KETTLENESS

Remote cove to the east of Runswick Bay. Tricky access via an uneven path and a rope for the final descent to reach the sand and rocky beach. Beautiful views along the coast to Runswick Bay. Check tide times.

→ From Whitby follow the A174 N for 2 miles to R turn to Goldsborough just after Lythe. Bear R for Kettleness, past Fox and Hounds (YO21 3RX). Park at bottom near Kettleness Farm (YO21 3RY). Take path in front of two benches (not coast path) down onto headland with landslips and mine workings. After 300m find very steep path L down landslip to beach. Rope provided for final descent.
10 mins, 54.5306, -0.7204 ⛰🚻🔺🚲📷⦿🐚

11 HOB HOLES, RUNSWICK BAY

Four small caves in the cliffs at the far end of Runswick Bay, possibly the result of jet mining. Hobs are creatures from northern folklore. Parents brought their children to the caves to cure them of whooping cough while reciting a rhyme. Great fossil hunting. Look out for ammonites, belemnites, bivalves and coprolites.

→ From Whitby, continue along the A174 and turn R for Runswick and parking. Walk 500m S on sand, beyond sailing club, to caves.
10 mins, 54.5318, -0.7482

12 PORT MULGRAVE

Fascinating small sand and rock beach with an end-of-time atmosphere. This once-thriving port was used for shipping ironstone to Jarrow on Tyneside. Rustic beach shacks built by local fishermen sit under precarious cliffs, and the remains of its industrial past are scattered among the rocks.
→ Turn R off the A174 in Hinderwell, signed 'Port Mulgrave'. Parking at end of road on cliff (TS13 5LH) after 1 mile. Very steep and tricky descent via a rope. Sandiest at N end near old pier.
10 mins, 54.5467, -0.7693

13 HUMMERSEA, SKINNINGROVE

Hidden shingle beach at the foot of Hummersea Cliff. Tricky descent by way of steps and handrail. At LT there is a rocky shore and wave-cut platform. Embedded in the cliffs are the remains of an old alum house, part of the Loftus Alum Works. The cliffs are resplendent with wildflowers in spring and summer.

→ Turn off the A174 in Loftus, opp Golden Lion Hotel/church (TS13 4HG), down narrow North Rd. Continue over 1 mile to and through Hummersea Farm (TS13 4JH) and park by gate on L (200m). Follow track to coast path and steep N1 steps to beach by bench.
20 mins, 54.5702, -0.8770

14 SKINNINGROVE JETTY AND SANDS

Old ironstone mining village with long stretch of sandy beach and an old jetty. Popular with surfers and fishermen.
→ From Staithes follow the A174 for 5 miles, then turn R onto Mill Lane to Skinningrove. Find parking in village. Beach is straight ahead. Cleveland Ironstone Mining Museum is here with haunted tunnel tours (TS13 4AP, 01287 642877).
5 mins, 54.5729, -0.8992

15 CATTERSTY SANDS

Wide, unspoilt golden expanse of sand and little-known bay, sheltered behind high cliffs and grassy dunes. One of the most beautiful beaches along this coastline, cherished by locals.
→ Directions as for Skinningrove Jetty and Sands. Beach is on far side of jetty.
5 mins, 54.5766, -0.9069

HILLTOPS

16 ROSEBERRY TOPPING

With its fin-like peak, Roseberry Topping is an outlier among the Cleveland Hills. A small stubborn slab of hard Middle Jurassic sandstone on its summit is responsible for its character. It is a fun 'mountain' to climb, with panoramic views from the top, 320m up. In spring a spectacular display of bluebells carpets the ancient Newton Wood at its base. Some good rocks for scrambling near the top.

→ Park in the car park just N of Great Ayton (54.5075, -1.1208), then follow Roseberry Lane for the quickest route, around 1¼ miles (1 hour circular). Alternatively, for Newton Wood and the bluebells, start along Roseberry Lane but turn R into the woods, following a gentler path up to the summit.
30 mins, 54.5053, -1.1073 📷🏃

17 CAPTAIN COOK'S MONUMENT

The monument to Captain Cook, who lived in nearby Great Ayton as a boy, was raised in 1827, almost 50 years after his death. It occupies a commanding spot on the hills, close to Roseberry Topping. A short distance from the monument, there are outcrops

and small quarries for bouldering, including Cook's Crags, Cockshaw Hill, Potter's Quarry and Easby View Quarry.

→ From Great Ayton follow Station Road, which passes over the railway and becomes Dikes Lane. Continue until you reach woodland on R and Gribdale Terrace parking with Gribdale Gate on R. The path leads up onto Easby Moor and the monument is visible ahead. If time permits, paths to the R offer fine views of Roseberry Topping.
20 mins, 54.4830, -1.0908 📷🏃

18 BOULBY CLIFFS

At 203m tall, the highest sea cliffs in the east of England offer spectacular views of the coastline in both directions. Beneath them you can see quarries and workings left behind from the alum and ironstone industries. This section of the Cleveland Way, from Staithes to Skinningrove, is exceptional for the spectacular coastal scenery.

→ Travelling N on the A174, continue past the R turn for Staithes to the next R, signposted 'Cowbar'. There is a lay-by here. From here walk towards Cowbar to join the Cleveland Way heading N along the clifftop.
20 mins, 54.5632, -0.8298 📷🏃

RUINS, FOLLIES & HOLY WELLS

19 GISBOROUGH PRIORY

The ruins of this 14th-century Augustinian priory, destroyed during Henry VIII's dissolution of the monasteries, are quite possibly the best example of early Gothic architecture in England. It was one of the first priories to be built in England by the Bruce family, ancestors of Robert the Bruce, King of Scotland. What remains is the shell of the church's east end, which is an extremely photogenic backdrop at sunset. Afterwards, head to Guisborough Woods for a hike up to Highcliff Nab, a spectacular rocky outcrop with magnificent views.

→ In Guisborough, the priory is at the E end of Westgate, the town's main street, beside St Nicholas Church. Park in short-stay car park 500m from site.
10 mins, 54.5488, -1.0412 🏛📷

20 WHITBY ABBEY

Quite possibly the country's most romantic ruin, inspiring Bram Stoker's Dracula, a link the town has embraced with its famous Whitby Goth Weekend. However, its true legacy goes back 1,400 years to a landmark meeting of the Synod of Whitby in 664 which

decided to follow Roman rather than Celtic practices as well as determining the date for Easter by adopting the lunar calculation we use to this day. The ruins are the shell of the 13th-century Benedictine Abbey. Explore the churchyard and St Mary's Church. Spectacular town and coastal views.

→ From Whitby, follow Green Lane for ½ mile then turn L to Abbey Lane to parking on L. Or climb the 199 steps, once a test of Christian faith.

5 mins, 54.4883, -0.6074 🖼️ ✝️ ✉️ 💷

21 MULGRAVE CASTLE

Hidden deep in the woods are the ruins of 13th-century Mulgrave Castle perched on an escarpment surrounded by the old curtain wall. Once a prison for captives of King John, it was garrisoned by Royalist troops in the Civil War and blown up in 1647. Mulgrave Woods are steeped in folklore: PadPad (part goat, panther and human) and an ill-tempered fairy, Jeanie, are said to inhabit the forest. Beautiful picnic spot with magnificent views across the valley and coast.

→ Park in Sandsend then cross stone bridge and bear L to gate into woods. Follow footpath for 1½ miles, keeping straight. Pass tunnel

on R to path on R to castle. Open Wed and weekends. Closed May.

30 mins, 54.4936, -0.7054 ✉️ 💡 🚶 🧗

22 ALBERT MEMORIAL FOLLY

Small classical temple at the top of Valley Gardens, sited as a focal point to look out over the landscape. It was originally built as the portico to Barnard Castle station in 1854 but became redundant when the town gained a second station. It was moved here in 1864, at a cost of £300, as a memorial to Albert, Prince Consort to Queen Victoria, who had died in 1861.

→ There are three entrances, the most straightforward being from the Cat Nab car park (TS12 1HH), following the miniature railway into the valley. Follow path leading R to find memorial on side of the valley.

20 mins, 54.5820, -0.9705 ✉️ 💡

23 BROTTON FAN HOUSE

Ruins of the Guibal fan house of Huntcliff Ironstone Mine, situated next to the railway line on Warsett Hill along a stunning coastal section of the Cleveland Way. You can crawl in through a tunnel at the back of the building to emerge in a large pit in the interior of the building.

→ Park in Skinningrove and follow the Cleveland Way coastal path for 1 mile in the direction of Saltburn.
15 mins, 54.5834, -0.9227

24 ST HILDA'S WELL, HINDERWELL

Situated in the corner of St Hilda's churchyard, this sacred spring has much earlier origins than the original 12th-century church. St Hilda, the most renowned female saint of Anglo-Saxon England, was the Abbess of Whitby Abbey. The fact that the village name derives from the well and the church is also dedicated to her, suggests she had a strong connection with this place. The spring water collects in a covered chamber, filled with coins from hopeful wish makers.
→ Travelling N on the A174 through Hinderwell, turn R just before the end of the village onto the old high street. Parking on L. Well is at the bottom of a S-facing slope in the churchyard.
2 mins, 54.5424, -0.7784

ANCIENT WOODLAND

25 SALTBURN GILL NATURE RESERVE

This wildlife-rich SSSI woodland, with a winding path that runs the length of the valley beneath a dense canopy of oak and ash trees, is a fine example of the type of woodland that would once have covered East Cleveland. The river flowing through it also goes by the name of Saltburn Gill.
→ There is free parking at a lay-by on the Saltburn Road towards Brotton, next to the playing fields at 54.5757, -0.9490. Follow the bridleway across playing field to woodland. Uneven paths. It is also possible to access the woodland from Saltburn, parking at Cat Nab and entering from the S.
5 mins, 54.5797, -0.9607

26 VALLEY GARDENS AND RIFTS WOOD

You could spend a day exploring this secluded valley, cut through by Skelton Beck, partly laid out as Saltburn's pleasure grounds by Quaker Henry Pease in the 19th century, with summerhouses, the Albert Memorial (see entry), footpaths and an Italian Garden. To the S is Rifts Wood: a semi-natural, mixed, ancient woodland with a species-rich understorey, upper and lower paths and a magnificent 11-arch brick viaduct.
→ There are three entrances; the most straightforward being from the Cat Nab car park (TS12 1HH), following the miniature railway into the valley.
5 mins, 54.5791, -0.9720

PUBS & MICROBREWERIES

27 BAY HORSE INN, HURWORTH

Gastropub serving hearty classics alongside modern dishes. Originally a 15th-century coaching inn, the Bay Horse Inn blends traditional charm with a modern style. Lovely walled garden and terrace.
→ 45 The Green, Hurworth, DL2 2AA, 01325 720663
54.4859, -1.5266

28 THE COD AND LOBSTER

Hunker down to watch the waves roll in at this iconic Staithes pub which is practically on the seashore. One large room wraps around the bar. Good, varied menu, including their signature pan-fried cod on a bed of lobster bisque, as well as traditional fish and chips.
→ 61 High St, Staithes, TS13 5BH, 01947 840330
54.5588, -0.7903

29 THE DUKE OF YORK, WHITBY

Situated at the foot of Whitby's famous 199 steps, this historic pub dates back 1,000 years to the Domesday book when monks serviced the monastery above from this spot, landing what they needed from the harbour below. Today it's a friendly traditional pub with a decent range of ales, cider, pub grub and great harbour views.
→ 124 Church St, Whitby, YO22 4DE, 01947 600324
54.4890, -0.6122

30 THE BLACK HORSE, WHITBY

Pint-sized traditional pub in Whitby's old town serving award-winning cask ales, craft beers and a 'Yapas' (Yorkshire Tapas) menu, including Yorkshire cheeses, mixed seafood pot and kipper pâté. On the walls are pencil portraits of regulars over the years.
→ 91 Church St, Whitby, YO22 4BH, 01947 602906
54.4877, -0.6118

31 WHITBY BREWERY

This popular microbrewery, in the shadow of Whitby Abbey, uses only floor-malted barley and whole hops to create Yorkshire ales, including Whitby Whaler, Smuggler's Gold and Abbey Blonde.
→ East Cliff, Whitby, YO22 4JR, 01947 228871
54.4888, -0.6062.

TEAROOMS & DELIS

32 VALLEY GARDENS TEAROOMS

Step into this lovely Victorian-themed tearoom hidden in the Valley Gardens and you'll feel like you're in your great-grandmother's front room. Expect slices of lemon and orange drizzle, fruit cupcakes and Oreo cake, all served with proper Yorkshire tea. Vegan and gluten-free options.

→ Rose Walk, Saltburn-by-the-Sea, TS12 1JS, 01287 626792

54.5786, -0.9709 🍴

33 BRICKYARD BAKERY

Small artisan bakery and tearoom with a huge passion for what they do and an ethos to make good local food available to all. You can even hone your baking skills at their Brickyard Academy.

→ 4–6 Westgate, Guisborough, TS14 6BA, 07507 934651

54.5358, -1.0521 🍴

34 CLARA'S

Cute coffee shop and ice-cream parlour in the Old Spa Pavilion theatre booking office overlooking the beach. Panoramic views from the clifftop terrace and amazing sunsets.

→ Esplanade Cres, Whitby, YO21 3EN, 07748 680212

54.4905, -0.6176 🍴

35 THE WHITBY DELI

Freshly baked goods and locally sourced produce, including cheeses, preserves, craft beers, English wine and Whitby gin. Grazing boxes and gourmet picnic hampers.

→ 22–23 Flowergate, Whitby, YO21 3BA, 01947 229062

54.4863, -0.6166 🍴🍷

36 FLETCHER'S FARM COFFEE SHOP

Snuggle up by the log burner or enjoy magnificent views from the balcony of this converted straw barn. Also well-stocked farm shop and campsite in the old pony paddocks beside a small stream. Ten pitches and five van/motor home pitches. Open year-round.

→ Woodhouse Farm, Little Ayton (Great Ayton), TS9 6HZ, 01642 723846

54.4858, -1.1187 🍴⛺

SEAFOOD & RESTAURANTS

37 MAGPIE CAFÉ

This former merchant's house is a Yorkshire institution offering up fish and chips and

responsibly sourced local fish and seafood dishes. Tuck into Whitby kipper with brown bread and strawberry jam or pacific oysters grown on the seashore at Lindisfarne National Nature Reserve.

→ 14 Pier Rd, Whitby, YO21 3PU, 01947 602058

54.4891, -0.6149 🍴

38 ROYAL FISHERIES, WHITBY

The Magpie Café is justifiably famous, but Royal Fisheries, run by the Fusco family since 1968, also serves great fish and chips and homemade fishcakes.

→ 48 Baxtergate, YO21 1BL, 01947 604738

54.4855, -0.6163 🍴

39 FORTUNE'S KIPPERS

Follow your nose along the cobbled streets to one of Whitby's most famous attractions, to indulge in Fortune's legendary oak-smoked kippers. They have been in business for 140 years and if the fires aren't burning, they might allow you a peek into the smokery.

→ 22 Henrietta St, Whitby, YO22 4DW, 01947 601659

54.4894, -0.6105 🍴

40 THE FISH COTTAGE

Situated just yards from the sandy beach, this pretty café with terrace serves up locally caught seafood. Perfect for a relaxed lunch or a takeaway from the hatch: fish and chips, fish tacos, lobster and chips, and crab fries.

→ Sandsend Rd, Sandsend, Whitby, YO21 3SU, 01947 899342

54.5008, -0.6711 🍴

41 THE FISHERMAN'S SHACK

Laid-back beach bar and grill, serving fresh grilled seafood and cocktails to enjoy on the terrace, which has great sea views.

→ 1–5 Battery Parade, Whitby, YO21 3PY,
01947 229188
54.4905, -0.6145 🍴

42 THE SEAVIEW RESTAURANT, SALTBURN

Light & airy restaurant serving up delicious
seafood platters dictated by the sea & the local
fishermen. Opt for their famous Saltburn crab
brioche or take away fish & chips to eat on the
beach. Large terrace with amazing sea views.
→ Lower Promenade, Saltburn-by-the-Sea,
TS12 1HQ, 01287 236015
54.5859, -0.9699 🍴

43 THE WAITING ROOM

Excellent neighbourhood vegetarian
restaurant and winner of the Vegetarian
Society's best UK restaurant. Serves up
creative dishes, such as Roast Jackfruit &
Peanut Satay Curry. Craft ale and organic
wine. Cocktail bar in the old chemist shop
next door. Organic bakery on the other side.
→ 9 Station Rd, Stockton-on-Tees, TS16 0BU,
01642 780465
54.5297, -1.3478 🍴🍷

44 THE GLASSHOUSE AT WYNYARD HALL

Smart modern restaurant, in one of the
UK's largest garden glasshouses, offering a
seasonal menu in a relaxed setting.
Nice views over the kitchen garden.
Perfect for a special gathering with friends
and family.
→ Wynyard, Stockton-on-Tees, Billingham,
TS22 5SH, 01740 665419
54.6281, -1.3538 🍴🍷

CAMP, GLAMP & SLEEP

45 FOLLY HALL FARM CAMPSITE

Family-friendly campsite with 15 pitches
over two acres with panoramic views over
the Esk Valley. EHU. Cars park away from
the campsite. BBQ on stone slabs but no
campfires. B&B in converted stable.
→ Tranmire, Whitby, YO21 2BW, 07774 415395
54.4914, -0.8049 ⛺

46 THE STIDDY AND LYTHE CARAVAN AND CAMPING

Choose a wild pitch if you want to camp
off-grid at this campsite behind the
traditional Stiddy Pub. Fire pits can be
hired. Outstanding coastal views. On a good
coastal bus route.
→ High St, Lythe, Whitby, YO21 3RT,
07496 987688
54.5063, -0.6928 ⛺

47 RUNSWICK BAY CARAVAN AND CAMPING

You can wander down the lane to lovely
Runswick Bay from this campsite at the
top of the village. Best for campers and
caravans (grass standing), with tent
pitches available during Jul and Aug. Can
feel a little exposed but the border of
trees helps.
→ Hinderwell Ln, Runswick Bay, Saltburn-by-
the-Sea, TS13 5HR, 01947 840997
54.5356, -0.7558 ⛺

48 SERENITY CAMPING

Spacious pitches on a two-hectare
campsite overlooking the North York
Moors. The potting shed is a delightful
wooden cabin with its own secret garden
for enjoying sublime sunsets. Less than
1 mile from Runswick Bay.
→ High Street, Hinderwell, Whitby, TS13 5JH,
01947 841122
54.5396, -0.7780 🛖

49 BABY MOON CAMP

Off-grid boutique glamping in Mongolian
yurts and bell tents heated by stick stoves.
Solar lighting, gas-heated showers and
fire pit. Mingling around the communal

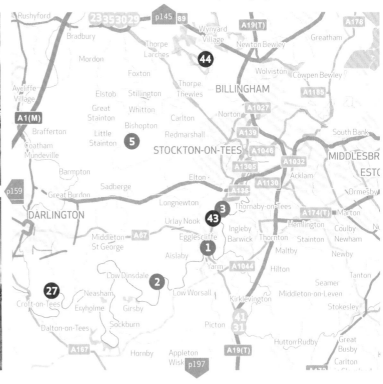

campfire. Guaranteed digital detox as there is no Wi-Fi or electricity (there is a mobile signal).

→ Redcar Rd, Dunsdale, Guisborough, TS14 6RH, 07764 928487
54.5595, -1.0611

50 NORTH SHIRE

Whimsical themed accommodation, including the Shire House and Ground Keeper's Cottage, which are straight out of The Hobbit and Harry Potter. A magical place for families. If you don't meet any hobbits or wizards, there are always the peacocks, hens and goats. Hook-ups for camper vans and tent pitches.

→ Liverton, Saltburn-by-the-Sea, TS13 4TJ, 01287 642228
54.5121, -0.8903

51 WHITBY ABBEY YHA

You may have bagged the best location in town when you bed down for the night in this Grade I listed mansion turned hostel in the grounds of Whitby Abbey at the top of the 199 steps.

→ Abbey House East Cliff, Whitby, YO22 4JT, 01629 592700
54.4873, -0.6083

52 BOULBY GRANGE HOLIDAY COTTAGES

Two one-bedroom cottages and a lovely barn conversion, sleeping 8-10, perched high on the cliffs at Boulby with spectacular sea views and a short walk to the delightful fishing village of Staithes.

→ Boulby Grange, Easington, Saltburn-by-the-Sea, TS13 4UW, 07515 378394
54.5601, -0.8246

53 LA ROSA HOTEL

Quirky boutique hotel with eight exquisitely designed rooms sourced from bric-a-brac finds, creating a retro and fantastical vibe. Author Lewis Carroll often stayed here. Picnic hamper breakfast in bed, overlooking the harbour and abbey ruins.

→ 5 East Terrace, Whitby, YO21 3HB, 01947 606981
54.4894, -0.6164

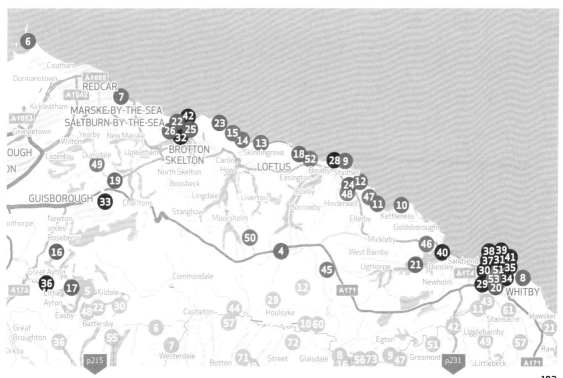

CLEVELAND & HAMBLETON

Our perfect weekend

→ **Stroll** through the ancient woodland of Garbutt Wood to picnic by the glistening shores of Gormire Lake

→ **Summit** the twin towers of the steeple and the needle at the Wainstones, a jumble of magnificent sandstone crags

→ **Hike** up to Barker's Crag, then brave a dip in Brian's Pond, a secret moorland tarn

→ **Pitch** a tent at the Lord Stones Country Park and watch the sun go down behind the ancient lord stones

→ **Enjoy** sublime views towards the Yorkshire Dales from the Hambleton Drove Road, once used by cattle drovers travelling from Scotland to the south of England

→ **Seek** out the Three Witches Oak, a majestic 600-year-old tree where a trio of sorceresses used to meet

→ **Follow** the Cleveland Way to High Paradise Farm Tearoom and tuck into home-baked scones

→ **Visit** the charming 16th-century cruck-framed Spout House, a historic alehouse that was once the heart of Bilsdale's rural community

This is a place to choose your climb; whether it is the lofty heights and crags of the Cleveland Hills or the gently rolling slopes of Hambleton, there is something here to suit all tastes. Rugged heather-clad moorland, inhabited by sheep and grouse on the hilltops, gives way to gentler pastures and tranquil wooded valleys where you will find rivers, becks and waterfalls.

The magnificent Cleveland Hills mark the north-west edge of the North York Moors, gradually sloping to the south and with a precipitous drop to the north and west into the flood plain of Teesside. The Hambleton Hills run north–south, meeting the Cleveland Hills in the north and forming the western edge of the national park, separated from the moors by the valley of the River Rye.

Wild and windswept, these hills are strewn with Bronze Age burial mounds, a hint at how populated these remote uplands were 4,000 years ago. Roulston Scar, marked out by the Victorian White Horse of Kilburn, is one of Britain's largest Iron Age hill forts. One of the biggest influences on this landscape were the monasteries and priories of the religious communities that settled here, from the Cistercians at Rievaulx Abbey in 1132 to the Carthusians at Mount Grace Priory in 1398. The monks were successful farmers, acquiring land and establishing farms further away from the abbeys.

Ancient pannier routes, footpaths and trods cross these fells, and the park's highest peaks are here: Urra Moor, Cringle Moor and Carlton Bank. As such, this area is a magnet for hill walkers, climbers and mountain bikers, who wheel along the disused ironstone railway. Two long-distance trails pass through; Wainwright's Coast to Coast and the Cleveland Way, which follows the ridge line of the hills towards the coast at Saltburn. Rocky outcrops at the Wainstones, Scugdale and Park Nab offer excellent bouldering and scrambling in superb locations.

Trees cover almost a quarter of the North York Moors, and this area retains precious fragments of ancient woodland which hark back to the wildwoods that covered the moors thousands of years ago. The legendary 600-year-old Three Witches Oak and enchanting Birch Wood and Garbutt Wood, leading down to sparkling Gormire, the only natural lake in the North York Moors, are all links to our past.

If you've worked up an appetite enjoying the outdoors, this whole area is brimming with wonderful places to eat, from gastropubs and cosy inns to artisan cafés and farm shops stocked with locally sourced, seasonal produce.

LAKES, RIVERS & WATERFALLS

1 GORMIRE LAKE

Sheltered by ancient Garbutt Wood and abundant with birdlife, this enchanting tarn, which is fed by an underground spring, was formed by glacial erosion more than 20,000 years ago. According to local legend, beneath Gormire's inky depths lurks a hidden city, the devil or – most chillingly – a bottomless pit. However, don't let this put you off. It's a tranquil place at any time of year.

→ Park at Sutton Bank Visitor Centre. Follow footpath signs for Cleveland Way. Continue for 500m. Take L and descend into Garbutt Wood to lakeshore. Path is steep and can be boggy when wet.

30 mins, 54.2427, -1.2283 🏊🌲🚶

2 COD BECK, OSMOTHERLEY

Surrounded by a coniferous woodland beneath remote moorland, this lovely lake has a shoreside footpath and sheltered beaches.

→ Leave the A19, taking the A684 Northallerton, and follow signs to Osmotherley. Turn L in village and continue 1½ miles to 2 car parks. 'No Swim' signs but many do. Use your own judgement.

2 mins, 54.3854, -1.2829 🏊🌲🚶

3 SHEEPWASH, COD BECK

Beauty spot on an ancient drovers' road by the ford at Cod Beck, where shepherds brought their sheep from the surrounding moorland to wash them. Mostly paddling but a delightful spot for a picnic, with some shade from trees.

→ As for Cod Beck Reservoir but continue to parking by ford or park in Cod Beck Reservoir car parks.

1 min, 54.3882, -1.2759 🏕🍴🏊🌲📷

4 CASCADES, DUNCOMBE PARK

Gnarled ash trees line the banks along this lovely section of the River Rye in Duncombe Park. The Cascades are popular with local kids, who come here to cool off in summer. Deeper bathing pools up and downstream. This was the former medieval deer park for Helmsley Castle, and many of the ancient trees date back to this time, including ancient pollarded oaks, ash, lime and beech.

→ Heading into Helmsley on the A170 from Thirsk, turn L onto Buckingham Square, then L again through gates to Duncombe Park parking (YO62 5EB). Follow footpath through woods.

30 mins, 54.2373, -1.0665 🏊🌲🏊

5 OLD MEGGISON FALLS

Located in a peaceful mixed woodland, this tumbling waterfall cascades across a rock face into a wide pool at the bottom. There are viewing points from the path. People have made steps down to the falls themselves, although they are now fenced off.

→ Take the Cleveland Way out of Kildale, where you will find a lay-by on L to park, just before the road passes under a railway bridge. Walk under the bridge and the road runs alongside a meadow for ¼ mile. At the top of the meadow on L there is a gate to the permissive path; the falls are ½ mile along this path.

25 mins, 54.4812, -1.0732 🚶

6 BRIAN'S POND AND BARKER'S CRAGS

This pond and crag are found by climbing onto the moor at the end of this beautiful dead-end valley. The crag offers an assortment of climbing. The pond is a wonderfully isolated moorland tarn, which makes it feels like it's on the top of the world.

→ From Swainby, off the A172, follow the high street and take a L fork onto Scugdale Road. Follow this road to the very end, to a lay-by before a group of houses. A bridleway to the L of the houses leads up through Barker's Crag

and onto the moor. Keep to the bridleway as it runs directly to the pond.

30 mins, 54.3990, -1.1972 🚗🚴🚶🏕️📷🏞️⛰️

7 JOHN BUNTING'S CHAPEL

Simple stone building tucked away from the world on the promontory of a hill. It was created from an earlier farmstead by sculptor John Bunting in 1957, as a memorial to those who lost their lives in WWII. The Battle of Byland took place at this spot in 1322 between the English, under Edward II, and the Scots; hence the name, Scots Corner. It's a tranquil place with spectacular views across the Vale of York and the distant Pennine range.

→ From A170 at Sutton Bank, park where road to Yorkshire Gliding Club bears R at junction with two tracks (54.2329, -1.2013). Follow track as it turns R then continues straight ahead with wood to your L. Path steepens at end of wood. Chapel is in clearing on R.

25 mins, 54.2261, -1.1928 🚶🏕️📷🔲⛰️

8 THE SLIPPER CHAPEL, RIEVAULX ABBEY

The atmospheric ruins of 12th-century Rievaulx Abbey nestle in the beautiful River Rye valley. Nearby is the lesser-visited 13th-century slipper chapel, where pilgrims changed into slippers before entering the abbey, possibly drinking from and cleaning footwear in the obscured spring-fed trough here. The large wooden cross outside the west door is the Earl of Feversham memorial. The 2nd earl's body and cross were brought back to England after he was killed in the 1915 Battle of the Somme.

→ From the car park at Rievaulx Abbey, walk up hill for 300m. Church gate is on R. Spring is up road, opp row of cottages.

2 mins, 54.2591, -1.1156 ✝️🔲

9 MOUNT GRACE PRIORY

The best-preserved Carthusian priory in England, situated at the foot of the Cleveland Hills. There are reconstructed monks' cells and a herb plot to explore and a colony of priory stoats to spot. Nice café.

→ Located 6 miles NE of Northallerton, well signposted off the A19 (DL6 3JG).

2 mins, 54.3796, -1.3118 🍴♿🚻

10 LADY CHAPEL, SHRINE OF OUR LADY OF MOUNT GRACE

Situated on a hill with far-reaching views, this historic chapel was once the site of a hermitage funded by Katharine of Aragon,

and it remains a place of devotion for pilgrims. It was built by Carthusian monks from nearby Mount Grace Priory in the 15th century, although it has earlier origins. The pub in the village is the only pub named after Henry VIII's first wife.

→ From parking in Osmotherley, follow the road N for 500m to a signpost on L for the Cleveland Way and chapel (½ mile). Pass the houses and then take a R, signposted 'Lady Chapel'.

20 mins, 54.3771, -1.3023 🔲🚶✝️

11 ST MARY MAGDALENE CHURCH

Surrounded by a churchyard of rhododendrons in a remote location, this enchanting church was built in 1882 to serve the scattered farming community. The painted wagon roof and stepped bell tower are characteristic of its designer, Temple Moore. Charmed by this lovely building, poet Sir John Betjeman devoted a poem to it, which you can read inside the church. The vicar used to ride up here on a Saturday evening and sleep in a hammock in the south aisle, ready for the Sunday service.

→ From Helmsley, follow the A170 towards Scarborough for 275m, then turn L on Carlton Road and continue 4½ miles to roadside parking. Church is hidden behind a red telephone box on R.

1 min, 54.3052, -1.0641 ⛰️✝️ℹ️

12 ST NICHOLAS CHURCH

The charm of this tiny parish church is the solitude of its wondrous setting in the hamlet of Cockayne, at the head of the remote valley of Bransdale. This has been the site of a church since 1282, probably connected to the Priory of Keldholme. The ancient font lies in the graveyard, where there are several old graves, some dating back to the 1760s. It is a much-loved place where volunteers ensure tea and coffee are available for visitors. Snowdrops, daffodils and bluebells in spring. Bench for a picnic.

→ From Helmsley, follow the A170 for 4½ miles, then turn L at Starfits Lane and continue 10 miles, following an unclassified, gated road to parking and church at 54.3774, -1.0463.

1 min, 54.3773, -1.0463 🔲✝️🏕️🚶

13 WHORLTON OLD CHURCH

All that remains of the abandoned village of Whorlton are the ruins of the church of the Holy Cross and the ruined castle (see

entry). It was built on the site of an earlier Saxon church, but only the chancel and tower remain. The nave was dismantled in the 1970s, leaving just the original Norman arches standing and the chancel intact.

→ From Swainby, cross the bridge onto Church Lane towards Whorlton House. After 500m the ruined castle is on L. Continue 100m to church and parking on R.

1 min, 54.4152, -1.2567 ✝ ▦

14 THE LORD STONES

The main stone here is the Three Lords' Stone, named after three landowning lords whose estate boundaries met here. The stone is marked with prehistoric cup marks and is one of a number defining the perimeter of a Bronze Age burial mound on a hillside covered in ancient holloways. Stupendous sunset views. Great café and deli, plus camping, including pods.

→ Heading N on the A19 from Thirsk, continue for 14 miles. Take R, signposted 'Carlton-in-Cleveland', onto Alum House Lane then Raisdale Road for 2¼ miles to car park at Lord Stones Country Park.

5 mins, 54.4204, -1.1910 ▣▲⛺¶✝✖

ROCKS, TOPS & BOULDERING

15 THE WAINSTONES

The largest jumble of weathered sandstone rocks across the whole of the moors perch in a spectacular location to the northeast of Cold Moor. A popular place for rock climbers, this is also a great spot for a scramble, with excellent bouldering beneath the crag.

→ From the car park at Clay Bank, off the B1257, walk S for several hundred metres, then cross road to join the Cleveland Way onto the moor.

15 mins, 54.4245, -1.1402 ▣▨⛺✖🏊▣▲🚶

16 WHITESTONE CLIFF, SUTTON BANK

Sheared off by glaciers in the last ice age, this towering 140m wall of limestone is one of the most spectacular inland cliffs in the UK. Also known as White Mare Cragg, it has magnificent views down to the glacial Gormire Lake, the tree-covered mound of Hood Hill and the Vale of York and beyond.

→ From the car park at Sutton Bank, walk N along the scarp edge on the Cleveland Way to a bench with spectacular views. Optional circular walk to Gormire Lake and Garbutt Wood for return.

25 mins, 54.2477, -1.2236 ▣⛺🚶

17 KILBURN WHITE HORSE

When a local schoolmaster carved the figure of a white horse into the limestone rock of Roulston Scar in 1857, he had no idea he was chiselling into one of the most important prehistoric monuments in the country. The promontory is the site of a massive Iron Age hill fort, built around 400 bc. This blustery location is also home to the Yorkshire Gliding Club, one of the oldest in the world; pioneering pilot Amy Johnson was a member. Spectacular views across the Vale of York and the Vale of Mowbray.

→ Park in lay-by off the A170 just N of Sutton Bank Visitor Centre (54.2394, -1.2032), then follow Cleveland Way for 1 mile. Or paid parking option at visitor centre. Follow Cleveland Way.

25 mins, 54.2249, -1.2127 🚗♿🅿⛱

18 BLACK HAMBLETON, HAMBLETON DROVE ROAD

The highest point on the Hambleton Drove Road, part of an ancient highway from Scotland to the south of England, and the best-preserved drovers' road in Yorkshire. Along its entire length, flints, axes and pottery dating back to the Stone Age have

been unearthed. A short stroll along this stretch of the path offers up sublime views.

→ From Osmotherley, head S on South End Road towards School Lane. Continue onto Burnthouse Bank for 2 miles to parking at Square Corner. Follow Cleveland Way path up onto drovers' road.

5 mins, 54.3408, -1.2623 🅿⛱⛰

19 HANGING STONE, THIMBLEBY BANK

Hanging precipitously from the cliff edge, this hammer-shaped sandstone rock can be reached by a short leap over a small gap. Judging by the collection of initials etched into the stone, many do. A fun climb to find it and superb views across the Vale of Mowbray and the Pennines.

→ From the A19 travelling N, take a R signposted 'Thimbleby'. After ¾ mile, find parking on R by entrance to Thimbleby Shooting Ground. Don't block gates. Follow track to plantation and take R, then look out for a steep path on L cutting through trees, leading up to stone.

25 mins, 54.3418, -1.3089 🅿⛱🚶🐕

20 BRANSDALE

Known as the 'lost dale', this small, remote valley, managed by the NT, is the North York

Moors' hidden jewel. It is neither on the way to nor from anywhere, but those who venture here will find beautiful moorland scenery, fields criss-crossed by dry-stone walls and breathtaking views.

→ From Helmsley, follow the A170 for 4½ miles, then turn L at Starfits Lane and continue 10 miles, following an unclassified, gated road to parking by St Nicholas Church at 54.3774, -1.0463. The road then makes a U-turn over Bransdale Beck and winds 9 miles back over the moors to Kirbymoorside.
1 min, 54.3669, -1.0528 🖼️📓⛰️👣

21 CRINGLE MOOR

An adventurous climb over Cringle Moor, this loop takes in panoramic views across Middlesbrough, the Cleveland plain, Roseberry Topping and Cook's Monument. Turf-roofed café-restaurant, camping pitches and pods at Country Park (see entry). Superior location.

→ Park at Lord Stones Country Park, Carlton Bank, TS9 7JH. Follow Cleveland Way sign, then turn L, leaving Cleveland Way by stone wall. At crossing of tracks, continue ahead, following path around Cringle Moor. Turn sharp R before stream and climb steep bank on Cleveland Way to top of Cringle Moor. Turn L at viewing seat to retrace steps down hill.
90 mins, 54.4187, -1.1740 🖼️♿🚶🌳

22 PARK NAB

Park Nab looms on a ridge line over the Cleveland Way just before it descends into Kildale. A short scramble across the heather gets you to the jumble of crags. Some smaller boulders for beginners, plus more challenging ascents and overhangs. Scaling them affords you magnificent views across the fields below towards the hills in the distance.

→ Take the Cleveland Way W out of Kildale and after ¼ mile it turns L up onto the moor. Follow the track for ¼ mile to roadside parking. Multiple tracks across the heather lead you up to the crag, which lies to the L-hand side of the track as you ascend.
15 mins, 54.4699, -1.0628 🧗🖼️🪑

ANCIENT TREES & WOODLAND

23 THREE WITCHES ANCIENT OAK

Once one oak, this extraordinary tree has split and grown into three and is thought to be more than 600 years old. Legend has it three witches used it as a meeting place.

191

Accessible via the track running through the woodland in this quiet valley.

→ From Ingleby Greenhow, take main street out NE onto Stone Stoup Hill. After ¼ mile turn R on to road marked as dead end. Follow to the end and park on verge at beginning of bridleway on R towards woodland. Follow trail for 2 miles and at Ingleby Incline take R fork. Tree is on L next to track.

40 mins, 54.4207, -1.0802

24 GARBUTT WOOD

Situated below the dramatic Whitestone Cliff and bordering the shores of Gormire Lake, this enchanting woodland dates back to Tudor times. Twisted oaks and birch dominate, interspersed with rowan, holly and hazel. Giant moss-clad boulders that have tumbled from the rock face are strewn amid the undergrowth. Summertime resonates with birdsong from chiffchaffs and blackcaps, while autumn is a great time for a fungi foray, so keep an eye out for the fairy-tale red caps of the fly agaric.

→ Park at Sutton Bank car park. Follow Cleveland Way signs along the escarpment. Then turn L after 300m, following steep path into Garbutt Wood.

20 mins, 54.2446, -1.2273

25 BIRCH WOOD

Managed by the YWT, this magical and secluded ancient woodland is filled with twisted oak, birch, sycamore, rowan, hazel and ferns. Wildflowers grow out of mossy stumps, fungi thrive in fallen wood and the area is abundant with wildlife, including greater spotted woodpeckers, redstarts, deer and badgers.

→ Follow the B1257 N from Helmsley for 7 miles. Birch Wood is adjacent to road on opp side. Park in large lay-by, immediately past gate to Birch Wood. The Spout House (see entry) is 1 mile further on.

2 mins, 54.3191, -1.1245

26 ASHBERRY NATURE RESERVE

Bordered by steeply wooded slopes, with a crystal-clear stream flowing through a wildflower-rich grassland valley, this hidden ancient woodland reserve is a piece of paradise. Get there early and you might spot red, fallow and roe deer grazing the valley bottom. Rare plant and insect species thrive, and freshwater shrimps and white-clawed crayfish inhabit the stream.

→ From Helmsley, take the B1257 Stokesley Road for 1½ miles, then turn L onto Scawton Rd. Descend through woods and turn L across

28

River Rye. After ¼ mile, turn R, signposted 'Old Byland'. Limited roadside parking on L of road. Gate to reserve further downhill on R.
2 mins, 54.2553, -1.1295 🐾🏕🚗🐾

RUINS, CASTLES & HERITAGE

27 WHORLTON CASTLE

This ruined 14th-century tower house on the site of a Norman motte and bailey fortification was raised by William the Conqueror in the 11th century to keep control of the north. Only the castle and gatehouse remain, as well as the well-preserved vaulted undercroft of the tower house. Views of Roseberry Topping, and Whorl Hill is near enough if you fancy a walk.

→ From Swainby, cross the bridge onto Church Lane towards Whorlton House. After 500m the ruined castle is on L. Parking here or further down by ruined church on R (see entry).
1 min, 54.4157, -1.2600 🏠📷🐾

28 HELMSLEY CASTLE

This impressive 12th-century castle was built for Walter Espec, who founded nearby Rievaulx Abbey and Kirkham Priory.

Unusually for a medieval castle, it had a double bailey system rather than a motte or single keep. It was also a Tudor mansion and a Civil War stronghold in 1644. Afterwards, you can follow an ancient pilgrim's route through fields and woodland along the Cleveland Way to Rievaulx Abbey.

→ Park in the Cleveland Way car park (YO62 5AB). The Cleveland Way is signposted to L of car park, following a 3-mile route to Rievaulx Abbey (1 hr).
2 mins, 54.2447, -1.0642 🔲⚙🐾

29 THE SPOUT HOUSE

An exceptionally well-preserved 16th-century thatched cruck-framed house, once the village inn, which closed in 1914 when the new Sun Inn was built next door. Wander through the rooms, still furnished, and reflect on the importance of this historic alehouse to the people of Bilsdale 400 years ago. Open Easter to 31 Oct, 11am – 4pm.

→ Bilsdale, TS9 7LQ, 8 miles N of Helmsley on the B1257.
1 min, 54.3343, -1.1166

30 WARREN MOOR MINE

Situated in Leven Vale, Warren Moor Mine has the only fully intact Victorian ironstone

27

29

193

mine chimney in existence. The chimney has withstood the test of time and remains very well preserved. The site has the remnants of associated buildings, including the shafts sunk in what turned out to be an unsuccessful quest for ironstone.

→ The mine lies about 1½ miles SE of Kildale in Leven Vale. Turn R down Greengate Lane to the E of Kildale and follow the road into the woodland. Towards the top of the lane there is parking on the verges. The road becomes a track that runs along the R-hand side of a house at the top of the vale, and you will see the mine in the vale beyond, on the L of the path.

25 mins, 54.4716, -1.0372 🏞🔺🚶🏕

PUBS & MICROBREWERIES

31 THE CRATHORNE ARMS

Gorgeous village pub at the heart of the community. Owners, Barbara and Eugene, who live upstairs, have furnished the place with their own fabulous furniture, including sumptuous sofas and a canoe for the condiments. Suntrap courtyard, tipi tent and a pizza oven. Check out the Jimi Hendrix memorabilia.

→ Crathorne, TS15 0BA, 01642 961402
54.4624, -1.3214 🍴🍷

32 BLACK BULL, MOULTON

Award-winning upmarket pub with a contemporary restaurant championing the region's best produce, including Yorkshire Wagyu burger and veg from the kitchen garden. Lovely outdoor terrace.

→ Moulton, Richmond, DL10 6QJ, 01325 377556
54.4285, -1.6364 🍴🍷

33 THE STAR INN AT HAROME

It is more than 25 years since chef Andrew Pern transformed this Michelin-starred 14th-century thatched inn into one of the UK's top eateries. Much-loved by visitors and locals, the restaurant offers locally sourced, modern Yorkshire food.

Following a devastating fire in 2021, the pub is only just reopening. Some of the charred roof timbers have been preserved to acknowledge the latest episode in its 600-year-old history.

→ High St, Harome, York, YO62 5JE, 01439 770397
54.231, -1.0101 🍴🍷

34 THE HARE AT SCAWTON

Tiny, multi-award-winning gastropub with rooms in a 12th-century coaching inn offering a fine-dining tasting menu.

Contemporary country-style bedrooms with indulgent bathrooms.

→ Scawton, Helmsley, Thirsk, YO7 2HG, 01845 597769
54.2434, -1.1591 🍴🍷🛏

35 THE CARPENTER'S ARMS

Award-winning traditional village inn with lodge-style accommodation. The kitchen garden at historic Mount St John provides the chef with seasonal produce for an appetising menu. Raised decked terrace at back overlooking pretty landscaped gardens.

→ Carpenters Arms, Felixkirk, Thirsk, YO7 2DP, 01845 537369
54.2555, -1.2841 🍴🍷🛏

36 THE DUDLEY ARMS

A friendly local pub that also houses the popular Café 1756. A wide variety of food available, from café snacks to formal dining in the pub's restaurant. Outdoor tables and cabins. Beers and locally brewed cask ales.

→ Ingleby Greenhow, Great Ayton, TS9 6LL, 01642 722526
54.4496, -1.1053 🍴🍷

37 HELMSLEY BREWING COMPANY

Friendly microbrewery and shop in the heart of Helmsley offering a good range of artisan beers, including Yorkshire Legend, Howardian Gold and Striding the Riding, all brewed on site.

→ 18 Bridge St, Helmsley, YO62 5DX, 01439 771014
54.2448, -1.0601 📍

CAFÉS & FARM SHOPS

38 VINE HOUSE CAFÉ

Tuck into a scrumptious seasonal menu at this lovely restored Victorian glasshouse in the 18th-century Helmsley Walled Garden, which once supplied fruit, vegetables and flowers to Duncombe Park.

→ Helmsley Walled Garden/Duncombe Pk, York, YO62 5AH, 01439 772314
54.2449, -1.0674 🍴📍

39 HIGH PARADISE FARM TEAROOM

Wonderful family-run tearoom just off the Cleveland Way. Also offers semi-wild camping in a superb location. Self-catered rooms, evening meals and packed lunches. Cottage. Café open Mar to Sep, Thur and Fri 11am – 4pm, weekends/bank holidays 10am – 4pm. Camping runs Mar to Sep. Walkers should text a day ahead on 07739 498255 (£10.00 pppn).

→ Boltby, Thirsk, YO7 2HT, 07739 498255
54.2921, -1.2284

40 GLIDING CLUB CAFÉ

Enjoy a brew or tuck into hearty home-cooked food at this good-value, friendly café at the Yorkshire Gliding Club, where pioneering pilot Amy Johnson was once a member. The unique cylindrical building offers superb views of the gliders and countryside.

→ The Yorkshire Gliding Club, Sutton Bank, Thirsk, YO7 2EY, 01845 597237
54.2293, -1.2096 🍴

41 FIVE HOUSES FARM SHOP AND DELI

Family-run farm shop with a well-stocked deli and excellent butchery. Pop into the Kitchen Café for coffee and cake or a leisurely lunch in the pretty courtyard garden.

→ Crathorne, TS15 0AY, 01642 700333
54.4689, -1.3197 🍴

42 ROOTS FARM SHOP AND CAFÉ

Farm shop selling quality local produce, with homemade quiches, scones, cakes and its famous steak and ale pie available in the café. The meat is from its own butchery.

→ Home Farm, East Rounton, Northallerton, DL6 2LE, 01609 882480
54.4244, -1.3414 🍴

43 LEWIS & COOPER

An amazing Tardis-like gourmet emporium with a food hall, delicatessen, wine store, tearooms and hamper department. Impressive cheese counter with artisan selections, such as Flat Capper Northern Brie.

→ 92 High St, Northallerton, DL7 8PT, 01609 772880
54.3404, -1.4337 🍴📍

44 HUNTERS OF HELMSLEY

Stock up for your picnic hamper at this multi-award-winning, family-run deli selling a fantastic range of food and drink. Their delicious deep-filled sandwiches are always a hit.

→ 13 Market Pl, Helmsley, York, YO62 5BL, 01439 771307
54.2462, -1.0611 🍴

45 THE BAKER'S HOUSE

Eco-micro-bakery offering a tantalising array of cakes, pastries and bread using local & seasonal ingredients. Open Thur-Sat, 8am–4pm.

→ 8 Borogate, Helmsley, YO62 5BN, 01439 771429

54.2457, -1.0608 ⏹

46 THOMAS THE BAKER

Award-winning deli and butchers. Excellent cheese counter – and a curd tart master who ensures the pastry cases are filled with the juiciest currants and curd cheese.

→ 18 Market Pl, Helmsley, York, YO62 5BL, 01439 770249

54.2463, -1.0620 ⏹

CAMP, GLAMP & HOSTELS

47 SENTRY CIRCLE CAMPING

Toast marshmallows over the campfire at this friendly campsite for tents and campers with its own stone circle. Three artist-decorated glamping pods and bell tents also available.

→ Stokesley Rd, Northallerton, DL6 2UD, 07801 515287

54.3638, -1.4007 ⏹

48 KILDALE CAMPING AND BARN

A quiet campsite on a working farm. Also offers a barn (sleeps 12 in two sleeping areas) and byre (sleeps 5) to guests. Beautiful scenery surrounds the site, with the Cleveland Way a short distance away. Hot showers, toilets. Dog friendly.

→ Park Farm, Kildale, Whitby, YO21 2RN, 01642 722847

54.4678, -1.0715 ⏹

49 WHORLTON PODS

Three stylish cedar-clad pods with en suites and hot tubs nestled within a row of willow trees next to a pond in a secluded setting. Follow the footpath to the abandoned ancient village of Whorlton to find an ancient church and ruined castle (see entries).

→ Four Wynds, Whorl Hill, Faceby, DL6 3HU, 07508 108222

54.4222, -1.2504 ⏹

50 LARK AND COULTER, A PLACE IN THE PINES

Snug Scandi-style cabin and a rustic safari tent tucked away in woodland on the fringes of the North York Moors. Cosy log burners, fiery enough to rustle up a stew. Outdoor bathing deck with two luxurious tubs for a moonlit soak beneath the stars. Duck eggs from the honesty box by the pond.

→ Keepers Cottage Thimbleby, DL6 3PY, 07590 558986

54.3547, -1.3079 ⏹

51 MORNDYKE

Five award-winning shepherd's huts on a working farm with storybook names like Flopsy, Mopsy and Cottontail after the family's rescue sheep. Beautifully furnished and exquisite attention to detail. Sorry, no kids.

→ Morndyke Farm, Thirsk, YO7 4EH, 01845 587544

54.2197, -1.4216 ⏹

52 YHA OSMOTHERLEY

Beautifully situated hostel in a converted linen mill with a camping field. Campers can use all main facilities. On C2C and Cleveland Way.

→ Cote Ghyll, Osmotherley, Northallerton, DL6 3AH, 0345 260 2870

54.3764, -1.2916 ⏹

53 BRANSDALE MILL BUNKHOUSE

NT-managed bunkhouse in a former 18th-century mill in beautiful Bransdale. Ideal for groups. Sleeps 12 in 2 dormitories.

→ Fadmoor, York, YO62 7JL, 0344 335 1296, National Trust Holiday Cottages

54.3731, -1.0463 ⏹

COSY COTTAGES

54 BONFIELD GHYLL FARM, BRANSDALE

Charming 18th-century cottage, with quarry-tiled floors, a Victorian range and a bed in the rafters, on a working sheep farm generating its own electricity on the National Trust's Bransdale Estate. Poor Wi-Fi and dodgy TV signal.

→ The Old Back Kitchen, Bonfield Ghyll Farm, Helmsley, York, YO62 5GZ, 01439 771493, Yorkshire-cottages.info

54.3448, -1.0669 ⏹

55 BAYSDALE ABBEY AND COTTAGES

Fabulous place for a large family gathering, this beautiful stone farmhouse is located in a secluded valley on the site of a 12th-century Cistercian Abbey. Sleeps 18. Three barn conversions sleep 4 to 6.

→ Baysdale Abbey, Kildale, YO21 2SF, 01642 722836

54.4519, -1.0460 ⏹

48

52

56 COCKAYNE COTTAGE

Rural farmhouse situated in beautiful
Bransdale. Exposed beams, low ceilings
and a toasty log burner. Sleeps 5. Sweeping
views and a historic church next door.

→ Bransdale, Fadmoor, YO62 7JL, National
Trust Holiday Cottages
54.3777, -1.0469

57 REFECTORY COTTAGE

Soak up the serenity of atmospheric
Rievaulx Abbey at this traditional cottage
situated in its grounds and owned by English
Heritage. Sleeps 5.

→ English Heritage Holiday Cottages
54.2581, -1.1168

58 PRIOR'S LODGE

Pretty 18th-century cottage, sleeping 5,
in the grounds of Mount Grace Priory and
overlooking the Carthusian Monastery.

→ English Heritage Holiday Cottages
54.3789, -1.3109

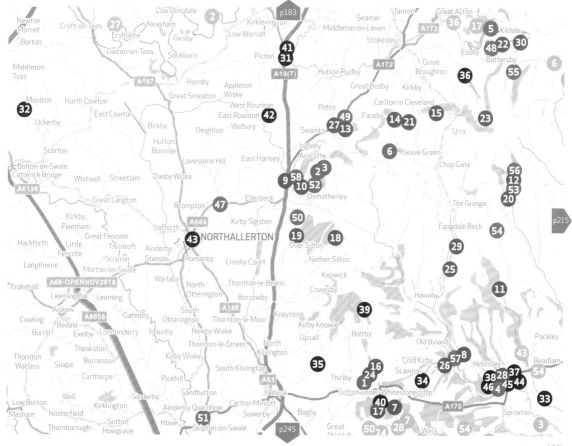

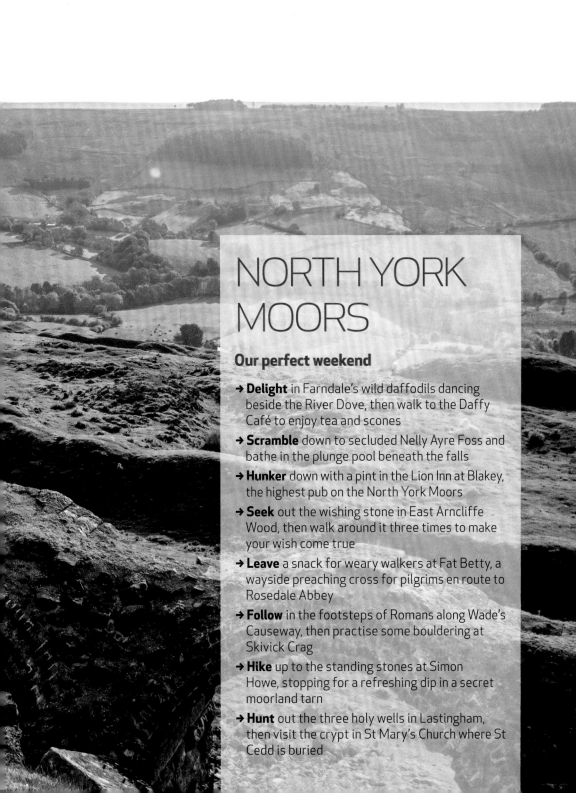

NORTH YORK MOORS

Our perfect weekend

→ **Delight** in Farndale's wild daffodils dancing beside the River Dove, then walk to the Daffy Café to enjoy tea and scones

→ **Scramble** down to secluded Nelly Ayre Foss and bathe in the plunge pool beneath the falls

→ **Hunker** down with a pint in the Lion Inn at Blakey, the highest pub on the North York Moors

→ **Seek** out the wishing stone in East Arncliffe Wood, then walk around it three times to make your wish come true

→ **Leave** a snack for weary walkers at Fat Betty, a wayside preaching cross for pilgrims en route to Rosedale Abbey

→ **Follow** in the footsteps of Romans along Wade's Causeway, then practise some bouldering at Skivick Crag

→ **Hike** up to the standing stones at Simon Howe, stopping for a refreshing dip in a secret moorland tarn

→ **Hunt** out the three holy wells in Lastingham, then visit the crypt in St Mary's Church where St Cedd is buried

The landscape here speaks to its history – whether it's the Ice Age's sculpting of the hills and dales, the standing stones left by Bronze Age tribes, the camps and roads laid by the Romans or ancient crosses erected by our Christian forebears.

The North York Moors has one of the largest unbroken expanses of upland heather moorland in England and Wales. These rugged slopes were cut through by glacial meltwater overflowing from the north to form its dales. Looking across spectacular Newtondale from Skelton Tower, with heritage steam trains chugging along the valley bottom, you will see one of the best examples of a meltwater channel in the country.

Each of these dales has its own delights: the wild daffodils at Farndale; the abandoned ironstone railway at Rosedale, now a scenic trail for walkers and cyclists; Eskdale cut through by the lovely River Esk; and Fryup Dale, a picturesque patchwork of meadows dotted with rustic farmsteads and hamlets.

The first farmers began clearing the woodland plateau 5,000 years ago. The vast number of burial mounds and well-preserved settlement sites dating to the early Bronze Age is a distinctive feature of the moors. Some you will easily stumble across; others like the atmospheric standing stones at Simon Howe and Temple Beeld require perseverance to find.

The moors are a joy to explore at any time of year, offering a sense of space and solitude, only broken by the cries of curlews, skylarks and red grouse and the buzz of bees and insects. They all find a home in the heather, which is particularly beautiful in August when a haze of purple covers the landscape. Much of the moorland of the North York Moors is open access land, meaning you can explore for miles without having to follow defined paths or tracks.

For those seeking adventure, bouldering and scrambling opportunities abound with fantastic crags at Rosedale Head, Breckon Bank and Wheeldale. Wild swimmers can clamber down to secluded waterfalls around Goathland. The rivers here, namely the Esk and the Seven, which can be trickling streams in summer and raging torrents in winter, provide plenty of water adventures for swimmers and kayakers.

Wherever you venture here, you are never far away from a country pub, whether it is tiny Birch Hall with its own traditional sweet shop; the New Inn at Cropton, home of the Great Yorkshire Brewery; or the spectacularly situated Lion Inn at Blakey – and if you are lucky, you might even get snowed in.

WATERFALLS

1 MALLYAN SPOUT

This picturesque waterfall, the highest in the North York Moors, has charmed visitors since Victorian times. Water tumbles over a steep-sided 20m drop. Spectacular after rain but take care as rocks can be slippery. Plunge pool and more pools and swing upstream.

→ Heading N on the A169, take L turn at signpost for Goathland, passing Goathland Viewpoint car park on L. Continue to Goathland village and take L at roundabout to park on verge. Walk back towards Mallyan Spout Hotel and follow signpost 'Footpath Mallyan Spout' and descend into woods. At junction at bottom, path to L leads upstream to Mallyan Spout.

20 mins, 54.3978, -0.7321 🚶🏊

2 NELLY AYRE FOSS

A secluded waterfall hidden down a slope with a plunge pool and some nice stone slabs for lounging. More plunge pools downstream.

→ Head SW out of Goathland with Mallyan Spout Hotel on R and go across roundabout. Continue for ¾ mile to parking on R before cattle grid. Find footpath on L, signposted 'Nelly Ayre Foss', alongside New Wath House. Continue to end of wall and start of perimeter fence. Follow fence round and find narrow path down to falls. Scramble down last bit.

20 mins, 54.3858, -0.7490 🚶🏊🏊🎣🚶🏕🍴🏃

3 THOMASON FOSS WATERFALL

This small, pretty waterfall with a great plunge pool in a wooded ravine on Eller Beck is reached by a narrow path. Afterwards, call in at the tiny Birch Hall Inn at Beck Hole, which has a traditional sweet shop (see entry).

→ Heading N on the A169, take L at signpost for Beck Hole. Continue to roadside parking on hill before you descend into Beck Hole. Walk into village (½ mile). Follow signposted footpath by bridge in centre of village to falls.

25 mins, 54.4079, -0.7284 🚶🏊🍴🏕🏊

4 WATER ARK WATERFALL

Spectacular, little-known waterfall with plunge pool upstream of Thomason Foss. Further plunge pools and large flat rocks to L and R of footbridge. Tricky to reach so take care.

→ From Goathland follow signs for Beck Hole and park at top of this road. Find footpath opp, through a snicket, and head into a field towards railway bridge (look out for steam train) and steep steps down to riverside. Cross footbridge and turn L along footpath to end, then take steep path on L down to falls.

15 mins, 54.4079, -0.7243 🚶🎣🏕🍴🚶

RIVERS & TARNS

5 THE TARN, OLD KIT BIELD

Nestled in the bowl of upland hills and circled by swallows and skylarks, this peaty moorland tarn is just a short distance from Goathland village. Spongy shore but decent access south of tarn.

→ From Goathland, pass the Mallyan Spout Hotel on R and go straight ahead at roundabout to parking on grass verge on R (54.3944, -0.7318). Follow footpath sign onto moor for ½ mile.

15 mins, 54.3900, -0.7345 🏊🎣🏕🏃🍴

6 HOB HOLE

Local beauty spot next to Baysdale Beck in a steep bracken-carpeted valley with a ford crossing the ancient medieval road from Castleton to Guisborough. Some deeper pools in between shallows that tumble over the rocks and stones. Perfect picnic spot for families.

→ From Young Ralph Cross, take L signposted 'Westerdale'. Follow road for 2½ miles to village, then continue on Upper Esk Road for 1 mile. Parking after ford on L.
2 mins, 54.4575, -0.9963

7 HUNTER'S STY BRIDGE, RIVER ESK
Small beach and shallow pools beneath an ancient packhorse bridge over the River Esk. Ideal for a secluded picnic, paddle or bathe.
→ From Young Ralph Cross, take L signposted 'Westerdale'. Follow road for 2½ miles to village, then continue on Upper Esk Road for 1 mile. Lay-by parking on R next to bridge.
2 mins, 54.4464, -0.9794

8 BEGGAR'S BRIDGE, RIVER ESK
Pleasant stretch of the River Esk with deep pools beneath the medieval Beggar's Bridge and a beach and shallower water a few metres downstream. For a longer swim, follow the footpath into East Arncliffe Woods, where there is a longer, deeper section of river.
→ From Glaisdale, follow road towards Egton Bridge. Beggar's Bridge is about ½ mile along on R, just under railway bridge. In East Arncliffe Woods, entry point is at 54.4367, -0.7922.
2 mins, 54.4387, -0.7921

9 GROSMONT, RIVER ESK
Calm bend of the River Esk near Grosmont with deeper pools for swimming. Just off the old toll road between Egton Bridge and Grosmont.
→ From Grosmont, follow road towards Egton, passing footbridge on L, to parking at end of toll road. Follow track to path to river on L.
5 mins, 54.4379, -0.7350

10 LEALHOLM, RIVER ESK
There are three crossings of the Esk at Lealholm: the bridge, a ford and this set of stepping stones, which are definitely a favourite with younger visitors. Deeper pool upstream of the Board Inn.
→ Park in car park at Lealholm. Stepping stones are by the green.
2 mins, 54.4583, -0.8257

11 SINNINGTON, RIVER SEVEN
A pebble beach at a bend in the river beneath a canopy of trees and in dappled light on summer days. Rope swing and fallen tree trunk to scramble across.
→ From Pickering, follow the A170 for 4 miles then turn R to Sinnington. Continue on Main Street to parking at village hall (donation).

Follow road to L of village hall, with river on L, to woodland footpath. Continue along riverside path, round a sharp L-hand bend in river, to a shallow ford used by horse riders. Beach is to L. Also paddle spot at 54.2669, -0.8596 with small beach and pool.
20 mins, 54.2691, -0.8691

SACRED & ANCIENT

12 TEMPLE BEELD STANDING STONES

A set of five stones in a cross. Some have a wall built between them to provide a – 'beeld' a shelter for sheep. The site takes some finding as they are set in a hollow on the moorland, but it is worth the effort. The stones are thought to have been erected around 1500 bc. There are bogs on three sides, so may be best to visit in summer.

→ From Lealholm, head uphill along the Esk Valley Walk (a road). Take the L turn to remain on the walk and park on the verge a little further up where the road takes a sharp L turn. Ahead is a track, follow this for approx ¼ mile to a T-junction with another track. Take a L here and after ¼ mile there is a track on the R with a row of grouse-shooting butts on the L-hand side. Follow this track to Temple Beeld. The stones are clearly visible on Google Earth

if you need assistance finding them. There are a few barrows in the area and if you climb any, they will help you spot the stones.
30 mins, 54.4809, -0.8327

13 SIMON HOWE CAIRN

Simon Howe has a variety of stones from various times. The prominent cairn and low wall are modern additions by walkers, but the circle of standing stones and row of stones date back much further, and finds at the site indicate it has been occupied for 5,000 years. The views from the cairn are stunning and you can understand why people have chosen to live here, or just pause while walking, for thousands of years.

→ Follow directions as for the tarn at Old Kit Bield, then choose path carefully. Ignore the path running parallel to the tarn and take the track at 90 degrees to the tarn, which heads uphill and leads you over the moor, past Two Howes, and on to Simon Howe.
30 mins, 54.3716, -0.7237

14 ALLAN TOFTS

Occupying a superb location on Goathland Moor, this ancient site comprises a cairn field, a field system, burial cairns and excellent examples of prehistoric rock

art. Some of the cup-marked stones are encrusted with lichen; others are clearly patterned. There were once more than 220 cairns scattered over the area, along with paths, tracks and holloways and post-medieval sheep beelds. It is a peaceful and remote place and the views over the Murk Esk Valley are splendid.

→ From Goathland, head NE towards the A169. Take first L after 1½ miles towards Beck Hole. Lay-by parking on R (54.4162, -0.7055). Follow footpath across moor towards Hawthorn Hill Farm to join track. Search for rock art stones in field to R, near beeld at top.

25 mins, 54.4151, -0.7223 🚶⛺🔦📷✝♻

15 MAULEY CROSS

Medieval roadside cross whose survival as a single piece of carved gritstone is remarkable. It lies east of the Roman road. Its use as a wayside religious symbol for the ancient trackway is a reminder of the piety expected of the travellers of that period.

→ From Stape village, head N on Stape Road for ½ mile. At T-junction, turn L then veer R onto Keys Beck Road for ⅓ mile. Turn R into Brown Howe Road (track). Mauley Cross is on L after few metres.

1 min, 54.3384, -0.7767 ✝

16 WISHING STONE, EAST ARNCLIFFE WOOD

This ancient wishing stone lies in an enchanting woodland. The stone had a yew (since rotted) growing through the middle, and it is said that if you walk round the stone three times, you can make a wish that will come true. Rare species of Tunbridge filmy fern and hay-scented buckler fern thrive in the damp and shaded conditions here. Sandstone glacial blocks for bouldering just off the footpath, near the stone.

→ From Whitby, follow the A171, signposted 'Guisborough', for 6½ miles. Turn L onto Egton Cliff then Smith's Lane for 3½ miles. Parking in tiny lay-by on right by entrance to woods at 54.4310, -0.7789.

15 min, 54.4340, -0.7893 🚶❓🌀

17 WHEELDALE ROMAN ROAD

Also known as Wade's Causeway, this excavated mile-long stretch of flagstones is thought to be the Roman road running between the Roman fort at Cawthorn Camp to another fort at Lease Rigg. However, it could be much older as a stone burial cist set into one side of the path may predate Roman occupation. According to legend, Wade was a local giant who built the road for his wife, Bell, so she could herd her

18

sheep to market. Beautiful, remote location. Continue to Skivick Crag (see entry).

→ From Stape village, head N on Stape Road for ½ mile. At T-junction turn L then veer R onto Keys Beck Road for 2 miles. Parking on L opp gate to Roman road.

2 mins, 54.3658, -0.7634 🚶🏊

18 ABRAHAM'S HUT ROUND CAIRN

Buried and earthwork remains of a Bronze Age stone burial mound situated on top of a hillside overlooking the River Seven. This well-preserved, mainly stone-built cairn was probably used for more than one burial. Such cairns are a feature of the uplands of the North York Moors and are the stone equivalent of the earthen burial mounds of the lowlands.

→ From Hutton-le-Hole, take R turn along Moor Ln, signposted 'Lastingham'. After ¼ mile, take a slight L to Chimney Bank and continue for 3 miles. Parking at Chimney Bank car park. Cross road to footpath sign a few metres up the hill. Pass Ana Cross on R and continue to cairn on L.

25 mins, 54.3272, -0.8643 🏊📷👪

19 ANA CROSS

This round barrow and wayside cross on a prehistoric burial mound mark a medieval route across the moors from Lastingham to Rosedale Priory. It is the tallest cross on the North York Moors at 3.5m, replacing the original pre-Norman cross which stood at twice its height, the top of which still survives, now held in the crypt of St Mary's Church, Lastingham.

→ From Hutton-le-Hole, take R turn along Moor Ln, signposted 'Lastingham'. After ¼ mile, take a slight left to Chimney Bank and continue for 3 miles. Parking at Chimney Bank car park. Cross road to footpath sign a few yards up the hill. Follow path to Ana Cross.

10 mins, 54.3352, -0.8871 📷🚶▲🪑

19

20 OLD RALPH CROSS

An older Ralph Cross stands a few hundred metres from its more famous brother, but you will need to heather bash to reach it, as it is neither visible from the road nor from Young Ralph. This 11th-century weathered gritstone cross is located on Ledging Hill, the highest point on Blakey Ridge, with Roseberry Topping in the distance. Don't forget to follow tradition by leaving a few coins on top of the cross.

→ Travel N on Blakey Ridge and pass the Lion Inn. The cross is just before the L turn to Westerdale. Use parking place on R – good

20

picnic spot with magnificent views across Rosedale Valley. Cross road and Old Ralph is 300m across the moor directly ahead of you.

5 mins, 54.4088, -0.9628

21 FAT BETTY

Standing beside an ancient track, the medieval cross known as Fat Betty has marked the way for travellers for hundreds of years. It also served as a Christian wayside preaching cross for pilgrims en route to Rosedale Abbey. Today, people leave snacks for walkers on the beautiful Esk Valley Walk.

→ As for Old Ralph Cross but continue along Knott Road for 450m. Fat Betty is on the L.

2 mins, 54.4088, -0.9503

22 CAWTHORN CAMP

One of the north's lesser-known Roman sites, Cawthorn Camp is unique for the variety of its features and its survival almost 20 centuries after the Romans left Britain. The two forts and camp are unusual in shape, as they form an elongated hexagon rather than the regular square or rectangle shape. A Bronze Age barrow lies in the woodland to the south-east.

→ From Pickering on the A170, take Middleton Road, then follow Swainsea Lane. After 3½ miles turn L at T-junction. In ½ mile turn R onto track to parking. Follow markers to camps. Follow woodland path behind wooden barrier to barrow at 54.2986, -0.7959.

10 mins, 54.3001, -0.8024

23 CHURCH OF ST PETER AND ST PAUL

The stunning medieval wall paintings in Pickering's parish church are the most important of their type in Northern Europe. Originally painted in 1450, they were covered over in the Reformation, rediscovered in 1851 and almost immediately re-covered. In 1870 they were fully restored.

→ The church is easily located from Pickering, sitting on top of a small hill in the marketplace (YO18 7AW).

5 mins, 54.2456, -0.7755

24 ST GREGORY'S MINSTER

Just a hundred years or so after Christianity arrived in Britain, the foundations were laid for a church at Kirkdale. This tiny minster, rebuilt around 1060, is in a lovely wooded dale alongside Hodge Beck. Its Saxon sundial, described as the finest in England, is an extraordinary survival having been covered in plaster for seven centuries.

→ From Kirbymoorside, head W on the A170 for 1½ miles, then turn R onto Kirkdale Lane to parking by church.
2 mins, 54.2632, -0.9623 ⛪🚲

HOLY WELLS & CRYPTS

25 OLD WIVES' WELL
This ancient spring, decorated with ribbons and pebbles, lies concealed on the edge of Cropton Forest. Further up the road are the Mauley Cross and Wade's Causeway, the old Roman road (see entry).
→ From Stape village, head N on Stape Road for ½ mile. At T-junction turn L then veer R onto Keys Beck Road for ⅓ mile. Parking on R side in tiny lay-by. Look for worn grass path into woods. Well lies just beyond.
2 mins, 54.3365, -0.7790 ⛪

26 HOLY WELLS, LASTINGHAM
There are three holy wells in Lastingham, each linked to the saints connected with founding the Celtic monastery here in ad 657. St Cedd's Well, a 19th-century construction, reused stone from Rosedale Abbey. Cedd was Bishop of the East Saxons and Abbot of Lastingham. When Cedd died, his brother, Chad, succeeded him as Abbot,

later becoming Bishop of Lichfield. The well is recessed into the boundary wall of Rosedale House, formerly White Garth. St Ovin's Well has arched access which may have had a door but lacks a trough.
→ In Lastingham the wells can be found as follows: St Cedd's Well – 54.3045, 0.8809, St Chad's Well – 54.3052, -0.8803, St Ovin's Well – 54.3042, -0.8802.
10 mins, 54.3044, -0.8820 ⛪

27 MARY MAGDALENE WELL
Inscribed 'Mary Magdalene Well', this roadside well is found in a tranquil hamlet and is surrounded by water mint. During excavations, 12th-century fragments were found, and the well often has offerings, showing it is still a special place. Opposite is a pretty gated garth and wildlife haven.
→ From Lastingham, head NW on Anserdale Lane for 800m. Parking in lay-by on R at hamlet before Spaunton Bank. Well is hidden down by spring on R. Secret garden is opp.
1 min, 54.3041, -0.8904 ⛪

28 THE CRYPT AT ST MARY'S, LASTINGHAM
Remarkable Norman crypt of St Mary's Church described as one of England's special places. Built on the site of an ad 654 monastery where

St Cedd, a missionary from Lindisfarne, is said to be buried. The original monastery was built from wood and the first stone church was built here in ad 725. The current church dates back to 1078, when it was refounded as a Benedictine Abbey. The crypt dates from this time and is unique for its apse, chancel and aisles.

→ The church is in the centre of Lastingham village, opp the pub. Roadside parking.
1 min, 54.3046, -0.8825 ⊕

ROCKS & HILLTOPS

29 DANBY BEACON

Less famous than its neighbour, Roseberry Topping, which lies at the end of the same moorland ridge, Danby Beacon offers equally stupendous views of the moors, dales and sea. Beacon Hill has been the site of a beacon since the 17th century, warning of the danger of invasion from France. An easy roadside summit or hill climb from Danby.

→ Head 1½ miles NE of Danby Visitor Centre on Park Bank then turn L to summit.
2 mins, 54.4734, -0.8656 🖼🏕

30 HOLE OF HORCUM

This stunning natural cauldron was created by a line of springs undermining the slopes above and eating away at the rocks to form an enormous bowl. Take in sunset views from Saltergate car park or follow the scenic Tabular Hills walk across Levisham Moor.

→ Take the A169 from Pickering towards Whitby for 10 miles to Saltergate car park on R. For walk, cross road and follow footpath along ridge line (Tabular Hills walk).
2 mins, 54.3319, -0.6901 🖼🚲🚶🐕🏕

31 GEORGE GAP CAUSEWAY

An old pannier way, possibly the longest line of paved trods across the North York Moors, linking Rosedale to Staithes and opening out to immense views northwards to Great Fryup Dale and the sea beyond. Superb picnic spot.

→ From Rosedale Abbey, follow New Road N for 1 mile, then turn R where road forks uphill for 3 miles. Bridleway (George Gap Causeway) is 1 mile along on R. Continue to parking on R where road forks (54.4014, -0.9265) and return to path. Follow path for 1 mile past ancient Causeway Stone boundary marker to junction with Cut Road (track) and views. Some trods are missing so can be boggy in places. Follow Cut Road track W past the solitary Trough House for circular walk back.
10 mins, 54.3959, -0.9197 🖼🚲🏕⛰

32 DUCK BOULDERS

Great bouldering site at Breckon Bank with plenty of good-sized boulders. Incredible views across Farndale.

➔ Park up on W side of the Castleton to Hutton-le-Hole moor road at 54.3246, -0.9376, in a lay-by just S of a public footpath post and just N of a sign indicating a sharp bend in the road. Follow the good track W down the hillside to a wall. Follow this until a gate is reached where a path breaks off R (N). From here the top of the boulders are visible but follow a path below to reach them.

20 mins, 54.3463, -0.9486 🖼️🔣

33 ROSEDALE HEAD

The walk along the old ironstone railway line around Rosedale Head to this secluded little boulder field offers spectacular views back down the valley. The crag itself is a peaceful location, invisible to anyone walking the track above. Red kites circle and dive and rare black ring ouzels have been spotted here. Ideal for bivvying or a wild camp.

➔ From the Lion Inn at Blakey car park (YO62 7LQ), cross road and follow a signed footpath down to the old railway line, continuing round Rosedale Head before descending steeply to

the boulders, marked by some trees. Look for the clearing on R and access is just after this, between the trees and the view. For an easier descent, continue to stone wall and approach from bottom of crag.

25 mins, 54.3979, -0.9473 🔣🖼️🔣🔣🔣

34 SKIVICK CRAG

This anvil-shaped boulder rising out of the ferns can only be seen as you crest a hill before descending into a beautiful, secluded valley. Fun for easy climbing. Fern bash along footpath to Wheeldale Beck for stepping stones and paddling. Nice for a picnic.

➔ As for Wheeldale Roman road (see entry). Then follow Roman road path for ½ mile and turn R along footpath into valley. For Wheeldale Beck, continue L of large boulder along narrow footpath between tall ferns.

25 mins, 54.3718, -0.7559 🔣🔣🔣🔣🖼️

35 HUNT HOUSE CRAG

Crag strewn with boulders and stones on a hillside with a commanding view of the valley below. The site is nestled in the heather, with buzzards wheeling in the skies above and summertime swallows darting over the moorland. Check out the largest jumble of boulders for scrambling.

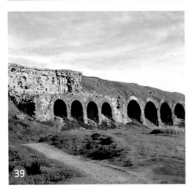

→ From Goathland, follow road S for ½ mile, then take Hunt House Rd S for 1 mile. Park in one of the small lay-bys (54.3784, -0.7462) just before Hunt House Farm and take the main path down the valley. Boulders are just off the path to the R.

25 mins, 54.3714, -0.7482 🖼️🧗🚶🌲🖼️⛰️

RUINS, CASTLES & CAVES

36 SKELTON TOWER

Romantic ruins of an early 19th-century shooting lodge built by the local rector who used to write his sermons here and, some say, enjoy a quiet tipple. Magnificent views across Newtondale. If you are lucky, you will have timed your visit to coincide with the NYM heritage steam train passing by.

→ From the Horseshoe Inn in Levisham, continue down the hill for 1½ miles to the car park at Levisham station. From the car park, continue R up the hill to a sharp bend in the road. Take the footpath L across the moor to the tower.

25 mins, 54.3258, -0.7399 🖼️📷🍴🚶⛰️

37 KIRKDALE CAVE

A slit in the rock face leads to this small cave discovered by quarry workers in

1821, along with the bones and teeth of elephants, hyenas, hippos, rhinos and bison dating back to the Ice Age. The bones, identified by William Buckland, Oxford University's first professor of Geology, were important evidence in establishing the idea of a deep geological past. The cave offers a short round trip near the entrance.

→ In Kirkdale, continue past St Gregory's Minster on L (see entry). Cross ford to lay-by parking immediately on L. Follow footpath for few metres, then turn R into a large bowl to cave in rock face. It's a scramble to get up into the cave, possible with care and basic safety equipment. Once inside, the cave divides, with both routes extending roughly 10m.

2 mins, 54.2627, -0.9617 🏵️✝️🔧▼

38 PICKERING CASTLE

A superb 13th-century castle, originally of wooden construction, founded under William the Conqueror and rebuilt in stone under Henry II. A perimeter path circles the castle. Behind is former quarry, Newbridge Park, and a short walk to Beacon Hill, a prominent summit 550m to the west and site of a former siege castle with views back to the castle and the town.

→ Roadside parking by castle. For Beacon Hill, take footpath through Newbridge Park. Cross road at end, over beck and railway line. Then take L along footpath to gate and across field. Continue through gate to follow footpath towards Beacon Hill (54.2495, -0.7845, private, fenced). Return same way or through town.
40 mins, 54.2502, -0.7757 ⊞£◲↩

INDUSTRIAL HERITAGE

39 BANK TOP KILNS, ROSEDALE CHIMNEY BANK

With only the song flight of skylarks to punctuate the silence, it's hard to imagine this area as a hive of industry in the 19th century when miners poured in to extract iron ore, swelling the population of Rosedale from 558 to almost 3,000. As you scramble over the old roasting kilns, you get some of the best views in the national park. The nine-mile route along the disused railway line is a spectacular walk or cycle along the ridge line.
→ From Hutton-le-Hole, take R turn along Moor Ln, signposted 'Lastingham'. After ¼ mile, take a slight left to Chimney Bank and continue for 3 miles. Parking at Chimney Bank car park.
2 mins, 54.3444, -0.8925 ◲▣◲↩⛺♿

40 ROSEDALE EAST KILNS

These two monumental sets of calcining kilns, relics of the huge ironstone mining and refining industry that dominated this valley from 1860 to 1926, can be seen from miles around. You can reach them from Dale Head or via a superb four-mile walk along the old railway line around the valley from the Lion Inn at Blakey Ridge.
→ Follow New Rd out of Rosedale Abbey. At fork in road keep L to find parking at Daleside Road in Rosedale East by Hill Cottages. Walk footpath and old railway line to kilns.
30 mins, 54.3814, -0.9151 ↩♿△◲▣◲⛺

NATURE & WILDLIFE

41 FARNDALE WILD DAFFODILS

The medieval monks at Rievaulx Abbey may have planted the wild daffodils that carpet the meadows and banks of the River Dove in a spectacular spring display. The petite wild daffodil is one of our native plants (protected here in Farndale). Follow the River Dove to the Daffy Caffy for a cream tea or bacon butty. Open daily in daff season and Fri to Sun, May to Sep (9am–5pm).
→ Park in Low Mill car park, Farndale (YO62 7UY), 4 miles NE of Hutton-le-Hole. Follow signpost to daffodil walk.
5 mins, 54.3484, -0.9665 ♿▣◲↩

42 FEN BOG NATURE RESERVE

Delightful hidden valley with magnificent views back across Newtondale and the steam railway. The area is home to many different species of butterflies, moths and dragonflies. Bog plants also flourish in a deep bed of peat. This is one of the last places in Yorkshire where the Large Heath butterfly, attracted by the wet boggy habitat, is found.
→ From Pickering, follow the A169 towards Whitby for 10 miles. The reserve is just N of RAF Fylingdales and S of Ellerbeck bridge and the turn-off to Goathland. Parking on track next to the gate.
2 mins, 54.3718, -0.6838 ◲⛺△♿

43 RICCAL DALE

Secluded woodland ravine cut through by the River Riccal with a gorgeous display of bluebells in spring. Follow the track towards Hasty Bank Farm on a circular walk for spectacular open views. Paddling and picnics in summer. An all-year-round delight.

→ From Helmsley, take the A170 in dir of Scarborough. After 1½ miles turn L along Wykeham Dale, signposted 'Pockley'. Just before Pockley village, park in lay-by on L before smaller lay-by further up with footpath sign. Follow track into Riccal Dale. Paddle and swim spots at 54.2688, -1.0437.
10 mins, 54.2620, -1.0375

CAFÉS & RESTAURANTS

44 DANBY BAKERY AND TEASHOP
Enjoy homemade cakes and light lunches at this small, licensed café in the heart of the North York Moors. Danby Health Shop next door sells organic produce.
→ 3 Briar Hill, Danby, Whitby YO21 2LZ, 01287 669126
54.4686, -0.9087

45 GRAZE ON THE GREEN
A pretty vintage-style café and tea garden, overlooking the village green in Rosedale, serving a hearty Yorkshire breakfast menu, soups, sandwiches and seriously good cakes.
→ Rosedale Abbey, Pickering, YO18 8RA, 01751 417468
54.3538, -0.8863

46 LOCKTON TEAROOMS & GALLERY
Tuck into a slice of Victoria sponge at this friendly café and art gallery situated in a delightful moorland village. Delicious home-baked cakes, breakfast and lunch or afternoon tea with fizz. Apartment-style loft for longer stays.
→ Hudgin Ln, Lockton, YO18 7QA, 01751 460467
54.2981, -0.7085

47 OLD SCHOOL COFFEE SHOP
Lovely, licensed café in a converted school near the Grosmont Station engine sheds. Delicious cakes, excellent coffee, light lunches and regular pizza nights. Pretty outside dining beneath a pergola of vines.
→ Grosmont, Whitby, YO22 5QW, 01947 895758
54.4351, -0.7244

48 LOWTHER HOUSE TEA GARDEN
Delightful tea garden next to a babbling brook in the steep-sided valley of Newtondale. Open Apr to Oct. Also does B&B.
→ Newbridge, Pickering, YO18 8JL, 01751 269121
54.2566, -0.7684

49 YORKSHIRE CYCLE HUB
Friendly cycle hub in one of the loveliest valleys of the North York Moors. Tuck into a hearty Great Fryup Breakfast bun at the café or bed down in the bunk house. Drying rooms, trails, magnificent views.
→ Fryup Gill Farm, Great Fryup Dale, Lealholm, Whitby, YO21 2AP, 01287 669098
54.4328, -0.8905

50 DALE HEAD FARM TEA GARDEN
Pretty tea garden on the edge of the North York Moors with spectacular views across Rosedale Valley. Traditional Yorkshire recipes made using locally sourced food. Shepherd's Hut.
→ Dale Head Farm, Rosedale East, Pickering, YO18 8RL, 01751 417353
54.3848, -0.9308

51 FEAST
Feast deli and café serving light bites, good coffee and cakes. Bike store. The White Swan Inn next door is a boutique bolthole with a cosy front bar and laid-back ambience.
→ 3 Market Pl, Pickering, YO18 7AA, 01751 470121
54.2459, -0.7773

52 THE HOMESTEAD KITCHEN

Rustic fine-dining restaurant in a converted 18th-century farmhouse. Changing seasonal menu using local produce or ingredients from the kitchen garden. Open Wed to Sat 12pm – 2pm and 6.30pm – 8.30pm. Sun 12pm – 2pm. Also tasteful Homestead Cottage next door, sleeps 6.

➜ Prudom House, Goathland, Whitby, YO22 5AN, 01947 896191
54.3958, -0.7266 🍴🏞

FARM SHOPS

53 NEWFIELDS ORGANIC PRODUCE FARM SHOP

Small organic farm shop selling exceptional seasonal vegetables straight from the field and eggs from their hens. Honesty box. Open 8am – 8pm. Check ahead as depends on what's in season.

➜ The Green, Fadmoor, YO62 7HY, 01751 431558
54.2959, -0.9634 🍴

54 BEADLAM GRANGE FARM SHOP AND TEAROOM

Well-stocked family-run farm shop and bistro. Own award-winning Limousin beef cattle. Good selection of Yorkshire cheeses. Fish van on Friday mornings. Small basic campsite.

➜ Beadlam, York, YO62 7TD, 01439 770303
54.2498, -1.0172 🍴⛺

55 CEDAR BARN FARM SHOP

Stock up for a picnic at this acclaimed farm shop and café with its high-quality meat counter plus delicious home-prepared dishes to take away. PYO in summer aboard the miniature railway.

➜ Thornton Rd, Pickering, YO18 7JX, 01751 475614
54.2381, -0.7497 🍴

COSY PUBS

56 HORSESHOE HOTEL, EGTON BRIDGE

Friendly village pub with a quirky style on the banks of the River Esk. Farm shop stocking local produce and bread from Danby Bakery. Rooms. EHU for motorhomes.

➜ Egton Bridge, Whitby, YO21 1XE, 01947 895245
54.4357, -0.7663 🍴🏞

57 FOX AND HOUNDS, AINTHORPE

Characterful 16th-century former coaching inn with a roaring log fire, beamed ceiling and vintage horse brasses. En-suite rooms. Popular with walkers and cyclists. Provides a pick-up and drop-off service, early breakfasts and pack-ups. Awesome dark skies.

➜ 45 Brook Ln, Ainthorpe, Whitby, YO21 2LD, 01287 660218
54.4599, -0.9150 🍴🏞

58 BIRCH HALL INN

Pocket-sized pub with two bars and a sweet shop. Hand-pulled cask beer. Butties and pies as well as its famous beer cake. Also the base for Beck Hole's 19th-century Quoit's Club, possibly the most famous in England.

➜ Beck Hole Rd, Beck Hole, Whitby, YO22 5LE, 01947 896245
54.4087, -0.7351 🍴

59 BLACKSMITH'S ARMS, LASTINGHAM

Country pub, with low beams and a roaring fire, serving high-quality homemade Yorkshire dishes, including a hearty signature steak and ale pie and real northern ales.

➜ Anserdale Ln, Lastingham, York, YO62 6TN, 01751 417247
54.3047, -0.8818 🍴🏞

60 BOARD INN, LEALHOLM

Quaint and cosy 18th-century coaching inn and hub of the community with a waterside decked beer garden and its own fishing rights.

→ Village Grn, Lealholm, Whitby, YO21 2AJ, 01947 897279

54.4580, -0.8254 🍴🚲

61 LION INN AT BLAKEY

Much-loved 16th-century pub situated on the highest point of the North York Moors with wide vistas over Rosedale. Open fires in ancient fireplaces and low-beamed ceilings all set the scene. Perfect for a Sunday roast. Rooms. Casual campsite.

→ Blakey Ridge, York, YO62 7LQ, 01751 417320

54.3884, -0.9560 🍴🚲🏕

62 HORSESHOE INN, LEVISHAM

Cosy pub situated at the head of the lovely moorland village of Levisham. Sit in the beer garden overlooking the village or settle in front of the roaring fire. Good pub grub and local ales.

→ Main St, Levisham, Pickering, YO18 7NL, 01751 460240

54.3047, -0.7211 🍴🚲

63 THE MOORS INN, APPLETON-LE-MOORS

Traditional 17th-century village inn with real fires, beamed ceilings and brasses. Seasonal menu offering high-quality Yorkshire food, including local meats, game and North Sea fish.

→ Appleton-le-Moors, York, YO62 6TF, 01751 417435

54.2817, -0.8728 🍴🚲

64 CROPTON BREWERY AT THE NEW INN

You are guaranteed a decent pint at the end of your walk as the New Inn is also home to the Great Yorkshire Brewery and Cropton Brewery which have been producing award-winning ales for more than 25 years – although Cropton has a brewing tradition dating back to 1613. Good value basic camping field.

→ Cropton Ln, Pickering, YO18 8HH, 01751 417330

54.2902, -0.8413 🍴🚲🏕

CAMP, GLAMP & SLEEP

65 BANK TOP CAMPING

Family-run camping and caravan site with grass pitches and EHU on a sunny, spacious site with spectacular views over the Vale of Pickering. Super walks and cycle trails from the site.

→ Rawcliffe Bank Top Farm, Newton-on-Rawcliffe, Pickering, YO18 8QF, 07771 911039

54.3089, -0.7751 🍴🏕

66 LOW BELL END FARM CAMPING

Gloriously situated campsite on a small working farm near Rosedale Abbey with stupendous views across the valley to Thorgill. Glamping barn and charming shepherd's hut. Sorry, no kids.

→ 3 Bell End Grn, Rosedale Abbey, Pickering, YO18 8RE, 01751 417997

54.3628, -0.8994 🏕

67 THORNHILL FARM CAMPSITE

Small, peaceful camping and caravan club campsite with gorgeous views across the valley, where the occasional steam train chugs along.

→ Thornhill Farm, Goathland, YO22 5NW

54.3892, -0.7080 🏕

68 OAK TREE FARM PARK

Small, friendly campsite with free-range hens, pigs and goats. Good showers with honesty box. Campfires allowed. Lovely site for families with young kids.

→ Yatts Rd, Pickering, YO18 8JN, 01751 472124

54.2789, -0.7585 🏕🚲

69 CROSSDALE CAMPSITE, FARFIELDS FARM

Enjoy stunning sunsets over the valley at this tiny camping field. Flat pitches. Friendly hosts. Basic facilities: water, chemical disposal and EHU. CC club-certified site.

→ Farfields, Lockton, Pickering, YO18 7NQ, 01751 460239

54.2855, -0.7103 🏕

70 BANK HOUSE FARM HOSTEL

Bunk barn for up to 10 on a working organic farm in beautiful Glaisdale. Also basic camping barn, ideal for walkers and cyclists, and farmhouse B&B. Stunning location.

→ Bank House Farm Hostel, Glaisdale, YO21 2QA, 01947 897297

54.4234, -0.8174 🚲

71 SHEPHERD'S REST, STONEBECK GATE FARM

Gorgeous shepherd's hut for two by a trickling stream. Campfire, composting loo, basic shower and hot tub. Jill is a cook so hampers for guests are available. Also larger Keeper's Rest shepherd's hut for small families.

→ Fryup, Whitby, YO21 2NS, Book through Canopy & Stars
54.4383, -0.8996

72 LAWNSGATE CAMPING AND LLAMA TREKKING

Camping pitches, a yurt, a Romany wagon and a cosy chalet repurposed from an original game larder on a working farm. Amazing views over the Esk Valley. Fresh produce from the farm. Resident llamas, Tina, Debbie, Dolly and Cher, can accompany you on walks.

→ Shaw End, Lealholm, YO21 2AT, 07887 401023
54.4471, -0.8442

CABINS & COTTAGES

73 THE RIVER LODGE

Snuggle under sheepskin throws by the log burner or enjoy a moonlit soak in the outdoor copper bath at this romantic wooden cabin tucked away in a quiet corner of Egton Manor, overlooking the River Esk.

→ The Egton Estate, Egton Bridge, Whitby, YO21 1UY, 01947 895466
54.4357, -0.7603

74 FOREST HOLIDAYS CROPTON

The perfect place for forest bathing and starry nights, these secluded log cabins are situated in a woodland meadow, deep in Cropton Forest. Keldy Cabins are situated nearby.

→ Cropton, Pickering, YO18 8ES, 0333 0110495
54.3163, -0.8364

75 RAWCLIFFE HOUSE FARM HOLIDAY COTTAGES

Four 18th-century cottages and two studio rooms next to the owners' home. Idyllic location with plenty of space for kids to play and with goats and ducks to feed and eggs to collect.

→ Stape, Pickering, YO18 8JA, 01751 473292
54.3146, -0.7766

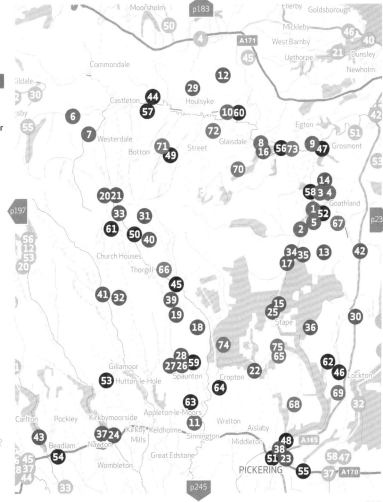

GREAT FORESTS & COAST

Our perfect weekend

→ **Crawl** through a smugglers' tunnel from the beach at Robin Hood's Bay

→ **Skinny-dip** beneath the double waterfall at the rocky cove of Hayburn Wyke

→ **Collect** driftwood to make a campfire at Osgodby Point, then wild camp in the woods

→ **Canoe** or stand-up paddleboard along the River Esk from Ruswarp and keep a lookout for herons and kingfishers

→ **Pack** a picnic and hike to the Lilla Cross, the oldest Christian monument in the north of England

→ **Bracken** bash your way to the summit of Blakey Topping, then hunt out the stone circle below

→ **Enjoy** an enchanting walk through Little Beck Wood to find a waterfall and a hermit's cave, then tuck into tea and cake at Falling Foss Tea Garden

→ **Take** in spectacular coastal scenery at Ravenscar, then explore the fascinating remains of the old alum works

From smugglers' tunnels, mysterious caves, surfing beaches and hidden coves to deep coniferous forests and pockets of ancient woodland, this is an area full of secret adventures.

This south-eastern corner of the North York Moors is marked out by the conifer plantations of Dalby, Wykeham, Langdale and Harwood Dale, which together form the North Riding Forest Park, the second largest in England. Dalby Forest is popular with cyclists and has hosted the UCI Mountain Biking World Cup. Its network of walking and cycling trails is so extensive that it is easy to find out-of-the-way places and hidden gems.

The wonderfully shaped sandstone rocks of the Bridestones stand atop Staindale Moor and have been sculpted by thousands of years of erosion from the elements. Happily, this wild, heather-clad moorland is not burnt to maximise grouse numbers, which means mosses and lichens thrive here. To the north lies the sacred hill of Blakey Topping, with the ruins of a stone circle, a place that remains off the radar for many but is well worth the climb for the stupendous views from the top.

In an area dominated by towering Sikta spruce and pines, there are still fragments of ancient woodland to be found: Raincliffe Woods with its glacial lake; Little Beck Wood with its own delightful waterfall, spectacular after heavy rain; and the lush wooded valley of Hayburn Wyke. The woods of Forge Valley link back to the ancient wildwoods, remnants of which still survive and are teeming with wildlife, including treecreepers, nuthatches, otters and crayfish. The majestic old horse chestnut, towering over the woodland canopy, is a wonderful place for children to stop and play.

These verdant uplands edge towards the coast, ending in precipitous cliffs at Robin Hood's Bay and a gradual slope towards the sandy beaches of Scarborough. This coastline was ideal for smuggling, with miles of secluded coves and caves to store contraband. Heavy import duties in the 18th and 19th centuries meant that tea, silk and tobacco were hauled in through secret subterranean passages. If you have the nerve, you can still crawl through one of these tunnels at Robin Hood's Bay.

The Cinder Track, the old railway route between Whitby and Scarborough, is a great off-road cycling or hiking trail. With a myriad of hidden rocky coves, this coastline is perfect for rock pooling and fossil hunting. Swimmers can enjoy a bracing early morning dip in the sea at one of Scarborough's lovely sandy bays and, for surfers, Cayton Bay has some of the best beach breaks on the east coast.

6

SECRET COVES

1 CROOK NESS

Victorians would come to gather rocks and stones for road building from this hidden rocky cove at the end of a ravine, carved out by years of ice and water. The beach is a mix of shale, sandstone and limestone outcrops containing fossilised plants and animals. Best explored at LT for rock pools.

→ Travelling N of Scarborough on the A171 to Burniston, turn R immediately after the Three Jolly Sailors pub. Continue on Field Ln, then take sharp R at kennels to limited parking. Follow paved path next to ravine to beach (not coastal path), then take stone steps to beach.

5 mins, 54.3263, -0.4215

2 CORNELIAN BAY

Sheltered, sandy beach situated beneath wooded cliffs. Rock pools and remains of WWII pillboxes. Generally peaceful, even on hot summer days.

→ From the A165 South Cliff roundabout, take the Filey Rd, then turn L into Cornelian Dr (YO11 3AL). Take second L to pumping station. Bear L on coast path and find wide gravel track down to beach.

10 mins, 54.2592, -0.3741

3 OSGODBY POINT, CAYTON BAY

Walk through a wooded valley to this isolated sandy beach at the north end of Cayton Sands, buffeted by the rocky headland of Knife Point. LT walk S along beach to Lucy's Shack for refreshments and clifftop surf school.

→ Continue SE along the Filey Rd to find footpath on L next to Knipe Point homes (YO11 3JT). Parking next R, Osgodby Way. At coast path bear R then take first L to beach.

15 mins, 54.2515, -0.3682

4 CLOUGHTON WYKE

Remote rocky beach with ledges just off the Cleveland Way coastal path and with good access from the Cinder Track cycle route. Great beach for fossil hunting, and plenty of opportunities for scrambling in Scarborough's most boulder-rich cove. Check tide times.

→ From the A171 in Cloughton, turn onto Newlands Rd (YO13 0AP, signed 'Staintondale'), then turn immediately R into Newlands Ln. Park at road end. Descend to coast path and bear R for 500m to find stream flowing down to Cloughton Wyke. Follow path carefully downstream. Explore far R of bay to find ledges good for snorkelling.

15 mins, 54.3409, -0.4307

5 HAYBURN WYKE

A picturesque, wooded valley leads to this magnificent rocky cove with its double waterfall and giant boulders. Children will love exploring the millions of colourful pebbles and rocks or spotting tiny sea creatures in the rock pools. The Hayburn Wyke Inn is recommended.

→ Turn off the A171 at Cloughton as for Cloughton Wyke (see listing) but continue towards Staintondale. After 1½ miles turn R for Hayburn Wyke Inn (YO13 0AU, 01723 870202). Parking at pub (fee, reimbursed if you eat/drink at pub). Follow signposted woodland path from car park down to sea.

20 mins, 54.3589, -0.4454

6 STOUPE BECK SANDS

Secluded sandy beach at the bottom of a flight of steps, which along with Boggle Hole forms part of Robin Hood's Bay.

→ Travelling S from Robin Hood's Bay on the A171, take L turn at the sign for the Falcon Inn, then L on to Stubbs Ln, signed 'Staintondale/Ravenscar'. Continue for just over 1 mile to junction and take L turn, signed 'Ravenscar'. Continue for 3 miles to small car park on L after Stoupe Bank Farm. Walk 300m down path and steps to beach.

Alternatively, follow the coastal path
S from Boggle Hole.
10 mins, 54.4174, -0.5226 ⬚⛰⚓ℹ️◎

7 BOGGLE HOLE

Small cove with carved-out hollows eroded
by the sea at the end of a wooded valley.
Smugglers once used the caves to hide their
contraband. The curious name comes from
local dialect for hobgoblin, the mischievous
tiny folk who lived in the sea caves here. Great
fossil hunting. The old watermill is now a hostel
and café, both recommended (see entry).

➔ 4 miles N of Cloughton (A171), take R
signed 'Boggle Hole'. Continue 2½ miles to
parking at corner (YO22 4UQ).
10 mins, 54.4242, -0.5284 ⚓ℹ️◎

8 SCALBY NESS SANDS

Two crescent-shaped bays at LT, with rocky
ledges and rock pools at HT. Stunning
stretch of coastline with views towards
Scarborough Castle and Oliver's Mount. Look
out for cormorants and oystercatchers.

➔ At LT it is possible to walk from
Scarborough's North Bay; otherwise follow
the A165 Burniston Rd N out of Scarborough.
After sharp R bend and bridge over Scalby
Beck, take immediate R to parking by pumping

station (54.3032, -0.4209). Follow footpath to
coastline and scramble down to beach.
10 mins, 54.3064, -0.4108 ◎⬛

9 RAVENSCAR OLD PEAK

This rocky promontory is home to large
colonies of seals. In June and July, you will
spot common seals, while in October and
November grey seals lounge around with
their pups. Sandy beach and rock pools. A LT
beach walk takes you to a pretty waterfall
and onto Stoupe Beck Sands. Keep your
distance from the seals.

➔ Roadside parking in Ravenscar. Follow the
rocky path between the Raven Hall Hotel and
NT shop to the golf course and a fingerpost.
Walk to the cliff edge to a steep path down to
the beach. Check tide times.
20 mins, 54.4063, -0.4940 ◎⚓ℹ️

WATERFALLS, RIVERS & LAKES

10 FALLING FOSS

Set in ancient woodland, this dramatic 10m
waterfall is steeped in myths. You will pass
smaller pools along babbling May Beck before
you reach the deeper plunge pool beneath the
falls. The walk to the base of the falls along the
beck is tricky, so good footwear is essential.

→ Follow the B1416 S from Whitby and turn R after 3 miles, signed 'Newton House/Falling Foss'. Follow Foss Ln for 1 mile to car park. Take footpath into the woods, signposted 'Hermitage', keeping R. Just before the Hermitage, take the L path down the slope along stone trods. Cross the first footbridge, then follow riverbed upstream to bottom of waterfall.
30 mins. 54.4190, -0.6327 🏊🚶

11 RUSWARP, RIVER ESK
Rent a canoe or rowing boat from Ruswarp Pleasure Boats and enjoy a lazy afternoon on the River Esk. You can use the slipway to launch your own canoe, kayak or stand-up paddleboard for a fee.
→ The Carrs, Ruswarp, Whitby, YO21 1RL, 01947 600109/07722113056. Follow the A169 from Sleights towards Whitby. On leaving village, turn R, signposted 'Ruswarp'. Roadside parking and boats after 1½ miles on R. Hire 10am – 4pm. Private launch from Duck Landing, 100m back along path. £5 per craft.
2 mins. 54.4687, -0.6342 🚣🏊

12 HACKNESS, RIVER DERWENT
A tranquil section of the Derwent flowing through beautiful Hackness, with a riverside footpath and little paths down to the river. Look out for kingfishers which nest here.
→ From Hackness, head S on Storr Ln, then turn L onto Mowthorp Rd for ½ mile. Before Everley, take R turn, crossing bridge to parking on L at Wrench Green. Cross road to follow riverside footpath and river access.
2 mins. 54.2957, -0.5137 🚶🏊🚶🏕🐕

13 NORTH YORKSHIRE WATER PARK, WYKEHAM
The largest natural water sports lake in North Yorkshire, with weekly open-water swimming sessions. Also stand-up paddleboarding, kayaking, wakeboarding and lakeside trails. Permits required for own stand-up paddleboards and kayaks. Picnicking by the lakeside. Café and gravel and grass camping pitches.
→ From Scarborough, follow the A170 in dir of Thirsk. Park entrance is 550m before village of Wykeham on L.
1 min. 54.2258, -0.4851 🏊🚶🐕🏕£

CASTLES & RUINS

14 AYTON CASTLE
Situated in a prominent position above the village, this ruined stone tower is all

that remains of an important medieval and post-medieval fortified keep. Earthworks surround the tower where the original buildings stood, and large rectangular depressions in the field to the R are the remains of the castle's fishponds, which were filled from the River Derwent.

→ Parking by the bridge in West Ayton (54.2489, -0.4858). Cross the road and head N up Yedmandale Rd to a footpath signposted 'Forge Valley'. The castle is through a gate at the end of this road. A scenic walk leads to the Forge Valley.

10 mins, 54.2539, -0.4880 🚉🏞

15 WYKEHAM ICE HOUSE

A restored 18th-century ice house near Fishpond Wood. The ice was removed from the pond when it was one-inch thick and brought to the chamber, where it was packed with straw to create an airtight seal, with more ice added as required. The path along the old railway track leads to the pretty village of Ruston Parva.

→ Follow the A170 E from Brompton-by-Sawdon to Wykeham. After the Dawnay Arms on the L, turn R to parking by café and buildings.

5 mins, 54.2376, -0.5212 🚶🚉

16 RAVENSCAR ALUM WORKS

Well-preserved alum works showing how the extraction process worked in this once thriving industry. Alum was an essential fixative for dyes in the 16th century. It was initially imported from Italy until a Papal monopoly cut off supply in the Reformation; the supply then switched to the North East, as fossils found on the Yorkshire coast were similar to those of the alum quarries of Europe. The works required 200 tonnes of human urine each year, often imported from as far as London. Spectacular coastal views.

→ From Whitby, follow the A171 S for 10 miles, then turn L into Gainforth Wath Rd to The Avenue in Ravenscar. Roadside parking in Ravenscar. Follow signs for Cleveland Way through woodland to alum works on R.

20 mins, 54.4056, -0.5019 🚶🏞🌳🏞🏕

17 SCARBOROUGH CASTLE

A natural fortress on a rocky promontory favoured by prehistoric settlers long before the 12th-century castle was built for Henry II and King John. The Romans sited one of their signal stations here, around ad 370, to send messages along the coast and to inland forts, warning of enemy invasion.

During the English Civil War, Scarborough was one of the only Royalist ports on the east coast until it was forced to surrender to Parliament in 1645. Panoramic views extend over the coastline, and it is the only place in town you can admire both north and south bays.

→ Parking on Marine Dr (seafront). Then follow winding path up from skatepark to castle. Anne Brontë's grave is in St Mary's Churchyard nearby.

10 mins, 54.2873, -0.3859 ⊞£◫◩⬚⊠

18 WWII RADAR STATION

Considered the best example of a coastal WWII Radar Station in the North East, it was constructed in 1941 to detect approaching shipping and aircraft using the experimental radar system, the Coastal Defence Chain Home Low. The shells of the four original buildings survive intact, including the fuel store, engine house, communications hut and transmitter/receiver block.

→ From Raven Hall, Ravenscar, follow the Cleveland Way S for 1 mile to radar station on R. Glorious coastal views over Ravenscar to Robin Hood's Bay.

25 mins, 54.3932, -0.4745 🚶◫◪✳❄✿

19 LILLA CROSS

The oldest Christian monument in the north of England stands on the Bronze Age barrow of Lilla Howe, at the junction of two medieval trackways: the Old Salt Road and the Pannierman's Way. It has superb views north-east towards Robin Hood's Bay and west across the moors. The 10th-century cross commemorates Lilla, one of Edwin of Northumbria's officers who was killed by a poison dagger as he stepped in to protect the king in ad 626. Find skylarks and common lizards darting among the heather, a pretty waterfall and solitude at Eller Beck en route.

→ Park as for Fen Bog (entry) at 54.3718, -0.6838. Cross road at bridge, go through gate and follow track E. Path becomes boggy. Persevere, keeping beck to your L and be aware of RAF Fylingdales signs on R. Can be accessed via the Moors and Coast cycle route and longer, easier path from Jugger Howe car park (54.3887, -0.5458) in poor weather.

60 mins, 54.3760, -0.6325 🚶◫⛲◪

20 STANDINGSTONES RIGG

Comprising 15 stones, this stone circle stands in a prominent position near the top

of a gentle, south-west facing slope. The stones, originally totalling 24, measure between 40cm and 1.2m high and lean outwards or have toppled. This whole area is populated with prehistoric ritual and burial sites, as well as field systems and cairns.

→ From Cloughton, follow the A171 N for 2½ miles to roadside parking on L next to forestry track (54.3630, -0.4910). Walk SW along the track for 300m, then find grass track on L following fence line. Circle is 300m along, immediately behind fence through metal gate on private land.
25 mins, 54.3588, -0.4895 🖼🕇♻

21 T'AWD ABBA WELL, HAWSKER

This 18th-century red-brick roadside well house also goes by the more prosaic Old Boiling Well. Its Yorkshire dialect moniker suggests a more sacred history. In the 19th century water was piped from here to a reservoir in the grounds of Whitby Abbey to provide a clean water supply to parts of Whitby. It may have once fed the ponds at Whitby Abbey.

→ From High Hawkser, take the B1447 S towards Robin Hood's Bay for ¾ mile. The well is on the L side of the road. Parking is tricky but possible for a short stop on the verge just before the well on the R at a gap in the hedge.
1 min, 54.4531, -0.5565 🕇

22 BLAKEY TOPPING & STONE CIRCLE

Believed to be a sacred hill, Blakey Topping has the ruins of a stone circle, or alignment, lying several hundred metres to its south. Some stones may have been lost, making it hard to identify their original symbolism. The hill is a fun bracken-bashing climb. Fabulous views over Dalby Forest and Fylingdales.

→ From Pickering take the A169 towards Whitby. Park on R at Hole of Horcum. Walk N along roadside for 60m, then follow footpath E for 1 mile until track splits. Bear L through farmyard at Newgate Foot to a stream and gate into the field. The stones are in front of you and Blakey Topping is ahead.
30 mins, 54.3288, -0.6606 🖼🕇♻🌄🐾

23 ALL SAINT'S CHURCH, BROMPTON-BY-SAWDON

Poet William Wordsworth married his childhood friend, Mary Hutchinson, here on 4 October 1802. A copy of their marriage certificate is framed inside the church and a variety of wild daffodil, *narcissus lobularis*, has been planted in the churchyard in his honour. Sir George Cayley, father of aviation, is buried here. It would be easy to drive by and miss this delightful place, which overlooks fishponds and has a mill pond and pretty beck for paddling and picnics.

→ From the A170, turn R into Cayley Lane at Brompton-by-Sawdon. Continue through village, over small bridge, and turn R into Malpas Rd and parking by beck (54.2234, -0.5532). For church, follow beck and footpath to L of fishponds.

5 mins, 54.2261, -0.5551 🚶🏊⛺✝

CAVES & TUNNELS

24 THE HERMITAGE, FALLING FOSS

Located in a fairy-tale woodland near Falling Foss waterfall, the Hermitage is carved out of an enormous boulder and dates back to the 18th century. It was once the home of a hermit, who lived his life foraging for food and fuel in the surrounding woods.

→ Follow the B1416 S from Whitby and turn R after 3 miles, signed 'Newton House/Falling Foss'. Follow lane for 1 mile to car park. Continue down through woods on foot. Follow circular woodland path past tearooms to Hermitage.

25 mins, 54.4247, -0.6361 🚶⛺🏊☕

25 KING ALFRED'S CAIRN, CHAFER WOOD

Near the entrance to these lovely woods is King Alfred's Cairn, the site of a natural cave used as a burial chamber in Neolithic times,

which has its own enchanting story. King Alfred of Northumbria is said to have taken shelter here after defeat in battle in ad 705, and a commemorative monument was built in 1790. Walk through the woodland of characterful ash trees to reveal magnificent views over the Vale of Pickering. Bluebells in spring. Mosses and ferns in winter. Great year-round picnic spot.

→ From Pickering, head E on the A170 to Ebberston. Pass The Grapes Inn on R, then turn L up a narrow road. Parking on L at entrance to wood. Follow footpath to a clearing on R to find cairn (54.2375, -0.6219)

20 mins, 54.2366, -0.6214 🏊🚶📷✝🌲

26 SMUGGLERS' TUNNELS, ROBIN HOOD'S BAY

This secret tunnel was once used by smugglers to shift contraband, which had been rowed ashore, into one of the village's higgledy-piggledy houses above. A small ledge, which soon peters out, leads to a steeper passage with a boarded, beamed roof, most likely beneath a house, before it opens out into a steep moss-and-fern-covered gully.

→ From the Bay Hotel, walk down the slipway onto the beach and the tunnel is immediately to the L. Low ceiling and rocky, uneven floor. Torch necessary.

2 mins, 54.4303, -0.5320 📷📧🏊🔦ℹ🔦

27

28

29

ROCKS & HILLTOPS

27 BRIDESTONES, DALBY FOREST

Teetering sandstone boulders high on the moors, surrounded by ancient trees, open heather moorland and wildflowers. The Bridestones are, in fact, what remains of a much higher sandstone cap. Sheets of hard sandstone alternating with softer calcareous layers have been eroded over thousands of years, resulting in their peculiar shapes. Plenty of scrambling and bouldering. Look out for the Pepper Pot and the Tunnel at the High Bridestones. Spectacular views.

→ From Thornton Dale head N on Whitby Gate. After 1½ miles, turn R at Dalby The Great Yorkshire Forest sign. Continue to Dalby Forest Dr (toll road £). Park at Staindale car park. Follow marked footpath up to Low Bridestones and further on to High Bridestones.

35 mins, 54.3107, -0.6601

28 JONNO'S FIELD

A little corner of Yorkshire which is forever Easter Island. An unlikely setting on the edge of a housing estate but persevere to seek out this surprising green space. It is worth a visit for the sensational views of Scarborough Castle, the rooftops and the coastline alone, but the added highlight is the circle of eight extraordinary wooden sculptures modelled on the Moai statues found on Easter Island, almost 8,500 miles away in the Pacific.

→ From Scarborough, follow the A171 N on Scalby Rd, then turn R on to Woodland Ravine. Turn L onto Prospect Mount Rd and continue on to Barrowcliff Road for parking at 54.2864, -0.4234 at junction with Redcliffe Rd. From here find green gate up hill on R into field and statues. Also accessible from the Cinder Track.

5 mins, 54.2888, -0.4260

29 CINDER TRACK, RAVENSCAR

The highest point on the off-road Cinder Track and one of the best coastal viewing points for unrivalled views across Fylingdales Moor and the red-tiled rooftops of Robin Hood's Bay.

→ Follow the A171 N from Scarborough for 9 miles, then turn R onto Scarborough Rd and Raven Hall Rd for 1½ miles to parking on L. Head towards visitor centre, then take L to join Cinder Track.

15 mins, 54.4074, -0.5064

ANCIENT TREES & FORESTS

30 HORSE CHESTNUT, FORGE VALLEY

Situated next to the River Derwent in the
ancient woods of the Forge Valley, this
impressive horse chestnut reaches almost
35m tall and has a substantial 7m girth. A rope
swing hanging from the tree, with another
dangling over the river, makes this a fun place
for kids. There was once a forge here and
the woods were coppiced to smelt the locally
mined ironstone. The woods are teeming with
wildlife. Trails through the woods along the
boardwalk from Old Man's Mouth Picnic Site.

→ Take the A170 S from Scarborough to East
Ayton. After church on R, take next turn R,
signposted 'Forge Valley'. Park in lay-by on L
after 700m, near tree.

1 min, 54.2559, -0.4828 🐕🅿🚼♿🧍

31 RAINCLIFFE WOODS & THROXENBY MERE

A steep-sided coniferous and broad-leaved
woodland, remnants of which have covered
this area for 1,000 years, bordering the
remains of a large glacial lake. Holloways and
a Bronze Age dyke system cross the path
near Throxenby Mere (Cock Hollow 54.2846,
-0.4557). Makeshift tree swings dangle over
the valley side.

→ From Scarborough, follow the A171 Scalby
Rd for 2 miles, then turn L onto Lady Edith's Dr
to Low Rd and mere and woods.

1 min, 54.2849, -0.4507 🚶🐕🍴🅿♿🏕

32 DALBY FOREST

Dalby Forest's 3,575 hectares of woodland
covers the southern slopes of the North York
Moors. Here there are hiking trails, mountain
bike tracks, babbling streams and picnic and
BBQ areas. It is also a Dark Sky Discovery
Site with Milky Way status, meaning it is
among the darkest sites in the country and
the Milky Way is visible to the naked eye.

→ Follow the A169 Pickering to Whitby road.
Look out for the brown Dalby Forest signs.
Parking is at the Low Dalby visitor centre
(toll road).

5 mins, 54.2786, -0.6882 💷🐕🚼♿📷

CAFÉS & TEAROOMS

33 THE FOULSYKE

Rustic coffee house and bistro in a converted
farmhouse serving excellent food all day.
Full English breakfasts and mouth-watering
pancake stacks, Sunday lunches and evening
meals. Relaxed atmosphere and impeccable
service. Also B&B.

→ The Foulsyke Farmhouse, Barmoor Ln, Scalby, YO13 0PG, 01723 507423
54.3070, -0.4515 🍴

34 FALLING FOSS TEAROOMS

Savour delicious homemade cakes and lunches from the rustic forest cabin while relaxing at one of the wooden tables at this magical tea garden by Falling Foss waterfall.

→ Midge Hall, Whitby, YO22 5JD, 07723 477929
54.4187, -0.6326 🍴

35 YEW TREE CAFÉ, SCALBY

Lovely café in the centre of Scalby serving excellent homemade food, including hearty breakfasts (served until 3.30pm), light lunches and mouth-watering cakes.

→ High St, Scalby, YO13 0PT, 01723 367989
54.3001, -0.4483 🍴

36 WATERMARK CAFÉ

With stunning views out to sea and towards Scarborough Castle, this is the place to come for a post-swim or surf treat.

→ Royal Albert Dr, Scarborough, YO12 7TY, 01723 506506
54.2921, -0.4062 🍴

37 HIP'N'SQUARE PIZZERIA

Small pizzeria tucked away behind the bike shed – a bike repair shop. Relaxed ambience, delicious pizzas, tapas and ale. The Loft, a luxury apartment sleeping 6, is above.

→ The Square, Maltongate, Thornton-le-Dale, YO18 7LF, 01751 476633
54.2363, -0.7220

FARM SHOPS & LOCAL FOOD

38 WYKEHAM MARKET

Thriving farmers market showcasing the best locally reared, sourced and produced goods, with a good turnout of stalls, including a fishmonger, baker, butcher and cheesemaker, as well as fruit and vegetables. Country inn and tearooms nearby. Fri 8am – 1pm.

→ Car park of Downe Arms, Wykeham, YO13 9QB, 01723 866600
54.2370, -0.5224 🍴

39 STEPNEY HILL FARM SHOP

Farm shop and café selling high-quality meat and local produce, surrounded by acres of clover, grass and wildflower paddocks where Swaledale sheep graze and Tamworth pigs roam.

→ Stepney Rd, Scarborough, YO12 5NL, 01723 373 443
54.2710, -0.4374 🍴

40 BETTON FARM SHOP

Friendly farm shop and tearoom run by a local charity. Sandwiches to order for your picnic and takeaway drinks. Bottled beers brewed by on-site North Riding Micro Brewery. Farm animals, bee farm and children's play area. Camping, camper and caravan pitches.

→ Racecourse Rd, East Ayton, Scarborough, YO13 9HT, 01723 863143
54.2547, -0.4667 🍴🛒

41 TREE TOP PRESS

Cider press, micro bakery and farm shop stocking cider, fruit cordials, honey, fruit and veg, plus store cupboard essentials. Free-range local meat. Open Wed 9.30am – 12.30pm and Fri 9.30am – 12pm.

→ Hillcrest Cottage, Suffield, Scarborough, YO13 0BJ, 07713 966990
54.3037, -0.4834 🍴

42 RADFORD BUTCHERS

Great place to stock up on goodies en route to the coast. High-quality meat, including free-range pork and also fresh fruit and vegetables, bread, cheeses and scrumptious award-winning pork pies.

→ 81 Coach Rd, Sleights, Whitby, YO22 5EH, 01947 810229
54.4551, -0.6644 🍴

43 JACKSON A P BUTCHERS

Don't be surprised to find a small queue for the hot bacon and sausage sandwiches at this friendly, traditional butcher's. Top-quality meat and amazing pork pies.

→ 10 High St, Ruswarp, Whitby, YO21 1NH, 01947 820085
54.4714, -0.6293 🍴

44 GLAVES B W & DJ BUTCHERS

Buy pork and lamb reared on the family farm as well as delicious pies, made from a secret family recipe, at this super friendly village butcher's that has scooped the best Yorkshire butcher award. Also fruit, vegetables, bread, eggs and locally brewed ales.

→ 37 Cayley Ln, Brompton-by-Sawdon, Scarborough, YO13 9DL, 01723 859523
54.2258, -0.5526 🍴

45 COD AND LOBSTER, SCARBOROUGH

You won't find fresher fish and shellfish than the recently caught offerings at this friendly, independent wet fish shop on West Pier. Also hot smoked salmon and mackerel, kippers and dressed crab. Open Thu to Sat 9am – 3.30pm

→ West Pier, Scarborough, YO11 1PD, 01723 374102
54.2833, -0.3921 🍴

WILDER CAMPING

46 HOOKS HOUSE FARM

Enjoy fantastic coastal views from your tent at this campsite near Robin Hood's Bay. A 10-minute walk through the fields takes you to the village with its quaint pubs and sandy beach with rock pools. No campfires. BBQs for cooking only.

→ Whitby Rd, Whitby, YO22 4PE, 01947 880283
54.4383, -0.5435 ⛺

47 LOW FARM CAMPSITE

Off-grid camping in a beautiful hidden valley by a babbling beck near Dalby Forest. On Saturdays tuck into stone-fired pizzas and cheesecake. With some of the darkest night skies in the country, look out for shooting stars. Limited mobile coverage and no Wi-Fi or EHU; this is the place to unplug from the modern world.

→ Ellerburn Rd, Ellerburn, Thornton-le-Dale, YO18 7LL, 01751 470208
54.2463, -0.7094 ⛺

48 BAY NESS FARM

Wake up to spectacular coastal views at this rustic clifftop campsite overlooking Robin Hood's Bay. Perfectly located for the Cinder Track and beach.

→ High Ln, Robin Hood's Bay, Whitby, YO22 4PJ
54.4425, -0.5313 ⛺

49 LOUND HOUSE FARM CARAVAN SITE

Rustic campsite with spectacular views over Whitby and the abbey ruins. Spacious pitches with basic facilities: toilets but no showers.

→ Littlebeck Ln, Whitby, YO22 5HY, 01947 810383
54.4458, -0.6288 ⛺

50 HIGH YEDMANDALE FARM CAMPSITE

Small, peaceful campsite with super views towards the coast. Basic but clean facilities. Friendly hosts. Resident hens, peacocks and geese.

→ Yedmandale Rd, West Ayton, YO13 9JZ, 01723 862188
54.2667, -0.5108 ⛺

51

51 MR MALCOLM'S MARVELLOUS CAMPING FIELD

Park up and transport your camping gear in a wheelbarrow to your chosen pitch at this small off-grid campsite for tents only. Hot showers and composting loo. Communal campfire and spectacular sunsets. Children over 12 only. No pets.

→ Partridge Nest Farm, Whitby, YO22 5ES, 07445 027516
54.4443, -0.6875 ⛺🔥

GLAMPING

52 PINEWOOD PARK, SCARBOROUGH

Wild West–themed site with tipis, cowboy shacks and wagons. You can also pitch your own tent or camper. Two-mile footpath to Scarborough. Same rate all year round.

→ Racecourse Rd, Scarborough, YO12 5TG, 07360 495607
54.2650, -0.4385 🏕⛺

53 ALUM HOUSE GLAMPING

Trio of boutique bell tents tucked away by the riverside in the delightful hamlet of Littlebeck. Stoves, outdoor kitchens, fire pits and stargazing from the wood-fired hot tub.

48

53

→ Alum House, Littlebeck, Whitby, YO22 5EY, 07456 523232
54.4267, -0.6634

54 HIGH LANGDALE HIDEAWAY

Gorgeous hand-built off-grid shepherd's hut, three miles from the nearest road in a beautiful, remote location. Super views over the North York Moors, and on a clear night you might spot the Milky Way. Campfire cooking, eco hot shower and compost loo. Sorry, no kids.

→ West Side Rd, Broxa, YO13 0LD, Airbnb
54.3357, -0.5768

55 MEADOWBECK SHEPHERD'S HUTS

Unwind in Deer's Leap and Hide and Sea, two insulated off-grid shepherd's huts situated in an idyllic meadow setting with handcrafted beds and wood burners. Rainwater shower and eco loo. Superb location close to Robin Hood's Bay.

→ Barnacres, Whitby, YO22 4QH, 01947 881274
54.3954, -0.5687

56 DALBY GLAMPING WAGON

Quirky glamping wagon, which could be home to a circus troupe, made from a reclaimed trailer and materials and kitted out in a Bohemian vintage style. Gas and oil lamp lighting. Magnificent views and tons of space for exploring.

→ Bickley Rigg Farm, Scarborough, YO13 0LL, 07854 908737
54.3149, -0.5836

57 COAST AND CAMPLIGHT

Completely off-grid woodland camp with individually designed safari tents with log burners, al fresco kitchen and hot showers. Laze in a hammock or paddle in the beck before snuggling up by the campfire beneath pristine dark skies.

→ Low Rigg Farm, Stainsacre, Whitby, YO22 4LP, 07415 655046
54.4445, -0.5895

58 GUMBOOTS AND WELLINGTONS

Choose from a shepherd's hut or a Skandi-inspired garden den at this rustic retreat in a secluded valley on the edge of Dalby Forest. Yummy breakfast supplies include granola, locally pressed apple juice, and toast and jam. Riverside walks and evenings spent beneath star-studded skies.

→ Ellerburn, Pickering, YO18 7LL, 01751 475703
54.2467, -0.7096

CABINS & HOSTELS

59 BOGGLE HOLE YHA

Converted watermill tucked away in an old smugglers' cove. Kids will love the pirate-themed decor of the original building or choose the eco-friendly Crow's Nest annexe. It's a 10-minute LT beach walk to Robin Hood's Bay. Also houses the cosy Quarterdeck Café.

→ Mill Beck, Whitby, YO22 4UQ, 0345 3719504
54.4228, -0.5313

60 BIKE AND BOOT INN

Contemporary hostel where your dog is as welcome as your surfboard or bike. Easy-going atmosphere and fabulous sea views. Washing/drying area for bikes/surfboards/boots/dogs, etc., and cycle repair station in the Wadobi. Bar and restaurant.

→ Cliff Bridge Terrace, Scarborough, YO11 2HA, 01723 655555
54.2798, -0.3992

61 WHITBY LOG CABINS

Rustic log cabins in a romantic woodland setting with cosy wood burners and a chiminea to keep you toasty on the terrace. Stream and waterfall and a haven for wildlife. Sorry, no kids.

→ Valley View Golden Grove, Glen Esk Rd, Whitby, YO22 5HH, 07962 505906
54.4636, -0.6024

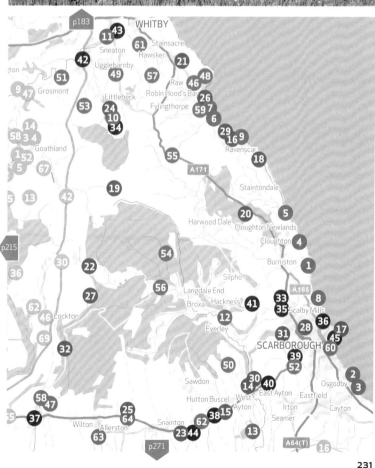

62 GALLOWS HILL BUNK BARN

Large two-storey beamed barn, sleeping
20, with lovely rear garden and views at
the former home of Mary Hutchinson,
who married poet William Wordsworth
in the local church. Ideal for large family
gatherings. Also B&B.

→ Gallows Hill, Gallows Hill Ln, Brompton-by-
Sawdon, YO13 9QF, 07494 964477
54.2326, -0.5409

COSY COTTAGES

63 OLD STATION, ALLERSTON

Quirky holiday accommodation in the
former Ebberston station on the old Forge
Valley Line. Stay in one of three self-
catering carriages or the Ticket Office.
Plenty of space for kids to play. Picnic
tables and BBQ.

→ Allerston, Pickering, YO18 7PG,
01723 859024
54.2255, -0.6532

64 CLIFF HOUSE COTTAGES

Cluster of five pretty stone cottages in the
grounds of an 18th-century manor house
with delightful gardens. Children will love
playing hide and seek in the ancient hollow
yew tree. Communal woodland fire pit and
heated indoor pool.

→ Ebberston, Vale of Pickering, YO13 9PA,
01723 859440
54.2354, -0.6216

HOWARDIAN HILLS

Our perfect weekend

→ **Cross** the wooden footbridge to the island at Howsham Mill for a picnic and swim in the River Derwent

→ **Hike** through the woods to Mount Snever Observatory and keep an eye out for wild ponies on the way

→ **Paddle** the River Derwent through the tranquil Kirkham Gorge and look out for herons, cormorants and, if you're lucky, an otter

→ **Pop** into Talbot Yard for an artisan coffee at Roost and marvel at the array of ice-cream flavours at Groovy Moos

→ **Relive** *Brideshead Revisited* with a walk past ancient oaks to the Temple of the Four Winds

→ **Wind** your way around the City of Troy, the smallest turf maze in Europe

→ **Lose** yourself in the woods at Baxby Manor with a night spent in the fairy-tale Rufus's Roost

→ **Discover** age-old trees, secret glades and wildflower meadows at the Yorkshire Arboretum

Rolling wooded hills, a mosaic of arable and pasture fields, scenic river valleys, honey-stone villages and historic country houses set in 18th-century parkland are all features of this Area of Outstanding Natural Beauty.

Sited as they are on the doorstep of the North York Moors and within easy reach of the Wolds and the Vale of York, the Howardian Hills are an excellent base for outdoor adventures, including walking, cycling, horse riding and fishing. You will find plenty of places to stay and eat and drink – after all, the food capital of Yorkshire is Malton with its artisan producers, independent shops, cafés and celebrated food lovers' festival.

The Howardian Hills stretch from Helmsley and Coxwold, on the edge of the North York Moors National Park, down to Kirkham Priory and the River Derwent, interspersed with several large country estates, including Castle Howard, Hovingham and Nunnington. These great houses are popular visitor attractions; their legacy is evident in the follies and monuments scattered across the landscape. Leave the crowds behind and have a picnic in a meadow beneath the Temple of the Four Winds, looking across at the mausoleum, or stand at the Exclamation Gates and admire the view that Queen Victoria enjoyed on her visit here in 1850.

Before these grand estates were established, it was the monasteries that dominated and shaped this landscape. Kirkham Priory and Byland Abbey are glorious ruins to explore, while Ampleforth Abbey is still a Benedictine monastery. It has the last sizeable monastery orchard in Britain, which is open to visitors, and the apples are pressed in its own cider mill.

This area contains a beautiful stretch of the River Derwent; it is a designated SSSI from Malton to its confluence with the River Ouse due to its outstanding array of wildlife, including river lamprey, otters, water voles and yellow water lilies. The relic wet pasture of tiny Jeffrey Bog lies in the tranquil setting of the deeply carved Kirkham Gorge and has an impressive variety of wildflowers, including purple orchids and betony in spring and summer.

A kayak or stand-up paddleboard adventure from Malton to Kirkham Abbey passes through the spectacular scenery of this ancient glacial gorge. The ruins of the priory provide a wonderful backdrop for a wild swim eye to eye with damselflies and dragonflies feeding on the water. Afterwards, spread out a rug on the grassy bank and tuck into a picnic of cheeses, meat, fruit and crackers, washed down with hand-pressed apple juice from local artisan producers.

2

RIVERS & LAKES

1 KIRKHAM, RIVER DERWENT

A beautiful stretch of the river as it meanders through the Derwent Valley past the ruins of Kirkham Priory. Grassy bank with steepish access to the river next to an overhanging tree. The bridge is a popular jumping spot with locals, who plunge into the pool below in summer. The Stone Trough pub is just up the hill.

➜ Travelling E from York on the A64, after the R turn for Barton, continue up hill and filter R, signposted 'Kirkham', onto Onhams Ln. Cross railway crossing to parking over bridge by abbey. Return over bridge to gate on L to access riverbank.

5 mins, 54.0827, -0.8801 🏊🛶🍴⛱

2 MALTON TO KIRKHAM, RIVER DERWENT

This beautiful river journey is around seven miles of fairly easy kayaking from Malton through the spectacular scenery of Kirkham Gorge to the 13th-century ruins of Kirkham Priory.

➜ From the A64, take the L exit towards Helmsley. Continue on York Rd (B1248), then turn R onto Railway St. Turn R before doctor's surgery onto Riverside View and roadside parking past the houses at the end of the road at 54.1318, -0.8008. Walk over banking to river and slipway.

5 mins, 54.1315, -0.8036 🏊🛶

3 RIVER RYE, NUNNINGTON

A tranquil stretch of the river just below the riverside path. Grass bank with easy entry into water and deeper water to the R for swimming. Deep pool further downstream by the old railway bridge.

➜ From Helmsley, follow the A170 towards Thirsk for ½ mile, then turn L onto the B1257 for 4 miles. Turn L after Birch Farm onto Lack Ln for ½ mile. Roadside parking with care. Walk past East Newton Hall to riverside footpath. Either cross ford or turn L to footbridge to cross over, then double back to swim spot.

20 mins, 54.2136, -1.0150 🏊🐾⛱

4 HOWSHAM MILL

Small island next to a Georgian Gothic watermill across a wooden bridge. Ladder access to river just past Archimedes Screw and weir (popular with kayakers). The island is occasionally closed for educational events.

➜ Follow the A64 E from York for 9 miles. Take R turn just before caravan showroom, signposted 'Harton'. Follow road for 1 mile, then turn R out of village. Continue straight for 1 mile. Parking on R just over bridge. Walk under bridge with river on L. Cross footbridge to island. The ladder is under the bank in a little hollow further along the island, past the buildings, in the woods.

10 mins, 54.0558, -0.8865 🏊🛶⛱

5 GILLING LAKES

Secluded lakes hidden in the woods down a country lane. This is the largest, known as the 'lower fish pond', with two others located further into the woods. You will find a number of wooden jetties stretching out into the water around the perimeter of the lake.

➜ From Gilling East, follow the road (Pottergate) past the Fairfax Arms as it becomes a narrower lane. Continue to the end for limited parking or park in the car park on the L by the cottages and walk to reach the footpath. Follow the footpath into the woods to the lake just ahead. For the other two lakes, follow the lakeside footpath on the L.

5 mins, 54.1816, -1.0969 🏊⛱

6 OULSTON RESERVOIR

A secluded freshwater lake and the source of the River Foss, a tributary of

the Ouse, which rises in Foss Crooks Woods near the reservoir.

→ From Yearsley village, take North Moor Ln, then turn L, signposted 'Oulston', for 1 mile. Park in lay-by on L at 54.1663, -1.1307. Walk up road to footpath sign on L. Follow track towards Pond Head Farm and turn R through kissing gate. Follow footpath beside the field then into woods. Reservoir is just off path on L. Technically no swimming but locals do.
20 mins, 54.1616, -1.1354

RUINS & FOLLIES

7 MOUNT SNEVER OBSERVATORY

Hidden in the trees on the edge of an escarpment overlooking Oldstead, this intriguing stone tower was built during the first year of Queen Victoria's reign in 1838 for John Wormald, son of the Lord Mayor of York. In the 19th century visitors climbed the tower for views of York Minster and beyond; it has since been used for stargazing. A wooden ladder gives access to a platform. Wild Exmoor ponies graze along the route.

→ Parking by Wass village hall (YO61 4AX). Walk downhill 180m to crossroads and turn R along road that turns into track through

woods. Keep bearing R through woodland. Turn L after footpath sign on R.
35 mins, 54.2170, -1.1777

8 TEMPLE OF THE FOUR WINDS, CASTLE HOWARD

Amble past Castle Howard's ancient oaks to reach this idyllic picnic spot at the foot of Vanbrugh's Temple of the Four Winds with its distant views over rolling landscape towards Hawksmoor's Mausoleum. Just across the whimsical New River Bridge is the Pyramid. On a hot day, cool off in the river at a shallow spot by the bridge.

→ Parking by village hall in Coneysthorpe (YO60 7DD). Cross road and turn L for 50m to white gateposts and follow adjacent footpath marked 'Welburn'. Turn R at fork onto path alongside Ray Wood, past ancient oaks. Pass through gate to meadow beneath Temple of the Four Winds.
20 mins, 54.1208, -0.8963

9 EXCLAMATION GATES

Two pillars framing a sensational reveal of Castle Howard on the horizon, with additional views either side of the follies and monuments across the estate. Their name derives from the cries of astonishment

from visitors, including Queen Victoria, as they approached the grand house from this original road from York.

→ From roadside parking in Welburn (54.1028, -0.8977), look for crossroads at E of village. Follow road uphill towards church, then follow path edging field for 500m to stone pillars at top for stupendous views. Follow bridleway along ridge line to return to village or retrace your steps and pop into the Crown & Cushion for refreshments.

10 mins, 54.0984, -0.9000 🚶🖼️📷

10 SHERIFF HUTTON CASTLE

Imposing ruins of a late 14th-century castle, once the grandest fortress in the north of England. It was the principal base of the 'Kingmaker', Richard Neville, Earl of Warwick, in the mid-15th century. After his death in 1471, it was seized by the Crown and granted to Richard, Duke of Gloucester, later Richard III. In 1525 Henry VIII gave the castle to his illegitimate son, Henry Fitzroy. A short circular walk follows the perimeter of the castle. Head to the church to see the tomb of Richard III's son and site of the original castle (see entry).

→ Park by post office on Main St in Sheriff Hutton (YO60 6SS). Follow footpath sign to L

of Castle Farm around castle perimeter for ½ mile.

20 mins, 54.0880, -1.0053 🚶🖼️🏃

11 SLINGSBY CASTLE

Ruins of a 17th-century Jacobean mansion built for Sir Charles Cavendish, grandson of Bess of Hardwick, on the site of a 13th-century moated castle. The house was never lived in, as Sir Charles chose the wrong side in the Civil War and fled to the continent in 1644.

→ From Malton, take the B1257 towards Helmsley. At Slingsby turn R into High St. Park next to castle on L. No access to ruins, but for a 1½-mile circular walk around the castle, take footpath by Castle Farm to Fryton. Turn R at Fryton and follow road to disused railway track. Turn R back to Slingsby.

2 mins, 54.1651, -0.9353 🚶🖼️

SACRED & ANCIENT

12 CITY OF TROY

The smallest turf maze in Europe often goes unnoticed sitting beside a remote country lane. Such turf labyrinths were once widespread throughout the British Isles, the old Germanic Empire and Scandinavia, but

this is one of only eight remaining in England. It measures just 8m by 6.5m and its exact age remains a mystery, with predictions ranging from the Viking Age or the Middle Ages to the 19th century. Whatever its true age, it is an atmospheric location.

→ Follow the B1363 out of Brandsby to crossroads. Turn R, signposted 'Terrington/ Dalby'. Then turn sharp L. Continue for 1 mile past a small wood on R. You will see the maze surrounded by a low wooden railing.

1 min, 54.1392, -1.0444 🖼🖼🖼

13 KIRKHAM PRIORY

Riverside ruins of an Augustinian priory nestled in the tranquil Derwent Valley. Note the heraldic carvings on the elaborate 14th-century gatehouse. During World War II, Kirkham was used by the military for testing equipment in preparation for the 1944 D-Day landings. Visitors to the top-secret base included Prime Minister Winston Churchill. Great place for kids to explore. Picnic spot and swimming by the river (see entry).

→ 5 miles SW of Malton (YO60 7JS). Heading S on the A64 towards York, turn L for Kirkham Abbey. Cross railway line and bridge to car park on R.

1 min, 54.0829, -0.8768 🖼🖼🖼🖼🖼🖼

14 BYLAND ABBEY

From inauspicious beginnings, only finding a permanent home in this tranquil setting after 43 years, Byland Abbey became one of the largest of the Cistercian orders in Britain. It is a magnificent example of early Gothic architecture; the towering remains of the great rose window on the west wall of the abbey church inspired the design for York Minster's rose window. The 13th-century floor tiles in the south transept of the church are the most extensive collection found anywhere today. Kids love playing hide and seek here. The Byland Abbey Inn is opposite.

→ From Wass, follow Wass Bank Rd in dir of Coxwold. Abbey is on L after ½ mile. Small car park.

2 mins, 54.2032, -1.1592 🖼🖼🖼🖼🖼🖼

15 ST HELEN AND THE HOLY CROSS

The only English parish church to contain a tomb of a member of the royal family. Edward Middleham, Prince of Wales, son of Richard III, died suddenly in 1484 destroying all hope of an easy succession and prolonging the War of the Roses. A gate in the SE corner of the graveyard leads to earthworks associated with the Norman

motte and bailey castle that preceded the 14th-century castle in the village centre. An enchanting location for a picnic, with wildlife, birdsong and wildflowers in summer.

→ Park by post office on Main St in Sheriff Hutton (YO60 6SS). Follow road E to church.
5 mins, 54.0883, -0.9964 🐾🎋👥✝

16 ST PETER'S CHURCH, DALBY

Tiny 12th-century church that looks more like a Northumbrian pele tower with its huge stone chancel and stepped buttresses and battlements, added in the 15th century. Pretty churchyard with magnificent views across the Howardian Hills.

→ Follow the B1363 out of Brandsby to crossroads. Turn R, signposted 'Terrington/ Dalby'. Then turn sharp L. Continue for 2 miles to R turn to church and parking.
2 mins, 54.1329, -1.0263 📷✝🎋

17 STONEGRAVE MINSTER

A tiny church with a grand name; it is in fact the smallest minster in the country whose origins date back to ad 757. A 10th-century Saxon wheel head cross, decorated with Celtic interlace and sculptural panels depicting biblical scenes, stands near the south door. The church was rebuilt in Norman times, around 1141, with later additions through to the 15th century.

→ Travelling from Hovingham to Helmsley on the B1257, the church is on the S side of this road (signed) as you enter Stonegrave. Turn off the road onto a narrow lane. The minster is straight ahead. There is just enough space to park here.
1 min, 54.1925, -0.9966 🎋✝

GARDENS, TREES & NATURE

18 YORKSHIRE ARBORETUM, CASTLE HOWARD

Wander off the beaten track to explore peaceful glades, hidden ponds, wildflower meadows and age-old trees with stories to tell at this lovely arboretum with more than 6,000 trees from around the world. The perimeter path towards Sata Pond is a delightful trail with enormous veteran sweet chestnuts growing on the ancient bank that surrounded the medieval deer park linked to Henderskelfe Castle. Head to the lesser-visited Sand Banks area to seek out the enchanting fly agaric fungi. Spectacular for autumn colour and beautiful spring blossom. Open Feb to Nov 10am – 4pm. Nice café with great views.

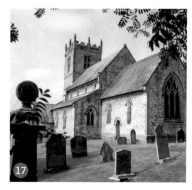

21

19

20

→ From the A64, follow signs for Castle Howard. At roundabout take first exit to Yorkshire Arboretum parking.
2 mins, 54.1183, -0.9219 ⛴🚶🧗🧺👣🍴🚻🐾

19 SHANDY HALL GARDENS
Delightful two-acre garden, where 18th-century author Laurence Stern wrote *Tristram Shandy*. The Wild Garden has been created within a former stone quarry and has a truly natural feel. The entire garden is an incredible wildlife haven and its moth project has recorded 450 species so far.
→ Shandy Hall (YO61 4AD) is on Thirsk Bank, Coxwold, near church (19 miles N of York on A19). Open 1 May – 30 Sep, 11am – 4.30pm, Tue – Sun and bank holiday Mondays. May be possible to visit out of season. Tel 01347 868465.
1 min, 54.1887, -1.1874 🚻💷

20 NUNNINGTON HALL GARDENS
Lovely organic walled garden of Nunnington Hall, situated on the banks of the River Rye. Drifts of snake's head fritillary and firework spikes of camassia carpet the wildflower meadows in spring. Idyllic spot for lazy summer picnics. For far-reaching views, walk S along The Avenue to Caulkleys Bank. Café.

→ From Hovingham, follow the B1257 towards Helmsley. After 1 mile turn R onto The Avenue and continue to Nunnington. In village cross bridge to car park for Nunnington Hall on the R.
2 mins, 54.2068, -0.9736 🧗⛴👣🐾

21 AMPLEFORTH ABBEY ORCHARDS
The last sizeable monastery orchard in Britain, planted in 1900 to supply the school and Benedictine community with fruit. Gorgeous situation in the heart of the Howardian Hills and open to visitors. Pop into the Abbey Tearoom afterwards for a slice of the famous Ampleforth apple cake.
→ Ampleforth Abbey, York, YO62 4EN, 01439 741111
1 min, 54.2026, -1.0780 🚶

22 KING OAK, PRETTY WOOD
A living piece of history, the King Oak is the oldest oak tree on the Castle Howard Estate, predating the stately home itself. At 400 years old, it towers above a footpath in Pretty Wood, an ancient woodland that has existed since ad 1600. Further along at a crossroads of tracks is one of Castle Howard's hidden follies, Hawksmoor's

Four Faces Monument, built around 1727 for Charles Howard, 3rd Earl of Carlisle (54.1093, -0.8838).

→ From roadside parking in Welburn, retrace road out of village to footpath sign after houses on L (54.1022, -0.8942). Head diagonally across field to signpost for Centenary Way. Keep L and continue into woods and oak on R. Continue further, keeping R to Four Faces monument. Several paths back to village.

25 mins, 54.1063, -0.8839 🚶🐕👁🚲

23 JEFFRY BOG NATURE RESERVE

Tiny nature reserve in the idyllic setting of Kirkham Gorge. Displays of cowslips and primroses in spring with glossy marsh marigolds in the wetter areas. Summer wildflowers include purple orchids. Stay for a picnic or keep an eye out for kingfishers and even otters on the riverside walk to beautiful Kirkham Abbey.

→ 6 miles SW of Malton. From Malton follow Welham Hill S for 3 miles, then turn R at Eddlethorpe towards Westow for 1½ miles. Park opp Church Farm on R. Follow track to reserve.

5 mins, 54.0910, -0.8392 🚶🐕🏕🌼🐾👁

24 FORRESTERS ARMS, KILBURN

Really good food and ales are served in this friendly village pub nestled below the White Horse at the foot of Sutton Bank. We enjoyed tasty burgers and chicken shawarma in the cosy bar area which welcomes walkers, dogs and muddy boots.

→ The Square, Kilburn, YO61 4AH, 01904 947570

54.2095, -1.2143 🍴🥾

25 THE GRAPES INN, SLINGSBY

Cosy up by the fire or bag a table in the heated wooden cabin with its cosy sheepskin throws at this popular village pub. Weekends (Fri – Sun) are pizza nights with hand-made, traditional Neapolitan-style pizzas cooked in a wood-fired oven and served from the outside 'organ bar'.

→ Railway St, Slingsby, York, YO62 4AL, 01653 628076

54.1666, -0.9326 🍴

26 THE DURHAM OX, CRAYKE

Award-winning 300-year-old hilltop pub run by the same family for the last 20 years. Enjoy regional pub classics like Yorkshire

beef and black sheep pie with horseradish scone dumpling. A beautiful historic village situated on an ancient Celtic trackway leading from Scotland to York.

→ West Way, Crayke, York, YO61 4TE, 01347 821506

54.1274, -1.1419 🍴🛏

27 CROWN & CUSHION, WELBURN

Locally sourced Yorkshire produce. Seasonal ingredients and menus. Own kitchen garden. Secluded back patio area with views towards Castle Howard Estate. Friendly, easy-going atmosphere whether you're here for a pint or a meal.

→ Welburn, York, YO60 7DZ, 01653 618777

54.1031, -0.8992 🍴

28 BLACK SWAN AT OLDSTEAD

High-end Michelin-starred pub restaurant with field-to-fork ethos, owned and run by the same family who have lived and farmed here for centuries. Just one tasting menu, inspired by flavoursome ingredients grown and foraged locally. Cocktails crafted from local produce and forage finds.

→ Oldstead, York, YO61 4BL, 01347 868387

54.2122, -1.1880 🍴🛏🛒

29 THE FAIRFAX ARMS, GILLING EAST

Pretty village pub with a traditional oak-beamed bar, light and airy orangery and plenty of outdoor seating on rattan chairs by a roadside stream. Good modern menu and friendly ambience.

→ Main St, Gilling East, Helmsley, York, YO62 4JH, 01439 788212

54.1849, -1.0592 🍴🛏

30 FAUCONBERG ARMS, COXWOLD

Picturesque pub with tables on the cobbles at the top of a pretty village. Very friendly staff. Modern country-style rooms and a stylish cabin garden room.

→ Thirsk Bank, Coxwold, YO61 4AD, 01347 868214

54.1878, -1.1832 🍴🛏

31 PLUM AND PARTRIDGE

Small upmarket hotel in the pretty village of Husthwaite with splendid views of the White Horse. Perfect for a romantic retreat as well as for cyclists or walkers. Beautifully furnished rooms and an excellent restaurant.

→ Low St, Husthwaite, York YO61 4QA, 01347 868642

54.1692, -1.2093 🍴🛏

32 THE WHITE SWAN, AMPLEFORTH

Popular village inn serving good pub classics. Convivial, relaxed atmosphere. Three dining areas, including a locals' bar with beamed ceiling and log fire, a lounge bar with French windows opening out onto a patio area and a cocktail bar.

→ East End, Ampleforth, YO62 4DA, 01439 788239

54.2008, -1.1072 🍴

CAFÉS & TEAROOMS

33 HEARTS OF AMPLEFORTH

Enjoy delicious homemade cakes and light lunches at this small family-run tearoom which also has a pretty garden at the back. Occasional evening menu.

→ Fir House, West End, York, YO62 4DU, 01439 788166

54.2009, -1.1086 🍴

34 LUTT AND TURNER COFFEE HOUSE & EATERY

Charming artisan café offering up a delicious selection of cakes, scones and pastries and freshly prepared breakfasts – full English, pancake stacks, cinnamon toast – and light lunches. Afterwards, pop into Kemps General Store, fast becoming a Malton institution, with its superbly curated bookshop.

→ 12–14 Market St, Malton, YO17 7LY, 01653 692555

54.1346, -0.7997 🍴

35 TEAHEE!

Sit at a table on the cobbled pavement and watch the world go by at this cute café which also has a pretty courtyard garden at the rear. Good coffee, cakes, breakfast and lunches.

→ 3, Tollbooth Cottage, Market Pl, Easingwold, York, YO61 3AB, 01347 823533

54.1219, -1.1921 🍴

36 HOVINGHAM BAKERY AND ROLLING PIN CAFÉ

Popular village bakery and tearoom by Hovingham beck, run by husband-and-wife team Simon and Victoria. Expect a Scandinavian touch to the baked goods on offer as Victoria is from Sweden. Be sure to try their delicious cinnamon buns.

→ Brookside, Hovingham, York, YO62 4LG, 01653 628898

54.1737, -0.9789 🍴

37 THE COXWOLD TEAROOMS

Delightful café and B&B housed in the

former village headteacher's home with a pretty tea garden. Delicious homemade cakes and scones. Also holiday cottage to let. Open Wed to Sun 11am – 4.30pm.

→ Coxwold YO61 4AD 01347 868138
54.1872, -1.1795 🍴

38 QUARMBY'S CAFÉ AND DELI
Contemporary coffee house, eatery and deli with an outdoor terrace overlooking Sheriff Hutton. Light lunches and delicious cakes, including plenty of vegan and gluten-free options.

→ The Square, Sheriff Hutton, YO60 6QX, 01347 878779
54.0892, -1.0068 🍴

39 DOGH
Bakery, deli and café where locals, walkers and cyclists grab a seat at the outside table to enjoy a coffee and watch the world go by. Takeaway pizza on Fri and Sat.

→ Welburn, York, YO60 7DX, 01653 618352
54.1028, -0.8991 🍴

FARM SHOPS & MARKETS

40 MALTON FOOD MARKET
Popular gourmet food market in the food capital of the North. Specialist stalls, street food and music bring the town to life on the second Sat of the month, 9am – 3pm. Malton Food Lovers Festival takes place each June.

→ Malton Market Square, YO17 7LX
54.1352, -0.7994 🍴

41 MALTON RELISH
Convivial deli and good spot for a relaxed coffee, cake or light lunch, with a small treasure trove of antiques upstairs. Owner Sophie will also deliver dishes, such as Lamb Keema Shepherd's Pie, to your holiday accommodation or create a delicious picnic for you.

→ 58 Market Pl, Malton, YO17 7LW, 01653 699389
54.1360, -0.7984 🍴

42 TALBOT YARD FOOD COURT
A converted coaching yard and gastronome's delight in Yorkshire's food capital. The courtyard is home to artisan food producers, including Roost, an excellent family-run coffee roastery; Groovy Moo's gelataria; the Bluebird Bakery; and Florio's, a macaron maker. The elegant Talbot Hotel is opposite.

→ Yorkersgate, Malton, YO17 7FT
54.1344, -0.8008 🍴

43 THE BAGGINS FARM GATE SHOP
Free-range pork, lamb and chicken farmed on a small scale. The meat – Pippins Pork, Legolas Lamb and Proudfoot Poultry – is named after characters in Tolkien's Lord of the Rings. Also sells organic fruit and veg, honey, cereals and their own pasteurised milk.

→ Thornton Ln, Easingwold, York, YO61 3QB, 01347 868894
54.1659, -1.1821 🍴

44 CASTLE HOWARD FARM SHOP
Popular farm shop stocking as much local produce as possible. Good cheese counter, small vegetable stall and freshly baked bread. Friendly butchers selling high-quality meat from the Castle Howard Estate or local partner farms.

→ The Courtyard, Castle Howard, York, YO60 7DA, 01653 648615
54.1204, -0.9117 🍴

45 WASS FARM SHOP
Award-winning farm shop selling free-range, grass-fed meat from the farm. Nick holds a deer-stalking licence so wild game from the woodlands is a speciality, and there is even an option of pigeon and squirrel.

42

44

40

→ Hollie Cottage, Wass Grange, West End, Ampleforth, York, YO62 4ED, 07779 340799
54.1983, -1.1380 🍴

46 SPILMAN'S, CHURCH FARM

If it's not from Yorkshire, it won't be on the shelves of this family-run farm shop, which sells home-reared beef and lamb and herb-fed chicken, PYO soft fruits and seasonal asparagus. On-site café, takeaway kiosk and breakfast van serving bacon sausage baps. Play barn for kids.

→ Church Farm, Sessay, Thirsk, YO7 3NB, 07754 857284
54.1665, -1.2856 🍴

47 GREETS FARM CAMPSITE

Enjoy camping as it used to be at this small, award-winning, family-run caravan and camping site. Beautiful views. Pub and bakery down the road. Well placed for visiting the moors, coast and Howardian Hills. Sorry, no kids.

→ Greets Farm, Welburn, YO60 7EP, 01653 619453
54.0959, -0.8855 ⛺

48 COTRIL FARM CAMPSITE

Pop-up wild camping field on a working family farm with plenty of space for kids to burn off energy. Portaloo but no shower. Level, well-maintained pitches and campfires. Collect fresh eggs for breakfast. The well-stocked Terrington Stores is a short stroll away for local produce and everyday essentials.

→ Terrington, York, YO60 6NT, 07761 123677
54.1341, -0.9768 ⛺🔥

49 CHAPEL COTTAGE CAMPING

Small-scale campsite for 10 tents and 5 vans run by very friendly owners. Peaceful location on edge of village and a good base for exploring the southern North York Moors.

→ Chapel Cottage, Normanby, York, YO62 6RH, 01751 431984
54.2237, -0.8733 ⛺

50 BUTTER HILL CARAVAN PARK

Tiny site with flat pitches for vans only in a super location in the shadow of the White Horse and within walking distance of Kilburn village and the Forresters Arms pub. Beautiful scenery.

→ Church Farm, Kilburn, York, YO61 4AG, 01347 868318
54.2108, -1.2168 🚐

51 STILLINGTON MILL SHEPHERD'S HUT AND POP-UP CAFÉ

Situated in the grounds of an 18th-century former watermill, this pretty shepherd's hut is decked out in vintage style and has a small pond and island to explore. It is also possible to camp out next to the hut, and there is a campfire and BBQ too.

→ Mill Lane, Stillington, York, YO61 1NG, 01347 811503
54.1037, -1.0964 🚐🔥

52 THE DEN AT HUSTHWAITE GATE

Surrounded by the wooded and tranquil valleys of the Hambleton Hills, this secluded retreat, hidden away by the side of the former railway station, was once the railway sidings. Stylish decor and quirky cabin-style bedrooms. Green electricity from an on-site wind turbine and the timber floorboards came from the village hall.

→ Old Station House, Husthwaite Gate, YO61 4QF, 07745 057807
54.1786, -1.2116 🚐

53 THE HIDEAWAY AT BAXBY MANOR

Beautiful glamp site on the 770-year-old Medieval Baxby Estate, nestled in the rolling countryside of the Howardian Hills. Something for every type of camper, from the enchanting Hobbit houses to rustic Rufus's Roost. Otherwise, pitch your tent or park up your camper on the 2½-hectare site with excellent facilities; several times winner of loo of the year!

→ Baxby Manor, Husthwaite, York, YO61 4PW, 01347 666079
54.1685, -1.2216 🚐

54 STUDFORD LUXURY LODGES

If high-end glamping ticks your boxes, check out these architecturally designed lodges. Elevated among the treetops in a secluded woodland with a huge decked area and far-reaching views, this is luxury in a wilderness setting.

→ High St, Nr Ampleforth, York, YO62 4BH, 01439 788991
54.2112, -1.1074 🚐

55 HALL FARM B&B, STITTENHAM

Traditional B&B with an adjoining holiday cottage in a charming setting overlooking the village pond and the Howardian Hills. Owner Sally trained as a chef at the Savoy so expect scrumptious cooked breakfasts. Stittenham Woods is right behind, with a beautiful display of bluebells in spring.

→ High Stittenham, Sheriff Hutton, York, YO60 7TW, 01347 878386
54.1001, -0.9629 🚐

56 CARR HOUSE FARM B&B

Surrounded by meadows, orchards and ancient bluebell woods, this charming 16th-century farmhouse B&B has been welcoming guests for more than 40 years. After a scrumptious Yorkshire breakfast, pull on your boots to explore the 160 hectares of woodland, streams and waterfalls.

→ Ampleforth, York, YO62 4ED, 01347 868526
54.2027, -1.1330 🚐

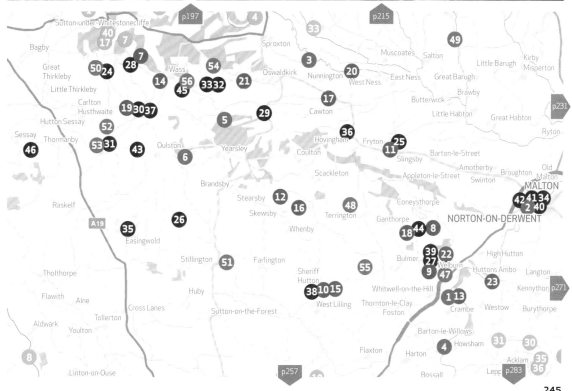

VALE OF YORK

Our perfect weekend

→ **Wander** through wildflower meadows at Three Hagges Woodmeadow, then tuck into homemade scones at Miller's Tearoom

→ **Watch** the sun setting over the memorial to the Battle of Marston Moor, the largest battle fought on English soil

→ **Bring** your binoculars to the flooded meadows of Wheldrake Ings to spot overwintering birds, including whooper swans, teals and peregrines

→ **Enjoy** a pot of tea and a slice of lemon drizzle served on vintage china at Tea by the Lock

→ **Cross** the river on the ancient ferry boat at Nun Monkton, then find a tranquil beach for a picnic and a swim in the River Ouse

→ **Stroll** along the boardwalk at Askham Bog and hunt for the giant royal ferns

→ **Enjoy** a paddleboard adventure on the Pocklington Canal and keep a look out for red-eyed damselflies flitting across the water

→ **Build** a den in the woods at Jollydays and toast s'mores on a crackling campfire

While visitors might flock to York with its host of historic attractions, just a few miles outside the city walls you can find wild and untamed places. Whether you are looking for a day out of town for a micro adventure or planning a longer trip, there is plenty to do, from river swims beside wildflower meadows to rambles through ancient landscapes abundant with birds and wildlife.

Strensall Common is a magnificent heathland only five miles from York and one of a handful of lowland heaths left in the north of England. You may not see a soul as you wander across the varied terrain of wet and dry heath, woodland and acid grassland. More than 150 different species thrive here, including the fascinating carnivorous round-leaved sundew, which lives among the sphagnum mosses at the edge of bog pools. On warm days common lizards bask on the stumps of silver birch and, if you arrive early enough on a spring morning, you may be serenaded by a cuckoo or hear the beautiful song of the woodlark.

Moorlands Nature Reserve is a remnant of the ancient hunting forest of Galtres, created by the Norman kings, which once stretched from Crayke in the north to Bootham Bar in York. This pocket of woodland is a wonderful place for children to revel in pond dipping, fungi forays and bug hunts.

The idyllic waterway of the Pocklington Canal is one of the best canals in the country for wildlife, with three SSSIs along its route, its lower reaches lying within the Lower Derwent Valley NNR. Pootling down the canal on a paddleboard on a summer's day is a joy when the winter flood water has receded and the meadows are ablaze with wildflowers. Nearby are beautiful stretches of the River Derwent, where you can indulge in a wild swim at Wheldrake and Elvington.

Skipwith Common is another remnant of northern lowland heath, and a walk through this ancient terrain is akin to venturing out on a mini wildlife safari. Encounters with Longhorn cattle, Exmoor ponies and Hebridean sheep are guaranteed, and, if you are here long enough, adders, grass snakes and lizards may make an appearance.

To the north-west is historic Nun Monkton with an excellent pub, the Alice Hawthorn, overlooking one of only two working greens in the country, where cattle graze and the tallest maypole in England stands. The village is at the confluence of the rivers Nidd and Ouse, which is crossed by way of an ancient ferry.

RIVERS

1 WHELDRAKE, RIVER DERWENT
Tranquil section of the River Derwent, before its confluence with the Pocklington Canal, as it weaves its way through the seasonally flooded hay meadows of the wildlife-rich Lower Derwent Valley. Tiny beach just below the footpath to Thorganby.

→ From Wheldrake, head E on Main St, then continue onto Church Ln for 2 miles to a L turn on to Ferry Ln and parking at end. Follow footpath along river.

5 mins, 53.8758, -0.9396 🏊🏕️⛺

2 SUTTON BRIDGE, RIVER DERWENT
Situated just below the weir and lock, this lovely grassy-banked stretch of the Derwent has an easy entry point and a secluded basin for swimming or for a stand-up paddleboard and kayak launch (take out at Wheldrake Ings by bridge).

→ From Elvington, follow the B1228 for 300m to parking in Riverside Gardens on L. Cross road and follow footpath through snicket to churchyard. Then find metal gate on L to riverside path and river.

5 mins, 53.9179, -0.9303 🏊🚣⛺

3 THE BREIGHTON FERRY, RIVER DERWENT
Easy slipway for stand-up paddleboards or kayaks onto a beautiful, flat, calm stretch of the River Derwent from this popular riverside pub, which has boat moorings and a campsite. You can paddle upstream to Bubwith and get out at the historic Derwent Bridge.

→ From Bubwith, head S on Breighton Rd for 2 miles onto Gunby Rd which then becomes Clay Ln. Turn R onto Ferry Ln and sign for pub. Slipway is by pub.

2 mins, 53.8021, -0.9336 🚣⛺🍴

4 BISHOPTHORPE, RIVER OUSE
Easy stand-up paddleboard or kayak launch from the boatyard onto the River Ouse. Paddle upstream past Bishopthorpe Palace, the official residence of the Archbishop of York, or downstream to Naburn lock and refuel at the Blacksmith's Arms. Refreshments at Bosun's Oven Café.

→ From Bishopthorpe, follow Main St, then turn R onto Acaster Ln, then L onto Ferry Ln and boatyard parking. (You can also launch/ get out upstream at University of York Boat Club at 53.9370, -1.0806)

2 mins, 53.9217, -1.0902 🚣

5 NETHER POPPLETON, RIVER OUSE
Easy sloped access to the Ouse from a sandy beach reached via a pleasant walk past a lovely 16th-century tythe barn and through a moated field.

→ Follow the York ring road (A1237) anti-clockwise and take the R turn for Nether Poppleton onto Millfield Ln, then R turn onto Church Ln (1¼ miles) to parking at end by tythe barn. Follow footpath through moated field under Skelton Bridge then along riverbank to beach access.

20 mins, 53.9908, -1.1347 🏊⛺

6 NUN MONKTON FERRYBOAT, RIVER OUSE
Ancient ferry route at the confluence of the rivers Ouse and Nidd connecting Nun Monkton, Moor Monkton and Beningbrough. A ferry was first recorded here in 1174, when the priory of Benedictine nuns was founded. Until 1952 a small passenger ferry operated, where villagers rang a loud bell to cross the water. Today, a trip across on the *Bryan Ferry* leads to a pretty riverside walk that opens out to glorious views across the parkland of NT Beningbrough Hall. Beaches for swimming on other side (see entry).

→ YO26 8ES. Follow ferry boat signs through Nun Monkton to parking in field at end of

village, then follow avenue through Priory Estate to ferry boat pontoon. (Runs Apr – Sep; check website – Nunmonktonferryboat.org)
5 mins, 54.0143, -1.2189 🐕🛆🏕🏃🧍

7 BENINGBROUGH, RIVER OUSE

A popular spot with families, who swim and picnic here in the summer. Several beaches, good paddling and the opportunity for a longer, deeper swim. Tree swing for jumping into the deep water. The ancient ferry boat crosses this section of the river from Nun Monkton. There is a small area to launch a kayak/paddleboard before the beaches at 54.0163, -1.2097.

→ From Beningbrough, head N for ½ mile, then turn L at T-junction to parking by gates in small parking area (54.0207, -1.2012). Follow riverside footpath through woods to river.
10 mins, 54.0149, -1.2182 🛆⛵🍴🏕🐕

8 ALDWARK TOLL BRIDGE, RIVER URE

Ideal launch or landing for a stand-up paddleboard or kayak adventure, as well as swimming beneath the old toll bridge on a pleasant section of the River Ure before it becomes the Ouse a little further downstream. Jetty is to L of bridge. A toll keeper still collects a small

fee for crossing the bridge. Locals often swim here.

→ Follow the road S out of Aldwark for ½ mile, then turn R at T-junction to cross bridge. Toll at end (coins). Turn immediately R after bridge to car park by river.
1 min, 54.0534, -1.2887 🛆⛵🏕🏃

9 BOROUGHBRIDGE, RIVER URE

Interesting stretch of the River Ure with an impressive fish ladder allowing salmon and lamprey to pass over the weir. A short section of the river has also been canalised from here to Milby, making a great place for a stand-up paddleboard or kayak launch.

→ In Boroughbridge, at the main roundabout Langthorpe car park is on the L as soon as you leave the roundabout. Launch point to Milby Cut is to L of bridge.
2 mins, 54.0983, -1.3976 🛆🏕

LAKES & CANALS

10 BRAYTON BRIDGE, SELBY CANAL

Perfect launch for a stand-up paddleboard along the Selby canal from the arched stone bridge, where there is also a canal boat café serving full English breakfasts, tea and cake (9.30am – 4pm). Paddle N to Selby lock or S

to Burn Bridge, where you can also launch (53.7586, -1.0954).

→ From Selby, follow the A19 S for 1½ miles to Brayton, then take L at crossroads to bridge and parking area on L.
1 min, 53.7654, -1.0758 🏊🌲🍴

11 EAST COTTINGWITH, POCKLINGTON CANAL

Delightful, navigable stretch of waterway surrounded by the SSSI wetland landscape of the Lower Derwent Valley with its stunning summer wildflowers and overwintering wildfowl. Yellow water lilies and water forget-me-nots float on the clear waters, and unusual aquatic plants, including fan-leaved water crowfoot, thrive below the surface. Section is navigable for seven miles to Bielby Basin, with permanent moorings at Melbourne Arm, where the Pocklington Canal Amenity Society run short boat trips. The clear waters are suitable for a swim.

→ From Sutton-upon-Derwent, follow the B1228 for 3¾ miles, then turn R at crossroads for 1 mile to East Cottingwith. Park by church then follow footpath to canal. For boat trips visit Pockingtoncanalsociety.org.
10 mins, 53.8758, -0.9358 🚣🏊🌲🚶🎣🐾

12 POOL BRIDGE FARM

Two beautiful swimming lakes, including the Monet Lake, afloat with water lilies in summer, which feels like you're swimming through one of the artist's paintings. A wild swim experience in a lovely setting run by a friendly, laid-back team. Showers and toilets. Worth the small fee. Also campsite and wildlife photography hides.

→ Wheldrake Lane, Crockley Hill, York, YO19 4SQ, 07928 359 420. From the A64 at the A19 turn-off, head towards Selby for about 1 mile. At traffic lights, turn L onto Wheldrake Ln and follow this road for almost exactly 1 mile and the entrance to the farm is on L, just before the road passes over a small bridge.
2 mins, 53.9097, -1.0254 🏊🌲💷

ANCIENT COMMONS & WILDLIFE

13 WHELDRAKE INGS NATURE RESERVE

With big skies, rustling reed beds and flood meadows, this magical nature reserve feels remote, yet it is one of the busiest international airports for migrating birds. In winter, look out for whooper swans, coots, cormorants, widgeons and lapwings. You may also get the chance to spot an osprey or black tern during migration. In early summer,

251

the unique flood meadows support up to 25 plant species per square metre, including crimson great burnet and cream sprays of meadowsweet.

→ From Wheldrake, follow Church Ln towards Thorganby for 1¾ miles, then take L turn down track to the reserve. Park next to the bridge and follow linear walk to hides.
5 mins, 53.8913, -0.9454

14 ASKHAM BOG NATURE RESERVE

Site of an age-old lake left by a retreating glacier 15,000 years ago and a remnant of the ancient fenlands of Yorkshire. This small suburban reserve, abutting the A64, is home to the 500-year-old royal fern which thrives in wet, boggy places. Follow the boardwalk or clamber over the stiles to discover meadows, secret gardens and ponds. We stumbled across two grazing Exmoor ponies on our visit.

→ Approaching York on the eastbound A64, take the A1036 turn-off and then turn sharp L into the car park just after the first set of traffic lights. The ancient royal fern is right next to the boardwalk. Wellies advisable for exploring as boggy.
5 mins, 53.9261, -1.1286

15 MOORLANDS NATURE RESERVE

A remnant of the ancient royal forest of Galtres that was established in the Norman period and at its largest during Henry II's reign. It is now a small Edwardian woodland reserve with a display of rhododendrons and azaleas which dazzle with colour in the spring. These non-native exotic blooms are carefully managed to ensure they coexist alongside native species. Beautiful displays of snowdrops, bluebells, primroses and wood sorrel. Amazing fungi in autumn. Wooded glades, picnic areas, dipping ponds and a tree house.

→ Located 5½ miles N of York. From York, take the A19 Thirsk road for 3½ miles to Skelton. Turn R off A19 and continue through village for 2 miles to reserve on L of road and parking.
1 min, 54.0224, -1.1164

16 BISHOP WOOD, SELBY

A planted ancient woodland, named after Cardinal Wolsey, which provides an excellent habitat for butterflies and moths. The large, fast-flying silver-washed fritillary returned here in 2018 following a 150-year absence, and the wood is now one of the best places in Yorkshire to see them.

17

→ From Selby, take the B1223 to Sherburn Rd, then continue on to Dutchman's car park on Scalm Ln.
5 mins, 53.7968, -1.1539 ⬛

17 THREE HAGGES WOODMEADOW

Heavenly 10-hectare site rewilded from a barley field thanks to the pioneering work of the Woodmeadow Trust. The area features lowland wet meadows, species-rich dry meadows as well as a groundwater-fed pond, humming with dragonflies and damselflies, at the far end. Afterwards, pop across to Miller's Tearoom for coffee and cake.

→ Travelling S on the A19 from York, after 7 miles take the L turn after York Timber Products into York Rd, signposted 'Hollicarrs'. After 300m, turn L into Hollicarrs Holiday Park. Parking for Three Hagges Woodmeadow is on R.
1 min, 53.8473, -1.0465 ⬛🅰️⚙️ℹ️

18 SKIPWITH COMMON

One of the last remaining areas of northern lowland heath in England, formed around 3,500 years ago. Today open heath, ponds, mires, fens, reed beds, woodland and scrub are conserved to sustain a living ancient landscape with an incredible variety of plants and animals. The common was home to RAF Riccall in WWII, and you can see the bomb bays (53.8281, -1.0097) where munitions were stored. Danes Hill is the site of Iron Age tumuli and, according to local folklore, Danish King Harold Hardrada went into battle with the armies of Northumbria and Mercia at this spot in 1066 (53.8312, -1.0228). Exmoor ponies and Longhorn cattle roam and graze the pastures. Follow the footpaths and immerse yourself in this beautiful landscape.

→ From York, follow the A19 S for 7 miles, then turn L onto King Rudding Ln for 1 mile to car park (YO19 6LJ) and footpaths.
1 min, 53.8284, -1.0214 ⬛🅰️🚶⚙️📍🔄

18

19 STRENSALL COMMON

Just one of a few remaining lowland heaths in the North, this diverse 600-hectare common includes areas of heather, acid grassland, woodland, wetland and ponds. It was bought by the war department in the 1870s and preserved by the army, who train here. Look out for old military boundary stones dotted along The Sike area. It is a haven for wildlife, including a nationally important population of dark-bordered beauty moths. Visit in August when the heather is out. Leave the beaten path and your only encounters will be with the Hebridean sheep grazing here.

19

→ Park in car park on Lords Moor Ln in Strensall. Cross road to follow paths across common. Military boundary markers are along The Sike at the NE corner of the common (54.0461, -0.9952). Also parking area here.
2 mins, 54.0401, -1.0105 🐄🌳🧍♿♀🚗

20 ALL SAINT'S CHURCH, BOLTON PERCY

Deconsecrated churchyard and now a delightful cemetery garden teeming with flowers thanks to the dedication of local volunteers. Graves rise out from among clumps of *Alchemilla*, geraniums and agapanthus, and tall spires of *Acanthus mollis* form a backdrop to weathered stone crosses. After visiting pop into the lovely family-run Doylys Tearoom, a restored cow shed with courtyard seating.

→ From York, follow the A64 S, then turn L before Bilbrough services and follow signs to Bolton Percy. Turn L at Doylys Tearoom to churchyard on L opp church.
1 min, 53.8650, -1.1923 ♿♀🍴

RUINS, SACRED & ANCIENT

21 ST ANDREW'S OLD CHURCH FACADE

Whimsical Gothic-style ruins of St Andrew's old church, of Anglo-Scandinavian origin, situated in a tranquil spot on the banks of the River Ouse in Bishopthorpe, the centuries-old home to the Archbishops of York. By the 19th century its location so close to the river began to cause concern when a flood in 1872 washed bodies out of graves. The church was abandoned and the facade left as an eye-catcher.

→ From York, follow the A1036 and Bishopthorpe Rd to Acaster Ln in Bishopthorpe for 3 miles. At turn for Ferry Ln on L, there is roadside parking (53.9206, -1.0934). Walk down Ferry Ln and follow riverside footpath to L to old church.
15 mins, 53.9226, -1.0909 ♿🖼

22 DEVIL'S ARROWS

Three colossal Neolithic or early Bronze Age monoliths remaining from an original four or five. The tallest stone stands higher, at 7m, than those at Stonehenge, making it the second tallest standing stone in Britain after Rudston Monolith. Originally standing in a south-east to north-west alignment, their location, wedged between a housing estate and the A1, is incongruous. Nevertheless, their size and stature are awesome. According to legend, the devil threw the huge stone arrows to earth in a fit of rage.

→ Leave the A1 at junction 48 and continue

½ mile along the A168. Take 3rd exit at roundabout onto Roecliffe Ln. Park up 100m on R for first monolith next to the road. Gate entrance to other two in the field.

1 min, 54.0933, -1.4036 ✝♿🏛

23 ST MARY'S CHURCH, NUN MONKTON

Sole surviving structure of medieval Benedictine nunnery. Magnificent stained-glass east window designed by Edward Burne-Jones and William Morris in 1873. It is a work of art in praise of women, dedicated to Ann, wife of the Lord of the Manor, Isaac Crawhall. The priory survived until 1536 when Henry VIII ordered its dissolution. Cattle graze the ancient village green, one of only two working greens in the country, currently being restored to semi-natural grassland. The 27m Scots pine maypole is the tallest in England.

→ Follow the A59 towards Harrogate, then R to Nun Monkton after Ainsty Farm Shop on L. Church is at end of village, with Alice Hawthorn pub on R.

5 mins, 54.0148, -1.2209 ✝♿

24 MARSTON MOOR

The Battle of Marston Moor in 1644 was one of the largest battles on English soil and a significant victory in the English Civil War for Cromwell's Parliamentarians, who defeated Royalist forces to gain control of the north. This obelisk at the corner of a field marks the midpoint of the battlefield, and a display board shows where the two armies were drawn up.

→ Follow Tockwith Road from the village of Long Marston, and the obelisk is at the roadside on the L-hand side. There is parking in a lay-by opp.

1 min, 53.9621, -1.2537 ♿🖼

FRIENDLY PUBS

25 THE DROVERS ARMS, SKIPWITH

Award-winning pub in a picturesque village offering a seasonal menu. Hand-pulled cask ales and more than 60 gins. In summer, dine beneath the stars in the heated garden tipi or enjoy wonderful walks across Skipwith Common, on its doorstep.

→ York Rd, Selby, YO8 5SF, 01757 288088
53.8395, -0.9923 🍴🍷

26 ALICE HAWTHORN INN, NUN MONKTON

Charming village pub next to one of Yorkshire's oldest working greens where cattle roam freely. Stylish interiors, log fires and Yorkshire Heart Hearty Bitter, brewed in the village. Creative menu. The real Alice Hawthorn was one of the greatest English

race mares of all time. Twelve lovely rooms, above the pub or courtyard garden rooms.

→ The Green, Nun Monkton, York, YO26 8EW, 01423 330303
54.0136, -1.2253 🍴🍷🛏🚲

27 DAWNAY ARMS, NEWTON-ON-OUSE

A handsome 18th-century village inn with a large beer garden stretching down to the river. Excellent seasonal menu.

→ Newton-on-Ouse, YO30 2BR, 01347 848345
54.0211, -1.1579 🍴

CAFÉS & TEAROOMS

28 THE COFFEE BIKE, GREAT OUSEBURN

Grab your flat white or espresso from this roaming coffee shop, which pitches up at different locations around Great Ouseburn, including the village shop and village hall.

→ Great Ouseburn, York, YO26 9RL
54.0533, -1.3197

29 TEA BY THE LOCK

In the old banqueting hall next to Naburn lock, this lovely vegan tea hall is open for lunches and cakes. Eat inside or al fresco by the lock. Admire the impressive weir or take a riverside stroll to Naburn village and spot kingfishers, herons and red kites.

→ Naburn Lock, York, YO19 4RU, 07711 105741 (Ignore private road signs)
53.8935, -1.0969 🍴

30 STILLINGFLEET LODGE TEAROOM

Enjoy afternoon tea in the converted barn at this delightful organic plant nursery. Wildlife-friendly 1½-hectare gardens, including a stunning traditional wildflower meadow in summer. Picnic benches in the grass car park. (Entry fee for gardens not for café.)

→ Stewart Ln, YO19 6HP, 01904 728506
53.8620, -1.1060 🍴

FARM SHOPS

31 BALLOON TREE FARM SHOP AND CAFÉ

Award-winning farm shop which harvests its crops each morning for super fresh produce with the best flavours. PYO trail. Freshly baked cakes and bread. Rare-breed meats, specialising in Gloucester Old Spot pork. Provenance is king so everything is labelled – you even get to know which field your veg was harvested from.

→ Stamford Bridge Rd, Gate Helmsley, York, YO41 1NB, 01759 373023
53.9905, -0.9377 🍴

26

27

28

29

32 YOLK FARM & MINSKIP FARM SHOP

The world's first egg restaurant and also an award-winning farm shop with a tempting array of seasonal vegetables picked daily from their market garden or sourced from close by. Wander through the paddock where the hens scratch and meet alpacas and pygmy goats. Highly recommended.

→ Minskip Rd, Minskip, Boroughbridge, YO51 9HY, 01423 329063
54.0832, -1.4023 🍴

CAMP, GLAMP & SLEEP

33 POPLAR FARM CARAVAN PARK

Although this is a larger site with caravans, campers have their own field by the stream that runs into the River Ouse. It is in a pretty village only four miles from York, so well situated for exploring the historic city or for cycling and water activities. The Ship Inn is right next door.

→ Acaster Malbis, York, YO23 2UQ, 01904 706548
53.9029, -1.1030 ▲

34 YORKSHIRE HEART VINEYARD

Glamp in a bell tent next to the vines at this award-winning family-run vineyard. There's an on-site café and microbrewery as well as seasonal tent and camper van pitches in a spacious camping field (Apr to Oct), plus you've got the delightful ancient village of Nun Monkton on your doorstep.

→ Pool Ln, Nun Monkton, York, YO26 8EL, 01423 330716
54.0125, -1.2407 🏕

35 ACORN GLADE GLAMPING

Romantic glamping retreat with a chic yurt and two cosy log cabins set in a 1½-hectare lakeside meadow and woodland site on the fringes of the Yorkshire Wolds. Renewable energy and solar powered, with a communal kitchen. Sorry, no kids or pets. No Wi-Fi.

→ Kidd Ln, Melbourne, York, YO42 4QF, 01759 319151
53.8852, -0.8709 🏕

36 BEECH NUT SHEPHERD'S HUT

Off-grid shepherd's hut tucked away in an apple and pear orchard at the bottom of the garden on a working family farm. Superb views across open countryside and walks from the door. Collect eggs from the hens and enjoy freshly baked bread in the mornings. Fire pit for cosy evenings round the campfire.

→ Beech Farm, Buttercrambe, YO41 1AS, 01759 371297
54.0138, -0.8998 🏕

37 DEER WOOD, JOLLYDAYS GLAMPING

The original woodland camp. Christian and Carolyn Van Outersterp led the UK's glamping craze, and the promise here is comfort without the stresses of modern life, so expect hot water, comfy beds and wood burners but no Wi-Fi, so your focus will be the campfire rather than your screen. Woodland kitchen and bar with tree trunk scaffolding and tea tent. Accessed by a private road.

→ Buttercrambe Rd, York, YO41 1AN, 01439 748457
54.0054, -0.9146 🏕

38 THE OLD FORGE, SAND HUTTON

Follow secret paths through the gardens and picnic beneath the willow tree while the kids make dens or play on rope swings at this magical hideaway haven

with its gorgeous rustic outdoor area and communal fire pit. Choose from the Garden Shed for two or Next Door for families. There is an honesty shop for homemade meals and an allotment with a veg patch for guests.

→ The Old Forge, Sand Hutton, York, YO41 1LB, 07926 381022
54.0182, -0.9394 🏕

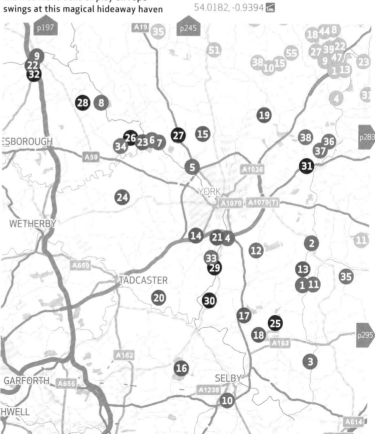

FLAMBOROUGH & EAST WOLDS

Our perfect weekend

→ **Paddle** your kayak around the spectacular coastline of Flamborough Head to explore sea caves, stacks and arches

→ **Follow** the course of the prehistoric Gypsey Race, a mysterious stream revered by our Neolithic and Bronze Age ancestors

→ **Clamber** down to the remarkable natural amphitheatre at Thornwick Bay and watch the sun go down over the chalk cliffs

→ **Follow** the path along the top of Filey Brigg and scramble down to the Emperor's Bath below

→ **Watch** the puffins swooping in an out of crevices at the UK's largest mainland seabird colony at Bempton Cliffs

→ **Hike** up to Knapton Brow to enjoy panoramic views and see the sky mirrored in the shimmering dew pond

→ **Take** a bracing dip in the North Sea at Hunmanby Gap, then warm up with a steaming mug of hot chocolate from the beach café

→ **Measure** yourself against the 2,000-year-old Rudston Monolith, England's tallest standing stone, which towers above the gravestones around it

From the dramatic headland of Filey Brigg, the sandy beaches of Hunmanby and the soaring chalk cliffs of Flamborough to the broad swathe of the Great Wold Valley, this region is rich in spectacular scenery and antiquity.

Filey Brigg juts out into the sea to the north of Filey bay, bestowing an instantly recognisable feature on the seaside town. It was formed around 150 million years ago, when hard rocks were laid down as silt and layers of sandstone and limestone built up over subsequent millennia. At low tide, rock pools crammed with miniature marine life are revealed at its base. A steep scramble down its rocky northern escarpment leads to the Emperor's Bath, a large sea pool refreshed by the tide.

Flamborough boasts some of the most magnificent chalk cliffs in England and the UK's largest mainland seabird colony at Bempton, home to puffins and a rare colony of gannets. In spring and summer, colourful displays of common spotted orchids, pink thrift and sea chamomile line the clifftop paths.

The coastline around Flamborough Head offers some of the most spectacular canoeing on the north-east coast, with vertical chalk cliffs eroded into natural arches, sea caves and stacks. The best time to paddle here is at high tide, as you can get in close to the cliffs as long as there is no swell. Tidal streams off Flamborough Head are strong so a reasonable knowledge of tides and weather is needed.

From Hunmanby, the Great Wold Valley sweeps inland. This large, broad basin cuts into the Yorkshire Wolds, carrying the Gypsey Race, a curious, intermittent chalk stream. The only water course on the high Wolds, it runs from the Neolithic round barrow at Duggleby Howe to the sea at Bridlington. Its erratic behaviour, flowing both above and below ground, suddenly changing direction as well as disappearing and then reappearing some years later, has long been a source of local legend. A series of important Neolithic and Bronze Age monuments are situated along its length, including Duggleby Howe, Willy Howe, Rudston Monolith and Danes Dyke, reminders of the symbolism it held for prehistoric communities.

While evidence of prehistoric activity here is clear to see, the plains and waterways around Star Carr go unnoticed. Yet this area hides one of the most archaeologically important sites in the world. Excavations here have unearthed remarkably well-preserved deer skull headdresses, possibly used by shamans in ritual practices, and harpoons for hunting and fishing, dating back more than 10,000 years.

2

HIDDEN BEACHES & SEA CAVES

1 THORNWICK BAY, FLAMBOROUGH

Shingle and pebble cove beneath magnificent chalk cliffs with smugglers' caves to explore by kayak or paddleboard. At LT, walk round to Little Thornwick Bay to find a spectacular natural amphitheatre and 'rapids' to swim through. Plenty of rock pools. Thornwick Bay Café serves basic snacks. Open summer, Mon – Fri 10.30am – 6pm; spring/autumn, Mon – Fri 11am – 5pm. Every weekend 10am – 6pm, except winter.

→ From Flamborough village, follow the B1255 on North Marine Road. After ½ mile take L, signposted 'Thornwick Bay'. Pass parking kiosk (£1.50 all day). Continue 300m to clifftop parking. If you plan on staying late, move car outside barrier before 6pm.
2 mins, 54.1318, -0.1148

2 NORTH LANDING, FLAMBOROUGH

Small, pretty beach flanked by high chalk cliffs. Soft sand at HT and pebbles at LT. Lots of caves to explore. Rockpools galore. Café by car park.

→ From Flamborough, follow signs to North Landing (1 mile). Park by café (YO15 1BJ). Plenty of rock pools and caves to explore on L

but largest cave is on R, after first inlet (50m) beyond arch. The narrow cave entrance leads to a major cavern with access to sea. Strong tidal races offshore so stay close if you swim.
2 mins, 54.1294, -0.1052

3 SELWICKS BAY, FLAMBOROUGH

Popular sand and pebble bay at the foot of high cliffs. As the tide goes out, a rocky shoreline with many rock pools is revealed. Amazing caves, tunnels and inlets to explore.

→ From Flamborough, follow signs to Flamborough Head (2 miles) and park by lighthouse/café (YO15 1AR). On beach, bear L and scramble round into deep inlet cove, with further tunnel out to sea. Further swims/scrambles around the headland and many more coves. At the R end of beach, a LT scramble (HT swim) leads to a cave with skylight (100m).
2 mins, 54.1181, -0.0825

4 HIGH STACKS, FLAMBOROUGH

Isolated pebble cove with spectacular sea arch known locally as the 'Drinking Dinosaur'. From above, the rock formation does resemble a sauropod drinking from the sea. In summer, common seals sprawl out along the beach.

→ From Flamborough, follow signs to Flamborough Head (2 miles) and park by lighthouse/café (YO15 1AR, 01262 851020). Follow coastal path S and then follow steep scramble down cliff with care.
10 mins, 54.1148, -0.0773

5 SOUTH LANDING, FLAMBOROUGH

A peaceful wooded ravine, part of a 14-hectare nature reserve, leading to a sand and cobble beach beneath spectacular chalk cliffs that continue underwater to form part of the largest underwater chalk reef in Europe. At LT an underwater world of anemones, limpets, crabs and starfish is revealed in the many rock pools. Lifeboat station.

→ Signed on R from Flamborough village (YO15 1AE). Paid car park at Living Seas Centre. Follow signed sculpture/nature trail to beach. Then take steep flight of 75 steps from trail. Or walk from car park down steep road to lifeboat station.
5 mins, 54.1044, -0.1179

6 DANES DYKE, FLAMBOROUGH

Follow a woodland path alongside the ancient fortified 'wall' of Dane's Dyke to a large cobble beach flanked by chalk cliffs.

Great for rock pooling and fossil hunting, the beach becomes sandier nearer the shore. The impressive 2½-mile long Dane's Dyke earthwork, built as a defence in the Iron Age, cuts across the Flamborough peninsula, creating a 1295-hectare defendable area. Café by car park, once the site of a grand house, built in 1873 and demolished in 1953. Some of the exotic parkland trees remain, including a monkey puzzle tree.

→ Located 2 miles E of Bridlington on the B1255. Car park signed on R (YO15 1AA). Or 2-mile walk from Bridlington North Sands.
10 mins, 54.1058, -0.1413 🚗🏖🚻🍴

7 FILEY BRIGG

Dramatic rocky promontory, the brigg, jutting out into the sea, its steep cliffs formed of layers of sandstone and limestone topped with boulder clay. A Roman signal station once stood at Carr Naze, at the landward end. A walk along the top offers superb views across the bay to the chalk cliffs of Bempton and Flamborough and N towards Scarborough. At LT you can walk to the end of the brigg from the beach. Great rock pooling. Check tide times.

→ From Filey, the brigg is easy to reach from parking in the Country Park car park at Church Cliff Drive (YO14 9ET).
10 mins, 54.2185, -0.2769 🏖🚗🚻🍴🚻🚲

8 THE EMPEROR'S BATH, FILEY BRIGG

According to legend, Emperor Constantine the Great liked to bathe in a large sea pool refreshed by the tides on Filey Brigg. Whatever its real history, you will see the Emperor's Bath, a large rock pool with ledges, as you peer down over the Scarborough side of Filey Brigg.

→ Follow signs for Country Park (YO14 9ET) from Filey. To access, follow a tricky LT scramble down the north base of the cliffs, along a narrow path then a metal ladder, to ledges and along to pool.
20 mins, 54.2182, -0.2709 🏊🚻🏖

9 HUNMANBY GAP SANDS

A gap in the hillside between Filey bay and the chalk cliffs of Bempton takes you down to this wide sandy beach. Friendly beach café: outdoor decked seating with fabulous coastal views. Toilets.

→ From Hunmanby, follow Stonegate, Filey Rd and Moor Rd for 2 miles to roundabout. Take 1st exit onto Sands Rd. After ½ mile, parking

is in field on L (fee). A there-and-back beach walk to Filey, passing Billy Butlin's art deco holiday home, The White House, on L, takes 1½ hrs. Apparently, Charlie, Billy's elephant, is buried near the house.
5 mins, 54.1805, -0.2688 🐾

10 SPEETON SANDS

The clamber down a rugged cliff path to this stunning stretch of wide sandy beach is well worth the effort. Even in the height of summer, you are likely to have the beach to yourself. The remains of the barnacle-encrusted shipwreck *Laura* is a landmark rooted in the seascape here. Read stories of more wrecks back at the tiny clifftop chapel of St Leonard's.

→ Heading S on the A165, turn L onto the B1229 at Dotterel roundabout. Take L to Speeton village. Continue along Main St. Turn L at pond. Parking (donation welcome) at St Leonard's Chapel (YO14 9TD). Follow footpath across fields to coastal path. Descend cliff path to beach.
5 mins, 54.1619, -0.2332

11 FRAISTHORPE BEACH

Wide, sandy beach backed by low clay cliffs with plenty of space in either direction

to walk for miles and have the beach to yourself. Popular with dog walkers. Remains of old pillboxes left over from WWII. Rustic, contemporary beach-front café, the Cowshed, serves food, wine and beers.

→ There is a brown sign off the A165 from Hull. Take L in village of Fraisthorpe. Follow narrow, winding road to beach and paid parking. Walk 5 mins S to quiet stretch of beach.
2 mins, 54.0492, -0.2135

12 GYPSEY RACE

The northernmost chalk stream is the only watercourse on the high Wolds. Because it flows on chalk, it is a winterbourne stream, which means it is intermittent, sometimes disappearing for miles then reappearing unexpectedly, conferring on it an air of mystery. It was revered and honoured with several prehistoric monuments deliberately sited close to it. One of the villages to see the Gypsey Race at its best is Kirby Grindalythe, where it runs along the main street in front of St Andrew's church, also worth a visit for the stunning mosaic that takes up its entire west wall.

→ From Sledmere, follow signs to Kirby Grindalythe from the B1252. Parking by St Andrew's church.

2 mins, 54.0954, -0.6183 ✝ ☸

13 DUGGLEBY HOWE

Impressive late Neolithic round barrow, one of the largest in the UK, built in several stages, reaching a diameter of 38m and 6m high. Excavations in 1890 uncovered a deep grave pit with several adult and child skeletons and artefacts, including a bowl, flint cores and flakes, dating back to 3500 bc. Significantly, the mound is just 300m from the source of the Gypsey Race, an intermittent stream steeped in mystical folklore (see entry).

→ Leave Duggleby on the B1253 towards Sledmere. The howe (tumulus) is almost immediately on the L-hand side. Park on roadside then follow the hedge across field.

5 mins, 54.0904, -0.6553 ✝ ☸ ☙

14 WILLY HOWE

A massive Neolithic round barrow, the largest on the Yorkshire Wolds, standing 200m from the mysterious Gypsey Race (see entry). Thought to be roughly the same age as Stonehenge, it is believed to be a monument rather than a burial mound, as excavations have unearthed no human remains. According to local folklore, if you run around it nine times, you can hear the fairies dancing and singing inside.

→ From Wold Newton, follow the Bridlington Road which becomes Burton Fleming Road for 1½ miles, then turn R and R again at T-junction to parking on R and Willy Howe on L.

5 mins, 54.1360, -0.3767 ✝ ☸

15 RUDSTON MONOLITH

The tallest standing stone in the UK is in the small Wolds village of Rudston. At 7.6m high, the towering monolith, in the churchyard of All Saints' Church, stands taller than any of the Stonehenge circle stones. It is hewn from sandstone from the Cleveland Hills, many miles away, and how it got here is one of its mysteries. It seems likely it marks a prehistoric holy place. The spot is also close to a dramatic bend in the Gypsey Race (see entry). The novelist Winifred Holtby, author of *South Riding*, was born in the village and is buried here.

→ From Rudston village, turn off the B1253 (Thwing Rd) onto School Ln. Parking next to church.

2 mins, 54.0935, -0.3230 ✝ ☸

16 FLIXTON BRIDGE, STAR CARR

Below the surface of a humble field lie the waterlogged remains of an incredible Mesolithic settlement that once stood on the eastern shores of the now vanished Lake Pickering. Headdresses made from red deer skulls, barbed points for hunting and fishing and the earliest evidence of carpentry were unearthed here, making it one of the world's most important archaeological sites. Flixton Bridge is a good place to conjure up an image of the place, marking the centre of the paleo lake. The slight rise in the landscape to the north was a paleo island, with Mesolithic activity contemporary with Star Carr.

→ From the Staxton roundabout on the A1039, continue to Flixton. Best to park in village and walk along Flixton Carr Ln to the bridge. Several footpaths and bridleways lead here.

20 mins, 54.2152, -0.4074 🚶🏃🚴

17 ST MARY'S CHURCH, COWLAM

Accessed through a farmyard and abutting Nissen huts, this tiny, almost forgotten church is pretty much all that remains of a former village. The highlight though is its font, which is an exceptional tub-shaped 12th-century Norman creation, covered with rare decorative carvings depicting various biblical stories.

→ From Sledmere head E on the B1253 towards Bridlington for 2 miles, then turn R, signposted 'Cowlam', for ½ mile. Church is on L behind farm. If locked, the key is at Manor Farm, next door. Beautiful walks from here along Cowlam Well Dale to Phillip's Slack.

2 mins, 54.0765, -0.5250 ✝🏃

18 ST JAMES CHURCH, FORDON

Enchanting church in a hidden Wolds valley, believed to be the smallest active church in Yorkshire and one of the smallest in the UK. The oldest parts of the church are Norman. Note the 18th-century rustic organ and decorated font. During its 900 years, it has been a hideout for smugglers and a shelter for sheep and lambs. Afterwards, explore North Dale (54.1648, -0.4000), chalk grasslands that have been a feature of the Wolds since the Ice Age, and Fordon Chalk Banks (54.1607, -0.3886), a nature reserve and butterfly conservation area.

→ From Wold Newton, head N, signposted 'Fordon', for 1½ miles. Church is on L at bottom of hill, just before crossroads. Keys for church – Call Marshall on 01262 470276

1 min, 54.1611, -0.3938 ✝🏃⛺

19 ST MARTIN'S CHURCH, LOWTHORPE

Former collegiate church, with the roofless ruin of a chancel at one end, located down a leafy lane. Inside the doorway of the church is a curious effigy of a couple lying beneath a sheet from which a tree emerges with the heads of 13 children. Above is a Saxon cross head. The medieval cross in the churchyard is from nearby Kilham, which lost much of its population to the Black Death.

→ Heading NE from Nafferton on the A614, at crossroads take R turn for Lowthorpe. Parking after ½ mile on L. Follow the footpath sign to the church. Alternatively, the church can be reached via a pleasant walk from Bracey Bridge picnic site, which is off the A614 (54.0429, -0.3568).

2 mins, 54.0319, -0.3540 ✝

20 SYKES CHURCH TRAIL

Arguably the most important collection of small rural churches in the UK, rebuilt and refurbished by the Sykes of Sledmere between 1866 and 1913. Employing illustrious architects, G.E. Street (Royal Courts of Justice in London), Temple Moore and leading stained-glass artists, the Sykes family financed the restoration of the 18 churches using their family fortune. Highlights include

St Michael and All Angels in Garton-on-the-Wolds for its astonishing wall paintings; St Edith's at Bishop Wilton with its floor tiles modelled on the Vatican; and the lavish interiors of St Mary's, Sledmere.

→ Parking by war memorial in Sledmere village for St Mary's Church (YO25 3XH). Follow trail at Eychurches.org.uk.

5 mins, 54.0687, -0.5805 ✝

HOLY WELLS

21 ST JOHN'S WELL, HARPHAM

Circular well dedicated to St John of Beverley, born here in ad 640. On his feast day (7 May) the well is decorated with spring flowers and a procession walks from the village church. As well as healing properties, it is said to tame ferocious beasts. The Drummer Boy's well, an artesian spring, is in a field next to the church surrounded by earthworks from the St Quintin family manor. Interesting church.

→ Heading N from Driffield on the A614, take R after Bracey Bridge for Harpham. Continue for 1 mile to village crossroads and roadside parking. Well is 200m ahead on R. Drummer Boy's well is in field W of church (54.0385, -0.3335).

5 mins, 54.0402, -0.3290 ✝

22 SAILOR'S WELL, FILEY

Attractive old stone well situated next to a gorge on the site of several springs which have been a source of water here for centuries. They were used by locals as well as visiting Dutch fishing fleets, who rolled their barrels up from the beach to fill up while fishing off the coast here.

→ Follow signs for Country Park (YO14 9ET) from Filey. Walk across the iron footbridge that crosses Ravine Rd in dir of town. Take the steps down on R-hand side. Well is at the bottom of the steps on R.

5 mins, 54.2127, -0.2882 ✝ ⚹

RUINS & FOLLIES

23 HOLY TRINITY CHURCH, COTTAM

All that remains of the abandoned medieval village of Cottam is the evocative Holy Trinity Chapel, left to crumble over time in the middle of a field. The village was thriving in 1698; however, following the 18th-century enclosure acts, all but four houses were lost. Terraces indicating past streets and houses undulate around the chapel. Walk down Cottam Well Dale to explore the tranquillity of the remote dry valley of Phillip's Slack.

→ From Driffield follow the A614 for ¾ mile

to roundabout. At the second roundabout, take 1st exit onto the B1249 for 3½ miles, then turn L at sign for Cottam. Continue (road swings to R) past Newhouse Farm on R to crossroads (signed Driffield and Langtoft) and take L turn (at footpath sign) to where road bends and carefully park here. Pass through gate into field to chapel.

5 mins, 54.0707, -0.4833 🖼🎣🏃⛰ℹ

24 FORMER RAF COTTAM

It is baffling why this remote hilltop location was chosen as a satellite airfield and bomber station for RAF Driffield in 1939. Its close proximity to the North York Moors meant it was at the mercy of wind and perpetual fog, rendering it completely unsuitable as an airfield. By winter 1941, it was all but abandoned. A section of runway still exists along with the remains of an air-raid shelter and standby set house. Combine with a visit to Holy Trinity Church (see entry).

→ As for Holy Trinity Chapel. Follow path behind chapel and cross road to airfield site and the remains of two runways. Footpaths extend across the site, where further debris can be seen along with fabulous views over the Wolds.

15 mins, 54.0672, -0.4779 🖼

25 WOLD COTTAGE METEORITE

The UK's oldest-known surviving meteorite plummeted through the Earth's atmosphere and landed here in 1795, weighing 56 pounds and measuring 76cm by 71cm; it was the stone that proved meteorites came from space. Farm worker James Shipley was standing so close he was struck by the soil and rocks it threw up into the air. The meteorite was sold to the Natural History Museum for £250, although only half of it made it there. An obelisk was erected at the site by playwright Edward Topham, who lived at Wold Cottage after which the meteorite was named.

→ The obelisk is on private land; however, the owners at Wold Cottage give permission to access it. Ring Mrs Katrina Gray on 01262 470696 to make an appointment.

5 mins, 54.1363, -0.4121 🖼

26 FLAMBOROUGH OLD LIGHTHOUSE

The lighthouse that was never used stands several hundred metres inland from the precipitous cliffs of the Flamborough coastline. Built in 1674 as a business venture, it is the earliest known lighthouse still in existence in the UK. It was never used due to lack of donations from passing ships.

→ From Flamborough, follow Lighthouse Rd (B1259) for 1¾ miles. The lighthouse is on L. Use car park next to new lighthouse.

5 mins, 54.1180, -0.0895 🖼

27 BURTON AGNES MANOR HOUSE

A magnificent Elizabethan stately home that retains the feel of a family home with an impressive art collection and beautiful gardens, including a jungle garden, a yew maze and a breathtaking display of snowdrops in spring. Less visited is the old hall, a 12th-century manor house with its rare, well-preserved Norman undercroft with an impressive vaulted ceiling.

→ Signed from Burton Agnes village, 5 miles SW of Bridlington on the A166. Manor house is by entrance to Burton Agnes Hall.

2 mins, 54.0534, -0.3173 💷☕🖼

HIDDEN DALES & WILDLIFE

28 RSPB BEMPTON CLIFFS

The UK's largest mainland seabird colony at Bempton Cliffs is alive with puffins, gannets, guillemots and razorbills, many arriving between March and October each year. The spectacle, and the sounds and smell, of these swooping creatures at this amazing seabird

28

27

29

city is unforgettable, as is the spectacular seascape. The puffins are undoubtedly the main draw; however, the massive albatross-like gannets are an equally wonderful sight as they plunge into the sea at speed. These magnificent birds pair for life, returning to the same nest each year. Viewpoints, exhilarating coastal walks, café.

→ RSPB Bempton Cliffs, Cliff Lane, Bempton YO15 1JF. From High St, Bempton on the B1229, turn L onto Cliff Ln. Continue 1 mile to RSPB visitor centre parking.

5 mins, 54.1474, -0.1686 🚲🚶‍♀️📷🗑️🛤️🍴

29 CAMP DALE

This area around Folkton Wold is archaeologically rich; the Folkton Drums, three of the most extraordinary objects from Neolithic Britain, were unearthed from a child's grave above Camp Dale in the late 19th century. A perfectly positioned oak bench, part of the Wolds Way WANDER art trail, is sited here with glorious views across the valley. If you continue along the trail through a hawthorn-lined dale, you will reach leafy Stocking Dale, a fragment of ancient woodland and a surprising contrast with the classic dry Wolds valleys.

→ Travelling E on the A1039, just before Flixton turn R at the sign for Fordon and

Wold Newton on to Flixton Brow for around 1½ miles to parking on R with Wolds Way fingerpost opp. Follow Yorkshire Wolds Way path for 1 mile.

25 mins, 54.1771, -0.3759 🚶‍♀️📷🔀📷

HILLTOPS

30 KNAPTON BROW

Spectacular views of the North York Moors and the Vale of Pickering from Knapton Brow, where there is an intriguing art installation, part of a series along the Yorkshire Wolds Way. The artwork is inspired by ancient archaeological remains found in the area and has reinstated a traditional East Yorkshire feature, a dew pond, enhancing the view as a sky mirror. There is a wildflower meadow and carved white figures, inspired by artefacts found near Iron Age settlements in the Derwent Valley.

→ Travelling E on the A64, after turn on L for West Knapton, turn R at the sign for Yorkshire Wolds Way Caravan and Camping. Follow road uphill to parking on roadside at Yorkshire Wolds Way footpath sign on R. Follow footpath alongside earthwork on L to artwork at hilltop.

5 mins, 54.1569, -0.6376 📷🔀🚶‍♀️📷

33 THE FARMHOUSE BAKERY

Scrumptious bakery and coffee shop in a pretty courtyard setting. Sells artisan chocolates, including the most delish hot chocolate.

→ Outgang Rd, Scampston, Malton, YO17 8NG, 01944 759153
54.1672, -0.6841 🍴

34 BEACH CAFÉ, HUNMANBY GAP

Easy-going beachside café in a superb location overlooking Filey Brigg and Bempton cliffs. Cosy interior with a larger decked area. Homemade cakes, bacon rolls and full English breakfast. Summer 9am – 5pm.

→ Sands Rd, Hunmanby Gap, Filey, YO14 9QW, 01723 892945
54.1791, -0.2694 🍴

35 SALT ON THE HARBOUR

À la carte seafood restaurant with cracking views of the waterfront. The menu comprises lobster, crab and fish all landed in Bridlington harbour right outside, the largest shellfish port in Europe.

→ South Pier, Bridlington, YO15 3AW, 01262 606040
54.0803, -0.1933 🍴

FARM SHOPS & DELIS

36 HUNMANBY PANTRY

Stock up your picnic basket with cheeses, chutneys, pies and pastries from the deli counter or ask one of the team to create one of their award-winning hampers for a gourmet al fresco feast.

→ 10 & 12 Bridlington St, Hunmanby, Filey, YO14 0JR, 01723 891300
54.1801, -0.3216 🍴

37 TROTTERS FARM SHOP

Roadside farm shop selling pork from its own outdoor pig herd, bred without antibiotics; beef from three miles away; and lamb from local farms. Award-winning sausages with 30 different flavours.

→ Trotters Farm Shop, Gladvic Farm, Main Rd, Potter Brompton, YO12 4PF, 01944 710721
54.1783, -0.5164 🍴

COSY PUBS

38 THE OLD STAR, KILHAM

Excellent-value home-cooked food and ales are served at this friendly Wolds inn. A traditional pub in the best possible way

31 SYKES MONUMENT

Looming above the Wolds landscape, this elaborate 36m Gothic spire was erected as a memorial to Sir Tatton Sykes, 4th Baronet of Sledmere House, in 1865, two years after his death. Stroll along the adjacent green lane for far-reaching views across the Wolds. This entire area is steeped in ancient history, with burial mounds, earthworks and an important Roman road, Low Street, which ran from York to Bridlington.

→ From Sledmere, follow the B1252 towards Garton-on-the-Wolds for 2 miles. The monument is on the R.
2 mins, 54.0436, -0.5390 📷🖼🚶

CAFÉS & RESTAURANTS

32 GARDEN CAFÉ, SCAMPSTON HALL

Light and airy licensed café overlooking the pretty walled garden and serving light lunches, soups and paninis using local produce and seasonal ingredients from the kitchen garden. Open Mar to Oct.

→ Back Ln, Scampston, Malton, YO17 8NG, 01944 759000
54.1693, -0.6801 🍴

in a historic village, once the Capital of the Wolds. Pull up a bar stool and join in the banter with the locals. Artist David Hockney was once a regular.

→ Church St, Kilham, Driffield, YO25 4RG, 01262 420619
54.0639, -0.3759 🍴

39 THE TRITON INN, SLEDMERE

There is no dressing up of menus at this down-to-earth 18th-century inn, so you won't find *tarte aux pommes avec crème anglaise* but you will find apple pie and custard. Good traditional fare. Nice village. Book ahead for Sunday lunch.

→ Sledmere, Driffield, YO25 3XH, 01377 236078
54.0712, -0.5765 🍴

40 SEABIRDS INN, FLAMBOROUGH

A popular 200-year-old pub serving a traditional pub menu and making the most of its proximity to the North Sea with plenty of fish and seafood dishes. Cosy log fires and a good ambience in the beer garden in summer.

→ 14 Tower St, Flamborough, Bridlington, YO15 1PD, 01262 850242
54.1156, -0.1248 🍴

CAMP, GLAMP & SLEEP

41 WOLDS WAY CARAVAN AND CAMPING

Set up camp at this much-lauded camping and caravan site on a working farm overlooking glorious Wolds scenery, with walks and bike rides on your doorstep. It is a larger site with caravans, but the situation is beautiful and the facilities are top class, including a shop stocking local produce.

→ West Farm, West Knapton, Malton, YO17 8JE, 07960 169219
54.1581, -0.6268 ⛰🏕

42 WOLD FARM CARAVAN AND CAMPING

Pods and bell tents plus camper/caravan pitches (EHU and non-EHU, no tents) on the edge of Flamborough, with fabulous coastal views and its own private path to Bempton Cliffs for spotting puffins, gannets and guillemots.

→ Bempton Ln, Flamborough, Bridlington, YO15 1AT, 01262 850536
54.1324, -0.1380 🏕

43 HUMBLE BEE FARM

Stargaze around a campfire on the terrace of a timber wigwam lodge and collect fresh eggs from the farm for breakfast. There

are also yurts, bell tents and a campsite, all located in an idyllic part of the Wolds, not far from the coast.

→ Flixton, Scarborough, YO11 3UJ, 01723 890437
54.1874, -0.4071 🏕

44 WEST HALE GATE GLAMPING

Lincoln Longwool, Blue Texel and Swaledale are a trio of high-end shepherd's huts named after rare-breed sheep. Rural farm setting and tasteful decor. Also camper van/caravan pitches. Good coastal bus links from the village. Sorry, no kids or dogs.

→ Grindale Rd, Burton Fleming, YO25 3HR, 01262 470336
54.1321, -0.3252 🏕

45 DALE FARM HOLIDAYS

What could be more magical than a rustic nest for two high in the treetops? Alternatively, opt for a quirky yellow 1970s caravan with a hammock for lazy afternoons under big Wolds skies. The fabulous summerhouse, converted from the old cowshed, has large bi-folding doors opening onto the kitchen garden.

→ Bartindale Rd, Hunmanby, Filey, YO14 0JD, 01723 890175
54.1579, -0.3167 🏕

46 LAHTLEWOOD GLAMPING

Friendly off-grid site with 12 glamping pods in a woodland glade. Stock up with tasty treats in nearby foodie Malton to cook in the alfresco kitchen. 'Scrub shack' with toilet and wood-fired hot showers. Kids will love exploring the woods.

→ Carr Ln, East Heslerton, Malton, YO17 8RP, 01944 728510
54.1792, -0.5794 🏕

47 WOLDS WALK GLAMPING

The view of the North York Moors and the Scarborough coastline from these glamping pods is magnificent, not to mention the star-studded night skies. The Yorkshire Wolds Way is on your doorstep should you wish to explore the area's lovely dry valleys.

→ Manor Wold Farm, East Heslerton, Malton, YO17 8RN, 07494 101795
54.1662, -0.5777 🏕

48 THE FOLLIES HUNMANBY & POSH PODS

Stay in a Grade II listed folly that was built as a ruin in 1825 using stone from Filey Brigg and which has now been transformed into two gatehouses. Set in an acre of grounds, it is surrounded by an abundance of wildlife, including owls, squirrels and bats. Posh pods also available.

→ 126 Bridlington St, Hunmanby, Filey, YO14 0LS, 01723 891697/07514 746468 54.1749, -0.3175 🏠

49 DRAGONFLY LODGE

Handcrafted rustic cabin for two with a bespoke hand-built double bed, kitchen and cosy log burner to brew your tea. Solar-powered fairy lights create a magical ambience outdoors. Pizza oven, BBQ and hot tub overlooking a pretty pond.

→ Spring Farm, Grindale, YO16 4XY, 07515 931152 54.1262, -0.2701 🏠

50 FLAMBOROUGH GLAMPING AND VINEYARD

After a day exploring Flamborough's sea caves and rock pools, hunker down in one of the cosy luxury pods on this small family-run vineyard. With names like Gannet, Puffin and Kittiwake, they all sleep 4 and have a kitchen, en suite facilities and underfloor heating.

→ Lighthouse Rd, Flamborough, Bridlington, YO15 1AJ, 07922 598867 54.1137, -0.1187 🏠

51 THE WOLD COTTAGE B&B

Opt for luxury B&B in the Georgian manor house or choose one of the pretty cottages, including the cute Miss Wells Garden Room for two. Heating and water supplied from a straw burner, locally sourced food and fresh flowers from the garden. Perfect base for exploring the Wolds and the coast.

→ Wold Newton, Driffield, YO25 3HL, 01262 470696 54.1361, -0.4067 🏠🍴

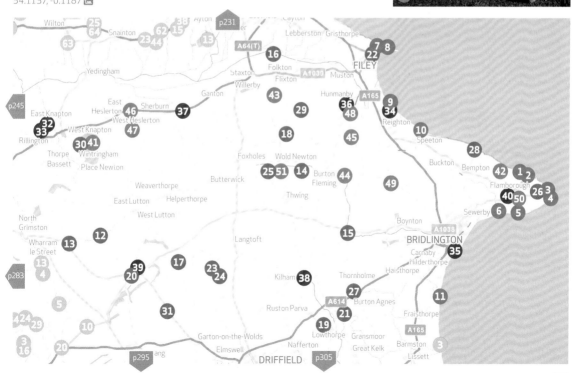

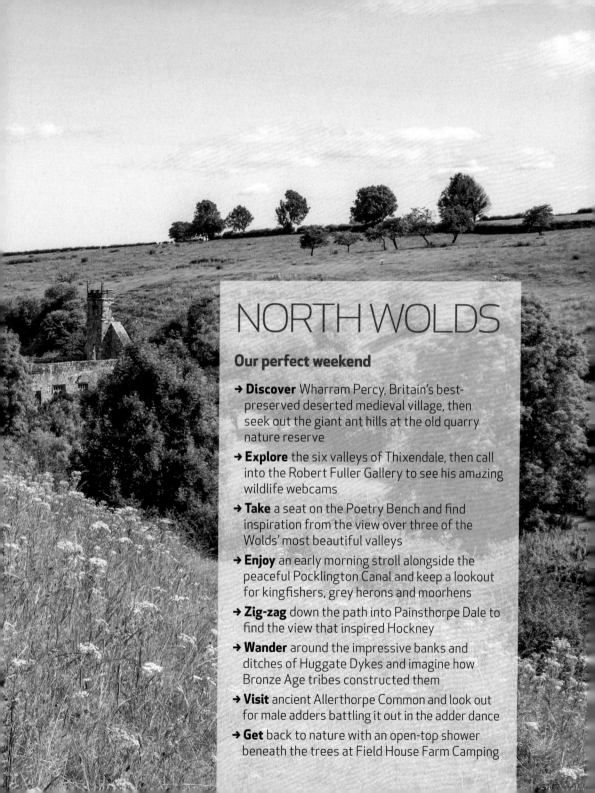

NORTH WOLDS

Our perfect weekend

→ **Discover** Wharram Percy, Britain's best-preserved deserted medieval village, then seek out the giant ant hills at the old quarry nature reserve

→ **Explore** the six valleys of Thixendale, then call into the Robert Fuller Gallery to see his amazing wildlife webcams

→ **Take** a seat on the Poetry Bench and find inspiration from the view over three of the Wolds' most beautiful valleys

→ **Enjoy** an early morning stroll alongside the peaceful Pocklington Canal and keep a lookout for kingfishers, grey herons and moorhens

→ **Zig-zag** down the path into Painsthorpe Dale to find the view that inspired Hockney

→ **Wander** around the impressive banks and ditches of Huggate Dykes and imagine how Bronze Age tribes constructed them

→ **Visit** ancient Allerthorpe Common and look out for male adders battling it out in the adder dance

→ **Get** back to nature with an open-top shower beneath the trees at Field House Farm Camping

The enchantment of the Yorkshire Wolds lies in its network of deeply incised dry valleys: the slacks and dales that weave beneath the rolling uplands of mainly arable landscape. In this topsy-turvy world, the wild is reached not by challenging ascents but by travelling downwards into the beautiful, remote dales.

The Yorkshire Wolds are something of a secret, unspoilt and devoid of tourists. This area takes in some of the Wolds' most beautiful dales around Huggate, Thixendale and Garrowby Hill. Above the slacks is a glorious, undulating landscape, immense skies and timeless villages – scenery that appealed to artist David Hockney, who drew inspiration from the countryside around here.

The dry valleys were created at the end of the last ice age, around 18,000 years ago, when fast-flowing streams carved out the valleys. This most northerly outcrop of chalk on which the landscape has formed drains water so efficiently that the valleys run dry.

On the high Wolds there are no springs or streams as the chalk is porous. Meres and dew ponds are a feature of many Wolds villages. These man-made ponds were created in the 18th and 19th centuries to provide water for farm animals. So precious was this commodity that in the hot summer of 1826, a ferocious battle broke out between neighbouring villages when the pond at Fridaythorpe ran dry and men went to steal water from the pond in Fimber.

People have inhabited the Wolds for thousands of years, leaving a rich archaeological legacy. The Wolds countryside today is the result of the 18th-century Enclosure Acts, designed to make a profit from the land. Despite the loss of many important archaeological sites to the plough, some spectacular finds have been unearthed: a rare Iron Age horse and cart burial at Pocklington and the biggest Middle Iron Age cemetery in the country at Wetwang. Even earlier and still visible are the impressive Bronze Age earthworks of Huggate Dykes. Wharram Percy is one of the best-preserved, deserted medieval villages in Britain and an evocative place to visit, as is the less well-known Hanging Grimston.

Wildlife abounds in the hidden pockets of this beautiful landscape. Above are red kites, skylarks, barn owls and buzzards, while in the fields hares are a frequent sight, and deer roam freely. For those seeking peace and an immersion in nature, they can be found in many places here. After a day's wandering in this unique wilderness, there are pretty villages and cosy pubs offering a warm Yorkshire welcome.

5

CANALS & LAKES

1 CANAL HEAD, POCKLINGTON CANAL

Having remained relatively undisturbed throughout its 200-year history, this idyllic, rural canal is one of the best in the country for wildlife. This is a particularly lovely stretch of the 9½-mile waterway, with dragonflies and damselflies flitting over crystal-clear waters where otters and water voles paddle and mute swans, coots and moorhens nest. Small picnic site with benches and information boards; the one at Silburn Lock has a photograph of children learning to swim in days gone by. Although only partly restored, the canal is in water for its entire length and navigable for seven miles between East Cottingwith and Bielby basin.

→ Located off the A1079 10 miles E of York. Follow brown signs to car park and picnic areas (YO42 1NW).

1 min, 53.9155, -0.7842 🎪🚶🏊

2 ALLERTHORPE LAKELAND PARK

If you are looking for a wild-swim experience in an organised setting, Allerthorpe Lake is a good option. The man-made lake has a maximum depth of around 2m with a sandy bottom and no weeds. Being reasonably shallow, it warms up quickly in summer. Water sports available, including stand-up paddle boarding, kayaking and canoeing. Set in 22 hectares of woodland with lakeside walks. On-site café and camping.

→ From Pocklington follow West Green, then continue on to Hodsow Ln. Go straight across at roundabout onto Main St, then continue on to Back Ln, past the Plough Inn on R. Continue to L turn to lakeland park (YO42 4RL).

1 min, 53.9037, -0.8145 🏊🚣🎪🚶🏊

3 WOLDS DEW PONDS

These shimmering oases of water are a distinctive feature of the Yorkshire Wolds landscape. Created in the 18th and 19th centuries, they were an essential source of water for farm animals when a natural supply of surface water was not always available in the dry chalk landscape. The ponds are of important historical value and are part of a conservation project. This walk up out of Thixendale takes you past one of the best examples in a lovely setting.

→ Roadside parking in Thixendale. With pub on your L walk to junction, turn R and walk up Huggate Hill for ½ mile. When you reach Gill's Farm (YO25 9SB) on L, turn R down footpath to carved Dew Pond sign. Dew Pond is through gate on R.

20 mins, 54.0231, -0.7115 📷🚶

RUINS & FOLLIES

4 WHARRAM PERCY

One of the country's best-preserved deserted villages, tucked away in a tranquil Wolds valley. It is best approached along Deep Dale, where the evocative ruins of St Martin's church gradually come into view. After you have explored the church and medieval fishpond, climb onto the plateau to trace the outlines of more than 30 lost houses. Settled in prehistoric times, Wharram flourished between the 12th and 14th centuries before it was abandoned around 1500; however, the church continued to be used long after this.

→ From Wharram-le-Street on the B1248, take the signposted R turn after ½ mile. Continue past parking for Wharram Percy to sharp R bend and lay-by parking. Follow road to Centenary Way footpath then through gate into Deep Dale and path to Wharram Percy.

20 mins, 54.0704, -0.6872 📷🚴🚶📷

5 BURDALE TUNNEL

The southern portal of a disused railway tunnel on the abandoned Malton and Driffield Railway, burrowing beneath Wharram Percy Wold. When the line closed in 1958, the tunnel

6

4

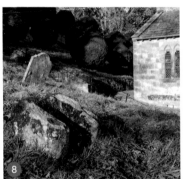

8

was bricked up. It is a gem of a place in a picturesque and remote setting. At nearby Fimber Garth, the Yorkshire Wolds Railway has restored part of the track, offering short cab rides in its locomotive.

→ From Wharram-le-Street, take the R turn for Wharram Percy after crossroads. Follow road for 1½ miles to small green and roadside parking. (The inspiration for David Hockney's *Three Trees at Thixendale* is across the field.) Walk under brick bridge, then turn L to tunnel. The Yorkshire Wolds Railway, just off Fimber roundabout on the B1248 Beverley Rd on L (YO25 3HG), offers short rides on its locomotive, the *Sir Tatton Sykes*. Open Sun and bank holidays, Apr to Oct. There is a rustic café in the woods opposite.

15 mins, 54.0499, -0.6686 🏕🏔🚗🏕

SACRED & ANCIENT

6 HUGGATE DYKES

A series of mysterious Bronze Age mounds and channels carved out of the earth to mark important boundaries in the landscape. Lying close to an ancient trackway, now the Yorkshire Wolds Way, they stretch across 80–100 miles of high ground. These dykes are one of the best-preserved remnants of

an earlier more complex system. Wander through these peaceful dales to marvel at these impressive ditches, reflecting upon how our ancient forebears divided land for social, ritual and agricultural purposes.

→ From Huggate, head out on York Ln for 1½ miles to park at Waterman's Hole (54.0008, -0.6950). Follow the Chalkland Way through Tun Dale and Frendal Dale. Impressive dykes sit at the intersection of these two dales.

5 mins, 53.9887, -0.7001 🚶🦮🚗🔭🏕🏔

7 ST ETHELBURGA'S CHANCEL

An exquisite church hidden down a wooded slope on an ancient site overlooking a picturesque valley and large pond. Rebuilt in 1849, the church retains its Saxon font and Norman chancel arch, with two rows of chevron carvings and intricately carved capitals above the pillars. Services are conducted by candlelight as it has no electricity. Visit in spring for displays of snowdrops and aconites. The Minster Way, an old pilgrim's route, runs past it.

→ From Pocklington, follow the B1247 then The Mile to Grimthorpe Hill for 2½ miles. Follow Grimthorpe Hill to Givendale Ln for 1½ miles. Church is on R with lay-by parking.

2 mins, 53.9746, -0.7614 ⛪🚶🏕ℹ️

7

8 ALL SAINT'S CHURCH, KIRBY UNDERDALE

Perched on a slope leading down to Hundle Beck, this characterful Norman church is found in one of the loveliest and less frequented corners of the Wolds. Set into the wall in the north aisle is a small Roman carving of Mercury, dating back to the 2nd or 3rd century, which was discovered in the rectory garden a hundred years ago. In the churchyard lies the base of a cross once situated at the top of Garrowby Hill. It is known as 'King Harold's Chair' as local legend tells of how the king once sat in it to admire the view after the Battle of Stamford Bridge in 1066.

→ From Fridaythorpe, follow the A166 towards York for 4 miles, then turn R down Roman Rd for 1 mile. Turn L to lay-by parking on R by church.

1 min, 54.0171, -0.7677 ✝🚶

9 ST JAMES' CHURCH, NUNBURNHOLME

An ancient stone cross carved by Anglo Saxon and Viking sculptors stands inside the church. It had been discarded and built into the church's fabric and was only rediscovered during the restoration of the church in 1872 by architect George Gilbert Scott (Albert Memorial). There

is also a Norman arch and medieval font. Rev Francis Orpen Morris, a famous ornithologist, was rector here from 1854 to 1893. The village was abandoned during William the Conqueror's wasting of the North and re-established on the south side of the beck, a distance from the church.

→ From Nunburnholme, head down Church Ln to end of village to church on L and parking.

1 min, 53.9194, -0.7106 ✝

10 ST MARY'S CHURCH, FIMBER

A Sykes' church and the site of a Bronze Age burial mound. Stunning stained-glass windows by prestigious stained-glass makers, Clayton and Bell. Inside the church there is an interesting display about the work of archaeologist J. R. Mortimer, who was born in Fimber and was responsible for the excavation of many significant barrows in the Yorkshire Wolds, including Duggleby Howe.

→ From the A166 at Fridaythorpe, pass petrol station on L, then turn L for 1 mile along the B1251. Turn L into Fimber village. Church on R. Parking near green.

3 mins, 54.0339, -0.6361 ✝

9

10

12

11

13

11 ALLERTHORPE COMMON

An ancient landscape of river and lake sands deposited around 12,000 years ago to create an area of lowland heath with a huge variety of habitats, of which only one per cent remains in England. Look out for adders in early spring, easier to spot after they have shed their skin, exposing extraordinarily colourful bodies. If you are lucky, you may see male adders engaged in battle, performing the adder dance, to establish their territory as the breeding season begins in late spring.

→ Heading S on the A1079 near Barmby Moor, turn R, signed 'Sutton-on-Derwent and Thornton'. Take next L, signposted 'Thornton', to parking in Forestry Commission car park ½ mile along road on R. Cross road and follow forest track until you come to a line of pylons. Turn R and nature reserve is a short distance along on R.

10 mins, 53.9187, -0.8448 🚶♿️🐕🛈

12 MILLINGTON WOOD

A beautiful ancient ash wood covering Lily Dale, dating back nearly 1,000 years. This is a typical dry valley of the Yorkshire Wolds, with the distinctive features of a chalk landscape and many rare botanical woodland species. Bluebells carpet the woodland floor in spring, and bell flowers, at home in the calcareous soil, tower above the flower-filled verges in summer. Follow the paths to end of the woods for glorious views over the treetops and the Yorkshire Wolds beyond.

→ Located 1 mile N of Millington village and 4 miles NE of Pocklington. From Pocklington, head towards Millington on the minor road, then follow brown road signs to Millington Wood.

2 mins, 53.9685, -0.7261 🅿️🚶⛽️🛈♿️

13 WHARRAM QUARRY NATURE RESERVE

A disused chalk quarry, now home to a riot of wildflowers that thrive on the thin Yorkshire Wolds soil. Admire the different species, including rare autumn gentian, woolly thistle, quaking grass and lady's bedstraw, once used for stuffing mattresses because of its sweet smell. Undisturbed anthills also cluster beneath the chalk cliff face; some of the more sizeable ones may be almost 50 years old, as ants extend their homes by the size of a fist each year. Best time to visit is mid-summer.

16

→ At the crossroads in Wharram-le-Street, follow sign for Birdsall. The reserve is on L after ½ mile. Limited parking by main gate.
2 mins, 54.0774, -0.6890 ⚅ 🎋 ⛵

14 ROBERT FULLER GALLERY

World-renowned wildlife artist Robert Fuller runs this excellent gallery of his artwork from his home at Fotherdale Farm. He also has more than 100 cameras, hidden in the nests of barn owls, tawny owls, kestrels and stoats, positioned in his garden and the surrounding countryside, which relay images to screens you can view inside the gallery.
→ Fotherdale Farm, Thixendale, YO17 9LS, 01759 368355
1 min, 54.0294, -0.7257 🚗

HIDDEN DALES & VALLEYS

15 MILLINGTON PASTURES

The dry chalk valleys of Millington Pastures, some of the loveliest in England, are grazed by sheep and highland cattle and crossed by ancient sheep tracks, a Roman road and the Wolds Way. One of the steepest valleys is Sylvan Dale, which has a series of earthworks, including lines where an Iron Age tribe cut into the chalk. There are several springs in the area, including one forded by the Romans centuries ago. The Huggate Sheep Walk nearby is an old drovers' road. Pack a picnic for a mooch around this sublime corner of the Wolds.
→ From Millington, follow Wood Gate N for 1½ miles, past entrance to Millington Woods. Continue along this beautiful road to parking on R at 53.9667, -0.7180. Look for spring on L and continue through gate to Sylvan Dale.
5 mins, 53.9635, -0.7099 🚶 🛶 ⛵ 🏕 🎋 ⛵

16 WORM DALE

Swirls in the grass decorate the bottom of Worm Dale, conjuring up images of an ancient earthwork. These are, in fact, *Waves and Time*, a modern art creation. The spirals sit at the intersection of three lovely dry Wolds valleys and with a nearby signpost and footpaths, this is a great place for an adventure into other hidden dales.
→ Roadside parking in Thixendale. With pub on your L walk to junction, turn R and walk up Huggate Hill for ½ mile. When you reach Gill's Farm (YO25 9SB) on L, turn R down footpath to carved Dew Pond sign. Then pass through gate and turn L down into dale.
25 mins, 54.0194, -0.7113 🚶 ⚅ 🎋 🐾 🎋

14

15

17 PAINSTHORPE DALE

This delightful dale, hidden away in the most captivating Wolds scenery, inspired a Hockney painting. Perhaps hoping to keep it his secret, he called this steep-sided valley on the western escarpment of the Wolds 'Bugthorpe Valley'. A gravel track zig-zags to the dale bottom, where there is a crystal-clear stream running into a pretty pond. Pure Yorkshire paradise.

→ Travelling E from York on the A166, take L at top of Garrowby Hill, signposted 'Uncleby'. Follow road for 1 mile, then turn L. Gate on to access land and dale is a few metres down on R.

5 mins, 54.0146, -0.7470 🚶🚴🛈⚙🦎🌊🏔

18 HORSE DALE

At the intersection of three of the loveliest dry Wolds valleys, Horse Dale, Holm Dale and Harper Dale, take a seat on the sculpted Poetry Bench, one of six along the Yorkshire Wolds Way; you will find a notebook to leave a poem for others to read. Also a prime location to spot the marbled white butterfly in summer. Nearby Huggate is the highest village in the Wolds and has one of the deepest wells in the country, as well as a beautiful ancient church, a good pub and a café.

→ Park in Huggate and follow road to the end of village past church on R. Follow Yorkshire Wolds Way signpost N into Horse Dale.

20 mins, 54.0018, -0.6561 🚶⚙🛈🌊🚴🦎🏔🛈

19 DEEP DALE, BISHOP WILTON

This lovely meandering dry dale, part wooded, part grassy slopes, appears as a beautiful vista at the end of a forested track. Nearby is Bishop Wilton Wold, the highest point in the Yorkshire Wolds (250m), better known as Garrowby Hill. The superb views from here over the Vale of York were famously captured by artist David Hockney. Afterwards, tuck into coffee and cake at the community café in charming Bishop Wilton.

→ Travelling E from York up Garrowby Hill, after the R turn for Bishop Wilton, turn R into Beacon Rd. After ½ mile park in lay-by on R (53.9931, -0.7626) opp footpath on L. Follow footpath through field and woodland track to Deep Dale: open access land and footpaths.

15 mins, 53.9898, -0.7475 🚶🦎🛈🏔🌊⚙🛈

20 FRIDAYTHORPE

One of the best places to begin an adventure into the network of unique dry valleys sculpted by glaciers that characterise the Wolds – it is also the mid-

way point of the 79-mile Yorkshire Wolds Way. Don't forget to seek out the tiny 12th-century Norman church.

→ In Fridaythorpe, park near duck pond. With pond on L, follow road, taking L fork until you pick up Yorkshire Wolds Way footpath, passing a large animal feed plant on R. Continue along track to gate that opens out into glorious Wolds scenery.
10 mins, 54.0202, -0.6665 🚶🌲🐄⛰️ℹ️📷✛

21 HANGING GRIMSTON
Little-known deserted medieval village situated in a secluded corner of the Wolds, inhabited in 1381 but abandoned by the 16th century. Only ridge and furrow earthworks survive; nevertheless, it remains an atmospheric setting from which to soak up stunning views down Open Dale. Neolithic and Bronze Age barrows are scattered across Hanging Grimston Wold to the N, parallel to the Roman road. More lovely views extend towards the Vale of York through Deep Dale. An absolute gem of a place to explore.

→ Travelling from York on the A166, continue up Garrowby Hill, then turn L, signposted 'Thixendale', following Roman road for 3 miles. Turn L, signposted 'Hanging Grimston'. Parking

space at 54.0375, -0.7793. Walk S to gated road to Hanging Grimston earthworks, or head N (over stile) to Hanging Grimston Wold and Deep Dale.
10 mins, 54.0313, -0.7809 🚶🌲⛰️🏊🚲ℹ️✛

CAFÉS & TEAROOMS

22 RACHEL'S WALNUT COTTAGE TEAROOM
Enjoy homemade cakes, mouth-watering walnut scones and bowls of soup from pretty china crockery at this friendly tearoom situated in the highest village in the Wolds. Delicious locally made ice cream. Take a seat in the tearoom or beside the vintage tractors in the sunny garden.

→ Pocklington Ln, Huggate, YO42 1YJ, 01377 288378
53.9842, -0.6595 🍴

23 WORLD PEACE CAFÉ, KILNWICK PERCY
Explore acres of parkland, lakeside walks and woodlands at this friendly café in the gardens of Kilnwick Percy Hall, a Buddhist meditation centre. Paninis, quiches, soups and delicious cakes. Vegetarian and vegan.

→ Kilnwick Percy Hall, Pocklington, YO42 1UF, 01759 304832
53.9388, -0.74322 🍴

24 THIXENDALE VILLAGE HALL

Tea, coffee, homemade cakes and scones are served by volunteers from the village at this friendly pop-up café most Sunday afternoons throughout the summer, 11am – 4pm.

→ Thixendale, Malton, YO17 9TG, 01377 288647
54.0390, -0.7160 ⏹

25 RAMBLER'S REST, MILLINGTON

Popular hub for walkers, cyclists and locals, who come for the homemade family recipes cooked on a range that once sat in the farmhouse kitchen. Tearoom and restaurant inside or tables outside overlooking the village. Also B&B in the old granary.

→ The Ramblers Rest, Main St, Millington, York, YO42 1TX, 01759 305220
53.9551, -0.7351 ⏹

26 BISHOP WILTON COMMUNITY SHOP AND CAFÉ

Located in a converted Methodist chapel, this community village store and café stocks fresh fruit and vegetables, own Bishop Wilton wine and preserves. Saturday pop-up bakery. Good spot for coffee and cake after a walk to Bishop Wilton Wold, the highest point in the Yorkshire Wolds. Mon to Fri 9am – 5.30pm, Sat 9am – 5pm, Sun 9am – 3pm.

→ Main St, Bishop Wilton, YO42 1SR, 01759 369774
53.9855, -0.7848 ⏹ ⏹

COSY PUBS

27 WOLDS INN, HUGGATE

Cosy 16th-century inn popular with locals, walkers and cyclists and known for its legendary steak pies – and its claim to be the first pub David Hockney got drunk in after stooking corn in the fields here as a boy.

→ Driffield Rd, Huggate, YO42 1YH, 01377 288217
53.9837, -0.6559

28 GAIT INN, MILLINGTON

The little village of Millington is blessed with two fine eateries, including this friendly, traditional country pub. Expect pub classics like lasagne, beef and potato pie and burgers, as well as vegetarian dishes and a good choice of real ales.

→ Millington, York, YO42 1TX, 01759 302045
53.9546, -0.7357 ⏹

29 THE CROSS KEYS INN, THIXENDALE

Traditional one-room village pub nestled in the deep valley of Thixendale, popular with walkers and cyclists. Guest ales and pub grub – it is a pub that serves food, not a restaurant that serves beer. Accommodation next door.

→ Thixendale, Malton, YO17 9TG, 01377 288272
54.0383, -0.7112 ⏹ ⏹

30 THE JOLLY FARMERS INN, LEAVENING

Friendly village local with up to five regional ales and good-value pub grub, including the popular local's favourite, beef stew and Yorkshire pudding.

→ Main St, Leavening, Malton, YO17 9SA, 01653 658276
54.0574, -0.8026 ⏹

LOCAL FOOD & DRINKS

31 RYEDALE VINEYARDS

The most northerly commercial vineyard in Britain producing delicious award-winning wines from 16 grape varieties, plus cider and apple juice from its heritage apple orchard. Also has a small B&B. The rustic Fox Room is in the eaves of the 500-year-old cruck-beamed farmhouse.

→ Farfield Farm, Westow, York, YO60 7LS, 01653 658035 or 07792 276713
54.0589, -0.8333 ⏹ ⏹

WILDER CAMPING

32 BROWN MOOR FARM

Secluded wild camping on an organic working farm with spectacular views of the Wolds, run by friendly hosts. Eggs and cold drinks from an honesty box. Beautiful situation and walks. Pristine night skies.

→ Brown Moor Farm, Leavening, Malton, YO17 9SS, 07341 119319
54.0496, -0.7694 ⏹

33 FIELD HOUSE CAMPSITE

Off-grid wild camping with rustic, open-air, solar-powered hot showers – cold option for the brave – offering a magical bathing adventure. Secluded, peaceful location with sustainability at its core.

→ Field House Farm, Tibthorpe, Driffield, YO25 9JZ, 07974 379181
53.9853, -0.5838 ⏹

34 COUNTRY HUTS ON THE WOLDS

A beautiful pair of traditional shepherd's huts, Wool and Wicket, created from reclaimed timber, insulated with sheep's wool and with log burners. On warmer days relax on the veranda, overlooking the landscape that inspired artist David Hockney.

→ Thixendale, Malton, YO17 9TG, 07824 312514
54.0395, -0.7198

35 PRIVATE HILL GLAMPING

Small, award-winning luxury glamping campsite with four geodesic domes named after the farm's Aberdeen Angus cattle. Electric vehicle charge point. Magnificent views across the Vale of York.

→ Thrussendale Rd, Acklam, Malton, YO17 9RG, 01653 917288
54.0461, -0.7938

36 THE HOBBIT'S DELL

Off-grid Landpod with a canvas and half-timber cladded roof that flips up to let the fresh air in and to soak up the far-reaching views. Shower shack and compost loo. Also spacious wild-camping field (tap with running water) for five tents. No Wi-Fi but very good mobile signal.

→ Manor Farm, Acklam, Malton, YO17 9RR, 07846 269128
54.0455, -0.7946

37 WOLDS EDGE HOLIDAY LODGES

Hire bikes and pootle along quiet country lanes, collect eggs for breakfast and delight in the early morning birdsong. There are two snug huts; seven lodges, including the delightful Mill Pond Lodge, tucked away by a wildlife pond; and a treehouse with a large wrap-around decked area overlooking the glorious Wolds countryside.

→ Main St, Bishop Wilton, York, YO42 1RX, 07768 534434
53.9823, -0.7910

38 THE BLACKSMITH'S SHOP, NORTHFIELD LODGE

If the stunning views from the south-facing terrace over the undulating Hockney landscape inspire you, then sign up for painting courses at this gorgeous rustic log cabin. There's also bread baking with Anna, who is a passionate cook. Also two more cottages available.

→ Northfield Farm, Huggate, York, YO42 1YN, 01377 288298
54.0003, -0.6470

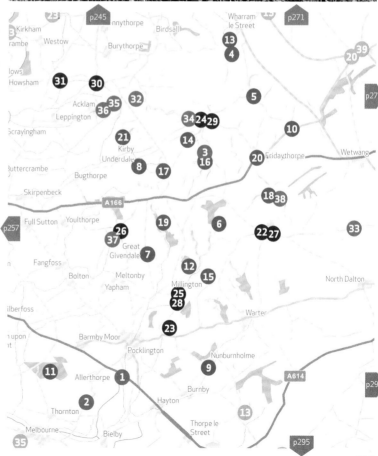

SOUTH WOLDS & HUMBER

Our perfect weekend

→ **Paddle** the River Hull to Pulfin Bog to see cormorants, herons and little egrets

→ **Hike** a section of the Yorkshire Wolds Way, stopping for a drink at the Green Dragon in Welton, where Dick Turpin was captured

→ **Indulge** in an al fresco meal at the Pipe and Glass, then explore the garden with its 400-year-old yew tree

→ **Climb** the staircase to the tower at St Mary's Church in Kirkburn to discover two rooms where monks stayed on their journey to Bridlington Priory

→ **Cycle** the old railway line along the Hudson Way and make a wish at St Helen's Well

→ **Hunt** for the steps from nowhere to nowhere at Londesborough Park, then enjoy a picnic overlooking the lake

→ **Go** fishing in the crystal-clear waters of Driffield Beck, the most northerly chalk stream in the country

→ **Wander** along Hessle Foreshore beneath the monumental Humber Bridge to watch passing ships and wading birds

The rolling chalk hills of this southern corner of the Wolds extend in an arc from the Humber estuary and take in some of Yorkshire's prettiest villages and its finest gastropubs. To the north is beautiful Beverley, and the upper Hull Valley lies further east with its delightful chalk streams and wetlands abundant with wildlife.

The Humber Bridge is one of the world's longest single-span suspension bridges. The structure is even more magnificent when viewed from the wildflower-fringed Hessle Foreshore or the green oasis of the Humber Bridge Country Park. At North Ferriby, the discovery of three Bronze Age boats in 1937 was one of the most important finds in maritime history, revealing that people were contemplating crossing oceans 4,000 years ago.

From here the Yorkshire Wolds rise as gently undulating hills dotted with picture-postcard villages: Brantingham, Welton and North Newbald. This is a walkers' paradise, taking in sweeping views and the most tranquil dales of the Wolds, including the scenic dry valley of Swin Dale. The ancient village of Goodmanham was a religious site for the Celts with a holy spring, St Helen's Well, and a temple where All Hallows Church now stands. In a pivotal moment in history, King Edwin of Northumbria converted to Christianity here in ad 627. At Londesborough, the evocative 18th-century parkland, with its lakes, woodland, deer shelter and solitary stone staircase, is all that remains of a lost stately home.

The Georgian town of Beverley, with its minster and historic Westwood, is a good base for exploring the southern Wolds and East Yorkshire. The main river here is the chalk-fed River Hull, which rises from a series of springs west of Driffield. The gin-clear waters of these most northerly chalk streams provide an important habitat for aquatic plants and fish, including grayling and brown trout.

Those seeking water adventures should look to the Driffield Navigation, which includes the Driffield Canal, with launches for kayaks and paddleboards at Canal Head, Brigham Bridge and Frodingham Landing, also popular with wild swimmers. The canal forms the River Hull, and the stretch from Baswick Landing makes for a particularly scenic paddle.

Nature lovers will appreciate the sheer variety of wildlife offered by the diverse habitats at Tophill Low and Pulfin Bog, which flank the River Hull, and the wetlands of Skerne and North Cave. Otters, kingfishers, water voles, grass snakes and all manner of birdlife have made their homes here.

RIVERS & LAKES

1 BRIGHAM BRIDGE, DRIFFIELD CANAL

A restored swing bridge along the 11-mile Driffield Canal with a launch for paddleboards, kayaks or canoes. The northern section is the canal and the southern section is the River Hull, which meanders through the plain of Holderness. Pleasant paddle to Wansford Lock (take out at 53.9926, -0.3815). There are a number of locks to portage, so may be more suitable for experienced paddlers.

→ From North Frodingham, follow the B1249 W for 1¼ miles, passing North Frodingham Wharf and continuing to L turn signed 'Brigham'. Continue to village and parking over bridge. Suggested donation of £5 to launch craft. Honesty box. Under 17s no charge.
1 min, 53.9680, -0.3605 🛶

2 BASWICK LANDING, RIVER HULL

Idyllic stretch of the River Hull with easy access for paddleboard or kayak launch or for a wild swim. The nature reserve at Tophill Low is upstream. Downstream take out at Wilfholme Landing or paddle past Pulfin Bog, a remnant of the fens that once occupied the river valley. Can be weedy in high summer.

→ From Brandesburton, follow Mill Ln for 3 miles, crossing bridge at Burshill to car park with honesty box.
2 mins, 53.9131, -0.3665 🏊🛶🎣📷🛶

3 WILFHOLME LANDING, RIVER HULL

Pleasant stretch of the River Hull for a paddleboard or kayak adventure. Head upstream towards the nature reserve at Tophill Low or downstream to Pulfin Bog. Can be weedy in high summer.

→ From Watton, head SW on Beverley Rd/A164 to Church Ln, then turn L onto Wilfholme Rd for 3½ miles to landing and parking. Walk over the bank to the launch spot.
1 min, 53.9098, -0.3836 🛶

4 TICKTON, RIVER HULL

A tranquil section of the River Hull for a stand-up paddleboard or kayak trip towards Pulfin Bog Nature Reserve. Launch at the tiny pebble beach beneath the bridge because it can be muddy elsewhere. Beach to get out further along before reserve (53.8735, -0.3984), which is a nice spot for a wild swim. The Crown & Anchor pub is good for refreshments.

→ From Beverley, follow the A1035 for 1¼ miles. After crossing River Hull, take R for Tickton, then immediately R again on to Weel Rd and verge parking. Launch is beneath road bridge.
5 mins, 53.8615, -0.3970 🛶🏊🎣🏕🚶🏴‍☠️ℹ️🛶

5 WEEL ROAD, RIVER HULL

Easy launch for paddleboards or kayaks just upstream of the historic Beverley Boatyard. You can enjoy a pleasant there-and-back paddle to the Crown & Anchor Pub in Tickton. The river is still tidal here, so be mindful of river levels, flow and wind.

→ From the Crown & Anchor at Tickton, follow Weel Rd S for just over 1 mile to a small parking bay on R and slipway.
1 min, 53.8445, -0.3994 🛶

6 WELTON WATERS ADVENTURE CENTRE

A water sports centre situated by a lovely stretch of the River Humber, offering kayaking, paddleboarding, sailing and wind sailing on its wide waters. Open-water swimming in the sheltered lagoons. You can also launch your own kayak or paddleboard for a launch fee.

→ Travelling E on the A63, take the turning for Elloughton/Brough/Welton. Follow the road to the L and at the traffic lights turn L. After 50m turn R onto Stanley Jackson Way. At the

T-junction turn R onto Common Ln. Follow the lane over a railway crossing and after ½ mile bear L at the junction and the WWAC is a red-brick building on the R. On-site car park and parking on the verges nearby. OWS £5 summer, £2 winter.

2 mins, 53.7149, -0.5489 🏊🚣🏄

SACRED & ANCIENT

7 ALL HALLOWS CHURCH, GOODMANHAM

One of the decisive events of British history took place at the site of this 12th-Century church in ad 627, when Edwin, King of Northumbria, converted to Christianity at this very spot – then the location of an important pagan temple. Edwin and his priest, Coifi, rode to Goodmanham, desecrated the temple and had it burned to the ground. The church's Victorian stained-glass windows depict the event.

→ From Market Weighton, head NW on Market Pl towards Londesborough Rd. Turn R on to Londesborough Rd, then turn R onto Goodmanham Rd for 1 mile. On-street parking by church.

2 mins, 53.8769, -0.6478 ✝🚲

8 WATTON PRIORY

This was once the largest house of the Gilbertine Order in England (founded in 1150); however, only St Mary's church, the nuns' and canons' cloisters, the prior's lodging and a barn remain. In the field behind the church are extensive earthworks indicating the scale of the monastic precinct, including remnants of monastic fishponds. The prior's lodging (Watton Abbey) is privately owned, but the early 16th-century church and beautiful old pasture with its mounds, embankments and walnut trees are worth exploring if you are in the area (Tophill Low Nature Reserve is round the corner).

→ From Driffield, take the A164 Beverley Rd S for 4½ miles to L turn for Watton. Continue ¼ mile down Church Ln to roadside parking by church on L.

2 mins, 53.9336, -0.4448 ✝🚲⛺ℹ

9 ST MARY'S CHURCH, KIRKBURN

Fascinating church of Norman origins with a surprise open stairway to the tower leading to two small rooms once used by Augustinian monks on their way between Gisborough and Bridlington priories. Take a close look at the fabulous Norman font with its characterful carved rustic figures before seeking out the old path behind the church, where the

origins of the River Hull bubble up in the woodland glade.

→ From Driffield, follow the A614 for 3½ miles, then turn R for Kirkburn onto Main St, and R again to church on L.

2 mins, 53.9823, -0.5076 ✝

HOLY WELLS

10 ST HELEN'S WELL, GOODMANHAM

Interesting holy well in a wooded valley above the old railway line, now the Hudson Way cycle route. The spring water rises from a natural grotto beneath an old elder tree and is channelled into a triangular stone bath; it may have been used for healing – or piped to the trackside for steam trains. Look for the wishing tree, adorned with ribbons. This is one of at least four wells in East Yorkshire dedicated to St Helen, mother of Constantine the Great.

→ From the Red Lion pub in Market Weighton, head SE on Beverley Rd, then at the roundabout take the first exit onto Finkle St. Continue onto Spring Rd for about 1 mile to roadside parking on L with path leading down to well. If on foot or bike, follow Hudson Way cycle and walking trail for 1 mile from Market Weighton.

5 mins, 53.8703, -0.6464 ✝👥👣↩

11 ST HELEN'S WELL, SOUTH CAVE

Former roadside well before the road was diverted in the 18th century when the 'castle' (now Cave Castle Hotel) was built in 1875 and the irregular lake created from the old formal canal. The well has been repaired over the years and lined with dressed rock and a pitched roof added. Cave Castle dates back to the 1700s as the site of a manor house and has secret tunnels leading to the adjacent church.

→ From Market Weighton, follow the A1034 to Church Hill in South Cave for 8 miles. Turn L up hill before entrance to Cave Castle to parking by All Saint's Church. Walk back to Castle and well is on R down by lake.

5 mins, 53.7669, -0.6104 ✝👥

12 ST HELEN'S WELL, NORTH CAVE

A holy spring hidden away in a beautifully tendered plot behind the old Quaker Meeting House. The well rises in a stone-lined chamber set at the base of a small mound surrounded by a lovely woodland garth, and the water seeps away to join a pretty, marshy stream. It was formerly used by the Quakers, who were very important in the village, and there was once a small burial ground at this site.

13

13

13

15

14

→ Follow the A1079 from Market Weighton. Continue on to Cliffe Rd for 5½ miles, then turn R onto Townend Ln and L on to the B1230 to Church St. Parking at 53.7821, -0.6437. The well is located behind Quaker Cottage and reached by a path to L and through two gates, where access is permitted.

5 mins, 53.7826, -0.6437

RUINS & FOLLIES

13 LONDESBOROUGH PARK

Remnants of a stately home, demolished in 1819, and surrounding parkland with chalk streams, woodland, two small lakes and a weir and original deer house. Find the steps from nowhere to nowhere, then seek out the secret garden. You may spot red kites circling above as well as other wildlife. The Norman All Saints church contains a treasure trove of historic artefacts, including a 10th-century Anglo-Danish cross.

→ Located 5¼ miles SE of Pocklington along Burnby Ln. Parking in village along Low St by church.

5 mins, 53.8975, -0.6795

14 RISBY HALL FOLLY

This lakeside folly is part of a lost country estate that once belonged to the Ellerker family. When Henry VIII came to stay in 1540, a 40-hectare deer park was created almost overnight to entertain the royal visitor. The 17th-century Risby Hall, built on the site of the former manor house, burned to the ground in 1784; well-defined earthworks are still visible. Walks and views from peaceful Folly Lake Café: open 7 days, 10am – 4pm, 07860 255981.

→ Follow the A164 from Beverley for 3½ miles, then turn R onto Dunflat Rd. Turn R again at signpost for Risby Park Fishing Ponds. For Risby Hall earthworks, continue past sign for 200m. Park on L opp information board and earthworks.

2 mins, 53.8046, -0.4664

WETLANDS & WILDLIFE

15 TOPHILL LOW NATURE RESERVE

A remote nature reserve with two huge lakes and lagoons for wildfowl. As a man-made natural environment, it has escaped the usual smattering of pesticides and is a haven for relict plants and invertebrates that are extinct in the surrounding farmland. Bird hides across the 120 hectares have recorded 270 species of bird since its creation in 1959. Wander through

the atmospheric woods, wetlands and grasslands to see all manner of wildlife at any time of year: butterflies, moths, grass snakes, otters and spectacular displays of cowslips in spring.

→ From Driffield, follow the A164 Beverley Rd to Watton, then turn L onto Church Ln and Carr Ln for 4½ miles to reserve.

5 mins, 53.9224, -0.3673 🚗🚌🚶🏊♿⛰

16 NORTH CAVE WETLANDS

A former sand and gravel quarry might not sound that promising but this site has undergone a huge transformation into a haven for wildlife. These wetlands hold one of the largest breeding colonies of sand martins and provide a superb habitat for passage, breeding and wintering wildfowl, waders, terns and gulls. Follow the 1¼-mile perimeter path around the reserve and marvel at the huge variety of birdlife as well as butterflies, dragonflies and damselflies.

→ From the A1079 Market Weighton bypass, head S on Cliffe Rd through North Cliffe to North Cave, then follow signs. The nature reserve is 15 miles W of Hull, off Cliffe Rd on Dryham Ln.

10 mins, 53.7844, -0.6560 🚗🚌🚶🚭🏕

17 SKERNE WETLANDS

The UK's most northerly chalk streams are the highlight of this biodiverse wetland on the River Hull floodplain, home to kingfishers, water voles and otters. The West Beck, with its crystal-clear waters, lush waterside vegetation and flowering beds of water crowfoot are a summer delight. As you listen to the cacophony of croaks from male frogs and the melodious birdsong, it feels like you have gatecrashed a party.

→ From Skerne village, head E on Main St, then take R at end of village. Turn L at fork, then turn R towards Cleaves Farm. Before farm at turning point, go through gate on L to grass parking. Paths are marked from here. Alternatively, Snakeholme Pastures lies S of Wansford Bridge off the B1249 SE of Driffield with lay-by parking. Follow footpath signs to reserve. It is possible to kayak here from North Frodingham.

10 mins, 53.9700, -0.3833 🚗🏕⛰👫🚭🚌

18 RIFLE BUTTS & KIPLINGCOTES QUARRIES NR

Former quarry and WWI rifle range, now a tiny reserve brimming with chalk-loving wildflowers and butterflies in summer. Interesting rock exposure on the quarry face with a unique Cretaceous

unconformity. An excellent interpretation board explains this geological anomaly. Further along the Hudson Way (a 10-mile stretch of disused railway line between Beverley and Market Weighton) is Kiplingcotes Chalk Pit NR, a haven for chalk-loving plants and animal species, including an array of butterflies in summer.

→ From Market Weighton, continue past the secondary school to next junction. After 1 mile turn sharp L between the embankments (crosses the Hudson Way). Reserve is on R at end of first field. Kiplingcotes (53.8783, -0.6118) is 5 mins to the E along the Hudson Way.

5 mins, 53.8720, -0.6350 🏊🚶🐾🚲ℹ️⛰️

19 PULFIN BOG NATURE RESERVE

A remnant of the expansive fens that once occupied the River Hull, this tidally influenced carr land and nature reserve (Pulfin is a corruption of 'pool fen') is a superb place to spot birdlife, with herons and kingfishers all making an appearance. High Eske lake borders the reserve and has several beaches – for a picnic and wild swim. Little egrets, oystercatchers, mute swans and cormorants gather on the two central islands

→ From Beverley, follow the A1035 for 1¼

miles. After crossing the River Hull, take R for Tickton then immediately R again onto Weel Rd and verge parking. Walk towards pub and follow footpath N on E of riverbank for 1½ miles.

25 mins, 53.8815, -0.4006 🏊🚻🐾⛰️ℹ️🅿️

20 NORTH CLIFFE WOOD

Surprisingly lovely roadside woodland nature reserve, best visited in spring for the lilac haze of bluebells that stretches out beneath the trees. This wet and dry mixed broadleaf woodland also has a small reed bed and areas of lowland heath. Several pools within the woodland and heathland areas provide homes for damselflies and dragonflies.

→ From the A1079 Market Weighton, head S down Cliffe Rd, then turn R after 4 miles down Sand Ln. Park on L in lay-by next to wood.

2 mins, 53.8258, -0.6958 🅿️🚶ℹ️

COMMONS & COUNTRY PARKS

21 BEVERLEY WESTWOOD

One of the loveliest areas of common land in the country, granted to locals by the Lord of the Manor in 1380. Residents still hold the right to graze cattle and sheep in a practice overseen by pasture makers. The Black Mill is a notable landmark; a mill has stood here

23

since 1650. The Michelin-starred Westwood Restaurant, set in the grounds of Beverley's former Georgian courthouse, is nearby.

→ Travelling E on the A1079 from Bishop Burton, at the roundabout take the 2nd exit onto the A1174 for ½ mile to Walkington Rd and roadside parking.
1 min, 53.8370, -0.4501 🚶🚲

22 HUMBER BRIDGE COUNTRY PARK

This 20-hectare slice of green lies between Hessle and the Humber, in the shadow of the mighty Humber Bridge. The site was once a quarry and the white chalk cliffs on either side lent it the nickname 'Little Switzerland' or 'Switzy', as local children call it. It has a network of paths through its woodland and meadows, home to a host of wildlife, including 22 species of butterflies as well as great crested newts and other amphibians that thrive in its ponds. A boat-shaped memorial marking the discovery of the oldest sailing vessels ever found (on display in Hull and East Yorkshire Museum) sits on the Hessle Foreshore at North Ferriby.

→ The park is accessed from the A63 and approach roads to the Humber Bridge, where its large free car park is clearly signposted.
5 mins, 53.7192, -0.4553 🚗🌳🚲🚻

HIDDEN DALES

23 SWIN DALE

Enjoy an early morning meander through this picturesque dale, typical of the chalk landscape of the Wolds. It is more of a ramble than a scramble along a grassy track between steep slopes fringed with trees along its upper brow. In the lovely village of North Newbald are the North Newbald Becksies, fed by clear chalk springs which almost never dry up, remaining at around 9°C year-round, and sometimes seen steaming on cold winter mornings.

→ Park by village green in North Newbald and follow Beverley Rd E for ¾ mile, past school on L and Newbald Becksies on R, to sign for Yorkshire Wolds Way on R into Swin Dale.
15 mins, 53.8181, -0.5840 🚶🏕️🚲

CAFÉS, DELIS & FARM SHOPS

24 SAILS CAFÉ

Courtyard café that is part of Skidby Mill, Yorkshire's last working windmill. The mill's original buildings are situated around the courtyard and house the East Riding Museum of Rural Life. At the time of writing the four-sailed mill is undergoing renovation.

22

24

→ Skidby Windmill, Beverley Rd, Cottingham, HU16 5TF, 01482 847831
53.7861, -0.4526 🍴

25 VANESSA DELI
Stock up on goodies for your picnic at this award-winning deli. All homemade or locally sourced produce. Delicious salads, good cheese counter, butchery and gourmet sandwiches. Popular café upstairs and terrace out front to watch the world go by.

→ 21–22 Saturday Market, Beverley, HU17 8BB, 01482 868190
53.8430, -0.4323 🍴

26 THE PICKLED FIG DELI
Popular and much-praised delicatessen and artisan bakery with top eco credentials stocking an impressive range of gourmet foods from Yorkshire and beyond. Excellent selection of cheeses with rarely less than 50 to choose from. Hampers and takeaway salads and sandwiches.

→ 24–26 Prestongate, Hessle, HU13 0RE, 01482 646115
53.7231, -0.4366 🍴

27 FARM SHOP AT CRANSWICK
Family-run farm shop selling locally sourced produce, including excellent homemade pies and pastries. Good range of cheeses, sandwiches to order and Yorkshire gin.

→ 2 Beverley Rd, Hutton Cranswick, Driffield, YO25 9PQ, 01377 271038
53.9570, -0.4457 🍴

28 DREWTON'S FARM SHOP
Popular farm shop on the Drewton Estate selling top-notch local produce, from fruit and vegetables to pantry staples, home-cooked prepared meals and meat sourced from the estate or elsewhere in Yorkshire. Open Mon to Sat 9am – 5pm, Sun 10am – 4pm. Award-winning tearoom and restaurant and two cottages: the Old Cowshed and the converted Dairy with sweeping Wolds views.

→ The Drewton Estate, South Cave, Nr Brough, HU15 2AG, 01430 425079
53.7892, -0.6103 🍴

PUBS & MICROBREWERIES

29 THE STAR INN AT SANCTON
One time 'grubby roadside boozer', now one of Yorkshire's best-kept secrets in the heart of the Wolds. Local food and beers. Creative menu and pub classics. Twice winner of the great Yorkshire pudding competition.

→ The Star Inn, King St, Sancton, York, YO43 4QP, 01430 827269
53.8421, -0.6325 🍴

30 PIPE AND GLASS, SOUTH DALTON
Michelin-starred former coaching inn set in the splendid surroundings of the Dalton Estate. Seasonal menu with vegetarian options and good kids' menu. Grab a sandwich and a beer in the friendly bar, then take a stroll in the adjacent parkland.

Boutique rooms in the Old Lambing Yard.

→ W End, South Dalton, Beverley, HU17 7PN, 01430 810246
53.8954, -0.5349 🍴

31 THE WELLINGTON INN, LUND
The 'Welly' is a traditional village pub with a relaxing farmers' bar area and a more formal restaurant serving traditional country pub food. Also offers a 'Welly Deli' takeaway menu for food to take home, heat and eat. Afterwards, take time to explore the delightful Wolds village of Lund.

→ 19 The Green, Lund, Driffield, YO25 9TE, 01377 217294
53.9201, -0.5237 🍴

32 GOODMANHAM ARMS, GOODMANHAM
Unpretentious country pub with quirky interior, including a Harley-Davidson. Four-times CAMRA East Yorkshire Pub of the Year winner. Six real ales, including at least two from the on-site All Hallows microbrewery. Unfussy pub grub from Italian owner. On Friday evenings there is often a cooking pot hanging over the open fire.

→ Main St, Goodmanham, York, YO43 3JA, 01430 873849
53.8766, -0.6493 🍴

33 GREEN DRAGON, WELTON
Handsome 17th-century former coaching inn overlooking a charming village with a church that looks like it is sitting in water. It is also where notorious highwayman Dick Turpin was arrested in 1739. Ancient rights exist at a piped spring in the village and if you have brought some cattle with you, they have the right to drink from this spring.

→ Cowgate, Welton, Brough, HU15 1NB, 01482 666700
53.7329, -0.54962 🍴

CAMP, GLAMP & SLEEP

34 CAMPING AT WILLIAM'S DEN
William's Den adventure attraction is hugely popular with families. Their Pitch up and Play, where you pick your own pitch, offers off-grid camping weekends between June and September. Includes free entry to the park. Your kids will love you for it!

→ Castle Farm, Wold Hill, HU15 2LS, 01430 472230
53.7883, -0.6210 ⛺

35 BUTT FARM
If you have ever dreamt of running away with the circus, this could be your dream come true.

Stay in an authentic showman's wagon with raised decking to enjoy magnificent sunsets. There is also a bowtop wagon and lodge, plus standard pitches set in 72 hectares and a rustic barn for cooking and eating (Apr to Oct).

→ Victoria Rd, Beverley, HU17 8PJ, 01482 870984

53.8191, -0.4522

36 LITTLE WOLD AWAY GLAMPING

Cosy up for the night in Badger or Bunny, two glamping pods with under-floor heating, en-suite showers, a brick BBQ and fire pit. There's also a safari tent on site, all tucked away in a peaceful woodland glade.

→ Woodside House, Low Rd, Everthorpe, HU15 2AD, 01430 470805

53.7738, -0.6355

37 NORTH STAR CLUB

Reminiscent of the American Great Camps of the Gilded Age, this enchanting retreat, situated in 200 hectares of English woodland in a hidden corner of Yorkshire, has rustic safari-style tents with sumptuous four-poster beds and indulgent roll-top baths. Mingle with fellow guests at The Woodshed, a communal chill-out area, or book a table at nearby award-winning gastropub The Star at Sancton.

→ Sancton, York, YO43 4RE, 01439 748457

53.8352, -0.6410

38 BROADGATE FARM HOLIDAY COTTAGES

A complex of self-catering cottages converted from period farm buildings. High Barn, sleeping 12, is perfect for families holidaying together. As well as the 8 hectares of meadows and woodland, you have the Wolds on your doorstep and the unique common pastureland of Beverley Westwood nearby, a relic of a bygone era and spot on for kite flying and picnics.

→ Beverley Rd, Walkington, HU17 8RP, 01482 888111

53.8265, -0.4650

39 TICKTON GRANGE

Georgian country house hotel, home to the same family for the past 40 years. Back in the day Edward VIII played cards here. Meals are served on bespoke hand-painted Royal Crown Derby china. Gardens and woodland to explore. Hampers and packed lunches of fruit loaf and Wensleydale cheese for day-long adventures.

→ Tickton, Beverley, HU17 9SH, 01964 543666

53.8653, -0.3713

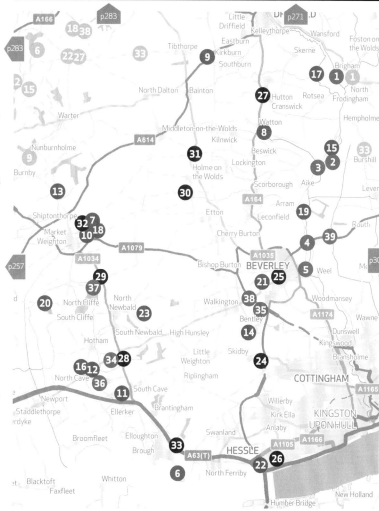

HOLDERNESS & SPURN HEAD

Our perfect weekend

→ **Walk** to the very tip of Spurn Head, which feels like the end of the earth

→ **Visit** the sublime churchyard that inspired *Lord of the Rings'* author J. R. R. Tolkien to weave one of his Middle-earth myths

→ **Track** down the Kilnsea Sound Mirror, a wartime relic from the days before radar

→ **Stroll** along the golden sands at Easington to find a hidden lake in the dunes

→ **Explore** the woodland on the Humber Estuary to find the colossal ruins of Sunk Island Battery, then picnic on the embankment and watch the boats go by

→ **Dive** in for an early morning swim at Mappleton Sands, then tuck into a hearty breakfast at the Old Post Office Tearooms

→ **Climb** the 144 steps to the top of Withernsea Lighthouse for fabulous views of the coastline and the Humber Bridge

→ **Paddle** across the lake at sunset, then toast marshmallows over the campfire beneath starry skies at Kingfisher Lakes

It is hard to pinpoint what makes this region so beguiling, but when you arrive, you know you are somewhere like nowhere else in the country. Whether it is the spit of sand of Spurn Point, ever threatened by the sea, or the abandoned wartime ruins that emerge from the landscape, this area has a sparse, other-worldly beauty that rewards the explorer.

The Holderness coastline sweeps south from the chalk stacks and stumps at Flamborough, ending in the spit of Spurn Head. It is one of the fastest eroding coastlines in Europe due to the weak boulder clay cliffs and destructive North Sea storms, and it now lies around two and a half miles inland from where it was in Roman times. Since then, 23 towns and villages have been lost to the sea. Coastal erosion is a constant threat and one of the area's most startling features; it is not unusual to be driving down a road, only to discover it has collapsed into the sea.

Inland, the Holderness plain extends as far as the eye can see; lonely lanes wind through an expanse of arable fields beneath big skies. Village names like Skeffling, Fitling and Nunkeeling would seem better placed in a Tolkien novel. In fact, this area has been dubbed 'The Tolkien Triangle'. The author lived here in 1917 and his story *Beren and Lúthien* may have been inspired by his wife dancing among the hemlock in the churchyard at Roos.

Sunk Island, a sand bank of the Humber, is an intriguing place to explore with its eerie concrete remains of a WWI battery. Hidden in a nature reserve at Kilnsea is an acoustic sound mirror and strewn across the beach at Easington are the great hulking remains of Fort Godwin.

Undoubtedly, the wild of this area is the bleak edginess of Spurn Head, an iconic and constantly shifting peninsula that curves between the North Sea and the Humber Estuary. This thin spit of sand and gravel stretches 3½ miles but is as narrow as 50m wide in places. Grab a bike and cycle, as we did, to its tip, along wildflower-fringed paths flanked by dune-backed beaches, lagoons and mudflats, passing the lighthouse, the ruins of a wartime fort, the lifeboat station and the pier. It is probably one of the most subdued, wild places you will visit, and if the sea wins its war of attrition, it may not be here forever.

BECKS & MERES

1 FRODINGHAM LANDING, FRODINGHAM BECK

This short section of the Driffield Canal, leading onto the River Hull, is a popular spot to launch canoes, kayaks, paddleboards and dinghies. You can paddle from here to Skerne Wetlands with its abundance of wildlife (take out at 53.9764, -0.3779). Also a wild swim spot but can be reedy in summer. If swimming, be vigilant of river craft as it is a narrow waterway.

→ The wharf is off the B1249 on L, ¾ mile W of North Frodingham. Honesty box – suggested donation of £5 for upkeep of canal for launching craft. Under 17s free. Boat trips (01377 270508). Occasional pedaloes.
2 mins, 53.9674, -0.3418 🏊🚣🅿️🚻

2 HORNSEA MERE

The largest freshwater lake in Yorkshire, formed at the end of the Ice Age, and a remnant of a huge wetland that characterised the area. It is a haven for overwintering birds like gadwalls, goldeneyes and tufted ducks. It is 2 miles long and ¾ mile at its widest point and is reasonably shallow (3.6m at its deepest),

resulting in a diverse range of swamp and fen plants. It is determinedly uncommercial and all the more charming for that. You can sometimes rent a boat or take a boat trip, operated by a chap who has lived here all his life and who shares his knowledge of the mere and its wildlife. The Mere Café serves breakfasts, sandwiches and homemade cakes but is not always open.

→ From Hornsea, head SE on Market Pl/ B1242. After 300m turn R, opp Football Green, onto a narrow lane and continue to car park by mere.
2 mins, 53.9072, -0.1774 🍴🅿️🚻🚣

HIDDEN BEACHES

3 BARMSTON BEACH

A long, flat stretch of sand and pebble beach backed by low clay cliffs where migratory sand martins make their home between May and September. It is a delight to see swarms of them sweeping across the fields, which are peppered with coastal defence pillboxes, and to watch them flying in and out of the cliffs where they nest.

→ From Bridlington, take the A165 S for 5½ miles, then turn L, signposted 'Parkdean Resorts Barmston Beach', for 1 mile. Parking

by caravan park. Follow signs to beach in front of static caravans.
5 mins, 54.0165, -0.2147 🏊🚶🚻🌊

4 MAPPLETON SANDS

A lovely stretch of sand and shingle beach between two granite rock breakwaters, tucked away in a cute, timeless village with a small café for refreshments.

→ Follow the B1242 from Hornsea for 2½ miles to Mappleton. Take L onto Cliff Ln to car parking at end on R.
3 mins, 53.8807, -0.1357 🏊🌊

5 EASINGTON BEACH SOUTH

Long sand and shingle beach backed by dunes and clay cliffs which runs all the way to the Spurn Peninsula. Walk S along the beach and you will find a beautiful lake tucked away in the dunes – part of Kilnsea Wetlands.

→ Follow the B1445 from Hull to Easington. Turn R at T-junction into village and past church on L. Continue to Pines Caravan Park and parking. Access to the beach is via a sandy slipway a few metres to S of park.
2 mins, 53.6327, 0.1328 🏊🌊🚶

6 SPURN HEAD BEACH

For a bracing dip in the North Sea, you won't get much wilder or isolated than the beaches along Spurn Head. Walk past the first shingle beach and follow the path to reach a lovely sandy beach hidden behind the dunes, which stretches as far as the lighthouse.

→ From Hull take the A1033 to Patrington, then take the B1445 to Easington and continue to Kilnsea. Turn R onto Spurn Road for Spurn Discovery Centre car park. Walk along path, cross first section of pebbly beach and continue onto next section of path. Access to beach is through dunes onto sands after ¾ mile.

25 mins, 53.5933, 0.1403

7 JETTY BEACH, SPURN POINT

Wild, wind-ravaged beach at the tip of the peninsula. Very strong tidal currents.

→ From Hull take the A1033 to Patrington, then take the B1445 to Easington and continue to Kilnsea. Turn R onto Spurn Rd for Spurn Discovery Centre car park. Walk along path, cross first section of pebbly beach and continue onto next section of path. Continue as far as you can go along track to beach beyond jetty.

40 mins, 53.5749, 0.1101

SACRED & ANCIENT

8 TOLKIEN'S 'HEMLOCK GLADE'

Utterly charming churchyard said to have inspired *The Hobbit* author J. R. R. Tolkien to write his fantasy Middle-earth tale *Beren and Lúthien*. Tolkien was stationed at a nearby camp with his wife, Edith, during WWI. Watching his young wife dance and sing in a hemlock glade (cow parsley) in Dents Garth, he was inspired to weave the scene into his story. Seek out the three-trunked Linden tree (Lime), the 'treeish' gravestone and the heraldic hand on the railed-off area behind All Saints' church, all linking to Tolkien's tale.

→ From Garton follow the B1242 S, dir Withernsea. Continue along Rectory Rd, past signs for Roos village. Continue to All Saint's church at HU12 0LA. Turn L at church for parking.

2 mins, 53.7469, -0.0441

9 ST GERMAIN, WINESTEAD

This small towerless church stands in fields near the village of Winestead, surrounded by a ring of trees. The church was built in the 12th century and is still lit mainly by candles.

→ Heading E on the A1033 from Hull, pass turning for Winestead on the L, go round bend

to R and the church is a ¼ mile further on the R. Go through gate off the road and there is parking directly in front of the church.

1 min, 53.6940, -0.0346 ✝

10 ST PATRICK'S CHURCH, PATRINGTON

This glorious Gothic church, whose spire is a soaring feature of the flat agricultural landscape of the Holderness peninsula, is located in a village immortalised by poet Philip Larkin in 'Bridge for the Living'. Dubbed the 'Queen of the Holderness', St Patrick's, with its exquisite architecture, was created by stonemasons so skilled they went on to work at Westminster Abbey. Tours on open days or for small groups. Climb the spiral staircases and crawl on hands and knees through the rafters to marvel at the magnificent view from the tower pulpit. The King of the Holderness, St Augustine's, is in Hedon.

→ Church Ln, Patrington, Hull, HU12 ORE. Car park to front.

2 min, 53.6828, -0.0095 ✝

11 HALI-WELL, ATWICK

Spring-fed roadside pool situated 200m from the village church and said to be haunted by the boggle (spirit) of a hooded and cloaked one-eyed woman, murdered by her husband and buried near the well. This doesn't seem to deter the ducks whose wooden home overlooks the pond. One to visit if passing.

→ Located 3 miles S of Skipsea on the B1242. At the Black Horse Pub in Atwick, take R turn onto Bewholme Rd to well on L after 500m.

1 min, 53.9283, -0.1956 ✝ ♿

12 ST HELEN'S WELL, GREAT HATFIELD

Site of an ancient spring later dedicated to St Helen, mother of Roman Emperor Constantine the Great. Also known as the Rag Well because pieces of cloth or lace were dipped in the holy water and knotted on the hawthorn hedges as a thanksgiving for blessings received. Today ribbons are tied to the grid covering the well. Check out the unusual village cross with lions at its base.

→ Located 3½ miles SW of Hornsea, following Hull Rd then Hornsea Rd. Continue through village on Cross St then Withernwick Rd and just before leaving village, find verge parking on L and well further down on R by cemetery.

5 mins, 53.8662, -0.1940 ✝ ♿

15

13

14

MILITARY HERITAGE

13 SUNK ISLAND BATTERY

Sunk Island Battery was built in WWI to defend the River Humber and was abandoned after WWII. Hidden in a small woodland on the banks of the estuary, the giant concrete remains of the gun emplacements are an eerie sight. On the walk to the battery look out for the ruined anti-aircraft site visible from the footpath.

→ Follow the A1033 E from Hull to Thorngumbald. At the end of the village turn R onto Hooks Ln, then L onto Bellcroft Ln which becomes Thorn Marsh Rd. Follow all way to T-junction and turn L onto Cherry Cobb Sands Rd and continue to Stone Creek. Park on roadside verge. Take permissive path E by river. See remains of the anti-aircraft battery on L. Continue 1 mile to woodland next to embankment. Follow path until you see track into woodland on L with metal gate. Cross over stile into woods and battery is there.

30 mins, 53.6396, -0.1117 ▣

14 PAULL HOLME TOWER

An unusual late-medieval fortified tower overlooking the Humber Estuary. The design is unique for this area, and there is debate about whether it was a fortification or a luxury residence. It is on private land but is easily seen from footpaths nearby.

→ Take the A1033 E out of Hull and then turn R onto Paull Rd. Go through village of Paull and head E on Thorngumbald Rd for approx 1 mile until you see Paull Holme Strays Nature Reserve on R. Footpath heading E along top of river embankment and Paull Holme Tower is visible on L after about ½ mile.

10 mins, 53.7069, -0.2058 ▣

15 KILNSEA SOUND MIRROR

Tucked away behind Kilnsea Wetlands Reserve is this concrete acoustic sound mirror, a forerunner of radar that provided early warning of German Zeppelin bombing raids in WWI. The nature reserve's lagoon and coastal grassland are excellent places to spot golden and grey plovers and other wintering wading birds.

→ Follow the B1445 out of Easington and turn R onto Firtholme Rd and continue to parking at Kilnsea Wetlands Nature Reserve. The car park is on the L just after you go over the L-hand bend, which rises over Long Bank and before Kilnsea village. Follow paths through reserve to mirror in a field behind.

15 mins, 53.6274, 0.1316 ▣

16 GODWIN BATTERY

The colossal slabs of concrete strewn across Kilnsea Beach were once Fort Godwin, a coastal battery built to defend the ports along the Humber Estuary during WWI and reused in WWII. A casualty of coastal erosion, it originally had gun emplacements, barracks, an officers' mess and a hospital and was the terminus for a military railway running down to Spurn Point.

→ As for Spurn Head but find car park at the end of Easington Rd on R. Battery is a few metres N along beach.

2 mins, 53.6219, 0.1419

RUINS & FOLLIES

17 PIER TOWERS, WITHERNSEA

All that remains of the original 365m Victorian pier are two gateway towers modelled on Conwy Castle. The original structure, built in 1877, lasted three decades before it was completely destroyed by passing ships. Current plans include a staged rebuilding of the pier and a renewable energy centre. The plaque to the L commemorating the 13th-century Church of St Mary, lost to coastal erosion and now lying a mile out to sea, is a solemn reminder of the precarious nature of this coastline. For spectacular views across the Holderness coast, climb to the top of Withernsea Lighthouse (HU19 2DY, 01964 614834).

→ Follow the B1362 to Seaside Rd, Withernsea. Continue on Seaside Rd. Drive to Promenade for ¼ mile. Parking along Promenade. Towers on corner of Pier Rd.

5 mins, 53.7306, 0.0356

18 SKIPSEA CASTLE

Originally believed to have been a motte and bailey castle, built by William the Conqueror, this impressive mound was actually playing its part in history 1,500 years before the Normans recycled it. It is an Iron Age burial mound, believed to be the largest artificial mound of this date in Britain, measuring 85m in diameter and 13m high. Only the mound and scant earthworks remain; however, its historic importance and the interpretation board at the entrance help you gauge its former prominence.

→ Located 8 miles south of Bridlington. Follow the A165 from Bridlington for 6 miles, then turn L on to the B1242 for 3 miles to Beeford Rd. Castle is on R.

2 mins, 53.9789, -0.2295

LOCAL FOOD

19 MELBOURNE BUTCHERS AND BAKERY

Everything in this friendly bakery is made from scratch, including mouth-watering cakes, pastries and savouries. The meat is locally sourced and the bacon and ham are home-cured. Bespoke BBQ packs available in summer.

→ Main St, Roos, Hull, HU12 0HB, 01964 670241

53.7546, -0.0442

20 WHITEDALE COTTAGE FARM SHOP

Farm shop stocking heritage breeds meat, including Gloucester Old Spot pork, Shorthorn beef and game from local estates.

→ Beverley Rd, Hull, HU11 4TY, 07867 676991

53.8503, -0.2194

21 CAKEY BAKEY YUM YUM

A friendly, welcoming cake shop and tearoom serving an array of mouth-watering home-baked sweet treats. Also deli-style sandwiches, quiches, soups and salads. Bike store for cyclists at the back.

→ 12 Market Pl, Patrington, HU12 0RB, 01964 631954

53.6838, -0.0125

22 HALSHAM WATERSIDE CAFÉ AND FARM SHOP

Friendly café and farm shop, overlooking a fish pond, serving breakfasts, homemade cakes and light lunches.

→ Dalton Ln, Halsham, Hull, HU12 0DE, 07972 183436
53.7288, -0.0755 🍴

23 THE OLD POST OFFICE TEAROOMS, MAPPLETON

Quaint tearoom serving homemade cakes, including gluten-free and vegan options. Large patio with tables. Dog-friendly with water bowls and beds. The perfect place to refuel after a walk on lovely Mappleton Sands.

→ Cliff Ln, Mappleton, HU18 1XX, 01964 533424
53.8760, -0.1361 🍴

24 SPURN DISCOVERY CENTRE CAFÉ, KILNSEA

Wooden-clad eco café serving homemade food using local ingredients, including sustainably sourced seafood. Fabulous views of the ever-changing view of the Humber Estuary through the large window. Sheltered outside seating. Bike hire available.

→ Spurn National Nature Reserve, Kilnsea, HU12 0UH, 01964 650144
53.6156, 0.1397 🍴

25 CROWN & ANCHOR, KILNSEA

Convivial pub, with large windows overlooking the Humber Estuary, serving good food and real ales. A great place to watch the sun set over the water.

→ Easington Rd, Kilnsea, Hull, HU12 0UB, 01964 650276
53.6200, 0.1298 🍴

WILDER CAMPING

26 HIGHFIELD FARM

Working arable farm with three camping areas: the sheltered paddock, the strip with far-reaching views and the hard standing. Resident alpacas and free-range hens. The nearby disused railway line is great for exploring the local area by bike.

→ Highfield Farm, Station Rd, Ottringham, HU12 0BJ, 01964 622283
53.7065, -0.0783 ▲

27 SPRINGFIELD WOODS CAMPSITE

Pitch up at this rustic pop-up woodland campsite, then laze in one of the hammocks (rent or bring your own) while the kids build a den in the woods or paddle in the stream. Spacious pitches. Solar mobile phone charging. Operates as a forest school in term time. At the time of writing, the campsite opens mid-July to mid-August but this may be extended in future.

→ Springfield House, Rise Rd, Hull, HU11 5BH, book via Pitchup
53.8513, -0.2444 ▲ ⚑

28 WOOD LAKE CAMPSITE

Pitch your tent or van beneath the trees or out in the open to enjoy starry skies at this friendly campsite with its own lake and woodland. Sorry, no kids but pets allowed. A mile down the road is the beach at Mappleton.

→ Mappleton Rd, Great Hatfield, Hornsea, HU11 4UP, 01964 536869
53.8702, -0.1931 ▲

29 GARTH FARM CARAVAN AND CAMPING

Pitch up within walking distance of two nature reserves near the peaceful village of Hollym. Free-range hens strut between the hard standing and grass pitches (with EHU). A couple of miles from sandy beaches and ideal for exploring Spurn Head.

→ Back Ln, Hollym, HU19 2SJ, 07851 653026
53.7058, 0.0280 ▲

30 ELM TREE FARM CAMPSITE

Laid-back family-run campsite on the edge of a small Holderness village and within striking distance of Spurn Head. Hot breakfast sandwiches available and fresh eggs; they also have a licence to sell craft beers and ciders.

→ Holmpton, Withernsea, HU19 2QR, 01964 630957
53.6879, 0.0665 ▲

31 MILL FARM COUNTRY PARK

Family-run campsite for tents, campers and caravans plus a shepherd's hut created using recycled farm materials. Farm walk and playing field. Nearby is Skipsea Castle, one of the largest Iron Age mounds in the UK (see entry).

→ Mill Ln, Skipsea, YO25 8SS, 01262 468211
53.9816, -0.2187 ▲

32 DRIFTWOOD CARAVAN SITE

Tiny tree-enclosed caravan site with field for small tents (max 2-person) near the wonderfully wild and dramatic Spurn Head. A short walk to the friendly Crown & Anchor pub with amazing estuary views.

→ Driftwood, The Nookin, Kilnsea, HU12 0UB, 01964 650208
53.6219, 0.1284 ▲

33 KINGFISHER LAKES

Paddle across the lake in a kayak, enjoy a sunrise dip, catch a fish or marvel at the moonlight shimmering on the water at this idyllic lakeside glamping site. Safari tents and a safari lodge, sleeping up to 10. Otherwise there are cosy yurts and three luxury log cabins with balconies to enjoy spectacular Yorkshire sunsets.

→ Burhill, Brandesburton, Driffield, YO25 8LY (or 8NA for SatNav), 07843 548460
53.9208, -0.3299

34 LITTLE OTCHAN GLAMPING

Keep an eye out for roe deer and buzzards in the woods that fringe this lovely shepherd's hut and watch damselflies skit across the lily-strewn pond. Eco-fired hot tub and rustic campfire cooking. Also four bell tents in an idyllic meadow plus a microbrewery and a short jaunt to the wilderness of Spurn Point.

→ Hall Farm, Halsham, HU12 0BU, 01964 612201
53.7327, -0.0263

35 NORTH STAR SANCTUM

Six luxury lodges styled on the exotic locations owners Simon and Rupal have visited, including the Indian-inspired Raj and the Balinese-inspired Lotus. The entire site, surrounded by rolling fields, is named after the North Star, which you can spot here on a clear night from your own private hot tub.

→ Humbleton Rd, Fitling, HU12 9AJ, 07930 405530
53.7963, -0.1087

36 SHEPHERD'S RETREAT, PATRINGTON

Cosy shepherd's hut in a 5-hectare pasture surrounded by grazing sheep and extensive countryside views. Get fired up for a day of adventures with a full English or American pancakes from the breakfast options, then wind down at twilight in the wood-fired hot tub.

→ Highfields Farm, Ings Ln, Patrington, HU12 0ND, 07943 421970
53.6842, -0.0179

37 WHITE COTTAGE PODS, HORNSEA

Bo-Peep's hut and two luxurious pods with solar-powered wet rooms in a fenced-off part of a larger 4-hectare camping and caravan site. Boats and birdwatching at Hornsea Mere and the coast at Hornsea.

38 THE PADDOCK PODS

Caravan Club site offering a glamping experience with two cosy camping pods with wood-fired hot tubs.

For walkers and cyclists, the 215-mile Trans Pennine Trail borders the site.

→ Hull Rd, Hornsea, HU11 5RN, 07708 640769
53.8920, -0.1795

→ Homeland, Catfoss Rd, Bewholme, YO25 8DX, 07767 821038
53.9323, -0.2298

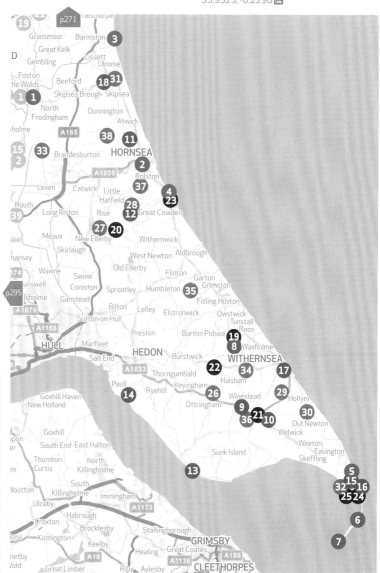

1 Northern Borders
1. NU 041 471
2. NU 028 487
3. NU 143 379
4. NU 127 437
5. NU 134 435
6. NU 104 439
7. NU 003 536
8. NT 925 395
9. NT 883 433
10. NT 939 374
11. NT 933 513
12. NT 897 476
13. NT 927 498
14. NT 982 367
15. NU 124 425
16. NU 126 416
17. NT 930 437
18. NU 122 415
19. NT 983 367
20. NU 235 376
21. NT 965 374
22. NU 136 417
23. NT 906 475
24. NT 882 434
25. NT 925 393
26. NU 129 416
27. NT 889 372
28. NT 945 375
29. NT 927 393
30. NT 910 382
31. NT 949 393
32. NT 945 373
33. NT 933 383
34. NU 126 419
35. NT 927 393
36. NT 858 392
37. NU 133 369
38. NT 996 531
39. NU 066 427
40. NT 932 368
41. NU 011 395
42. NT 858 392

2 The Cheviots
1. NT 958 170
2. NT 927 203
3. NT 901 284
4. NT 887 202
5. NT 996 166
6. NT 887 247
7. NT 909 205
8. NT 943 197
9. NT 967 282
10. NT 928 292
11. NU 004 316
12. NU 007 163
13. NU 081 253
14. NT 927 304
15. NT 939 336
16. NT 892 278
17. NT 913 302
18. NU 082 223
19. NU 067 221
20. NU 062 259
21. NT 986 270
22. NU 004 310
23. NU 059 352
24. NU 102 236
25. NU 070 247
26. NU 070 217
27. NU 064 333
28. NU 075 241
29. NU 062 261
30. NU 048 164
31. NU 019 163
32. NT 995 278
33. NU 043 163
34. NU 056 283
35. NT 935 338
36. NU 055 283
37. NT 893 325
38. NU 094 356
39. NU 061 260
40. NT 991 277
41. NT 881 225

3 Alnwick & Embleton Bay
1. NU 148 352
2. NU 181 355
3. NU 210 329
4. NU 235 266
5. NU 247 226
6. NU 173 359
7. NU 241 255
8. NU 242 243
9. NU 258 204
10. NU 262 173
11. NU 261 169
12. NU 258 163
13. NU 260 160
14. NU 262 156
15. NU 175 146
16. NU 183 350
17. NU 256 217
18. NU 163 157
19. NU 188 143
20. NU 178 349
21. NU 190 147
22. NU 230 227
23. NU 235 287
24. NU 191 345
25. NU 179 347
26. NU 258 198
27. NU 220 321
28. NU 258 199
29. NU 234 251
30. NU 240 245
31. NU 266 142
32. NU 168 257
33. NU 165 237
34. NU 229 292
35. NU 229 292
36. NU 247 174
37. NU 192 134
38. NU 152 299
39. NU 179 348
40. NU 154 350
41. NU 186 223
42. NU 249 147
43. NU 256 176
44. NU 209 308
45. NU 207 275
46. NU 172 331
47. NU 158 229
48. NU 261 175
49. NU 240 248
50. NU 159 355
51. NU 233 225

4 Kielder to Coquetdale
1. NY 779 999
2. NY 841 854
3. NT 890 072
4. NT 870 082
5. NT 957 031
6. NT 917 042
7. NY 946 824
8. NY 695 882
9. NY 641 902
10. NY 829 747
11. NT 789 085
12. NY 832 986
13. NT 920 044
14. NT 952 029
15. NY 837 831
16. NY 773 899
17. NY 802 769
18. NT 932 048
19. NY 934 757
20. NY 790 761
21. NT 866 103
22. NY 632 935
23. NY 661 766
24. NT 803 073
25. NY 937 934
26. NY 712 984
27. NY 962 907
28. NY 932 834
29. NY 871 736
30. NY 839 834
31. NT 934 046
32. NY 723 874
33. NY 630 934
34. NY 860 768
35. NY 722 865
36. NY 916 733
37. NY 932 913
38. NY 625 938
39. NY 835 826
40. NY 694 861
41. NY 916 733
42. NY 785 876
43. NY 819 835
44. NT 768 056
45. NY 745 832
46. NY 740 785
47. NY 670 924
48. NY 753 886
49. NY 792 857
50. NY 661 855
51. NY 664 771
52. NT 911 098

5 Rothbury & Simonside
1. NU 247 102
2. NZ 273 980
3. NU 258 064
4. NU 266 125
5. NU 241 058
6. NU 068 015
7. NU 060 017
8. NU 045 011
9. NZ 100 994
10. NU 230 114
11. NU 268 000
12. NU 116 092
13. NU 245 100
14. NZ 265 965
15. NU 247 057
16. NZ 023 986
17. NU 126 096
18. NU 047 020
19. NU 060 093
20. NZ 046 986
21. NZ 054 992
22. NU 027 009
23. NU 073 021
24. NU 246 104
25. NU 247 061
26. NU 184 003
27. NU 269 048
28. NU 184 002
29. NZ 137 985
30. NU 246 105
31. NU 246 105
32. NT 997 110
33. NU 228 044
34. NU 129 024
35. NU 002 122
36. NU 255 113
37. NU 181 024
38. NZ 128 981
39. NU 101 110
40. NU 013 032
41. NU 087 008
42. NZ 117 982

6 Morpeth & Wansbeck
1. NZ 219 858
2. NZ 240 864
3. NZ 238 804
4. NZ 268 806
5. NZ 170 854
6. NZ 259 863
7. NZ 049 934
8. NZ 082 819
9. NZ 302 849
10. NZ 336 767
11. NZ 086 864
12. NZ 154 943
13. NZ 028 842
14. NZ 043 887
15. NZ 054 822
16. NZ 044 900
17. NZ 092 825
18. NZ 334 760
19. NZ 321 764
20. NZ 237 772
21. NZ 313 875
22. NZ 289 937
23. NZ 034 803
24. NZ 013 824
25. NZ 102 785
26. NZ 030 718
27. NZ 313 880
28. NZ 338 766
29. NZ 195 770
30. NZ 197 859
31. NZ 216 761
32. NZ 165 729
33. NZ 030 718
34. NZ 338 767
35. NZ 178 831
36. NZ 184 856
37. NZ 198 950
38. NZ 044 908
39. NZ 035 803

7 Hadrian's Wall
1. NY 925 707
2. NY 675 583
3. NY 671 608
4. NY 675 618
5. NY 936 648
6. NY 797 613
7. NY 957 623
8. NY 640 696
9. NY 713 665
10. NY 767 680
11. NY 794 697
12. NY 789 688
13. NY 675 663
14. NY 914 700
15. NY 858 710
16. NY 931 719
17. NY 939 698
18. NY 659 661
19. NY 799 607
20. NY 940 607
21. NY 789 639
22. NY 761 677
23. NY 798 640
24. NY 840 611
25. NY 941 579
26. NY 828 612
27. NY 750 668
28. NY 715 660
29. NY 988 643
30. NY 953 655
31. NY 989 643
32. NY 730 657
33. NY 684 620
34. NY 744 667
35. NY 960 579
36. NY 884 717
37. NY 752 668
38. NY 787 712
39. NY 828 608
40. NY 677 588
41. NY 762 663
42. NY 807 597
43. NY 892 680
44. NY 752 674
45. NY 752 670
46. NY 975 634

8 Tyne & Wear
1. NZ 364 719
2. NZ 413 629
3. NZ 398 650
4. NZ 350 750
5. NZ 064 680
6. NZ 101 553
7. NZ 338 652
8. NZ 103 554
9. NZ 033 704
10. NZ 334 543
11. NZ 073 648
12. NZ 186 599
13. NZ 130 565
14. NZ 201 558
15. NZ 180 599
16. NZ 371 695
17. NZ 365 708
18. NZ 407 613
19. NZ 126 635
20. NZ 399 648
21. NZ 206 553
22. NZ 079 591
23. NZ 234 676
24. NZ 023 637
25. NZ 102 667
26. NZ 162 621
27. NZ 076 590
28. NZ 074 590
29. NZ 050 697
30. NZ 246 638
31. NZ 181 586

9 Durham & Coast
1. NZ 434 495
2. NZ 423 508
3. NZ 469 393
4. NZ 436 474
5. NZ 441 460
6. NZ 443 452
7. NZ 491 365
8. NZ 187 304
9. NZ 359 478
10. NZ 193 301
11. NZ 297 470
12. NZ 296 471
13. NZ 283 508
14. NZ 200 300
15. NZ 147 307
16. NZ 296 471
17. NZ 216 304
18. NZ 243 438
19. NZ 330 358
20. NZ 353 492
21. NZ 422 505
22. NZ 189 301
23. NZ 344 289
24. NZ 427 393
25. NZ 149 413
26. NZ 178 464
27. NZ 161 314
28. NZ 147 514

10 Teesdale
1. NZ 167 164
2. NZ 163 172
3. NZ 225 144
4. NZ 107 146
5. NZ 066 149
6. NZ 084 144
7. NY 814 286
8. NY 880 284
9. NY 903 279
10. NY 874 279
11. NY 909 286
12. NY 992 132
13. NY 976 124
14. NY 947 260
15. NY 947 270
16. NY 957 125
17. NY 813 303
18. NY 965 197
19. NY 919 185
20. NY 947 185
21. NY 938 224
22. NY 883 283
23. NY 935 186
24. NY 968 194
25. NZ 080 308
26. NZ 063 150
27. NY 992 135
28. NZ 128 217
29. NZ 077 122
30. NZ 210 156
31. NZ 214 155
32. NZ 179 123
33. NZ 059 083
34. NY 953 177
35. NZ 050 137
36. NZ 154 085
37. NZ 050 164
38. NZ 209 157
39. NZ 093 252
40. NY 994 135
41. NZ 010 197
42. NZ 210 159
43. NY 994 220
44. NY 946 236
45. NY 996 245
46. NZ 053 107
47. NZ 034 113
48. NY 853 312
49. NY 915 269
50. NY 860 304

11 Allendale & Weardale
1. NY 758 404
2. NY 724 467
3. NZ 074 499
4. NY 906 391
5. NY 697 496
6. NY 985 390
7. NY 876 385
8. NY 893 380
9. NZ 080 503
10. NZ 065 411
11. NZ 012 518
12. NY 903 392
13. NY 851 408
14. NY 845 466
15. NY 807 537
16. NY 924 429
17. NY 959 510
18. NY 784 433
19. NY 895 441
20. NY 910 391
21. NY 831 565
22. NY 955 464
23. NY 695 485
24. NY 839 512
25. NZ 042 552
26. NY 695 487
27. NY 699 494
28. NY 780 440
29. NZ 068 393
30. NZ 056 491
31. NY 781 437
32. NY 859 452
33. NY 697 488
34. NY 718 464
35. NY 965 503
36. NY 859 453
37. NZ 016 500
38. NY 717 464
39. NY 717 463
40. NY 766 450
41. NZ 042 522
42. NZ 063 356
43. NY 938 428
44. NY 792 559
45. NY 716 461
46. NY 771 513
47. NZ 017 500

12 Tees Valley & Coast
1. NZ 419 131
2. NZ 383 107
3. NZ 429 157
4. NZ 741 126
5. NZ 365 204
6. NZ 558 270
7. NZ 624 237
8. NZ 916 108
9. NZ 784 108
10. NZ 829 157
11. NZ 811 158
12. NZ 797 175
13. NZ 727 200
14. NZ 712 202

15 NZ 707 207	28 SE 610 836	36 SE 820 929	27 SE 872 913	30 SE 533 772
16 NZ 579 125	29 SE 575 935	37 SE 677 857	28 TA 025 892	31 SE 517 751
17 NZ 590 101	30 NZ 624 088	38 SE 798 845	29 NZ 970 023	32 SE 583 787
18 NZ 757 192	31 NZ 440 076	39 SE 720 948	30 SE 989 855	33 SE 582 787
19 NZ 621 174	32 NZ 236 037	40 SE 705 989	31 TA 009 888	34 SE 785 716
20 NZ 903 112	33 SE 646 821	41 SE 672 952	32 SE 855 877	35 SE 529 698
21 NZ 839 116	34 SE 548 834	42 SE 856 981	33 TA 008 912	36 SE 667 758
22 NZ 666 212	35 SE 467 846	43 SE 627 855	34 NZ 888 034	37 SE 536 771
23 NZ 697 214	36 NZ 581 063	44 NZ 708 086	35 TA 010 904	38 SE 650 663
24 NZ 791 170	37 SE 613 836	45 SE 724 959	36 TA 038 896	39 SE 720 679
25 NZ 672 209	38 SE 608 836	46 SE 841 899	37 SE 833 830	40 SE 785 717
26 NZ 665 209	39 SE 503 887	47 NZ 828 051	38 SE 964 833	41 SE 786 717
27 NZ 307 101	40 SE 516 817	48 SE 803 852	39 TA 018 872	42 SE 784 716
28 NZ 783 188	41 NZ 441 083	49 NZ 720 047	40 SE 999 854	43 SE 534 747
29 NZ 899 112	42 NZ 428 034	50 SE 695 993	41 SE 987 908	44 SE 712 699
30 NZ 900 111	43 SE 369 940	51 SE 797 840	42 NZ 866 074	45 SE 563 784
31 NZ 903 112	44 SE 612 837	52 NZ 827 007	43 NZ 889 093	46 SE 467 747
32 NZ 666 208	45 SE 613 837	53 SE 675 894	44 SE 944 820	47 SE 729 672
33 NZ 614 160	46 SE 612 838	54 SE 641 842	45 TA 047 887	48 SE 669 714
34 NZ 896 114	47 SE 390 966	55 SE 815 832	46 NZ 945 057	49 SE 735 814
35 NZ 897 109	48 NZ 602 084	56 NZ 801 051	47 SE 841 841	50 SE 511 797
36 NZ 571 104	49 NZ 487 032	57 NZ 704 077	48 NZ 953 062	51 SE 591 679
37 NZ 898 113	50 SE 450 956	58 NZ 821 022	49 NZ 890 064	52 SE 515 761
38 NZ 897 108	51 SE 378 805	59 SE 728 904	50 SE 970 866	53 SE 509 750
39 NZ 901 113	52 SE 461 981	60 NZ 762 075	51 NZ 852 062	54 SE 583 798
40 NZ 861 125	53 SE 620 979	61 SE 678 997	52 TA 018 866	55 SE 679 676
41 NZ 898 114	54 SE 607 947	62 SE 833 906	53 NZ 868 042	56 SE 566 788
42 NZ 666 216	55 NZ 619 066	63 SE 734 879	54 SE 926 942	
43 NZ 423 151	56 SE 620 984	64 SE 755 889	55 NZ 930 009	**17 Vale of York**
44 NZ 418 260	57 SE 576 850	65 SE 797 910	56 SE 922 919	1 SE 698 426
45 NZ 775 113	58 SE 448 983	66 SE 716 969	57 NZ 915 063	2 SE 703 473
46 NZ 847 131		67 NZ 839 000	58 SE 841 842	3 SE 703 345
47 NZ 806 163	**14 North**	68 SE 809 877	59 NZ 953 040	4 SE 598 476
48 NZ 791 167	**York Moors**	69 SE 840 885	60 TA 043 883	5 SE 568 553
49 NZ 608 186	1 NZ 824 009	70 NZ 768 037	61 NZ 906 084	6 SE 512 578
50 NZ 719 135	2 SE 813 996	71 NZ 714 053	62 SE 952 828	7 SE 513 579
51 NZ 902 111	3 SE 826 021	72 NZ 750 063	63 SE 879 819	8 SE 466 621
52 NZ 761 189	4 NZ 829 021	73 NZ 805 051	64 SE 899 830	9 SE 394 671
53 NZ 897 113	5 NZ 822 001	74 SE 757 918		10 SE 610 302
	6 NZ 651 073	75 SE 796 916	**16 Howardian Hills**	11 SE 700 427
13 Cleveland	7 NZ 626 061		1 SE 733 657	12 SE 641 463
& Hambleton	8 NZ 784 054	**15 Great Forests**	2 SE 782 712	13 SE 691 444
1 SE 503 832	9 NZ 821 054	**& Coast**	3 SE 643 802	14 SE 573 481
2 SE 466 991	10 NZ 762 076	1 TA 027 934	4 SE 729 627	15 SE 579 588
3 SE 471 994	11 SE 737 865	2 TA 060 860	5 SE 590 765	16 SE 558 337
4 SE 609 828	12 NZ 757 101	3 TA 064 852	6 SE 565 743	17 SE 628 394
5 NZ 601 099	13 SE 830 980	4 TA 021 950	7 SE 537 804	18 SE 645 373
6 NZ 522 006	14 NZ 830 029	5 TA 011 970	8 SE 722 700	19 SE 648 609
7 SE 527 814	15 SE 796 943	6 NZ 959 034	9 SE 720 675	20 SE 532 412
8 SE 577 851	16 NZ 786 049	7 NZ 955 041	10 SE 651 662	21 SE 598 477
9 SE 447 984	17 SE 804 974	8 TA 035 912	11 SE 696 748	22 SE 391 665
10 SE 454 981	18 SE 739 929	9 NZ 978 022	12 SE 625 719	23 SE 511 579
11 SE 609 903	19 SE 724 038	10 NZ 888 053	13 SE 735 658	24 SE 490 520
12 SE 620 983	20 NZ 674 019	11 NZ 886 090	14 SE 549 789	25 SE 664 386
13 NZ 483 024	21 NZ 682 019	12 SE 968 899	15 SE 657 662	26 SE 508 577
14 NZ 525 030	22 NZ 780 900	13 SE 988 821	16 SE 637 712	27 SE 552 586
15 NZ 558 035	23 SE 798 840	14 SE 986 853	17 SE 655 778	28 SE 446 621
16 SE 506 838	24 SE 676 857	15 SE 964 834	18 SE 705 696	29 SE 594 445
17 SE 514 813	25 SE 794 941	16 NZ 973 021	19 SE 531 772	30 SE 588 410
18 SE 480 941	26 SE 728 904	17 TA 051 891	20 SE 670 794	31 SE 697 554
19 SE 450 942	27 SE 723 904	18 NZ 991 008	21 SE 602 789	32 SE 391 654
20 SE 616 972	28 SE 728 904	19 SE 889 986	22 SE 730 683	33 SE 590 455
21 SE 536 028	29 NZ 736 092	20 SE 982 969	23 SE 760 667	34 SE 498 576
22 NZ 608 086	30 SE 852 937	21 NZ 936 073	24 SE 513 795	35 SE 743 438
23 NZ 597 031	31 NZ 702 005	22 SE 872 934	25 SE 697 750	36 SE 721 580
24 SE 504 834	32 SE 684 950	23 SE 942 821	26 SE 561 705	37 SE 712 571
25 NZ 570 918	33 NZ 684 007	24 NZ 885 041	27 SE 720 680	38 SE 695 585
26 SE 568 847	34 SE 809 980	25 SE 899 831	28 SE 530 799	
27 NZ 481 025	35 SE 814 980	26 NZ 953 048	29 SE 614 769	

18 Flamborough & East Wolds

1 TA 232 723	15 SE 847 527	28 SE 916 334	
2 TA 239 720	16 SE 845 589	29 SE 900 392	
3 TA 254 708	17 SE 822 583	30 SE 963 453	
4 TA 257 704	18 SE 881 570	31 SE 970 481	
5 TA 231 692	19 SE 822 555	32 SE 888 431	
6 TA 216 693	20 SE 874 590	33 SE 957 272	
7 TA 124 816	21 SE 799 601	34 SE 909 333	
8 TA 128 816	22 SE 880 550	35 TA 019 369	
9 TA 130 774	23 SE 826 499	36 SE 900 316	
10 TA 154 754	24 SE 841 610	37 SE 895 385	
11 TA 170 629	25 SE 831 517	38 TA 011 377	
12 SE 904 674	26 SE 797 550	39 TA 072 422	
13 SE 880 668	27 SE 882 550		
14 TA 061 723	28 SE 830 516	**21 Holderness**	
15 TA 097 677	29 SE 845 610	**& Spurn Head**	
16 TA 039 811	30 SE 784 630	1 TA 088 536	
17 SE 966 655	31 SE 764 631	2 TA 198 472	
18 TA 049 751	32 SE 806 622	3 TA 170 593	
19 TA 079 607	33 SE 929 552	4 TA 226 443	
20 SE 929 645	34 SE 839 611	5 TA 411 172	
21 TA 095 617	35 SE 790 617	6 TA 417 128	
22 TA 117 810	36 SE 790 617	7 TA 398 107	
23 SE 993 649	37 SE 793 547	8 TA 290 296	
24 SE 997 645	38 SE 887 568	9 TA 298 237	
25 TA 038 723		10 TA 315 225	
26 TA 249 708	**20 South Wolds**	11 TA 185 495	
27 TA 102 632	**& Humber**	12 TA 188 426	
28 TA 197 739	1 TA 076 536	13 TA 249 175	
29 TA 061 769	2 TA 073 475	14 TA 185 248	
30 SE 890 743	3 TA 062 471	15 TA 410 166	
31 SE 957 618	4 TA 055 417	16 TA 417 160	
32 SE 862 756	5 TA 054 398	17 TA 343 279	
33 SE 860 754	6 SE 958 252	18 TA 162 551	
34 TA 130 773	7 SE 889 431	19 TA 290 304	
35 TA 182 664	8 TA 022 497	20 TA 172 408	
36 TA 096 773	9 SE 979 550	21 TA 313 226	
37 SE 969 768	10 SE 891 424	22 TA 270 275	
38 TA 063 643	11 SE 916 309	23 TA 226 438	
39 SE 932 648	12 SE 894 326	24 TA 416 153	
40 TA 226 704	13 SE 868 454	25 TA 409 158	
41 SE 897 744	14 TA 010 353	26 TA 269 250	
42 TA 217 723	15 TA 073 485	27 TA 155 408	
43 TA 040 780	16 SE 886 328	28 TA 189 430	
44 TA 095 719	17 TA 061 538	29 TA 339 251	
45 TA 100 748	18 SE 898 426	30 TA 365 232	
46 SE 928 768	19 SE 852 439	31 TA 169 554	
47 SE 929 754	20 SE 859 374	32 TA 408 160	
48 TA 099 767	21 TA 020 389	33 TA 097 484	
49 TA 131 714	22 TA 020 258	34 TA 302 280	
50 TA 230 702	23 SE 933 366	35 TA 246 349	
51 TA 041 723	24 TA 020 333	36 TA 310 226	
	25 TA 032 396	37 TA 197 455	
19 North Wolds	26 TA 032 263	38 TA 163 499	
1 SE 799 472	27 TA 020 523		
2 SE 779 459			
3 SE 845 593			
4 SE 860 646			
5 SE 872 623			
6 SE 853 555			
7 SE 813 538			
8 SE 808 586			
9 SE 847 477			
10 SE 894 606			
11 SE 759 475			
12 SE 836 532			
13 SE 858 654			
14 SE 835 600			

Converting decimal degrees to minutes and seconds. The whole number of degrees will remain the same (i.e. 50.1355° still starts with 50°). Then multiply the whole decimal by 60 (i.e. 0.1355 x 60 = 8.13). The whole first number becomes the minutes (8'). Take the remaining decimal digits and multiply by 60 again. (i.e. 13 x 60 = 7.8). The resulting number becomes the seconds (7.8").

Wild Guide
North East England
Adventures in
Northumberland, North
York Moors, Wolds &
North Pennines

Words:
Sarah Banks

Photos:
Sarah Banks
and those credited

Editing:
Victoria O'Dowd

Proofreading:
Becky Hawkins

Design:
Gary Nickolls &
Rachel Malenoir

Distribution:
Central Books Ltd
50, Freshwater Road
Dagenham, RM8 1RX
020 8525 8800
orders@centralbooks.com

Published by:
Wild Things Publishing Ltd.
Freshford, Bath, BA2 7WG
hello@
wildthingspublishing.com

the award-winning, best-
selling adventure travel
series, also available as
iPhone and Android apps.

Author acknowledgements:
Huge thanks go to Daniel and Tania at Wild Things Publishing for entrusting me with such a wonderful project - this is the book I have dreamed of writing and for it to be part of the Wild Guide series is the pinnacle. I am also incredibly grateful to my editor, Victoria O'Dowd, for her meticulous editing and fact-checking and to Gary Nickolls, the designer, who put these pages together so beautifully. Several people have kindly shared their expertise, offering a unique insight into main places within these pages: Tim Burkinshaw on Star Carr, Nick Pepper on Thirlwall Castle, Paul Jones-King, and the managers of Alston, Langdon Beck and Wooler youth hostels - Linda, Rob and Cindy - with their invaluable local knowledge. Thank you to geograph.org.uk contributors and all those who provided photographs so generously. Finally, I could not have completed this book without the unswerving support of my family. As always, my husband, David, has been my rock - a companion on many trips as well as assisting with photography - and a constant source of encouragement. My sons, Joe, Will and Ted, have been unfaltering in their eagerness to seek out swim spots; scramble up crags and hill forts and explore lost ruins. I am immensely grateful to my parents, Margaret and Peter, who instilled in me, from a young age, a love of the outdoors. Thank you to friends and family who accompanied me on expeditions and shared recommendations: Camilla Simpson, Oscarine Vonk, Tilly, Kitty and Pamela Lewis, Jane Gledhill, Katharine Lockett and Jessica Shaw. I also met many friendly faces along the way, strangers with whom I struck up conversations and whose enthusiasm for this book made my road trips an absolute joy. Thank you to every one of you for all your support.

Health, Safety and Responsibility:
The activities in this book have risks and can be dangerous. The locations may be on private land and permission may need to be sought. While the author and publisher have gone to great lengths to ensure the accuracy of the information herein they will not be held legally or financially responsible for any accident, injury, loss or inconvenience sustained as a result of the information or advice contained in this book.

Other books from Wild Things Publishing

Wild Guide Wales
Wild Guide Scotland
Wild Guide Central
Wild Guide Lakes & Dales
Wild Guide South-West
Wild Guide South-East
Wild Guide Greece
Wild Guide Scandinavia
Wild Guide Portugal
Wild Guide French Alps

Wild Swimming Britain
Wild Swimming France
Wild Swimming Italy
Wild Swimming Spain
Wild Swimming Sydney Australia
Wild Swimming Walks Cornwall
Wild Swimming Walks Devon
Wild Swimming Walks London
Hidden Beaches Britain
Hidden Beaches Spain

Lost Lanes South
Lost Lanes Wales
Lost Lanes West
Lost Lanes North
Bikepacking
Magical Britain
Wild Running
Wild Ruins & Wild Ruins B.C.
Wild Garden Weekends
Scottish Bothy Bible & Bothy Walks